S0-FBB-756

Iraq: Power and Society

edited by

Derek Hopwood

Habib Ishow

Thomas Koszinowski

Published for
St. Antony's College, Oxford
by Ithaca Press, Reading
1993

Copyright © 1993 St. Antony's College, Oxford

All rights reserved. No part of this book may be produced in any form or by any electronic or mechanical means, including information storage and retrieval systems, without permission in writing from the publisher, except by a reviewer who may quote brief passages in a review.

First edition

ISBN 0 86372 172 9

Middle East Monographs Series Volume 29

British Library Cataloguing-in-Publication Data
A catalogue record for this book is available from the British Library

Typeset by Imprint, Oxford
Jacket Design by Mark Slader
Printed in Lebanon

Ithaca Press is an imprint of Garnet Publishing
Published by Garnet Publishing Ltd,
8 Southern Court, South Street,
Reading RG1 4QS,
UK.

Contents

Introduction	v
List of Contributors	viii

1. The formation of the new state and political aspects

Social Structures and the New State 1921–1958 *Derek Hopwood*	1
The Development of Internal Politics in Iraq from 1958 to the Present Day *May Chartouni-Dubarry*	19
Political Parties, Institutions and Administrative Structures *Peter Heine*	37
Liberation or Repression? Pan-Arab Nationalism and the Women's Movement in Iraq *Marion Farouk-Sluglett*	51
Sunnis and Shi'is Revisited: Sectarianism and Ethnicity in Authoritarian Iraq *Peter Sluglett and Marion Farouk-Sluglett*	75
The Iran–Iraq War and the Iraqi State *Charles Tripp*	91

2. Economic and Social Aspects

Iraq: Environmental, Resource and Development Issues *Peter Beaumont*	117
Iraq and its Oil: Sixty-five Years of Ambition and Frustration *Michel Chatelus*	141

The Development of Agrarian Policies since 1958 *Habib Ishow*	171
The Distribution of National Income in Iraq, with Particular Refernce to the Development of Policies Applied by the State *Aziz Alkazaz*	193
Egyptian Migrant Labour in Iraq: Economic Expediency and Socio-political Reality *Camillia Fawzi El-Solh*	257

3. Foreign Relations

Iraq as a Regional Power *Thomas Koszinowski*	283
Relations between Iraq and Kuwait *Habib Ishow*	303
Iraq and Saudi Arabia: from Rivalry to Confrontation *Andreas Rieck*	319
Relations between Iraq and its Turkish Neighbour: from Ideological to Geostrategic Constraints *Elizabeth Picard*	341
The Limits of Fertile Crescent Unity: Iraqi Policies towards Syria since 1945 *Eberhard Kienle*	357
Relations between Iraq and Iran *Paul Balta*	381
Index	398

Introduction
Iraq: Power and Society

In the last quarter of the twentieth century, several Middle Eastern countries have occupied centre stage in international politics, and in particular Iraq.

On its creation in 1921 Iraq was given a political structure which proved to be fragile as it did not sufficiently take into account the different religious and ethnic groups which inhabited the country. These unbalanced political structures have caused bloody and semi-permanent confrontations between the central power, controlled principally by a group of Sunni Arabs (largely a minority in the country, fifteen to twenty per cent of the total population) and the other ethnic and religious groups (Shi'i, Kurds, Chaldeans, Turcomans and Iranians).

These severe internal conflicts have created feelings of frustration and injustice among the major part of the population, particularly on the political, linguistic and cultural levels. Despite the frustration and discrimination caused by the state, the various ethnic and religious groups remain for the greater part attached to the concept of an Iraqi state, but they demand respect for their fundamental rights based on the principle of equality of all citizens in all fields.

Moreover, intolerance and violent struggles for power amongst the political forces have aggravated the internal situation and pushed the régime towards dictatorship and systematic repressive measures in government. This development also had unfavourable economic and social consequences for the development of the country.

However, thanks to its oil income Iraq, having become a military power, sought to impose its dominance in the region. To achieve this object it undertook a disastrous war against Iran 1980–88 and invaded Kuwait on 2 August 1990. These military operations brought in their wake ruin, misery and human dramas not only for Iraq but also for the other countries in the region.

Introduction

The importance of Iraq is undeniable and as a country it has long interested specialists on the Middle East. Scholars in Britain, France and Germany conceived the joint project of a conference to study the evolution of relations betrween society and political power in contemporary Iraq in various domains, and the country's relations with other states in the region. This collective work represents the fruits of their work which, it is hoped, will give readers a better understanding of the principal features of this contemporary Mesopotamia.

Habib Ishow
Aix-en-Provence, 1993

The organizers of the conference held in Aix-en-provence in September 1991 wish to thank for their support and cooperation:

L'Institut de Recherches et d'Etudes sur le Monde Arabe et Musulman, Aix-en-Provence

CNRS Paris, France

Middle East Centre, St. Antony's College, Oxford

ESRC, Swindon, UK

Deutsches Orient-Institut, Hamburg, Germany

> Derek Hopwood, Oxford
> Habib Ishow, Aix-en-Provence
> Thomas Koszinowski, Hamburg

List of Contributors

Alkazaz, Aziz   Researcher, Deutsches Orient-Institut, Hamburg.

Balta, Paul   Director of CEOC, Université de Paris III.

Beaumont, Peter   Professor of Geography, University of Wales at Lampeter.

Chartouni-Dubarry, May   Chargée de Recherche, Institut Français des Relations Internationales de Paris.

Chatelus, Michel   Professeur d'Économie Politique, Institut d'Etudes Politiques de Grenoble.

Farouk-Sluglett, Marion   Lecturer in Politics, University of Wales at Swansea.

Heine, Peter   Professor of Sociology, University of Münster.

Hopwood, Derek   Lecturer in Modern Middle Eastern Studies, Oxford University.

Ishow, Habib   Chargé de Recherche, IREMAM, Aix-en-Provence.

Kienle, Eberhard   Lecturer in Politics, SOAS, London University.

Koszinowski, Thomas   Researcher, Deutsches Orient-Institut, Hamburg.

Picard, Elizabeth   Chargée de Recherche, Fondation Nationale des Sciences Politiques, Paris.

Rieck, Andreas   Researcher, Deutsches Orient-Institut, Hamburg.

Sluglett, Peter   Lecturer in Middle Eastern History, University of Durham.

Solh, Camillia Fawzi el-   Researcher associated with Centre for Cross-Cultural Research on Women, Oxford University.

Tripp, Charles   Lecturer in Politics, SOAS, London University.

Social Structures and the New State 1921–1958

Derek Hopwood

At the end of the First World War the Arab provinces of the defeated Ottoman Empire were facing an uncertain future. The world that had been familiar to them and with which they had learned to live during the previous four centuries had been shattered. A system of relationships had been established between ruler and ruled and amongst the ruled themselves, based largely on a common religion, age-old economic links and a mutually acknowledged hierarchy founded on learning, wealth or land, or on a hereditary position of leadership. The Sunni majority enjoyed its status of being closest to the Sunni Ottoman Turks, the minorities had either acquired the wisdom of accepting their fate and blending into the majority or of choosing to dwell in remote fastnesses where they attempted to live their lives unhindered by outsiders. Loyalties of the inhabitants of the Ottoman Arab provinces were felt toward the local area (village or larger), or to the community, religious or ethnic, which, although experienced locally, might spread over a wider range (for example the Islamic *umma* or the Greek Orthodox Church or the Kurdish people). Possibly they had a particular feeling of belonging to an empire which taxed them, sometimes conscripted them, and which defined their world view. Within this view among an educated minority there had been growing since the

---

This chapter owes everything to work of other authors, particularly P. Sluglett *Britain in Iraq 1914–1932* (London, 1976), M. Farouk-Sluglett and P. Sluglett *Iraq since 1958, from revolution to dictatorship* (London, 1987), R.A. Fernea and W.R. Louis eds., *The Iraqi Revolution of 1958, the old social classes revisited* (London, 1991), H. Batatu, *The old social classes and the revolutionary movements of Iraq* (Princeton U.P. 1978) and S.H. Longrigg *Iraq, 1900 to 1950, a political social, and economic history* (London, 1953).

middle of the nineteenth century another awareness, that to be an Arab meant something more than being an Ottoman citizen. A shared language, history and culture set them apart, a separation which was emphasized at a time when Turkish nationalism was becoming more intense. Thus although the First World War physically put an end to the Ottoman Empire, psychologically a growing number of its Arab inhabitants had left it and were looking for a new way of organizing their society. Decentralization was a catch word at one time, complete independence at another. The area in which the latter would come about was only hazily defined, the concept of individual Arab states with recognized boundaries was not yet common currency.

Even before 1918 parts of the Ottoman Arab world had been detached by the actions of the European powers, Algeria occupied by the French in 1830, Egypt by the British in 1882, Libya by the Italians in 1911. European influence was spread in other ways, through education, missionary activity, trade and by treaties of protection with local rulers. Thus the Persian Gulf area fell into the British sphere (Aden had been occupied in 1839) and important trade links and communications had been established through Basra at the mouth of the Tigris–Euphrates and on the rivers themselves. Europeans were becoming familiar figures in the area and they brought with them an introduction to a new world, to new methods of thought and action, and an uneasy awareness of the power of Europe. Traditional society was having to change to accommodate these innovations, although only among a small urban minority in the beginning, those who went to foreign schools (mainly Christians), those who engaged in commerce or came into contact with or studied Western technology. Rural and mountain societies remained largely untouched and unchanged in their centuries old traditions.

The Ottoman Empire was divided administratively into provinces (and smaller units), each under a centrally appointed governor. The three provinces which were to come together to form the state of Iraq were based on the towns of Basra in the south, Baghdad in the centre and Mosul in the north. The area was united by the two rivers of the Tigris and the Euphrates and was generally known in Europe as Mesopotamia, the seat of the great civilization of Babylon. Under the Arabs it was termed Iraq, an undefined territory meeting the Persian Empire to the east and the deserts to the west. In the first three centuries of Turkish rule there had been only the one province of Baghdad, and even after 1879 when Mosul became separate and 1884 when Basra was detached Baghdad retained its primacy and its governor his seniority. The three chief towns had nevertheless looked in different ways, Mosul towards Aleppo and Turkey, while Basra faced down the Gulf and towards trade with India. Baghdad had long been a centre of Arab culture and learning and was a city of the transit trade from Persia.

If the territory that was to become Iraq was divided administratively and geographically it was also very diverse ethnically, religiously and socially. The population at the beginning of the century was very approximately between two and two and a half million people the majority of which was Arab, with a shared pride in language, history and culture. This did not mean, however, that they were a homogeneous group. They were divided by formidable differences, between towndweller and tribesman, and between the two main socio-religous communities, Sunni and Shi'i. In the north the Sunni Arabs predominated, in the south the Shi'i, in the more mixed central areas the Shi'i were in a majority. Relations between the two groups were brittle, sometimes violent, and there was little social mixing. The Shi'is were largely excluded from the Sunni educational system and also from the ranks of government. The Sunnis were closer to their Ottoman Sunni rulers, the Shi'is looked across the frontier to their co-religionaries the Persians.

The mountain people of Mosul province belonged to another racial group; the Kurds with their own language were largely Sunni. They had kin in other areas of the Ottoman Empire and together formed a very large group. Like most mountaineers they were fiercely independent and strongly resented and resisted attempts to impose outside control on them. However, they were gradually being brought into the imperial system. Some served as officials or soldiers for the Empire. Yet they showed far greater loyalty to their own leaders than to Turkish officialdom. They were the kind of problem disliked by all central governments, an unruly minority in inaccessible areas, unwilling to conform or pay taxes, liable to revolt. In Mosul province there were also smaller groups of Yazidis and Turkomans. More important were the Iraqi Jews, recognized as a community by Istanbul. They were found in most urban areas, hardworking, quietly supporting authority, holding aloof from public life, living as a minority trying to avoid persecution and to integrate themselves by specializing in certain crafts and professions. In Baghdad with a population of some 50,000 they almost outnumbered the Sunni Arabs and certainly the Christians. They were able to establish foreign trade links with their co-religionaries abroad and readily accepted Western education. Some were rich landowners, while others were very poor.

The Christians were spread though the three provinces. The Armenians were fairly numerous in the towns, the Assyrians (or Nestorians) few in number were mainly in the extreme north, while the numerically important Chaldeans (by origin Nestorian) largely in Mosul formed a Uniate (Catholic) Church. The Christians as a whole were poorer than the Jews yet above them in status. They owned land in the northern villages but not in the south where they specialized in retailing, hotel keeping, craftsmanship and the law. They too enjoyed higher educational standards than the Muslims and some girls went to school. Both Jews and Christians were exempt from army service on payment of a tax and both communities had the right to send members to the Administrative Councils of their districts.

The Assyrians need a special word of mention. They lived scattered amongst the Kurds on both sides of the Mosul province frontier (with other minority groups, Armenians, Chaldeans and Jews) and were particularly vulnerable to torment. They were an ancient community speaking Syriac and barely distinguishable from their Kurdish neighbours. They had kept themselves together by strong character and resolute faith (always difficult when living among a non-Christian majority) but just before the First World War they had been suffering particularly badly at the hands of the Kurds and had nowhere to turn. We shall see that they then appealed to the British.

The ethnic and religious groupings were cut across by social, economic and urban/rural divisions. Iraq was not one people or one political community and in pre-modern society loyalties were primarily local. It consisted of weakly interconnected societies, some concerned with money making and the expansion of private property, while the older groups preserved other values traditional in the Middle East societies, lineage, possession and transmission of religious knowledge or tribal honour expressed in fighting ability. Iraqi society was dominated by local bonds, a limited world view and small scale local economic links.

The social structures of the various towns and regions differed according to history and natural circumstances. These have been touched on above. They ranged from the tribal market town of Suq al-Shuyukh in southern Iraq to the cities of Najaf and Karbala centred round the Shi'i holy shrines to Baghdad as administrative centre. In most of the towns and cities there were also social hierarchies, in Baghdad one of wealth and religion, where Muslims had higher status than Christians and Jews, Sunnis above Shi'is, Christians above Jews, Turks above Arabs, Kurds and Persians. The larger towns were the most open to change where society was slowly evolving as communications improved and education spread. The beginning of an integration into the world market meant that new groups were gaining wealth and prestige, moving upwards in competition with the traditionally prestigious groups. These latter included the learned scholars, the notables, the old aristocracy of officials, and the *ashraf*, those who claimed descent from the family of the Prophet Muhammad.

The world outside the towns was that of the tribes who lived by their own codes and rules, traditional modes of hospitality and social customs. They formed the majority of the inhabitants and their world surrounded the towns and larger villages of Iraq. Ruled by their tribal sheikhs, the tribesmen although homogeneous in code and outlook differed amongst themselves in important respects. Roughly half were Sunni, half Shi'i. Some were mixed, some were Shi'i with Sunni ruling families. In Kurdistan Shi'i tribes were rare. Some of the tribes were settled cultivators, growing fruit and tobacco, wheat and vegetables, dates or rice, others were still nomadic. The size of the tribes could vary from a few tents to confederacies of several tribes under one paramount chief. Despite so many elements of variety, most tribesmen had a common feeling of separateness from the urban dwellers who came more closely under government control. The tribesman traditionally resented outside attempts at interference in whatever form.

Nevertheless, the tribal world was also slowly changing. Government control was spreading, courts had been set up which at least claimed overall jurisdiction, local Ottoman officials could appear in tribal areas, and communal tribal lands were beginning to be registered in the Tapu land records as the private property of the sheikhs. This introduced a new relationship of landlord and tenant rather than that of sheikh and follower. In the mountainous regions government control and influence was as tenuous as ever.

WORLD WAR

While change had been creeping gradually into the Ottoman Empire as a whole during the nineteenth century nothing was as great as the cataclysm caused by the First World War. Iraq itself was to move from one empire to another. The British were to come in as outsiders, non-Muslims, non-Asians, as conquerors to stay to rule this disparate country.

They had no prepared plan for the conquest of Iraq. They were drawn in ever more deeply until they ended in control of the three provinces. In November 1914 Imperial forces landed near Basra, and meeting little opposition moved up the river to begin a comprehensive military campaign. They moved too quickly and soon met stiff opposition. They were besieged in Kut al-Amara for five disastrous months, surrendered, were reinforced and captured Baghdad in March 1917. In 1918 Mosul was taken and a large part of the province occupied. The Turks had by then signed an armistice and abandoned control over all their Arab provinces. The British and the French had to determine the future of these large territories. The very mixed nature of the Iraqi provinces made this a far from easy task. In the beginning ad hoc arrangements had to be made until firm decisions were taken about the longer term future. At the very least law and order had to be maintained and missing officials replaced at, it was urged, minimum cost to the British taxpayer. There followed a lengthy search for an ideal solution, a system which would take account of the existing social structures of the country and provide a framework within which competing interests and different approaches could operate. The British were not expert in this and muddled along for the first three years.

They set up a civil administration in the areas under their control in the only way they knew, one based on their experience in ruling India by which the people were administered directly by British officials with the help of local leaders who were willing to collaborate. With the limited means and manpower available it was only possible to lay down general guidelines and leave much to individual initiative. British officers would ride out amongst the tribes 'where none of the Arabs had ever seen an Englishman' to show the flag, to try to settle disputes and keep order. One such officer wrote unblushingly in 1918 that 'I am the only white man who at present can manage the Muntafik (tribes)'.[1]

In the towns and in Baghdad in particular such men and women as Percy Cox, Gertrude Bell and Arnold Wilson battled with both the problems of central administration and with a government in

---

1. Colonel H.A.R. Dickson in D. Hopwood *Tales of empire* (London, 1990) p. 187.

London unable to give clear directives. Conditions of life were abnormal; the Ottoman administration had gone; many leading Iraqis of the urban Sunni upper class and more senior officials were absent, local politics were inactive. But the necessity to restart government and order society led to the taking of decisions which helped to shape public life for the medium term future, in such matters as law, tribal policy, the structure of the administration and the currency.

What were the approaches the British believed feasible in creating the state of Iraq? They sought a method of dealing with the tribes and tribal disputes (and introduced a series of regulations based on Indian practice). One way to run the country was to enlist men who might fall under British influence (and be in a sense a fifth column) and they singled out the Jews of Baghdad (who at one time asked for British citizenship), the notables of Baghdad and Basra, wealthy landlords and sheikhs of settled tribes. They saw them as stable elements in society and deeply mistrusted those they considered 'nationalist'—a term of criticism of men not amenable to British control. It was believed that the only trustworthy 'progressive' sections of the populations were the Jews and the Christians. There was a desire, however, to try to integrate the different sections of the country, to protect the minorities although well aware that it would be difficult to ensure such protection and that the Kurds, the Shi'is and the tribes would resist strong Sunni rule from Baghdad. One general conclusion was that Iraq (and therefore Britain) should have an administration with Arab institutions which could be safely left to rule with the British pulling the strings.[2]

As the British dithered over the form of government severe rioting broke out in 1920, led by a combination of several elements opposed to British rule. The revolt was put down but the British questioned whether it was worth remaining. But they had destroyed the existing form of government and had morally to stay at least to oversee the installation of a new one. The revolt was a first demonstration of some kind of Iraqi identity and clearly showed that new policies were needed to run the country.

The British did not have absolute freedom in making up their minds. In the post-war world envisaged by President Wilson of the United States Britain and France were not to be allowed to rule any

---

2. Sluglett, *op. cit.*, p. 37 quoting Sir Arthur Hirtzel of the India Office.

newly liberated parts of the Arab east directly. A new way of preparation for independence had to be found. Already in Egypt a widespread uprising had put the British presence at risk and yet British officials on the spot in Iraq had yet to admit that direct rule would be impossible. They did not believe the Iraqis capable of self-government. In practice a middle way was found. In April 1920 the League of Nations awarded a mandate for Iraq to Britain, a device whereby Britain would help to prepare the country for independence. Iraq's existence as an independent nation could be provisionally recognized subject to the rendering of administrative advice and assistance until such time as it would be able to stand alone. Behind this flimsy veil British domination would be exercised.

REVOLUTION 1958

In 1958 a military revolution swept away the institutions that the British set up in 1920. The revolution all too clearly showed the weaknesses of the structures first created under the mandate. The support for these structures had been the British presence, the Royal Air Forces bases, advisers in many parts of the administration and control of the Iraq Petroleum Company. On this foundation were built those institutions which it was hoped would help to create a new stable Iraq with a sense of national identity and within which the various social structures could develop and ultimately coalesce into the new identity, each with a role in the development of power and authority and a say in how it could be exercised or transferred. But the institutions which were created, the monarchy, government, parliament, civil service and army/police force, did not create this stable national political entity. The time frame was too brief, the complexities of the country too great and in many ways the policies too misguided for this to happen. A weak monarchy, too narrow a ruling class, a still developing military and civil control did not provide the motor force necessary for the creation of a nation. On the eve of the revolution Iraq was ruled by an élite of monarchy, rich merchants and property owners (including tribal sheikhs) and a group of civil servants, lawyers and politicians. The British were comfortable with this arrangement, the Iraqi leaders unwilling to change, and the scene was set for revolution.

Most historians now agree that the institutions set up by the British in Iraq failed. Perhaps given the situation nothing could have succeeded. In 1920 an attempt was made to find a solution based on past experience and on imperfect understanding of the working of Iraqi society. The British looked towards the Westminster system of government as their model, however inappropriate for a newly born country unprepared for democracy. It seemed though that the British never really believed that a fully independent democratic system would work on the ground, and consequently they had to work with those men who were willing to take office and who had some experience of government, turning a blind eye to actions which did not fully accord with ideal Westminster practice.

INSTITUTIONS OF GOVERNMENT

At the top of the administrative structure the British decided to place a king, not because local tradition demanded it, but because they sought a facade behind which to run the new system. Faisal, son of Sharif Husain of Mecca, had already been King of Syria for a short period (1920) until expelled by the French. He was chosen, partly from a sense of obligation for his help in the Arab revolt, partly from guilt over his treatment by the French, to be the figurehead of the regime, to reign, it was hoped, not to govern. The British claimed the choice was welcome to most Iraqis but it proved that few had much affection for or faith in him. He was weak and indeterminate ('If only he would be more firm!', cried Gertrude Bell) and irritated his British advisers. He owed his throne to the British and yet to make his own position secure he had to demonstrate that he was not their creature—in many ways a wretched role. For the British the fact of bringing Faisal to Baghdad entailed consequences detrimental to their prestige. Faisal in his turn was bound to a system with which he was identified and he was held responsible for its failures.

The British set up a government under Faisal recruited chiefly from Sunni Arab dignitaries and supported by a network of British advisers in the various ministries in Baghdad and in the offices of the local administrations. Iraq was to be ruled by this alliance of the monarchy and élite, with Britain part of a triangle of power. The élite formed by the propertied classes, the tribal sheikhs and the political and military leaders naturally favoured the existing social order, leaving aside the majority of Sunnis and Shi'is, the Kurds and the rank and file tribesmen. This élite supported by Britain was not particularly interested in reform, nor willing to share power with Shi'is or Kurds. In this situation lay the seeds of the disastrous end of the regime less than forty years on.

THE TREATY OF 1922

The British now had the elements of a system which included a two chamber parliament, the basis of a civil service, an army and police force. All arrangements were to be enshrined in a treaty which Britain drew up and against which Faisal had strong objections. The King was already forced into a position of trying to reject certain provisos which seemed to weaken his standing in the country. In the end, however, he had to acknowledge that he could either agree to British demands or lose his throne.

A treaty was ratified in October 1922. It did not give Iraq the complete independence sought by Faisal and retained the provisions of the mandate. Under its terms Faisal agreed to frame an organic law for a Constituent Assembly and to promise freedom of conscience for and non-discrimination against all the inhabitants of Iraq, regardless of race, religion or language. Other provisions regulated foreign representation, judicial matters, financial relations and the army. The organic law was ratified by the Assembly in June 1924. This dealt with and confirmed the above mentioned matters and defined such things as elections, local administration and taxation. Careful provision was made for the rights of minorities, their representation in parliament and their internal administration.

INDEPENDENCE 1930

Most Iraqis viewed the 1922 Treaty (quite correctly) as a veil for the continued British direction of their country. Therefore, continuous pressure was exerted in an attempt to modify its provisions. A new treaty was signed in 1930 which ostensibly gave Iraq full independence. It terminated the mandate and promised perpetual friendship between Britain and Iraq. Its title of 'preferential alliance' indicated the real nature of the relationship and an essential provision was the maintenance of British bases in the country. Although a step forward, few believed that Britain had really given up very much. Britain now exercised power more covertly and less directly.

As with all treaties and laws their effectiveness lies only in the zeal with which they are adhered to and put into practice. Fallible and inexperienced men often place immediate aims and short-term gains before the demands of the law. And this happened in Iraq where Britain was more concerned with power and influence than with the greater good of the community. Cooperation with existing centres of power was seen as the best way forward, and the Royal Air Force was always there as a means of encouraging the non-cooperators to toe the line.

THE STATE SOCIAL AND POLITICAL STRUCTURES 1920–58

The task of creating a unified state from the elements involved proved too much for the system installed by the British. The situation in 1990/1 once again proved the enormity of the problem. In 1953 a historian wrote that the Shi'i situation was inflammable, the Kurds restless.[3] The events of 1991 confirmed this analysis only too clearly. Despite economic and social progress since 1958 the two communities took the first opportunity to seek a more acceptable place within (or even outside) the Iraqi state. Under the monarchy the state had been weak and in a sense 'external' to the society it purported to rule, and no one group was sufficiently dominant to impose coherence at the centre or between rulers and ruled. What political power there was depended on the skill of the palace and the politicians in working together, with the British always there in the background (or as in the case of the attempted 1941 anti-British coup by the army stepping in directly with military force). The extreme fluidity at the centre was exemplified by the fact that forty-seven ministries fell in thirty years of political life, because of internal quarrels and not the organized withdrawal of public or parliamentary support. The system of two stage elections meant that the deputies were virtually independent of the electorate, and in any case rarely represented party interests. The parliamentary system was abused and failed as any kind of check on government.

The shortcomings of the state system stemmed from the institutions set up, by the British, from the weak and 'half-foreign' monarchy downwards. But once set up the British were reluctant to change them. They closed their eyes to abuses, tended to cover up

---

3. Longrigg, *op. cit.*, pp. 381, 382.

for the Iraqi government rather than to blame it, and when a strong man came along, Nuri al-Said (prime-minister fourteen times between 1930–58, assassinated 1958) the British were only too happy to encourage him. He personified that alliance between monarchy and the élite, created by the British in favour of the existing social order. As a member of the old guard he was reluctant to encourage social change through political participation and in alliance with him the British irrevocably identified themselves with the class and system he represented. Opposition was not tolerated and was thus driven underground. The crowd which murdered him and the King, Faisal II, in 1958 were as much murdering the hated British imposed system. It is no coincidence that at the same time they ransacked the British Embassy.

THE ÉLITE

The British in their empire were happiest ruling in cooperation with an élite, in the Gulf sheikhdoms, in India or Africa. With their public school, regimental or Oxbridge background they looked for those who by birth or heredity were natural rulers. In Iraq they looked first to the Arab Sunni urban notables, ex-Ottoman officials, ex-Sharifian officers, to form an administration supported by local tribal leaders. Around this group coalesced an upper class of richer landowners, businessmen, men of money and commerce, high officials, who became identified with the regime. In the early decades of the monarchy different elements within this group were vying for power, but later closed ranks in defence of the social order from which they all benefited and against the growing strength of other groups, the army, the Communists, the Shi'is. They dominated the political arena in Baghdad through the cabinet, offices of state and parliament which they controlled. They clung to power under Nuri and suffered together with him. It was almost as though government had been carried on merely for their sake.

THE SHI'A

Although the leadership was Sunni it did not follow that poor urban/rural Sunnis benefited from the system. The Shi'is felt themselves even more excluded and discriminated against, while the Sunni/Shi'i split was emphasized by class division. Few Shi'is had moved into the upper classes. By the end of the monarchy the distinction between the two remained, doctrinally, socially and politically. The Shi'is had never believed that the Ottoman Sunni government had had the right to govern them and only with difficulty accepted the monarchy, although Faisal was tolerant religiously and saw one of his tasks as the integration of the Shi'is. The growth of feeling of national unity depended on their assimilation (and that of the Kurds) into the political system. Not all was black though, as there was little discrimination in the bureaucracy and the professions, the army was open, and many Shi'is were making their way up in commerce, particularly in taking the place of those Jews who left for Israel after the foundation of the state. The influence of the *mujtahids* (religious leaders) had diminished but many Shi'i grievances remained. The British remained wary of what they considered Shi'i fanaticism.

Tribes and Tribal Leaders

The British saw the tribes as a distinct entity within the new Iraqi state, as a discrete body with which it was easier to deal separately. There was also some sympathy for tribal life and a desire not to change it too rapidly. Some British officials felt more at home amongst the tribal peoples than with urban, more sophisticated Arabs who they believed to be corrupted by ideas of nationalism. From the beginning the tribes were treated differently with the introduction of the Tribal Criminal and Civil Disputes Regulation in 1916 drawn up on the lines of a code from India. It gave the local British Political officer the right to call a tribal council/*majlis* to deal with all cases according to tribal custom in which one of the parties was a tribesman. This was done under the jurisdiction of the sheikhs and it enhanced their position by giving them absolute legal authority over their tribes. The Regulation was reissued in 1918 and became part of the general code of law in 1924. In this way a section of the population of Iraq was set apart, militating against national integration. Until 1958 Iraq remained legally subject to two codes, one for the cities and one for the tribal areas. The tribes had, however, made common cause with the townsmen in the uprising of 1920 against the British, but the agitation of the time was not nationalist, it was still largely a tribal affair.

The British had attempted to balance the influence of tribe and town, to stop detribalization and to prevent a nationwide alliance against their authority. Support for the tribal sheikhs was continued by the monarchy which thus was far from playing a unifying role. As the power of the sheikhs increased with their juridical authority and greater land holding they pressed down on their villages, exploited them in a system of extreme economic inequality. The greed of the sheikhs was a direct result of British policy.

Changes were on the way. Some distinctions were slowly being eroded. The arm of government was spreading everywhere. Better communications made it possible to control even the most remote areas. Local administrations were set up, irrigation was improved, commerce developed, and there was steady migration from the rural areas to the towns. High expectations were raised, not enough was done to satisfy them. The world of the tribesmen was thus expanding. They had to deal with the government through its officials, the outside world came to them through the radio and other means. The foundations of their lives were being modified and they were struggling with two ways of thinking, the traditional and the new. They were passing through a period of transition.

THE KURDS

The Kurds were characterized as a restless minority at mid century with no sign of their evolving into a contented or strengthening element in the Iraqi state.[4] In 1991 they were still restless. British and Iraqi policies of integration had clearly failed. The British in 1920 had insisted that Iraqi Kurdistan be included in the mandate and not revert to Turkey. The Kurds, although disunited and often in revolt, had not wanted to be ruled from Baghdad. The British believed that they should be with strict guarantees for their language and local administration. The Iraqis rejected any such guarantees and the Kurds were stranded among the higher demands of political and international considerations. The problem was complicated by the dispute with Turkey over the line of the northern frontier. It was not until 1926 that the League of Nations finally awarded the entire Mosul province to Iraq which had claimed that possession of Mosul was essential to its continuance as a state.

Although Britain had stressed the necessity of protecting Kurdish rights and of granting a form of autonomy by 1930 little had been done. The British tried to persuade the Iraqis to take

---

4. Longrigg, p. 382.

Kurdish aspirations seriously—to no avail. The Anglo-Iraqi Treaty of 1930 contained no special provisions for the Kurds. The League of Nations tried to insist that just treatment of the Kurds be made a condition for Iraqi entry. The British were embarrassed by obvious signs of continued discontent in Kurdistan which the Iraqis blamed on British weakness, and which the British laid at the door of Iraqi intransigence. The Kurds did not believe in any paper promises made by the Iraqis to the League or to the British. The latter after the 1930 Treaty had in any case abandoned the Kurds who staged a series of unsuccessful revolts against the central government until 1958. The British had left a problem for others to solve.

Christians and Jews

The Assyrians became a responsibility of the British after their advance in 1918 into north west Persia, where they found the Christians being persecuted by the Persians and harassed by the Turks. The British rescued them, perhaps one third of their original number, and led them to refugee camps in Iraq. Where repatriation was impractical in the face of Persian hostility or because their homes were in Turkish territory the British bore the financial burden of supporting them, lessened to some extent by recruiting some thousands into a special military force, the Iraq Levies. The officers were British, the soldiers Arab, Assyrian and Kurdish, and feelings between the different elements were never cordial.

The Assyrians were not an easy group to deal with, indisciplined, disunited, and their leaders making impossible claims for special status. Iraqi Muslims thought them not fully loyal to the state and there was much bitter feeling between them which led to attacks on the Assyrians who for their part felt discriminated against and insecure. It was impossible for them to return home (some who made the attempt were attacked by the Turks) and so they had to try to settle in Iraq.

The end of the mandate particularly disturbed the Assyrians as anti-Assyrian feeling grew. The British tried to reassure them but they continued to demand unacceptable privileges. In 1933 some tried to flee to Syria, were turned back by the French and great ill feeling flared. Rumours multiplied of Assyrian ambitions and atrocities which led to widescale attacks on Assyrian lives and property. There was worldwide revulsion at these massacres and Iraq apologized for the unjustifiable severity against the Assyrians.

Some of them went abroad and the remainder attempted to adapt to Iraqi conditions and to obtain citizenship. On the whole they settled down, tolerated but not assimilated, and not less prosperous than those amongst whom they lived.

Other Christians, largely the Chaldeans, wished to be accepted as equals in Iraqi society and the administration and were basically loyal to Faisal. Laws of 1930 defined the powers of priest and councils and they were given a measure of self-government, living as another minority who according to observers changed little in the period to 1958 in outlook, organization or their place in society. They had their patriarch in Baghdad and formed the largest non-Muslim group. They continued as professionals, hoteliers and teachers. Their position was never easy, although not persecuted as were the Assyrians, they constantly feared discrimination or attack. To preserve their status they kept an uneasy low profile and professed their loyalty to the state.

It was the position of the Jews which changed most drastically. After 1929 they remained a compact, assiduous, self-sufficient community, serving in the government, dominating many of the markets and owning property. They did not demur when Iraq was approaching independence in 1930. They maintained or even improved their position. Shops and hotels multiplied in Baghdad and elsewhere in the running and owning of which Jews and Christians were prominent. However, anti-Jewish feeling grew because of Zionist activities in Palestine, particularly during the 1936–39 Arab uprising. There were incidents of hooliganism against the Jews, attacks on persons and property which the government did little to prevent. After the foundation of the state of Israel the hostile pressure increased and for most Jews the only tolerable solution was to emigrate. Eventually some seven eighths of the community left, a great loss in human terms to Iraq.

THE END OF THE MONARCHY

The social, economic and political tensions which had been growing finally exploded in the 1958 revolution. No mechanisms had been developed to deal with them peacefully. The army, after major coups in 1936 and 1941 was the only body capable of the planning and organization and with the necessary power to sweep away the immobile regime of King and old politicians. The seeds of the end were sown in the beginning, in the institutions which the British created and left others to run. Most commentators, even the most balanced, admit that these institutions had failed to create a national, political community in the full sense. Britain had imposed a political system but not territorial integrity. A federal system representing the local populations could have better coped with the existing tensions. The frontiers imposed by Britain enclosed so many different demands and systems that a very strong central government was needed to cope with them. This was a tradition which was passed on to the post revolutionary state. By the 1950s a political culture had developed which could find no expression through the institutions of the state. In many ways Iraq is still reaping the fruits of the British legacy.

For an extremely critical assessment of the British legacy see E. Kedourie, 'The Kingdom of Iraq a retrospect' in *The Chatham House Version* (London, 1970) esp. p. 278.

The Development of Internal Politics in Iraq from 1958 to the Present Day

May Chartouni-Dubarry

When examining the development of internal politics in Iraq from 1958 to the present day, one is struck by the permanence of certain questions which have been posed almost continuously throughout the thirty-five years following the overthrow of the monarchy by a small group of Iraqi Free Officers and the establishment of the Republic on 14 July. These questions chiefly concern the endemic instability which has paralysed the administration of internal affairs, which has signed away every project of development and reform since the early 1970s, and which is once again threatening not only Saddam Hussein's régime, but also the cohesion of Iraqi society today.

In retrospect and on the scale of the Iraqi Republic's short history, this country has not known a period of real internal or external stability, except between 1975 and 1980, the signing of the Algiers accords and the start of the war with Iran. Beyond the inexperience or incompetence of the régimes which have succeeded each other since the revolution, and the external 'plots', or rather interference from abroad—Egypt and Qasim, the Shah's and then Khomeini's Iran, and finally the United States, which have been rightly or wrongly accused of attempting to destabilize the existing régime—how may we explain the country's apparent inability to achieve the harmonious reconciliation of growth and internal cohesion on the one hand, and the exercise of a regional role proportional to its real weight on the other?

This chapter is devoted to strictly internal aspects of Iraqi politics, and does not aim to explain why in 1992 the country was in the same position of regional and international isolation and extreme fragility on an internal level as it was in 1962, one year before Abd al-Karim Qasim was overthrown. However, an excessively factual approach would provide an imperfect interpretation of both the richness and the complexity of the period in question and of the position of impasse and political uncertainty in which Iraq finds itself today. A more analytical approach which will highlight the political constellation which causes the instability, the interaction between the 'inherent' difficulty of governing Iraq and the violent struggles for the seizure of power. This constellation led Iraq from crisis to crisis throughout the first decade of Republican government, one of the most unstable and violent periods in the history of the country: leaving aside the various aborted coup at- tempts, in ten years the country saw four coups d'état which led to a change in régime. This instability is above all due to the monopolization of power by a military engaged in constant factional struggles and, in the absence of any steps towards democracy, to the radicalization of political life. The main consequence of this was a progressive split between the first Republican régimes and civilian society. This decade is characterized by a form of political 'weakness'. but it is also a decade of transition, when elements of change and continuity are intertwined, from which the Baath Party drew a certain maturity and was able to impose its hegemony. Without settling the central problem of legitimacy, the régime succeeded in establishing a period of political stability unprecedented in the young history of the Iraqi Republic, a stability which would prove to be no more than a digression.

1958–1968: A Decade Of Political Weakness

The Origins of the Politicization of the Army

Relations between the army and the political powers are the determining factor in recent Iraqi history. The army's constant interference in the political domain goes back to 1936 when, four years after its accession to independence, Iraq saw its first aborted military coup, which inaugurated the officers' new style of intervention in political life, and which rapidly became the norm throughout the Arab world.

In fact the process of the politicization of the Iraqi army was set in motion with the creation of the new state in 1920, when King Faisal chose to place ex-Ottoman-army officers in principal political and administrative posts. Leaving the Academy of Military Sciences in Istanbul, these officers, the sons of prominent citizens, constituted an intellectual élite. Their aim was to exercise a leading role in both the political and military spheres,[1] having been set the task of creating a national Iraqi army by King Faisal. From its creation in 1921 onwards this army believed it had been invested with a vital mission: that it should constitute the backbone of the fragile nation-state which had just been born. It therefore had to serve as a catalyst for centrifugal forces, operating on all levels—including violence—in order to obtain the allegiance of the various communities of the Iraqi state; and on the other hand it had to be a factor of modernization and national integration. It is from this viewpoint, and with the clear aim of increasing the power of the army, that Faisal I decided to introduce obligatory conscription during the 1930s, and to open the military academies to all classes of the Iraqi population. Since the army was a source of prestige, the means of social promotion and/or of material security, this measure quite rapidly led to the emergence of a new class of young officer from more modest and sometimes very humble backgrounds,[2] which would soon outstrip in number the officer corps from the great families of the aristocracy, the bourgeoisie and the Muslim clergy. Of the 5,000 officers of which the Iraqi army was comprised from the 1940s onwards, the overwhelming majority came from the middle classes in the widest sense, composed of small businessmen, functionaries and employees.[3] However, despite their ever-increasing importance in the army, they were completely excluded from political life, which remained a privilege reserved for the traditional class of officers. Republicans and anti-imperialists, filled with nationalist and revolutionary ideas, these young officers were also convinced of the avant-garde role which the army had as its mission. In this they subscribed to the continuation of the narrow dependence of the monarchy on the military, and acknowledged the preeminence of the army in Iraqi political life. They embodied this awareness of the value and the 'superiority' of the military

---

1. A certain number of them later became Prime Ministers, the most significant example being that of Nuri al-Said.
2. A. Tahir, *Irak; aux origines du régime militaire*, (Paris, 1989).
3. H. Al-Shawi, 'L'intervention des militaires dans la vie politique de la Syrie, de l'Irak et de la Jordanie', *Politique étrangère*, no 3/74, pp. 343–374.

institution. It is true that on the eve of the revolution in this country entirely created by the will of a colonial power—one might also say 'embryonic' state with regard to its national construction, its political, administrative and socio-economic structures—the army emerged as the most 'advanced' institution in terms of modernization,[4] political awareness and organizational qualities. The disparity, particularly between the army and the political parties and groupings which suffered from lack of experience, structures and means of action, would cost Iraq dear during the first Republican decade in terms of chronic political instability.

The split at the heart of the officer corps reflects the real state of the profound schism into which Iraq gradually progressed, between the monarchical régime and civilian society. Thus, the new military élite, embodied by the Organization of Free Iraqi Officers, drew its roots and its strengths from two impulses with which it identified; the first was linked to the wave of nationalism which swept through the Arab countries after the Second World War; the second interprets the needs and frustrated claims of the new social categories, the majority of which come from the petit bourgeoisie. 'After the Second World War a new generation composed of intellectuals, technicians and functionaries began to evolve (. . .) It has often been wrongly defined as a middle class. In reality, however, the majority came from very humble backgrounds'.[5] Disappointed regarding its pan-Arabist aspirations, its hopes for social and economic reforms to improve living conditions, the impossibility of playing a political role proportional to its size, this new generation embarked on a silent struggle with the ruling class, conclusively judged to be corrupt and wedded to British 'imperialism'. This conflict reached an impasse in 1958. Indeed, despite the existence of a National Front of opposition, bringing together four parties, the Istiqlal, the National Democratic Party, the Baath Party and the Communists, the civilian opposition remained powerless in the face of the means of repression the government used unsparingly. The only alternative was to turn to this new class of officers, within which secret cells had spread, and who combined towards the end of 1956[6] to form the 'Free Officer' movement. A supreme committee of twelve members

4. A. Tahir, *op. cit.*, p. 27.
5. M. Khadduri, *Republican Iraq; a study in Iraqi politics since the revolution of 1958*, (New York, 1969), p. 6.
6. P.A. Marr, 'The Iraqi Revolution; a case study of army rule', *Orbis*, No. 3, 1970, pp. 714–39.

was elected, with Abd al-Karim Qasim at its head, whose immediate objectives were to overthrow the monarchy and liberate Iraq from colonialism. Even though permanent contacts had been established with the political parties in order to ensure their support, the Free Officers, in their capacity as a military organization, acted in no less an autonomous and independent fashion, all the more because they cherished the ambition, deeply rooted in their feelings of superiority and the historical role which had been assigned to them, of presiding over Iraq's destiny. The sole architects of the revolution, the military had no intention of allowing themselves to be dispossessed. They established a quasi-absolute monopoly of the army and made a central issue of the internal rivalries. This 'abduction' of the revolution by the military inevitably led to its decline, that is to say to the maintenance of Iraq in a state of under-development on a political, socio-economic and cultural level.

The military régime's powerlessness to induce real social and economic change in Iraq, whilst embarking the country on the path of stability, is due chiefly to the extreme fragmentation of the officer corps, even though the support of the army for the conspirators had been almost unanimous immediately after the seizure of power. This fragmentation on the one hand reflects the multiplicity of political cross-currents within the army, and on the other the traditional religious, ethnic and regional membership systems in Iraqi society, whose allegiance to the state remained fragile.

From its creation onwards, this fragmentation characterized the Organization of Free Officers, which, in contrast to the Egyptian model, suffered from a lack of cohesion and organization due, amongst other things, to the movement's relatively short gestation period. The absence of a leadership invested with real legitimacy, the absence of a programme of reforms or even a preliminary charter for the new constitution testify to the political immaturity and the impatience of the young officers. In fact, the year which preceded the coup was marked by an increase in the number of differences between the members of the movement; differences of an organizational nature regarding the strategy to adopt or of a more ideological nature. These rivalries, as well as the lack of dialogue, led to the progressive monopolization of power by a handful of men. Thus, the coup of 14 July which overthrew the former régime was executed by the duo Qasim and Abd al-Salam Arif, who at the time represented the most powerful faction within the Free Officers. This seizure of power heralded the 'factionalism' which would dominate the first revolutionary decade, of which the Arif/Qasim split would be the first clear example.

The origins of the instability then reside in the very genesis of the movement of Free Officers. Latent splits would crystalize after the seizure of power by the military and undermine the very foundations of Qasim's régime.

The Military Regimes

The first military régime under Qasim (1958–1963) showed similar characteristics or symptoms to that of the two Arif brothers which succeeded it: the concentration of power in the hands of a single man, supported not by the entire army, but by a faction within it. Part of a narrow and shrinking power base, Qasim's dictatorship carried within it the seeds of its own destruction. The explosion of the conflict which brought Arif into opposition with Qasim immediately after the revolution is only the first link in a long chain of coups and counter-coups in a climate of permanent conspiracy. From the very beginning Qasim's government was forced to fight for its survival. This test of strength between the two leaders disputing the paternity of the revolution was from the outset of a personal nature. Nevertheless it rapidly degenerated into a merciless political struggle, the central issue of which was unity with the United Arab Republic (of Egypt and Syria), and which divided Iraq into two camps, pushing it to the brink of civil war. In fact the permanent threat of a putsch executed by a rival faction,[7] reinforced by the elimination of Arif and the exclusion of part of the Free Officers from power, was coupled with an implacable struggle between the two most radical and most influential parties of the time, the Baath and the Communist Parties. This took the form of the polarization and extreme radicalization of political life, the cause of instability and violence, as the bloody events of Mosul and Kirkuk in March and July 1959[8] bear witness. Qasim himself, without precise ideological tendencies and with no political vision, practised a short-

---

7. According to Colonel Rifat al-Hajj Sirri, the spiritual father of the Organization of Free Officers, when Nuri al-Said got wind of a plot against the régime, offered him these premonitory remarks: 'If ever your plot should succeed a merciless factional struggle will oppose all of you until death', quoted by Khadduri, *op cit.*, p. 86.

8. A source of great controversy amongst historians, the events of Mosul and Kirkuk were triggered on the first occasion by a coup attempt by an Arab nationalist officer and on the second occasion by the commemoration of the first anniversary of

sighted policy by making use of these acute rivalries between political parties to keep himself in power. Thus, whilst the Baath party sought alliances and support within the group of pan-Arabist officers, increasing numbers of whom thought that Qasim had betrayed the revolution, for its part the Communist Party manifested unequalled support for the 'sole leader'. Far from sharing its ideology, Qasim nevertheless relied on the ICP to counter pan-Arabist propaganda. This contributed on the one hand to the alienation of the liberal parties' support (Istiqlal and the National Democratic Party), who were already on bad terms with a régime which was irreversibly moving further and further away from parliamentary democracy, and on the other hand it increased its dependence on the Communists who, having suffered the worst persecutions under the monarchy, reached their true peak under Qasim (by occupying positions not only in the mass organizations and syndicates, but also in radio and television, and by organizing cells throughout the country). Nevertheless, having used the ICP and the forces of popular resistance[9] to bring the Arab nationalists into line, he set about undermining the increasing influence of the Communists by once again granting certain of their most bitter adversaries amongst the pan-Arabist forces sufficient room to manoeuvre.

Qasim's behaviour towards the political parties testifies to the profound deficiencies of his government. Indeed, although this seesaw permitted him to contain the sources of opposition temporarily, it could only end with the inescapable isolation of his régime, alienating it from all its support and depriving it for good of a base of support indispensable for survival. In any case Qasim never stopped declaring that his power was 'above the party'. The direct contact with the Iraqi people had revealed itself to be insufficient to provide him with a true popular base and now Qasim increasingly found himself in the position of the 'emperor with no clothes' which stemmed from his lack of traditional familial or regional networks of allegiance. In addition, this policy of systematic division, described as 'Qasimism'—from the name Qasim which means the 'divider'—had been practised by the Iraqi leader to extremes, even in the ranks of the army, with the aim of neutralizing an officer corps teeming with potential 'putschists'. 'Each Communist officer nominated was

the revolution of 1958. Both degenerated into violent confrontations between Arab nationalist forces and the Iraqi Communist Party (ICP), which were dangerously coupled with intercommunity confrontations involving Kurds and Turkomans.
9. The paramilitary organisation under the command of the ICP.

followed by the nomination of a very much more moderate officer, and vice versa (with the exception of nationalists, who were considered to be too dangerous). In this attempt to divide the army Qasim used not only political but also social means(. . .), the reactivation of all sources of fragmentation: rivalries between sects, ethnic groups, the military (. . .)'.[10]

His inability to encourage the rise of a moderating political force at the centre,[11] his narrow assessment of social and economic matters and above all the renewal of the war against the Kurds in 1961 precipitated his fall. Already exposed on a regional level to the permanent attacks of Nasser of Egypt, Qasim's Iraq found itself virtually ostracized by the Arab countries following the disastrous attempt to claim Kuwait.

Was the Iraqi leader conscious of the precarious nature of his position? It is probable that until the end he held the private conviction that he was fulfilling his mission, that of embodying and obeying the principles of the 1958 revolution. The assassination attempt stirred up by the Baathists in October 1959, which he was very lucky to escape, led him to the belief that he was protected by divine providence. This distorted perception of the political realities of his country doubtless led him to underestimate the degree of vulnerability of his régime and conversely to overestimate his ability to control rivalries and internal conflicts.[12]

In any case Qasim thought that as a last resort he would be able to rely on the support of the army, which he purged regularly of suspect elements. However, the army was swarming with ideological cells and it was precisely by allying with certain of these factions that the Baath Party's first coup d'état succeeded in overthrowing the Qasim régime on 8 February 1963.

The first Baath régime (February to November 1963) did not survive the inexperience of its leaders or involvement in the war against the Kurds, or, above all, the profound rivalries which undermined the Baath party, an acute conflict between the right and left wings of the party.[13] Arif, returning to power on the occasion of the Baath coup d'état—appointed to the title of honorary President of

10. Al-Shawi, *op. cit.*, pp. 371–2.
11. Khadduri, *op. cit.*, p. 137.
12. M. Farouk-Sluglett and P. Sluglett, *Iraq since 1958*, (London, 1987), p. 74.
13. For a detailed study of the Baath regime of 1963 see E.F. Penrose, 'Essai sur l'Irak', *Orient*, 35, 1965; and 'L'Irak en 1963: une année de coups d'Etat', *Orient* 48, 1963, pp. 17–36.

the Republic because of his nationalist past—would skillfully exploit its internal rivalries in order to move the Party completely away from the government.

The third military coup d'etat, known by the name of the November Revolution, allowed Arif to concentrate power in his own hands from spring 1964 onwards. Like 'Qasimism' the short Baathist interlude was denounced as a deviation from the objectives of the revolution of 14 July 1958. Nevertheless, Arif himself, despite his attachment to the principles of pan-Arabism and his boundless admiration for Nasser, was a more conservative pragmatist, a strong supporter of Islam as a national culture. To this end his régime had a quite marked Sunni hue,[14] which did not fail to arouse distrust amongst the Shi'is and the Kurds. It is this which caused his reticence regarding socialism and when he was more or less forced by Nasser to adopt certain social reforms (including laws on nationalization), he carried them out whilst affirming that Arab Socialism was based on Islam and must not be influenced by external forms. His enthusiasm for the union of Egypt and Iraq, as stipulated by the tripartite accord of 17 April 1963, would decline in contact with Iraqi realities. In his capacity as President of the Republic, he had been able to measure the difficulties, if not impossibility regarding the reconciliation of the imperative of national unity with pan-Arabist projects, to the great discontent of Nasserist officers.

Following the example of Qasim, Arif emerged as the strong man of a military régime. Like him he had no intention whatsoever of anchoring the legitimacy of his power in a parliamentary and democratic system. But in contrast to Qasim, he did not try to play off one party against another, but quite simply proceeded to effect the dissolution of all political parties, no longer relying on the hard core of Nasserist officers. Nevertheless, this group became more and more influential within the military and began to threaten Arif's power. They were eliminated from power when, for the first time since 1958, he nominated a civilian to government, Abd al-Rahman Bazzaz. Did Arif realize that the logic of the factional struggle could only lead in time to the overthrow of his régime? Did the government of Abd al-Rahman Bazzaz constitute the first stage

---

14. Arif's regime relied equally on tribal connections, in contrast to Qasim whose family was completely urbanized. Thus, the majority of the National Guard was composed of members of the al-Jumaila tribe, from which he himself originated.

in the progressive transfer of power into the hands of civilians? We will never know, because the accidental death of Abd al-Salam Arif in April 1966 put an end to this brief experience of civilian government in Iraq. The arrival in power of Abd al-Rahman Arif, who had neither the charisma nor the strength of his brother, permitted the military to return in force to the political scene under the pretext that he was setting Iraq on a counter-revolutionary path which deviated from the objectives of an Arab Socialist programme.

On the eve of the second Baathist coup the struggle for power had undergone a profound transformation; indeed the conflict between the old and the new generation, the cause of the 1958 revolution, had been transformed into a conflict between the military élite and the civilian élite, both of whom belonged to the same young generation.[15] Before coming to the second part of this chapter, it is important to analyse the development of the test of strength between the military and civilians, and more precisely between the Baathists and the army, since to the present day no stable equilibrium has existed between the two.

Since 1958 the army has been the originator of all political change in Iraq and no régime is able to survive for very long if it loses the support of the officers who control the army. The monopolization of power by the military rests on three main factors.

In the first place, the very success of the 1958 coup d'état created a precedent, a model point of reference which inspired all officers without exception. This phenomenon was intensified by the fact that the reappropriation of the 1958 revolution had become the official issue in the factional struggles within the army. Each faction believed that the revolution belonged to them and that it was up to them to rectify deviations. This defence of interests vital and superior to the revolution which served to legitimize a military coup d'état could not, however, hide the majority of officers' irresistible appetite for power.

As emphasized above, the second factor rests on the inequality between the army and the political groupings, which ensured a de facto primacy of the former and this despite the indispensable alliances which were made on the eve of the takeovers by force, which guaranteed their success. In brief one might say that this collaboration between the military leaders and the civilian opposition movements was founded on a complementarity: the civilians

---

15. Khadduri, *op cit.*, p. 297.

supplied the ideology, the political programmes and the military supplied the force. But it is a false complementarity because it is force which since 1958 has been the decisive factor in political changes in Iraq. Thus, the first two coups in 1958 and 1963 were the fruits of an alliance between civilians and the military. But as soon as they tried to participate in and to organize power, this cooperation ceased. Qasim's and Arif's paths are similar in this respect: both members of an influential faction within the army, each relied on political parties (the National Front in 1958 and the Baath party in 1963) who participated directly in the coup. 'But after the seizure of power, instead of the anticipated cooperation, internal struggles were stopped with the elimination of political parties and the establishment of exclusively military régimes'.[16]

This imbalance was reinforced by the 'esprit de corps'. Indeed, despite its divisions and rivalries, the military displayed greater solidarity and cohesion than the civilians, who allowed one faction to retain power until another more powerful faction took over. This conflict between the civilian and military wing rapidly overcame the Baath Party—which from 1963 onwards contained an increasing number of officers—and precipitated the fall of the first Baath régime. Here, too, the esprit de corps acted to the detriment of the party membership, because the military wing of the party (the right wing of the party) chose to ally itself with non-Baathist officers (to whom they felt closer politically) in order to eliminate the left and civilian wing and also to occupy key posts both in the army and the state.

Finally, the third factor, which emerges from the preceding, is the disorganization, the lack of coherence and cohesion of the principal political forces under the military régimes in Iraq. Conscious of the weakness of their structures and incapable of realizing a viable political coalition, the political parties participated fully in the game of alliances and counter-alliances, coups and counter-coups, the rules of which were defined by Qasim. For these parties, launched on their frantic course to power, the military leader or leaders represented both a trump and a central stake. The realization of their ambitions has necessarily to cut across the alliance, either with the ruling faction (such as the support of the ICP for Qasim), or with a group of Putschist officers (such as the alliance

16. H. Al-Shawi, 'Le Baath et l'armée en Irak et en Syrie; interpenetration et conflit', *Maghreb-Machrek*, January-March 1976, pp. 66–72.

between the Baathists and the hard core of the pan-Arabist officers). All these parties seemed to support the principle of a coup d'état as an instrument of political change and thus contributed to the encouragement and reinforcement of factional struggles within the Iraqi army.

We must wait for the arrival in power of a strong party, endowed with a highly structured organization and already well-established in the country before the rules of this game become out of date. For in ousting all the other parties from the political scene the Baathists at a stroke reduced and simplified the internal struggles in an exclusively bilateral test of force between themselves and the army.

THE BAATHIST REGIME (1968–)

Bringing the Military to Heel and the Hegemony of the Baath Party

When the Baath Party returned to power in July 1968 there was a resurgence in the conflict at the very heart of the party, bringing the civilian and military wings into opposition. But the main leaders of the Party, their fingers burned by their failure in 1963 and by the Baathist experience in Syria, where the army dominated the party, were this time determined to 'bring to heel' 'undisciplined' Baathist officers.[17] For the Baathist leaders the cooperation between civilians and the military was not possible because it systematically turned to the advantage of the military, which intended to govern not only alone, but independently of the principles and directives of the party. The civilians were convinced that the only means of reducing the vulnerability of the new Baathist régime, thus guaranteeing its stability, was to subordinate the army to the party. It therefore acted in the first place to depoliticize the army, whose regular intervention in political life had made it into a powerful and autonomous actor, but above all a destabilizing element. And for the first time since the group of officers overthrew the monarchy in 1958 it was a one-party régime composed of civilians which became the 'guide and the guardian of the revolution'.

The transfer of power into the hands of civilians was above all

17 General Hardan al-Takriti, a Baath officer enjoying great popularity within the army and who manifested an independent will in relation to the directives of the Party, was dismissed in October 1970, having been one of the principal instigators of the coup of July 1968. His dismissal marks the beginning of the decline in military influence on political life. See M. Khadduri, *Socialist Iraq; a study in Iraqi politics since 1968*, (Washington D.C., 1978).

the act of Ahmad Hasan al-Bakr, President of the Republic. Himself a member of the Free Officers, respected in official circles, civilian as much as military, he had not, however, as Qasim and Arif had, succumbed to the temptation of absolute power, despite the effective control which he exercised over the army. In all probability this Baathist officer had not regarded his dual military and party membership as a dilemma. His loyalty to Baathism took precedence over all other considerations. Indeed, he remained faithful to the principles of his party, endeavouring to govern through a collegiate leadership, bringing civilian leaders together, so as to reinforce solidarity at the heart of the Party. One of the principal factors of the consolidation of Baathist power resides precisely in this complementary relationship between Hasan al-Bakr and his young protégé Saddam Hussein. It was throughout this period that the latter cleverly and patiently spun a web around the principal political actors, without ever challenging the leadership of Hasan al-Bakr. He would become the principal architect of the depoliticization and simultaneous 'Baathization' of the army, subjected to the narrow control of the Party. This policy led to the creation of a popular paramilitary militia and an intelligence service independent of the army, a system of material rewards, not, of course, forgetting imprisonments, purges and regular deportations. The aim of all these measures was fundamentally to transform the role of the armed forces and to avoid the emergence of a 'military identity' capable of rivalling and threatening the hegemony of the Party. This progressive but radical 'professionalization' of the military is well illustrated by the composition of the Revolutionary Command Council (RCC), the highest authority, which after June 1982 included no more than a single member from the ranks of the army, whilst in 1968 it was exclusively composed of Sunni officers.

Having established a sophisticated system to detect and neutralize any officer who harboured political ambitions, Saddam Hussein set to work to introduce exclusive Baath influence and in this case his own, in all sectors of civilian society and all echelons of power. Parallel to this he practised patronage and nepotism at the highest level of the state, surrounding himself entirely with relations or friends from the Takrit region (Takrit is a small town on the Tigris, north of Baghdad), placing them in key political posts. Indeed, after the decade of 1958–1968, when the permanent climate of conspiracy impregnated political life, support from familial and regional allegiances constituted the most certain guarantee for the conservation of power. In many respects Baathist power appeared to be the personal preserve of Saddam Hussein and his clan, who had created a vacuum around themselves by systematically eliminating all potential opponents. This strongly clan-like hue of Baath power made some suggest[18] that the Takriti clan governed Iraq through the Party rather than the reverse. Having completely deviated from the initial thoughts of Michel Aflaq—founder of the Baath[19]—the interpretation of Baathism in Iraq was indistinguishable from a merciless and totalitarian policing machine to achieve power and maintain it.[20] In effectively achieving the Presidency of the Republic in 1979 Saddam Hussein merged the functions of the President of the RCC, Secretary General of the Party, Prime Minister and Commander in Chief of the Army, thus exercising a quasi absolute monopoly on the decision-making process. Even the National Assembly, elected for the first time in June 1980, and intended to enlarge the popular base of the régime, would really serve to legitimize the supremacy of the President in all other state institutions.[21] The personality cult, practised to extremes from 1982 onwards—the year in which the Iraqi army suffered its first setbacks with regard to Iran—associated with the redoubtable efficacy of the intelligence services, spying on each other and charged with the control of the population, ended by convincing the latter if not of the fact of the ubiquity of Saddam Hussein, then at least the absence of a possible alternative to his power. The personalization of the different channels of power had achieved such a degree that one can just as well speak of 'Saddamism' as 'Baathism' in Iraq. In any case, the symbiotic relationship which binds Saddam Hussein to the Party[22] constituted the most solid foundation of his régime. He would certainly have failed to impose his personal power had he been forced to rely on the army.

18. H. Batatu, *The old social classes and the revolutionary movements of Iraq*, (Princeton University Press, 1978).
19. This distortion between the Baathist rank and file ideology and practice, as found in Iraq did not prevent Saddam Hussein from proclaiming himself the heir and guardian of Aflaq's ideas.
20. See on this subject the charges by M. Farouk-Sluglett and P. Sluglett, *op cit.*, pp. 269–82; and S. al-Khalil, *Republic of Fear; the politics of modern Iraq*, (University of California Press, 1989).
21. See the chapter by C. Tripp.
22. A. Dawisha, 'The politics of war; presidential centrality, party power, political opposition', in F.W. Axelgard, ed., *Iraq in transition; a political, economic and strategic perspective*, (Boulder, Colorado, 1986).

The Consolidation of the Iraqi Nation

In emerging victorious from the incessant political struggles which got the better of the preceding régimes and by not skimping on the means of terror to put an end to them once and for all, the Baathist leaders succeeded in stabilizing rather than legitimizing their power. The chief consequence of this unprecedented political stability was that for the first time since 1958 a régime was in a position to govern in the medium term, without being constantly haunted by the immediate imperative of political survival. This is not to say that the Baathist leaders had remedied the structural feeling of vulnerability which characterized their predecessors; they were simply 'past masters in the art of political survival'.[23] But what distinguishes this régime from its predecessors is above all an ideology, or rather a legitimizing discourse, an economic and social programme and a certain type of political maturation; in short a better comprehension of the realities and needs of the Iraqi people. The failure of the Republican powers since 1958 to establish a policy and introduce a programme of reform led, beyond the rivalries and factional struggles, to a fundamental underestimation of the internal problems of Iraq and notably of the degree of cohesion and homogeneity of the society. And in fact, in 1968 when the Baath Party came to power, the fragility of national feeling, diluted in the systems of ethnic or religious membership, was the most visible symptom of a decade of political deficiencies.

Once their power was consolidated the priority of the Baath leaders was wisely to get down to the construction of a viable Iraqi nation state. They rapidly realized that progress along the path of unity was vital and that the very survival of the régime depended on it. It was with a social programme and a process of national integration both cultural and economic that they attempted to form a bridge between the state and civilian society, thus anchoring their legitimacy.

It is an irony of history to observe that of all the régimes since 1958, none of which ever succeeded in deciding between the global notion of Arab nationalism, to which the Kurds and Shi'is were opposed, and the narrow notion of Iraqi nationalism, the Baath Party, the party of Arab resurrection, resolutely opted in favour of the second. Whilst continuing to take their inspiration from pan-Arabism, the Baathist leaders, under the influence of Saddam

[23] According to Batatu, *op. cit.*, p. 1133.

Hussein, would mobilize all their efforts to develop a clearly Iraqi-specific identity, distinct from the rest of the Arab world. This was done through an ideologico-cultural campaign aimed at highlighting and exalting the unique character of pre-Islamic Iraqi history, the unity of which can be traced back to Mesopotamian civilization. By establishing the continuity of history and culture, the Baath régime sought to reinforce the feelings of unity of the Iraqi people, more able to identify with a unique Iraqi civilization than the ethnic or sectarian sense of identity. This campaign for the revitalization and glorification of Iraqi culture took various forms: archaeological excavations to discover the ruins of the ancient Babylonian cities, the organization of popular festivals following pagan ancestral traditions (such as the festival of spring in Mosul which follows a Mesopotamian rite, in a town symbolically situated on the edge of the Kurdish country, the Turkoman regions and the zones with Arabo-Sunni majorities), permitting the Kurds, Sunnis and Turkomans all at the same time to recognize themselves as descendants of the Semitic Kingdom of Assyria.[24]

The Iraqis were thus strongly encouraged to be proud of their, in many respects, superior cultural heritage. But this superiority, based on its thousands-year-old Mesopotamian origins, was not an expression of Iraq's split with the Arab World. On the contrary, the Baathist régime conceived a new form of 'Iraqo-centrist' pan-Arabism. Thus, precisely by virtue of this prestigious past, only Iraq was entitled to take on the Arab leadership. With this ideological device the Baathists were in a position to legitimize their national egoism, to be proud of it and at the same time to resolve the hiatus between the development of an Iraqi culture and the maintenance of the official pan-Arabist credo of the Party.[25]

Economic and social development constitutes the second axis of this policy of national integration. Thanks to the system of redistribution through oil revenues, since the second half of the 1970s the régime has been able to put into place a policy of state as provider, by establishing social services and a certain material well-being for the entire population. Thus, in the second five year plan

24. A. Baram, 'Mesopotamian identity in Baathi Iraq', *Middle Eastern Studies*, 19 (4), October 1983, pp. 426–55.
25. A. Baram, 'National integration and local orientation in Iraq under the Baath', *The Jerusalem Journal of International Relations*, vol. 9, no. 3, 1987, pp. 38–51; and O. Bengio, 'Baathi Iraq in search of identity; between ideology and praxis', *Orient*, 28 (4), 1987, pp. 511–8.

of development (1976–1980), the emphasis was placed on the industrialization of the Shi'i south and on the promotion of rural zones with Kurdish and Shi'i majorities. The objective was threefold: to bind, on an economic and ideological level, the peripheral regions to the centre, dominated politically and geographically by Sunni Arabs, to reinforce the national consensus by alleviating sources of socio-economic tension which confirm the 'natural' lines of division between diverse communities, and finally to reinforce the legitimacy of the régime.

It cannot be denied that the Baathists' considerable efforts to cement national unity and promote the emergence in Iraq of national feeling have been successful, at least as regards the Shi'i community, whose allegience to the Iraqi state was clearly demonstrated during the eight years of the war with Iran.[26] On a political level, this translates into a Shi'i participation in power unprecedented in Iraq's modern history. (Since June 1982 thirty-three per cent of the members of the RCC and fifty per cent of the members of the regional command of the Baath party are Shi'i.) It would seem that very early on Saddam Hussein understood the national importance which the Shi'i community represents for the viability of the Baath régime and that he deliberately chose to treat the problem of its integration within the Iraqi nation as a priority, successfully practising a 'carrot and stick' policy towards it.

Clearly, the results are far less satisfactory in matters concerning the Kurdish community. It is rare to find Kurds today who challenge Iraqi frontiers. Nevertheless, there is a contradiction, which is hard to overcome, between the strongly centralized Baathist political system and the autonomous status, even in its minimal form, such as the Kurdish opposition movements claim. In any case, on the eve of 2 August 1990, the Kurdish question was still perceived as a threat by the government.

Did the insurrections in the Kurdish and Shi'i regions in Spring 1991 signify a failure of the process of national integration parallel to the total failure of the vast regional ambitions which Saddam Hussein cherished for his country?

It is possible to say that the first Gulf War against Iran served as positive proof of both the unity of the Iraqi people and the solidity of Saddam Hussein's power. However, this is far from the case with

26. F.W. Axelgard, *A New Iraq? The Gulf War and implications for U.S. policy*, (Washington D.C., The Center for Strategic and International Studies, 1988).

the second war, which largely damaged his credibility and his legitimacy, at the same time demonstrating that the national Iraqi entity remained even more fragile. It remains the task for for the country to find a middle way between the two terms of the dilemma in which it has been trapped for the last thirty-five years: dictatorship or chaos.

Political Parties, Institutions and Administrative Structures

Peter Heine

TRADITIONAL POLICIES

This chapter deals with the situation of Iraq at the beginning of the 1980s. That is the period about which there is some information. Very little information is available for the later period.

When Sati al-Husri, the famous theorist of Arab nationalism, was *mudir al-maarif* (Director of Education) of the Iraqi Ministry of Education he was once summoned to the office of the Prime Minister to meet his new Minister. He met a man in the traditional garb of a Shi'i *alim* and together they went by foot back to the Ministry. On their way al-Husri realized that there was a man following and entering the Ministry shortly after them. Very soon the new Minister came to visit al-Husri in his office and asked him for a job for this man. When al-Husri refused this for budgetary reasons the Minister tried hard to change his mind. He even said that there would be a cabinet crisis, if this man was not employed, because he was a client of the Minister.[1]

This story from the memoirs of Sati al-Husri illustrates the patron-client relations that were typical of great parts of the political system of Iraq until . . .?

THE PARTY SYSTEM

Hamid al-Shawi wrote that the Baath Party was founded among other reasons to combat the 'personalization of power' as seen in the anecdote of Sati al-Husri and al-Shawi adds that only the Communist Party in Syria and Iraq was a party organized as a mass

---

1. Sati al-Husri, *Mudhakkirati fi al-Iraq*, (Beirut, 1964), vol. 1, pp. 367–9.

party and a party in a European sense of the word at all.[2] For a long time the Baath Party in Iraq was just a conventicle of Arab nationalists of a certain ideology, a secret or semi-secret organization. That is one of the reasons why it is so difficult to get any information about the Party even today. Members only rarely talk freely about their membership, the organization or the political techniques of the Party. They even deny that they are members when questioned by foreigners. A neighbourhood sometimes considers someone to be a member, because of his behaviour or because he has an important post within the government or some other important institution, but they are not certain whether he is in the Party or not. Examining the candidates for the 1980 election for the National Assembly, Amatzia Baram had some difficulty 'in trying to determine who is indeed a party member and who is independent'. He therefore established three categories of candidate: those who are definitely party members, those who are probably party members and those who are independent or probably independent.[3] The other reason for the lack of information about the party is the deep suspicions of spies in the whole of the Middle East and especially in Iraq.

Until 1968 in Iraq the Baath Party was cellular in structure.

> 'A cellular organization such as the Baath allows no free transfer of information. Communication within the system occurs vertically, never horizontally, so that recruitment can be carefully controlled, information effectively restricted ... Low- and middle-ranking Baathists, therefore, may be not only reluctant but unable to discuss the party machinery; and even though members of the upper echelon are exceedingly articulate about Baathist policies, they remain reticent in discussing decision making and internal party debates'.[4]

The structure of the party is generally described as follows: the cell or circle constitutes the smallest party-unit. It is composed of a minimum of three persons. Two to seven cells form a division; at least two divisions a section, and at least two sections make a branch. There are twenty-two branches in Iraq, one in each of the

---

2. Hamid al-Shawi, 'Le Baath, sa technique d'action politique', *Maghreb Machrek*, 59 (Septembre/Obtobre 1973): 63.

3. A. Baram, 'The June 1980 elections to the National Assembly in Iraq; an experiment in controlled democracy', *Orient*, 22, 1981, pp. 399, 400.

4. C.M. Helms, *Iraq; the eastern flank of the Arab world* (Washington, 1984), pp. 84-5.

eighteen provinces and three in Baghdad. All the Iraqi branches form the region. 'At each level of the hierarchy are an elected command and congresses, that meet regularly'.[5] When the Baath Party finally came to power in Iraq in 1968 its membership-politics changed. The party was opened to new members and sympathizers and the number of members rose considerably. Early in 1979 Saddam Hussein said: 'Had I not been Baathi, today I would become Baathi. Please do not hesitate to become a party member now. We shall exclude no one from the party ship. The ship is big this time, as big as Iraq itself, and it includes those Baathis who are organized in the party as well as those Baathis who belong to this nation (and who are not yet officially organized)'. And in another speech Saddam said, 'that the only preconditions for joining the party were that the prospective members be authentic Iraqis and patriots, who reject imperialism . . . humiliation . . . the weakening of Iraqi sovereignty . . . and surrender to foreigners, and that they be diligent, precise and scientific'.[6]

Different sources estimate one and a half million supporters and members of the Iraqi branch of the Baath Party, which is about ten per cent of the total population after 1980.[7] Helms compares the recruitment procedure with a system of apprenticeship. The candidate has to pass successfully through the stages of sympathizer, supporter, candidate, trainee member, until he obtains full membership.[8] New members undergo a course of training in the *Madrasat al-idad al-hizbi*, the School for party preparation. Nearly two thirds of the members are government employees. Some of those in important positions who did not join the party were forced to leave their posts. Strict guidelines are said to govern the personal conduct of the members. Gambling, heavy drinking or adultery can be reasons for expulsion from the Party. Traditionally, the Party has made it clear that membership necessitates willingness to sacrifice and life-long devotion on the part of the member to the party and its ideals, and it strongly emphasizes that membership is not merely a formality. Most members of the Party leadership appear in public dressed modestly and have an aura of asceticism. The exception to this is the President himself who is said to have his own tailor and

5. Helms, *op. cit.*, p. 86.
6. Helms, *op. cit.*, p. 392.
7. Helms, *op. cit.*, p. 87; Samir al-Khalil, *Republic of fear; the politics of modern Iraq*, (Berkeley, 1989), p. 87.
8. Helms, *op. cit.*, p. 87.

the pictures and posters of him show him in different dress, in uniform, as a Bedouin, in traditional Kurdish dress, in a strange European style jacket with fur collar or wearing a Tyrolean hat. The asceticism of the top echelon of the Party is underscored by a weight-watchers programme, where all senior members of government and semi-government institutions are checked at certain intervals to ascertain whether they have kept their prescribed weight or not. If they fail to do so they are likely to be removed from their post. When the time of the checkup approaches, this point is taken very seriously, although it is not clear that anyone actually lost his position because of being overweight. 'Even Iraqis critical of the Baath have admitted that members of its upper echelon are perceived to lead relatively pristine lives as family men or women with little time for social life'.[9]

The opening of the Party to new members after 1968 led to some negative consequences:

> the speed with which the Party had to place its members in key positions led to some unfortunate results. On being promoted, some members lost their sense of proportion, committed serious mistakes and became arrogant. The Party was often forced to reconsider its decisions and reshuffle its appointments. Promotion also produced a sort of impermissible competition among some Party members'.[10]

This is the view of the Party adopted at its eighth regional congress in January 1984. Every person interested in becoming a member is urged to view himself as a vanguard of a social transformation, who should evaluate his daily performance in both a professional and a personal sense. The Party pervades the whole political system and other sectors of Iraqi society, which is why it attracts a wide following. 'Although membership in the party is not a prerequisite for government employment or even for advancement, a number of Baath and non-Baath Iraqis agree that "an incompetent Baathi is unlikely to be promoted, but all factors being equal, a Baathi has a greater advantage than a non-Baathi" '.[11]

The self-critical remarks of the eighth reqional congress are an indication that the client system has invaded the party. Typical for a

---

9. Helms, *op. cit.*, p. 88.
10. *The 1968 Revolution in Iraq: experience and prospects*, (London, 1979), pp. 41–2
11. Helms, *op. cit.*, p. 83.

client system is an uneven reciprocity between patron and client. The client depends more on the patron than vice versa. This is the situation at the base and at the top of the political system in Iraq. First some examples of the client situation in the lower strata of society: this is the *wasta* of so many Middle Eastern states.

> The *wasta* system is generalized in society and performs important functions within the family and clan as well as outside it. One needs *wasta* in order not to be cheated in the market place, in locating and acquiring jobs, in resolving conflict and legal litigation, in winning a court decision, a speeding governmental action and in establishing and maintaining political influence, bureaucratic procedures, in finding a bride ... The *wasta* procedure is complex, its rules varied depending on the sphere and nature of activity, whether it is legal, familial, economic, etc. ... the higher the degree of training and education the lesser the use of *wasta* procedure, except in the form of recommending and sponsoring'.[12]

This definition applies to a large extent to the way in which *wasta* is used in Iraq. However, unlike Lebanon, the use of *wasta* does not necessarily diminish with the higher degree of training and education. In fact in many cases it is quite the contrary. If you wish to build a house in certain parts of Baghdad, you may have difficulties in finding the necessary plot of land. When you approach a known party member, he may be able to help you, even if the required place is in the possession of somebody else. If you have an accident with your car and somebody is hurt, you can ask a party member for intervention. These examples raise the question whether this possibility of *wasta* is the consequence of party membership or of a certain official position. The pervasiveness of the Party at all levels of Iraqi society answers this question. The Baath Party has a clearly hierarchical structure. As an indication of this, Saddam Hussein said in 1989: 'More than one million organized persons practise democracy inside the party on a wide and deep scale, discussing the affairs of the people and what is decided about their affairs'.[13] Taha Yasin Ramadan is cited as saying: 'We try to discourage trends in the Party', and Dr Saadun Hammadi explained: 'We encourage an open, active debate over an issue, but once a vote has been taken it is expected that all members will accept the majority opinion as if it

12. S. Farsoun, 'Family structure and society in modern Lebanon', in L. Sweet, ed., *Peoples and cultures of the Middle East*, (New York, 1970), Vol. 1, p. 270.
13. A. Iskander, *Saddam Hussein, the fighter, the thinker and the man*, (Paris, 1980), p. 343.

had been unanimous. No further public debate is allowed'.[14] In his introduction to discussions over the model for autonomy of Kurdistan Saddam Hussein said: 'We stated at the outset, that we did not intend, neither do we intend now, to make such meetings a matter of formality. We actually intend to make them the interaction of views so that they may enable us to render the best services to our people'.[15] Thus, it seems from his words that the leadership decides after consultations with experts and it is the job of ordinary party members and sympathizers to explain these decisions to the public. Normally a neighbourhood knows who of the neighbours is a party member and who is not. Some members were given residence in traditionally non-Baath quarters of big cities by the authorities, and could therefore be readily identified. Others are known to be party members or sympathizers by their jobs. If they are working for a government institution or are army officers they are expected to be in the Party. One Iraqi said: 'You can see it from the way they walk and from their dress'. The party leadership expects these members to do the grass roots work by explaining the decisions of the leadership to the people. Opponents of the Baath regime claim that they control and even terrorize the population. On the other hand, they are sought after for *wasta*. They can help to get a driving permit or a taxi licence, enable a son to obtain a scholarship for study abroad without paying a deposit and so on.

A good example of the way the Baath Party acts to achieve a certain goal is the campaign for the eradication of illiteracy in 1978. The idea of fighting illiteracy had been put forward in the first manifesto of the Party in 1947 and was incorporated in Article 27 of the Iraqi Provisional Constitution of 1968. 'The campaign aimed at eradicating the illiteracy of all those between the ages of fifteen and forty-five . . . within a fixed limit of thirty-six months. The time limit was later reduced to twenty-one months'.[16] The campaign was accompanied by a huge mobilization programme that touched the population.

> The mass-media were fully employed to familiarize the public with the objectives and seriousness of the campaign and the benefits to be reaped therefrom. Special programmes were broadcast on radio and television and exhibitions depicting the various aspects of the battle

14. Helms, *op. cit.*, p. 93.
15. Saddam Hussein, *On current events in Iraq*, (London, 1977), p. 14.
16. A. Sousa, 'The eradication of illiteracy in Iraq', in T. Niblock, ed., *Iraq, the contemporary state*, (London, 1982), p. 104.

against ignorance were offered to the public. Daily evening literacy lessons were televised on all channels of the national networks'.[17]

One can find many opponents of the regime who acknowledge the efforts of the Baath Party and the mass organizations in this campaign, although there are also some critics who say that the campaign was without success and the evaluations were forged.

Since 1988 there have been several announcements that Iraq should change to a multi-party system and after the second Gulf War these announcements became more precise. A new party law was approved by the RCC on 2 September 1991. The law forbids activities of any parties having a regional or confessional base or with atheistic ideologies or programmes hostile to the Arabs. The right of activity within the armed forces is confined to the Baath Party. Parties are forbidden to have any direct or indirect relations abroad.[18]

OPPOSITION PARTIES

There are some other official or secret political organizations or parties. The Kurdish movement after the setback of the Algiers Agreement and the disaster that followed split into two main factions, the Kurdish Democratic Party—Provisional Leadership led by Masud Barzani and the Patriotic Union of Kurdistan led by Jalal Talabani. There is another Kurdish Democratic Party led by Aziz Agrawi and a Kurdish Revolutionary Party led by Abd al-Sattar Tahir Sharif and some splinter parties. Only one, the Progressive Nationalist Group collaborates with the central government.[19] Recent developments show that the two parties are in conflict for the leadership of the Kurdish movement in Iraq.

The main Shi'i opposition group is *Hizb al-dawa al-islamiya*, which was founded in 1959 in Najaf. In the mid-1960s *Munazammat al-amal al-islami* was established in Karbala. And finally there are *al-Mujahidun*, who were founded in 1980, whose first spectacular action was to blow up the Iraqi News Agency building in Baghdad in December 1981.[20] The reaction of a large part of the

17. *Ibid.*
18. Article of A.H. (= Arnold Hottinger) in *Neue Zürcher Zeitung*, 7/8 September 1991.
19. T. Koszinowski, 'Iraq', in U. Steinbach and R. Robert, eds., *Der Nahe und Mittlere Osten*, vol. 1, (Leverkusen, 1987), p. 108.
20. A. Baram, 'The radical Shi'ite opposition movements in Iraq', in E. Sivan

population concerning this attempt was not friendly. Iraqis distant from the regime said that those who were killed by this bombing were women because the men were fighting the Iranians, and acting in this way against women was seen as a crime.

NATIONAL FRONT

The National Progressive Front was founded in July 1973 after long discussions of more than two years and is composed of the Baath Party, the Communist Party and the Kurdish Democratic Party. From the beginning it was clear that the Baath would hold a privileged position within the Front. The Kurdish Democratic Party never joined because of conditions for participation which were not accepted by the Baath Party. Consequently rival Kurdish groups joined. In practice the parties other than the Baath had no real power. In 1975 relations between the Baath Party and the Communist Party became strained and in April 1979 the Iraqi Communist Party suspended its membership in the National Front.[21]

MASS ORGANIZATIONS

Mass organizations include those for the young such as the Pioneers for children of primary schools, the Vanguards for boys and girls between the ages of ten and fifteen, and those between fifteen and twenty join a youth organization called *Futuwa*. The Baath Party is very much concerned with these organizations: 'The Party itself must exert great and urgent efforts to promote the activities of youth organizations. They must come to embrace a majority of our young people, boys and girls, and contribute activily to cultivating pan-Arab and socialist principles among them'.[22] And Saddam Hussein wrote: 'To prevent the father and mother dominating the household with their backwardness, we must make the small ones able to expel it. Some fathers have slipped away from us for various reasons, but the small boy is still in our hands and we must transform him into an interactive radiating centre inside the family through all the hours that he spends with his parents to change

and M. Friedman, eds., *Religious radicalism and politics in the Middle East* (Albany, 1990), pp. 96 f.
21. 'The Progressive National Front', *Arab World File*, 13 June 1979, No. 1293.
22. *The Revolution in Iraq*, p. 174.

their conditions for the better. We must also keep him away from bad influences'.[23] That this position is turning upside down the traditional Middle Eastern family structure is quite clear. The activities of the youth organizations are participation in supervised sports, cultural and scientific programmes, and training camps. The members of the youth organizations wear uniforms, take an oath of allegiance to their country and so on. (Indoctrination of Iraqi youth was not invented by the Baath Party. The first youth organization in Iraq, called *al-kashshaf* and established in 1925 had as its aim the development of national and Arab feelings in the hearts of the young ones.[24] The difference is a stronger incorporation of girls into these organizations.) Some observers consider the Vanguard to be the most important of these organizations. It has national, regional and local congresses which elect a 'Central Office' which in turn elects a 'Core Committee'. None of these organizations, which together constitute the General Federation of Iraqi Youth, is part of the Baath Party. It has its own youth organization, the 'partisans'. In addition there are students' organizations and trade unions. People are not forced to become members of these organizations, but for a student it is easier to receive a scholarship if a member.

In the Party's view 'a prominent role' is played by the General Federation of Iraqi Women (*al-Ittihad al-nisai al-iraqi*). It has eighteen branches, one in each province, 265 subsections based in the major towns, 755 centres that incorporate villages with more than 200 families or quarters of cities with more than 6,000 people, and an additional 1,612 liaison committees which extend to all the remaining villages and quarters. Conferences and elections determine a General Council out of which a Central Council of thirty-eight women and an Executive Bureau is chosen.[25] This extensive and popular organization both initiates and implements programmes aimed at raising the social, economic, cultural and health standards of women. It cooperates with government establishments and other people's organizations in the achievement of its aims. It contributes to promoting women's work and performance through open discussions held at work—attended by all working staff, and possibly by relevant ministers or heads of departments. The

23. Saddam Hussein, *Al-dimuqratiyya masdar quwa li al-fard wa al-mujtama* (Baghdad, 1977), p. 14.
24. Sati al-Husri, *op. cit.*, pp. 213–137, 364.
25. Helms, *op. cit.*, p. 99

participation of the federation in arts, sports and other public activities has contributed significantly to the emerging image of the new Iraqi woman.[26] 'The Federation sponsors and operates a number of programmes aimed at women. These include "consciousness-raising" conferences and meetings, television and radio programmes that offer advice and information to women and rural centres where women come to learn to read, sew and embroider'.[27] But Amal Rassam says that the legislation on Personal Status does not free an Iraqi woman from the hold of her family and local group, but still limits her full autonomy and gives her a status that is still secondary to that of the man.[28]

Another mass organization is the Popular Army, a militia fomally established in 1970. In the beginning membership was only possible for members of the Baath Party, in 1975 membership was expanded to non-Baathists and to women in 1976. The number of militia members is estimated at about 450,000, ten per cent of them women. 'In addition to protecting strategic installations, guarding the frontier, and acting as a security force in rural areas, the Popular Army serves as a military reserve force and an instrument of political consolidation'.[29] Militia members have to undergo an annual training period of two months, when they receive lectures on political vigilance as well as training in weaponry, mobilization and military tactics from the graduates of the militia's own school, which was established in 1972.

GOVERNMENT INSTITUTIONS

Majid Khadduri considering the temporary constitution of 1974 finds four principal branches within the political machinery of Iraq: the Revolutionary Command Council, the National Assembly, the Presidency and the Judiciary.[30] Perhaps one should add the Legislative Assembly for the autonomous Region of Kurdistan. The question is, which of these branches is the most important and powerful. The temporary constitution states that it is the Revolutionary Command Council, as long as the National Assembly was not elected.

26. Amal al-Sharqi, 'The emancipation of Iraqi women', in Niblock, *op. cit.*, p. 85.
27. Amal Rassam, 'Revolution within the revolution? Women and state in Iraq', in Niblock, *op. cit.*, p. 91.
28. *Ibid.*, p. 97.
29. Helms, *op. cit.*, p. 100.
30. M. Khadduri, *Socialist Iraq*, (Washington, 1978), p.34.

This has since happened. Consequently the National Assembly should be the most important institution of Iraq. The Assembly is authorized to draft and propose laws, to legislate, to confirm the general budget and the national development plans, to confirm international treaties and agreements, and to debate questions of internal and external policy. Amatzia Baram, however, who adds the Regional Leadership of the Baath Party to the above mentioned branches of the government machinery, sees the Revolutionary Command Council as still the most important but finds contradictions concerning the Regional Leadership, referring to a statement of the Eighth Regional Congress of the Party in 1974:

> The Regional Leadership assumed its role of leading the revolution through the Revolutionary Command Council . . . There is no doubt that since 1974 the resolutions of the regional party congresses have been of paramount importance, if not serving as guidelines, then at least legitimizing the regime's policies retroactively and facilitating their pursuit. That the second interim constitution specifies that new RCC members be recruited from the RL also testifies to the importance of the latter.[31]

Concerning the government the situation is quite clear. According to the constitution it is appointed, dismissed and supervised by the chairman of the Revolutionary Command Council. Until the end of the second Gulf War he was also Prime Minister. The government has to carry out the orders of the Revolutionary Command Council, but it can issue administrative instructions subject to RCC approval.[32] That means that the Iraqi government has a dualistic character in the sense that, although the cabinet and all dependent institutions are autonomous entities, the Baath Party can influence or directly control government policies in two ways. The first is that government employees are members of the Baath Party. At the same time there are Party units at all levels of government institutions. They control or monitor activities at all levels. The Party itself has installed a parallel organization to all government institutions. But it is not clear by what means and how strongly the Party intervenes, considering the fact that most employees are Party members themselves.[33] What is interesting in the context of the RCC is the fact that

31. A. Baram, 'The ruling political elite in Baathi Irag 1968– 1986: the changing features of a collective profile', *International Journal of Middle East Studies*, 21, 1989, p. 449.
32. *Ibid.*
33. Helms, *op. cit.*, p. 90.

there seems not to exist any collection of orders, decisions or decrees of the RCC, so that there are contradictory decrees on one topic and repetitions of older decrees which were not necessary.

If we consider the role of the presidency in this rectangle of power we also can find different views. Some writers see Iraq now as the one-man-show of Saddam Hussein. He is the Godfather of the political elite or, as Miller and Mylroie put it, he is the Don of Takrit.[34] In a less spectacular way, is Saddam the patron of Iraq? First of all, it is difficult to get information about the decision making process within the Iraqi leadership, whether in the RCC or in the cabinet. Ordinary members of the Party refrain from answering questions on this matter. During the rule of Ahmad Hasan al-Bakr debates within the Revolutionary Command Council are said to have been often substantial and sometimes acrimonious. Saddam Hussein also stressed the importance of collective leadership in an interview with Christine Helms, when he said:

> The Revolutionary Command Council is a constitutional body with vested authority. It has an agenda which is distributed a sufficient time before meetings convene. Decisions are taken by majority. Usually a consensus develops through discussions so it is rare an actual vote must be called. In fact I can count these occasions on less than the fingers of my hands. We are mostly interested in unanimous decisions, but not necessarily identical mentalities. I have no veto power, but my opinion as a question of courtesy is viewed in a different way. Sometimes outsiders, such as Sadun Hamadi, are called to present special issues. If there is a tie vote, the president's opinion carries. In very sensitive issues, we desire even more a consensus and consultations among the National Command, Revolutionary Command Council, and the Regional Command.[35]

Since Saddam Hussein concentrated all power in his hands the members of the Council derive their actual authority from him.[36] From the perspective of a simple Party member Saddam Hussein is omnipotent in Iraq. This can be seen from the words of an Iraqi university teacher who, when passing the newly erected monument

---

34. J. Miller and L. Mylroie, *Saddam Hussein and the crisis in the Gulf* (New York, 1990), p. 24.
35. Helms, *op.cit.*, p. 96.
36. Helms, *op.cit.*, p. 128 has another impression and writes: 'Obviously Saddam Husain is on a different level than the other four, though it would be a mistake to assume that the power of the other four is necessarily derived from or contingent on Husain'.

to King Faisal I, commented: 'This monument was given to us by His Excellency, the President'. The whole situation may be described as a client system. The typical traditional Near Eastern client system is a system of power in a society, which can be described as lacking a law-abiding bureaucracy. Ernest Gellner, using instead of client system patronage, says:

> It seems to me of the essence of a patronage system that, ... it always belongs to some *pays réel* which is ambivalently conscious of not being a *pays légal*. Patronage may not always and necessarily be illegal or corrupt, and it does have its own pride and morality ... Real patronage seems to me to be a system, a style, a moral climate ... Patronage proper is an ethos: people know that it is a way of doing things, amongst others.[37]

Gellner sees the political field as more patronage prone than others. 'Typical is a stress on the fidelity to persons rather than to principles, a cult of honour and loyalty, violence and virility'.[38] One can add that the relationship of patron and client is unsymmetrical. One finds an exchange of labour, loyalty, money and so on for protection. But there is a certain interdependence between patron and client. The client can try to shift his loyalty to some other patron, if his former patron is not able to protect him. Does this description fit with the relationship between Saddam Hussein and the members of the RCC, the Regional Command of the Baath Party and the Cabinet? As far as is known, the members of the above-mentioned institutions are dependent on the President. He can dismiss them, take away their positions, properties, even their lives, if they lack in loyalty. But, as he well knows, if he was not able to protect them or to guarantee a good life for them, he could lose their loyalty and possibly be overthrown.

This may be a simplistic model of the actual political system in Iraq. But perhaps it serves to explain why Saddam Hussein is still the strong man of Iraq and will continue to remain in this position.

---

37. A. Gellner, 'Patrons and clients'. in E. Gellner and J. Waterbury, eds., *Patrons and Clients*, (London, 1977), p. 3.
38. *Ibid.*, p. 2.

Liberation or Repression? Pan-Arab Nationalism and the Women's Movement in Iraq

Marion Farouk-Sluglett

In common with most other genuinely authentic movements in Iraq, the women's movement has been transformed into an obedient instrument and mouthpiece of the state; along with the rest of the population, Iraqi women have been cowed into submission and acquiescence to the powers that be. This transformation has been the result of a conscious and comprehensive effort on the part of the Baath Party to establish its political hegemony in all parts of the country and throughout society in general, including areas hitherto not fully incorporated into the nation state. To the extent that this has been achieved by the most ruthless repression and fear,[1] the Baath record is well known and will only be of indirect concern here. What follows is an attempt to investigate the way in which the populist underpinning of Baath ideology served to justify and legitimate such measures and to socialize the whole population, including women, into the Baath polity. As such an investigation can only be undertaken within its historical context a brief outline of the events which led to the Baath's seizure of power in 1968 and its consolidation over the following decades will be given.

HISTORICAL BACKGROUND

The political system introduced into Iraq as part of the peace settlement after the First World War consisted of a constitutional monarchy and a parliamentary structure derived broadly from the

---

1. See especially Samir al-Khalil, *The Republic of Fear*, (London, 1989).

British models.[2] It was superimposed upon a society in which the forms and organization of production and the value systems of large sections of the population continued to be pre-capitalist on many levels. Lacking the social foundations and the consensus that could have formed the basis for a stable political system, the new structure remained inherently weak, and the monarchy and its supporters continued to depend largely on Britain for their continuation in power. A further factor which was to underpin Iraq's international linkages was its gradual development into a rentier state, deriving its principal revenue from a source largely external to the social relations of production. Although oil revenues in the 1940s and 1950s remained relatively modest in comparison with later decades, they were large enough to allow the expansion of state institutions, the modernization of education and other services, and the gradual development of the country's infrastructure.

In consequence, the state began to take on important developmental functions, and the availability of government contracts and the mediation of access to the various state authorities became crucial for members of the business community and other groups and individuals.[3] While the standard of living of many Iraqis improved as a result of public investments, the majority of the population remained extremely poor, especially those living in the rural areas and in the shanty towns around Baghdad and other major cities. In addition, a burst of conspicuous consumption on the part of the well-to-do further widened the gap between the rich and the rest of society.

One feature peculiar to Iraqi politics between the end of the Second World War and the Revolution of 1958 was that there was little room for the development and expression of a 'conventional' democratic political tradition. As a result no liberal democratic party was able to muster anything like mass support or to build up a well functioning organization. Effective political opposition was driven underground—a situation which promoted radical rather than liberal or reformist politics—and became increasingly dominated by the Communist Party and its front organizations, including the trade unions.

2. Much of the empirical data used here is taken from M. Farouk-Sluglett and P. Sluglett, *Iraq since 1958: from revolution to dictatorship*, 2nd extended edition, (London, 1990), pp. 227–254 where full references will be found.

3. Government contracts were generally carried out by local firms, and were often given to individuals with access to influential government officials.

More generally, the overall consensus of opinion by the early 1950s was that the country's most urgent needs were national independence and economic development, and that both these goals were being blocked or denied by the monarchy and its British sponsors. This kind of thinking, with its nationalist and populist characteristics—usually but not always associated with the desirability of some kind of 'socialism' (or more accurately, state-sponsored economic development)—had wide currency in the Arab world at the time. Such aspirations were widely accepted and articulated by members of the expanding middle and lower middle classes, including professionals, teachers, civil servants and students. Although there were considerable disparities in their political thinking and social consciousness, their common opposition to the status quo gave them a certain degree of cohesion and their desire for national independence was shared by members of most social classes and strata.

THE POLARIZATION OF IRAQI POLITICS

When the Free Officers seized power in 1958, the Communist Party and its sympathizers emerged as the most significant political force. As Qasim had neither kin nor regional networks at his disposal—unlike Abd al-Salam Arif at the time, or Saddam Hussein a few years later—let alone a political party, he found himself increasingly dependent on and identified with the Communists, for whom his own enthusiasm was distinctly lukewarm. Popular acclamation and the military constituted the twin support bases of his regime (1958–1963). As Qasim never attempted to institutionalize the mass support that the Revolution had engendered to create a more participatory political system, he was fatally exposed when the military abandoned him in 1963.

Although the Communists did not call for revolution but pressed for social reforms *within* the existing social order, the political atmosphere became increasingly polarized, and a pan-Arab nationalist and Baathist alliance emerged which began a fierce anti-communist and anti-Qasim campaign. Here a few words on the place of Arab nationalism in Iraq before 1958 are in order, largely because the notion of 'nationalism' and the controversies surrounding it and its precise meanings at different stages in modern Iraqi history have become confused through a certain looseness of terminology. The different but overlapping notions of 'patriotism',

'Iraqi nationalism' and 'Arab nationalism', which informed the thinking of a variety of very different political groups and organizations, have often been assimilated into the terms 'nationalism' or 'pan-Arab nationalism'. This has suggested a greater degree of coherence and continuity within nationalist thinking in Iraq under the monarchy than actually existed, and also gives the misleading impression that pan-Arab nationalism in its totality was deeply rooted in the political culture of the time. There has also been a tendency to generalize from the behaviour and thinking of fairly narrow political élites—most notably the Iraqi officer corps at particular conjunctures—while less attention has been directed towards the wider political culture as it evolved during the 1940s and 1950s.[4]

Substantially influenced by the communist left, this political culture was dominated by the desire to ameliorate or eradicate poverty and to realize greater social justice. As it was widely believed that genuine social reform could not be carried out until Iraq was fully independent from Britain, those who believed in these ideals considered that the struggle for social justice was inseparable from that for national independence. Hence, although it is true that national independence was the goal of the majority of politically conscious Iraqis (and to that extent it can correctly be said that they espoused nationalist sentiments), only a small minority of those who supported these aspirations were 'pan-Arab nationalists', in the strict sense of being in favour of merging Iraq into a larger Arab entity.

As the idea of national independence was ideologically inclusive rather than exclusive, the more fundamental political and ideological differences among the various otherwise competing political groups and organizations became, at least for the time being, relegated to second place. The centrality which national liberation assumed among the members of different political organizations and parties helped to blur the dividing lines between national, patriotic, nationalist or pan-Arab sentiments. Nevertheless, until the Suez crisis and the tripartite invasion of Egypt in 1956, the appeal of pan-Arab nationalism in Iraq was largely confined to sections of the Sunni Arab urban middle and lower middle classes, for two main reasons. In the first place, pan-Arab nationalism in Iraq has always

4. See for instance P. Marr, *The modern history of Iraq*, (Boulder, 1985); Majid Khadduri, *Independent Iraq 1932–1958: a study in Iraqi politics*, 2nd edition, (London, 1960); Majid Khadduri, *Republican Iraq: a study of Iraqi politics since the revolution of 1958*, (London, 1969).

been a predominantly urban phenomenon, and in the 1940s and 1950s, the Sunnis formed the majority of the urban population. Second, while the Arab world outside Iraq is overwhelmingly Sunni, over one quarter of the Iraqi population are Kurds and more than half are Shi'is. Although neither the Kurdish nor the Shi'i communities should be thought to be monolithic, it has not generally been the case that either has seen its interests being best served by Iraq joining a wider Arab federation.

Hence, by the end of the 1950s pan-Arabism had exerted relatively little influence in Iraq outside a number of suburbs in Baghdad (notably Adhamiya and Karkh), most parts of the city of Mosul and the small towns of Ana, Falluja, Haditha, Rawa and Takrit, where ideas of *uruba* had always been strong and where communism had generally not taken root. It was only after the revolution, when the political situation was particularly volatile and when the spectacular rise in the fortunes of the Communist Party created a profound sense of alarm among those who had no sympathy for communism, that the pan-Arab nationalists and Baathists were able to increase their support and to rally wide sections of the population behind them.

It was widely believed—by communists and non-communists alike—that communist support was so strong that free elections would bring in a genuinely left-wing government. As it was never put to the test, it is difficult to say whether this assumption was correct. Nevertheless, the *perceived* threat of a powerful communist advance in Iraq—and in the region—was sufficient to rally all those opposed to it (both at home and abroad) behind the pan-Arab nationalists and the Baath; the two seized power in a military coup in 1963 and took brutal revenge on the communists and their supporters.

Unlike Qasim, who had not subscribed to any particular ideology or political party, the regime which seized power in 1963 (though by no means politically uniform) based its social and economic policies on the broad premises of Arab nationalism and Arab socialism and thus constituted the first *ideological* regime in Iraq. As some of the premises of Arab socialism had anti-big business connotations, the regime—following Nasser—nationalized banking, insurance, foreign trade and a number of key industries in 1964. However, these policies were soon discontinued and apart from the nationalization of the oil companies by the Baath in 1972, no major nationalizations have been carried out in Iraq since.

The social and political foundations of the state remained weak and continued to be vulnerable to threats from disaffected groups within the military. Income from oil—although already decisive within the economy—was not yet exclusively under the control of any particular group within the state and had not yet attained the order of magnitude which it was to reach in later years. In addition political power was still relatively diffuse and was based largely on the kin or regional alliances of the principal office holders. On the whole the Arif regime wore its pan-Arabism rather lightly.

BAATH RULE SINCE 1968

The Baathists who seized power in July 1968 formed a disparate group with few real roots in the country. They were still highly unpopular in many quarters because of the reign of terror for which many of them had been responsible in 1963. Nevertheless, they were now in sole control of the state and its institutions and most importantly of the military. Determined to consolidate its position and to widen its support, the Baath began a vigorous ideological campaign in which it presented itself as a militant revolutionary organization which had the welfare and wellbeing of every Iraqi at heart. Its nationalist ideology enabled it to invoke general notions of anti-imperialism, anti-Zionism, social equality and economic development which had wide appeal, and to promote itself as a progressive and radical force whose objective was to complete the revolution inherited in 1958.

To this end, and especially through such policies as greater cooperation with the Soviet Union, the recognition of the German Democratic Republic and above all by determined moves in the direction of the nationalization of oil (which took place in 1972), the Baath managed to co-opt the Communist Party, still its main competitor, into a short-lived alliance in 1973. One of the by-products of this was that the Baath was able to incorporate most of the communist mass organizations, either by mergers with its own associations or by decrees prohibiting oppositional organizations. Together with the general loss of credibility which the alliance entailed, the measures left the Communist Party fundamentally weakened.

At the same time the leadership transformed the Baath Party into an effective instrument of the state, Baathizing the army and forming several competing forces, equipped with the most up-to-date instruments of surveillance and coercion. Individuals inside and outside the Party who disagreed with the leadership around al-Bakr and Saddam Hussein were either removed or eliminated. Thus a particular group within the party leadership manoeuvred itself into a position where it was able to use the state, its institutions and forces of coercion to assert its own power, and the *raison d'être* of most of its policies became the maintenance and consolidation of its hegemony. The state and its institutions were gradually transformed into instruments of the Party leadership.

Significantly, although membership increased substantially, the Party became less and less important as an arena of political discourse the more the regime entrenched itself, and was rapidly transformed into an instrument of co-option, manipulation and artificial mass mobilization. Typically for regimes of this kind, the systematic incorporation of all types of political association—including trade unions and all other mass organizations—into the party structures had the effect of containing and generally demobilizing the population.

One important factor working in the leadership's favour was the series of oil price rises after 1973, which meant steady and very substantial increases in oil revenues and a concomitant enhancement of the power both of the state and of the party élite. In addition, the nationalization of the Iraq Petroleum Company in 1972, which was universally acclaimed, not only meant that Iraq had full control over its oil resources; given that political power was increasingly concentrated in the hands of one man (Saddam Hussein) and his closest associates, these revenues were controlled directly by the Baath leadership. As well as bringing about a substantial rise in national revenue the new situation also brought about an enormous increase in the power of those who controlled these resources and mediated access to them.[5]

The availability of resources on such a scale enabled the Baath to undertake wide-ranging developmental and welfare programmes and to regard itself and its leaders as benevolent benefactors of the people and the nation. In common with similar regimes, its discourse adopted an increasingly paternalistic tone. Another important factor was that the degree to which and the way in which

    5. The Iraqi leadership is probably no more accountable for the expenditure of the oil revenues than the Saudi royal family; the division between the public and the private domain in equally blurred, since all decisive positions in the state are held by close relatives and associates of the ruler.

individuals might obtain access to these resources (in terms of contracts or career possibilities) was dependent on their access to the state and party organizations. This state of affairs not only resulted in a dependency relationship between state and society and in new forms of patron-client relations; it also militated against the development of a civil society and the formation of class alliances. Thus the relationship between the Baath leadership and society became essentially one of domination and subordination. The inherent powerlessness of the ordinary individual within this relationship had the effect of forcing men and women to resort to traditional networks of sect, locality and family and thus resulted in a general reassertion of patriarchal relationships.

By the second half of the 1970s the Baath began to stamp out any kind of genuine political discourse either inside or outside the party and once again turned against the Communists. It pursued a brutal campaign in the course of which hundreds of Communists experienced prison, torture and execution. Those who survived sought refuge in exile. At the same time, Saddam Hussein, who became president in July 1979, continued to assert his own authority within the state, a tendency which became more accentuated during the 1980s as political power came to be concentrated almost exclusively in the President's personal office, from which the incumbents of the most important ministries were recruited. Although its organizational structure remained formally unchanged, the real influence of the Baath Party and the Revolutionary Command Council (RCC) substantially declined.

Having systematically eliminated all other political organizations as well as any opposition from within the Baath Party itself, the President surrounded himself with a small coterie based on personal and family ties reinforced by marriage alliances. Typically for populist regimes, a widespread cult of personality around the charismatic leader developed, with Saddam Hussein presenting himself as the all-powerful but benevolent father of the nation. By the end of the 1980s he was in absolute control of the state and party apparatuses and the security services were controlled either by himself or by close relatives. Laws took the form of decrees carrying his signature. In addition he was in full control of the Ministry of Oil and the Ministry of Industry and Military Industries. These key sectors of the economy had 'autonomous' status, meaning that their inputs and outputs were confidential and accountable only to the President.

POPULIST NATIONALISM AND THE BAATH

Contemporary pan-Arabism and Baathism tend to be seen primarily within the framework of their attempts to assert or reassert the independence and identity of the Arabs and of the Arab world vis-à-vis the West and in terms of their developmentalist and modernizing aspirations. As a result insufficient attention has been paid to the populist underpinning which is at the heart of such nationalist ideologies. In what follows I shall focus on the role of populism or populist nationalism in Baath politics within the analytical framework developed by scholars working on authoritarian and totalitarian regimes in various parts of the world. Given the haziness of the term, there is still a good deal of disagreement about the exact meaning of populism and its overall analytical usefulness, particularly in the context of the contemporary 'Third World'. Peter Worsley defines populist movements primarily within the framework of peasant movements (especially in Russia and parts of America) and rejects the somewhat loose interpretation of the term which describes 'any movement invoking the name of the people' as 'populist'. He correctly points out that totalitarian parties in the twentieth century had 'similarly converted large segments of the lower orders into the organized mass base of totalitarian parties and had not hesitated to use appeals to popular sentiments—as well as force, blandishment, patronage, etc.—to recruit them'. He argues that populism was only 'an *element*, not a dominant feature of this kind of movement'.[6]

While generally in agreement I feel that this particular 'element', or more accurately the way in which populism and populist ideologies work, has not been given the critical attention it deserves, and that this should be made more central in analyses of authoritarian or totalitarian regimes. A similar point has been made by Forgacs in his recent study of fascism in Italy, where he stresses the centrality of the mass base and of the 'ideological construction of people by a whole set of trans-class or non-class ascriptions' such as 'nation', 'masses' and so forth.[7] Concepts like fascism, authoritarianism and totalitarianism, any one of which could probably be applied to Iraq at certain stages of Baath rule, seem too broad and all-embracing for a limited study of this kind. This is all the more true as the

---

6. P. Worsley, 'Populism', in G. Ionescu and E. Gellner eds. *Populism, its meanings and national characteristics*, p. 241.
7. D. Forgacs, ed. *Rethinking Italian fascism*, (London, 1986).

Baath regime has so far not been analysed comprehensively within any of these frameworks.

I have therefore decided to take a more limited approach and intend to take the 'classical' theory of populism developed by scholars working on Latin America as the framework of my analysis. This defines populism as 'a loosely organized multiclass movement united by a charismatic leader behind an ideology and programme of social justice and nationalism'; popular participation in such movements does not take on a 'class' character.[8] Looking at populism in terms of 'social control' Steven Stein has noted four characteristic features, three of which can be applied to the Iraqi situation under the Baath:

1. The formation of electoral coalitions of upper, middle, and lower social sectors with potentially conflicting interests.

2. The appearance of a popular and exalted leader figure capable of appealing to the emotions of large portions of the citizenry.

3. An overriding concern for gaining control of the existing state for power and patronage without envisaging a major reordering of society.

4. The explicit rejection of the notion of class conflict with the advocacy in favour of the creation of a corporate-style state to rule the national family hierarchically.[9]

As the Baath did not come to power through elections but through a military coup Stein's first point clearly does not apply; Saddam Hussein's popularity as 'exalted leader' was only achieved *after* the Baath had consolidated itself in power. This was, as we have seen, greatly facilitated by an enormous increase in oil revenues, which resulted in an economic boom and the introduction of substantial welfare measures, which could be attributed to the wisdom and benevolence of the party and its leader. Indeed, the notion of authoritarian charismatic leadership was not alien to Baathist thinking but had already been invoked by Michel Aflaq, the movement's principal ideologue:

---

8. I. Roxborough, 'Populism and Class Conflict', in E.P. Archetti, P. Cammack and B. Roberts, eds. *The sociology of developing societies: Latin America*, (London, 1989), p. 119.

9. S. Stein, 'Social Control', in Archetti *et al.*, *op. cit.*, p. 129. On the role of populism in Latin America see also: A. Hennessey, 'Latin America', in G. Ionescu and E. Gellner, *op. cit.*, pp. 28–61.

Liberation or Repression? 61

> The leader, in times of weakness of the 'Idea' and its constriction, is not one to appeal to a majority or to a consensus, but to opposition and enmity; he is not one to substitute number for the 'Idea', but to translate numbers into the 'Idea' he is not the ingatherer, but the unifier. In words he is the master of the singular 'Idea' from which he separates and casts aside all those who contradict it.[10]

The overriding aim of gaining control of the state for power and patronage is certainly present in Baath thinking. Aflaq did not believe in parliamentary democracy and did not consider the development of the party into a mass movement *before* the seizure of power as a necessary precondition for a Baath takeover. According to Aflaq, the party must become

> the nation of revolution before it achieves the revolution of the nation...[it] must be a smaller version of the pure healthy and elevated nation that it wishes to resurrect'.

More precisely, the nation's leadership was to remain in the hands of an enlightened minority, which 'represents the people before the people expressly delegate them to undertake this representation'.[11]

The state was considered to be 'purely instrumental', 'a body with no spirit'; to gain control of it 'speed' was 'of the essence in a revolutionary movement'. Hence, the Baath's seizure of power through military coups and its assertion of power by force and coercion was entirely consonant with the spirit of this version of pan-Arab nationalism. Regarding Stein's fourth point, Baathism explicitly rejected the notion of class conflict and did not envisage a fundamental transformation of society: Baath ideology was inherently paternalistic and authoritarian. Aflaq had no confidence in the people, whom he considered incapable of judging what was good for them. Stressing that the people were 'unable to understand any idea truly and quickly', he went on to explain: 'if a group of educated, active and moral youth were to unite powerfully, according to a fierce discipline, and in accordance with a hierarchy of grades [this would in itself be] enough to guarantee their influence over the people. The holiness that these people endow upon their leader is in reality a sanctification of the idea. . .'[12]

This paternalistic and tutelary attitude towards the people (or

---

10. Michel Aflaq, *Fi sabil al-Baath,*, (Beirut, 1959), quoted by al-Khalil, *op. cit.,*, p. 220.
11. *Ibid.*, pp. 196, 220.
12. *Ibid.*, pp. 221, 223.

the 'masses')—who were unable to determine what was good for them—in some sense underpinned the Baath leaders' perception of themselves as benevolent benefactors who knew best how and to whom to allocate the nation's resources. As it was in absolute control of these resources, and in a position to determine conditions of access to them, a power structure emerged which resulted in the 'political massification of paternalism', to use Stein's characterization of similar situations in Latin America.[13] The party, and subsequently the charismatic leader, became the focus of patronage, a relationship characterized by hierarchical subordination and dependency.

The political strategies pursued by the Baath over the years show that it has remained faithful to these central features of its thinking. This was true for the ruthless determination with which 'the party' set about gaining power, in spite of the fact that it had no strong political roots in Iraq, its use of coercion and fear to establish and maintain itself, its disdain for parliamentary democracy, its broad commitment to social reform, its rejection of the notions of class conflict and of radical social revolution and its overall perception of itself and its leaders. There is therefore a much more coherent core to the Baath's version of pan-Arab nationalism than has often been acknowledged.

Perhaps the must crucial populist component in Baathism was its rejection of class conflict and its substitution of the notion of the harmonious Arab nation, a vision of society which enabled it to address the population as a whole across class lines.[14] This meant that it could pick up more general but vital material and symbolic themes such as pride in Arab history and pride in Arab-Islamic tradition as well as addressing aspirations for social reform, the expansion of education, modernization and economic development and absorb them into 'Arab Socialism'. This kind of socialism did not threaten the vital interests of the expanding middle and lower middle classes, who had a vested interest in the maintenance of existing bourgeois property relations. On the contrary, its development and modernizing vision was all-embracing and was thought to benefit all members of society. In other words, by voiding leftist concepts like socialism and imperialism of their class content, the Baath

13. Stein, *op. cit.*, p. 212.
14. 'All existing differences between the members of the nation are superficial and false, and will be dissipated with the awakening of the Arab soul', Aflaq wrote in 1947, quoted by al-Khalil, *op. cit.*, p. 197.

could make use of these terms to respond to the needs of wide sections of the population without essentially threatening the material interests of the propertied classes and could also project itself as a progressive force which had the welfare of all Iraqis (and indeed of all Arabs) at heart.

This ideological framework helped to conceal both the generally system-maintaining and demobilizing nature of Baathism and the degree to which it was rooted in many of the traditional political, social and cultural norms of Iraqi society. This characterisitic of pan-Arab nationalism was also reflected in its capacity to absorb and reassert the traditional cultural norms of Islam, including those affecting the position of women and the family. The Baath did not attempt to address, still less subvert, these norms but 'harnessed the emotions called forth by Islam in the service of the Arab national movement. . . By stepping outside Islamic doctrine yet basing itself on its most fundamental normative rationale, Aflaq was able to provide a new and yet traditionally rooted justification of pan-Arabism'.[15] This theme is also addressed in a seminal article by Mai Ghossoub on women and Islam where she writes, 'The new nationalism also claimed many of the most patriarchal values of Islamic traditionalism as integral to Arab cultural identity as such... For Islam is not simply a religion—it is a total order that blends the spiritual and the practical, the political and the private, indissolubly together'.[16] The inherently moderate nature of pan-Arab nationalism meant that it was never forced to address many of the most deeply entrenched traditional norms and values within Arab society, and it was this, paradoxically perhaps, which broadened its political platform. On the other hand it also increased the inherent tension between the mobilization required for the modernizing effort and the concomitant need to demobilize and constrain.

15. *Ibid.*, pp. 200, 211. Amal Rassam also discusses this theme in terms of the Baath's reluctance to provoke the more conservative elements among the religious establishment, who might conceivably mobilize a following on the issue of women; see her 'Revolution? Women and the state in Iraq', in T. Niblock, ed., *Iraq: the contemporary state*, (London, 1982). Suad Joseph looks at Baathist policies towards women in terms of 'state construction' and comes to the rather questionable conclusion that the Baath has attempted to undermine 'or diminish the power of the extended patriarchal family'. See 'The mobilization of Iraqi women into the wage labour force', *Women and politics in twentieth century Africa and Asia, studies in Third World societies*, No. 16, 1981.

16. Mai Ghossoub, 'Women in the Arab World', *New Left Review*, 161, January/February 1987, pp. 8–9.

THE WOMEN'S MOVEMENT IN IRAQ BEFORE THE BAATH TAKEOVER IN 1968

The earliest Iraqi women's movement was 'Women Arise!', founded by Asma Zahawi in the early 1920s, but little is known about its programmes or activities. In the 1920s, two publications, *The Modern Woman* and *The Arab Woman*, took up the question of women's liberation, but these were shortlived and it has not been possible to trace either of them. Although no vocal independent women's movement emerged in Iraq under the mandate and monarchy, Iraqi women participated regularly in oppositional political organizations, which, given the constraints on legal political activity, meant primarily that they became members of underground organizations connected in some way with the Communist Party. Thus, The Women's League Against Fascism *(al-Rabita)* was founded in 1943; it continued to function after the war, holding literacy classes and educational meetings at which women's rights and other political issues were discussed. When the liberal period came to an end in 1947, *al-Rabita* was banned along with all other left-wing organizations.

Again, little is known about women's activities in the period which followed, apart from the fact that some clandestine activities continued. In 1950 the Communist Party founded another front underground organization, whose membership was largely based on *al-Rabita*, the League for the Defence of Women's Rights. The Revolution of 1958 ushered in a brief period of political liberalization, during which the left began to flourish. By the middle of 1959, when the Communist Party was at the height of its influence, the new *al-Rabita* had 42,000 members, but had to close down again in 1961 when the political tide turned. As a communist front organization, *al-Rabita* called for civil and political equality for women, and stressed the close relationship between social change and women's liberation.[17] This was a reflection on *al-Rabita's* orthodox Marxist underpinning and the belief that social change would inevitably bring about the liberation of women. In common with the other communist front organizations *al-Rabita* continued to function in a semi-legal fashion until the events of 1963 forced it underground; after 1968 it emerged into semi-legality once again.

---

17. See the *Report of the Third National Congress of the Iraqi Communist Party*, September 1970, where these principles continue to be reiterated, particularly pp. 106–7.

The Women's Movement under the Baath

As the Baath did not seek to establish a pluralistic political system in Iraq it had to legitimize its claim to power within an ideological framework. In other words its had to try to legitimize itself through a 'belief system or a cause, rather than the exercise of choice between different leaders and policies', to borrow David Beetham's formulation from a more general political context. Typically for political movements and regimes of this kind, the Baath had to claim a 'monopoly of truth in the realm of doctrine, and a monopoly of organization in the sphere of political activity'. Under such regimes, 'the public expression of alternative ideas, or even of opposition to official policy constituted a threat to the party's legitimacy' since such attitudes challenged 'the truth claims on which its authority was based'.[18]

As I have shown, in its attempts to establish its control over the whole of society, the Baath first incorporated (in 1973-76) and then suppressed, eliminated or forced into exile any potential or genuine oppositional forces. A massive and pervasive apparatus of security and repression was constructed, accompanied by a thorough-going policy of indoctrination and thousands of publications by the Party and the state owned media. A similar role was played by the literacy and other 'educational' campaigns carried out through the mass organizations, all of which were now controlled by the state and Party. These attempts to infuse every citizen with the principles of the Party—and since 1979 with love for the person of the President—have been carried out with great zeal since the inception of Baath rule.[19] The Party was presented as the standard bearer and vanguard of the new Arab nation and the struggle against imperialism and backwardness. While a more exclusive group within the Party leadership established its control over the key positions within the state—so that party and state became increasingly indistinguishable—the Party itself was transformed into an all-embracing mass organization. The expansion of the Party apparatus was accompanied by the formation of new Baath-controlled mass organizations, very much on the pattern of those led by the Communists a few decades earlier.

The *General Federation of Iraqi Women* (GFIW) was one of these

18. D. Beetham, *The legitimation of power*, (London, 1991), p. 157.
19. Thus the report of the Eighth Regional Congress of the Arab Ba'th Socialist Party (January 1974) stresses that it is 'in education that the battle of transformation will be decisive. The Party has consistently argued for better educational programmes at all levels from kindergartens to university', p. 181.

organizations, founded immediately *after* the Baath takeover in 1968. Like others of its type, the Federation expanded substantially over the following decades, and there were apparently some 200,000 active members by 1982.[20] Like the Party itself, the GFIW was organized in a hierarchical structure which consisted of eighteen branches, one in each province, with 265 sub-units based in the most important towns, 755 centres based in villages or towns and some 1,600 liaison committees.[21] As these figures indicate, as well as increasing its membership the GFIW also developed a substantial institutional framework from which it could reach out to every part of the country, which meant that its political influence was far from negligible.

The GFIW was involved in education, particularly illiteracy campaigns, and organized various volunteer activities. It also provided services for women, especially child care facilities, and organized technical training for women in industry. These activities were considered to be an integral part of the developmental and modernizing efforts of the Baath Party, and must also be seen against the background of substantial increases in the number of women at all levels of the educational system and in their increased employment in the professions and the civil service. The percentage of women employed in the non-agricultural labour force rose from seven per cent in 1968 to nineteen per cent in 1980.[22]

Law 139 of 1972, specifying the status, duties and function of the GFIW, stressed as its most important task the mobilization of Iraqi women 'in the battle of the Arab nation against imperialism, Zionism, reaction and backwardness'. The Federation was to function as an integral part of the Party's 'resurrection of the Arab nation and the restoration of the Arabs' historic role among the other nations of the world'. It was thus not to address more general or far-reaching issues of women's liberation but to provide a framework for incorporating women into the developmental effort and into the hegemonic political process. In other words the Baath did not regard the liberation of women as being in any important sense related to women's oppression or subordination in the division of labour but as an integral part of the effort for the 'nation's liberation'.

20. Suad Joseph, *op. cit.*
21. C.M. Helms, *Iraq: Eastern flank of the Arab world*, (Washington, D.C., 1984), p. 99.
22. Amal Sharqi, 'The Emancipation of Iraqi Women', in Niblock, *op. cit.*, pp. 83–85.

However, the socialization of women was not only considered desirable for its own sake (given that women formed half of the population); their cooption was considered vital because of the ideological influence they could exert on their children and hence over the next generation. Saddam Hussein's speech to the Third Conference of the GFIW in April 1971 illustrates the Baath's deliberate, purposeful approach. 'An enlightened mother', he said, 'who is educated and liberated can give the country a generation of conscious and committed fighters'.[23]

It was considered that the GFIW would serve the cause of women's liberation best by carrying out and supporting the policies of the Party. 'The liberation of women', says the report of the Eighth Regional Baath Party Congress of 1974, 'cannot be achieved through women's societies alone. It can only be achieved through the complete political and economic liberation of society. The Arab Baath Socialist Party has a leading role to play in the liberation of women since it leads the process of social and cultural change'.[24] Hence the nature of women's liberation was to be determined not by the members of the Federation but by the Party and its leaders.

Given the Baath's monopolistic ideological claims and its increasingly repressive stance, the GFIW developed into a Party mouthpiece and became yet another framework of surveillance and oppression. Together with the Party's other developmental efforts, the Federation's activities in extending educational, health and child care facilities served to legitimate Baath rule and to discourage women from making more far-reaching demands for their liberation. Nevertheless, the process of containing the women's movement does not seem to have been accomplished entirely without resistance. The limited pluralism of the early 1970s, which permitted a certain amount of political discourse, meant that GFIW members did try to exert pressure on the regime for more far-reaching reforms of the personal status laws in favour of women. This was probably also facilitated by the fact that the Federation had been merged with the communist *al-Rabita* in 1975 as the result of the Communist/Baath alliance in the Progressive National Front in 1973. At the annual conference of the GFIW in 1976 Saddam Hussein addressed these demands in the following manner:

23. Saddam Hussein, *Social and foreign affairs in Iraq*, (London, 1979), p. 16.
24. *Political report of the Eighth Regional Congress of the Arab Baath Socialist Party—Iraq*, 1974, p. 86.

A serious question may occur to any of the delegates or any woman in Iraq outside this Congress, one which may arise during her work and lead occasionally to discussions, concerned with the principles of the Revolution and having faith in their foundation and capacity to build up the new society. The question is: how could the Revolution strike and overcome the positions and interests of the oil monopolies and feudalism and wrest the exploiting ownership from their grip . . . and yet falter in attacking and dealing with some of the aspects of the legal position of women? This is a question which must undoubtedly arise in the minds of some of you. *We hear it in your discussions.*[my italics]

The Revolution has tackled those problems and positions with striking means and methods because in doing so it could lose only the exploiters while winning in return the whole people. But when the Revolution tackles some legal matters related to women without taking a balance of attitudes to the question of equality and its historical perspective, it will certainly lose a large segment of the people . . . There is a difference between balance and equality. We don't mean that women should be emancipated with equivalent methods to those used in the emancipation of the whole of society. Our meaning is this: in women's emancipation the principle of balance must be maintained—that is when the Revolution set women free, it must take into consideration the degree and the stage of development in our society . . .

The development of sections of society must be examined so that we may have an idea of the amount of pressure which can be accommodated or absorbed by each of them. By doing so we can avoid the unnecessary loss of a section of our people and its conversion to an anti-revolutionary position because of its lack of knowledge and realization of the significance and justice of our measures.

If we find, considering the legal questions pertaining to women or the historical position of women in building society, that some formulae are losing us a significant section of our society, we must not adopt them . . . More important than anything is the liberation of women through active work and sincere participation in the reconstruction of society.[25]

This extract from Saddam Hussein's speech provides a good illustration of the Baath's basic attitude towards women's liberation. As well as exemplifying the basically paternalistic tone ('if the revolution sets women free') characteristic of most Baath procouncements, it

25. Saddam Hussein, *op. cit.*, pp. 36–9.

also shows that the leadership was very conscious of the essential difference between measures such as oil nationalization and land reform (which had weakened the traditional landowing élite) which did not threaten the material or symbolic interests of the majority of the population—but would on the contrary be welcomed and enhance the party's popularity—and those which might well threaten such interests. Radical changes in the personal status of women would constitute an attack on deeply entrenched patriarchal structures and norms, and were therefore not to be addressed. The Baath's position in this respect was not merely opportunistic, in the sense of fearing the wrath of the religious establishment, but reflected the inherent limitations of pan-Arab nationalist populism. In common with most other moden populist nationalist movements,[26] pan-Arab nationalism was deeply rooted in traditional social structures and generally did not address relations of domination, whether of social class or of men over women.

The amendments eventually made to the Code of Personal Status in 1978 did not, as al-Khalil and others suggest,[27] constitute an attack on the power of the patriarchal family. They did not address the personal status of women within society and were largely confined to the question of forced marriages, especially of minors. The new legislation declared forced marriages void and judges were given the right to overrule the father's wishes in the event of such marriages taking place. In addition, the power of male members of the extended family such as uncles and cousins was curtailed. These amendments were extremely moderate and only addressed some of the most blatantly outmoded features of the Personal Status Code. Thus the contention that the legislation intended 'as a whole to diminish the power of the patriarchal family'[28] does not take the essentially patrimonial nature of the power structure of regimes of this kind sufficiently into account, and overlooks the fact that they tend to maintain and reassert rather than undermine patriarchal structures as a basis of social control.

In this context there are some striking similarities with populist regimes in Latin America. In his analysis of the relationship of populist politics and social control in Latin America, Stein emphasizes the link between the 'high concentration of power in the hands

26. This relationship is brought out clearly by L. Caldwell, 'Reproducers of the nation: women and the family in Fascist policy', in Forgacs, *op. cit.*
27. al-Khalil, *op. cit.*, p. 90. See also Rassam, *op. cit.*
28. *Ibid.*

of narrow élite groups' and their reliance on century old 'forms of repression' which have helped to 'spawn a system of patrimonial values and institutions that have strongly supported basic inequalities and worked to defuse mass protest'. As an ideology patrimonialism 'stressed hierarchy and organicism' and as an institutional framework for politics, patrimonialism:

> appeared in the form of party machines and corporatist government in which elaborate patronage organs exercised a seminal role in linking together the rulers and the ruled . . . In all its forms patrimonialism has encouraged the popular masses to look upwards, to reject individual, groups, or class protests of adverse conditions in favour of dependence of forces more powerful and influential than themselves for the amelioration of immediate and prolonged suffering . . . Through the distribution of material and symbolic concessions by a group of highly charismatic, personalistic leaders, these movements succeeded, for a time at least, in bringing large numbers of lower-class elements into politics while preventing them from 'subverting' the process of national decision making.

Stein concludes that populist movements increased 'popular participation' while 'at the same time directing it into paternalistic forms [serving] to bolster the exploitative status quo'.[29]

As well as helping to understand the nature of its fundamental power structures, an analysis of Baath politics in terms of its populist patrimonial features also indicates that its policies vis-à-vis women are not merely a reflection of something specific to Islam or to Islamic culture. In other words, while it is true that Arab nationalism, 're-claimed many of the most patriarchal values of Islamic traditionalism as integral to Arab cultural identity as such' (to quote Mai Ghassoub again), this was not primarly because of any elements specific to Islam, but because it is in the nature of populist regimes that their ideologies tend to be based on traditional social and cultural norms.

The similarities between this style of national populism and Italian fascism are striking. Discussing Catholic and Fascist positions on women in Italy in the 1930s, Caldwell writes,

> In many ways the overall orientation of Fascism towards women moved along paths already well trodden by Catholicism. For Catholicism had evinced an ongoing and extensive concern with the family and the position of women within it . . . In such a view the available roles for women are hierarchized, beginning with that of

29. Stein, op, cit., pp. 126–127, 134.

the mother . . . the fascist emphasis on women as mothers has to be read in conjunction with these Catholic traditions which precede the period of Fascism but reinforce the tendency to regard women primarily as biological reproducers and nurturers'.[30]

Evidently, the very close linkage between Muslim and Arab national identity in Arab culture has provided a particularly favourable base for the development of both Islamic and nationalist populism. 'What better symbol of cultural identity', writes Mai Ghossoub, 'than the privacy of women, refuge *par excellence* of traditional values that the old colonialism could not reach and the new capitalism must not touch? The rigidity of the status of women in the family in the Arab world has been an innermost asylum of Arabo-Muslim identity'.[31]

The family 'as a living cell' constitutes a central theme in Baath pronouncements on the position of women in society in the Baghdad daily *al-Thawra*, the President's speeches and other publications, particularly those of the GFIW.[32] Although women should have equal opportunities in public life, they are 'different' by nature, and their 'natural' role in life is and must be distinct from that of men. This emphasis on the role of women in the family and as mothers is typically infused with a sense of pride in the superiority of Arab culture; Western societies are accused of having 'neglected' this fundamental difference and of not properly appreciating women's unique role as mothers.[33] The chairwoman of the Federation declared in 1981:

> In Europe there is the idea that women should wrest ('strip') their rights from men, that they should demonstrate against men and ask them to carry out the duties of motherhood. That is an influence of a society that does not respect motherhood; otherwise women would be proud to be mothers. Society has pushed women into wrong attitudes . . .[34]

30. Caldwell, *op. cit.*, p. 114.
31. Ghossoub, *op. cit.*, p. 4.
32. Saddam Hussein, *op. cit.*, p. 35. This theme is repeated and emphasized in the Baath's newspaper *al-Thawra* over the years. See particularly the issues every 8 March (International Woman's Day) which usually include articles on the issue of women's liberation. It is also reiterated in Amal Sharqi, *op. cit.*
33. See for instance: Republic of Iraq: National Committee for the preparation of the Nairobi International Conference 15–26 July 1985, General Report presented to Nairobi International Conference: Review Assessment of the Achievements of the United Nations Decade for Women, Baghdad, 1985, p. 21.
34. Saddam Hussein, 'Women, one half of our society', (speech delivered to the

The centrality of this theme is also borne out in a study of Baath attitudes towards women entitled 'Values related to women in President Saddam Hussein's addresses to women', published in 1985, by Muna Yunis Bahri, a lecturer at Baghdad University. It concludes: 'The value of women's love of family is the first among the values which were emphasized in the President's speeches'. Connoisseurs of bizarre statistics will delight in Bahri's revelation that the president mentioned the theme of woman's love for her family 119 times.[35] She explains: 'The president cares for this value because religion, the revolution, the cultural heritage, and the ideology of the Arab Baath Socialist Party, put great emphasis on its importance'. The study ends with the following quotation from one of the president's speeches:

> Though any large-scale activity remains incomplete unless the woman has an active, serious role in it, this should not be at the expense of the process of building up her family since it is a living cell which expresses the unity of society. The family members' relationship should be solid and strong. The General Federation of Iraqi Women has many responsibilities. One of the most important is to strive to build a solid strong family, a cell filled with life in the society. Relationships among family members are to be based on mutual respect and human equality.[36]

The Baath's idealization of motherhood has served to justify women's subordinate role in the 'natural' division of labour and had a generally demobilizing effect on the women's movement. Such an ideal, Beetham has argued in another context, 'serves to obscure the power relations between the sexes under the rubric of "different but equal" and to reconcile women to the limitations of their condition of offering them a positive image to which to aspire, and a domain of their own, the domestic, within which to exercise a carefully circimscribed power'.[37]

The extent to which the GFIW has developed into nothing more than a mouthpiece for the regime is illustrated in the report which it

---

Third Conference of the General Federation of Iraqi Women, 17 April, 1971 in Saddam Hussein, *op. cit.*, p. 16.
35. 'Values relating to women in President Saddam Hussein's Address to Women', General Federation of Iraqi Women (GFIW), Information and Public Relations Secretariat, Baghdad, 1985, p. 13.
36. National Committee for the preparation of the Nairobi International Conference, *op. cit.*, p. 21.
37. Beetham, *op. cit.*, p. 78.

presented to the Nairobi International Women's Conference in July 1985. This document does not contain a single demand for reforms of any kind. Instead, it simply echoes the Party line by repeating the arguments put forward over the years in Saddam Hussein's speeches.[38] The report also embodies a new Islamic dimension hitherto absent from the Baath's language on the women's question. In a passage dealing with the civil status of women the report indicates the Federations's acceptance of the notion that as a legal system the *sharia* offers adequate safeguards for the emancipation of women, if only it were 'properly applied'.[39] Such abnegation of responsibility shows that the General Federation of Iraqi Women had itself become an active participant in the subordination of women in Iraq.

38. National Committee for the preparation of the Nairobi International Conference, *op. cit.*
39. *Ibid.*

Sunnis and Shi'is Revisited: Sectarianism and Ethnicity in Authoritarian Iraq

Peter Sluglett and Marion Farouk-Sluglett

In the last years of the Ottoman Empire, and even after the First World War when the Arab states were first mapped out by Britain and France, most of the inhabitants of the *Mashriq* would have tended to identify with their immediate social units, such as kin, sect, tribe, village, town or quarter. It was only rather hazily that some kind of identification with a nation state came into being, accompanied, as part of the rise of Arabism in the inter-war years, by the acceptance of a broader notion of an Arab nation. With the gradual emergence of market relations in town and countryside, the expansion of education and the growing awareness of a wider world on the part of ever increasing sections of the population, old sectarian and kinship relations began to be undermined and on some levels to break down. Society began to become stratified into elementary forms of social classes, an uneven process but one which moved slowly towards the gradual crystallization of some form of nation state.

It seems that in Iraq, and to a certain extent in other Arab states, such as Syria, this process slowed down or even came to a halt with the emergence of a series of authoritarian regimes in the second half of the twentieth century. In the mid-1970s we wrote an essay called 'Some Reflections on the Sunni-Shi'i Question in Iraq.'[1] Re-reading it fifteen years later, we realized that some of the ideas

This article has been reprinted from John Spagnolo (ed.), *The Modern Middle East in Historical Perspective: Essays in Honour of Albert Hourani*, Ithaca Press, Reading, 1992, pp. 279–294.

1. In *Bulletin of the British Society for Middle Eastern Studies*, vol.5 (1978).

needed further clarification and others needed a more fundamental reassessment, within the general context of the notions of nation formation and national integration which have just been described. In this essay, therefore, after briefly describing the main sectarian and ethnic components of Iraqi society, the Kurds, the Sunni Arabs and the Shi'i Arabs, we shall look at the policies of Iraqi governments towards the different groups in the intervening period. Our main contention is that much of our earlier optimism proved unfounded, and that the process of national integration was checked by an increasingly powerful totalitarian state.

Let us recapitulate the main features of the sectarian and ethnic situation. About ninety-five per cent of the Iraqi population are Muslims[2] who can be subdivided into three principal ethnic and/or sectarian groups: Sunni Kurds, Sunni Arabs, and Shi'i Arabs. Proportionally, the Kurds account for between fifteen per cent andtwenty per cent of the Muslim population, the Sunni Arabs for about twenty-five per cent, and the Shi'is for the rest, about fifty-five per cent. These divisions run through all social classes, but particular political, geographical and historical factors have influenced the social and regional distribution of the three groups.

THE KURDS

We shall take each of the groups in turn, somewhat oversimplifying the historical record in order to present a broad overview. We will begin the discussion with a brief summary of the Kurdish situation, a dimension missing in our previous paper. Apart from those who have migrated to the cities over the last forty or fifty years, most Kurds live in the area which constituted the Vilayet of Mosul before the First World War. Although there were always some small towns in what is now Iraqi Kurdistan, the bulk of the population was organized on a tribal basis and consisted either of transhuman pastoralists, sedentary share-cropping villagers, or landlords. For most of the Ottoman period the penetration of the area by the central government was extremely light, although sufficient to encourage the formation of separatist movements at the beginning of the twentieth century. However, in the aftermath of the First World War, and especially after the unratified Treaty of Sèvres of 1920 which promised the Kurds a state of their own,

---

2. The remaining five per cent are Christians, Yazidis and Sabaeans.

there were a number of attempts on the part of Kurdish tribal armies and political parties to create a Kurdish nation state on the borders of what are now Turkey, Iran and Iraq, none of which ever came to fruition.

In Iraqi Kurdistan the two principal leaders were Shaykh Mahmud Barzinji and Mulla Mustafa Barzani, who were prominent between 1919–1931 and 1937–1975 respectively. Until the overthrow of the Iraqi monarchy in 1958, Barzani was probably best known for his somewhat ambiguous role in the Kurdish Republic of Mahabad, a Soviet-backed separatist movement in Iranian Kurdistan which lasted from January to December 1946. After the Iranian Kurdish leaders surrendered to the Iranian authorities in December 1946, the republic collapsed; Barzani and some of his followers subsequently escaped to the Soviet Union, where they remained in exile until the Revolution of July 1958.

When the revolution came, it appeared that the new regime was well-disposed towards Kurdish aspirations, and indeed encouraged Barzani to return to Iraq. But the initial cordiality proved short-lived when the full implications of the implementation of any sort of Kurdish autonomy gradually became clear, and military confrontation eventually resulted. After nearly a decade of intermittent fighting between various Iraqi regimes and Barzani's forces, the second Baath government, which came to power in 1968, offered Barzani a form of limited autonomy in part of Iraqi Kurdistan in 1970, set to take effect in 1974. Barzani at first accepted the arrangement in principle, but rejected it when its practical limitations became apparent. Fighting broke out once more, but ended in March 1975 when the Iraqi government came to terms with the Kurds' main backer, the Shah of Iran, who withdrew his support for them after he and Saddam Hussein reached an agreement in Algiers.

Subsequently, the Baath regime attempted to impose its will more directly on the area, a process which culminated in the late 1980s in chemical weapon attacks on Kurdish villages and threats of large scale forcible deportations from the area.[3] It should be

---

3. Between 1975 and 1979 an estimated 200,000 Kurds were deported from the frontier area and some 700 villages burnt down as part of a scorched earth policy which aimed to create a depopulated cordon sanitaire along the border with Iran and Turkey. During and after the Iran-Iraq war the process was intensified with the result that by 1990 the majority of Kurdish villages had been destroyed and the population either moved to special regroupment centres within the Kurdish area or 'relocated' outside the area altogether.

stressed that although the ethnic division between Sunni Kurds and Sunni Arabs is in many ways more significant than their common sectarian affiliation, there had never been any systematic *racial* persecution of the Kurds before the 1970s and 1980s. Previous Iraqi governments had sought to bring a rebellious people to heel in order to control the mountainous north eastern region of the territory awarded to Iraq by the League of Nations; it was the scale of the operations of 1988–89 and the apparent desire of the regime to exterminate the Kurdish population which introduced an entirely new and horrifying dimension.

THE SUNNI ARABS

The Sunni Arabs are located primarily in what has been aptly called the Sunni triangle, whose apexes are Mosul, Baghdad and the small country towns on the Tigris and Euphrates in the north west of the country, such as Ana, Rawa, Haditha, Falluja, Hit, Takrit and Ramadi. Apart from Baghdad, which is mixed Sunni and Shi'i, this area has traditionally been entirely Sunni and Christian, with the Sunnis forming the overwhelming majority.

In Ottoman times, the area beyond the immediate hinterland of Baghdad and Mosul formed part of the grazing grounds of many of the great nomadic tribes of the Syrian and North Arabian deserts, notably the Anaiza, the Shammar and the Dulaim. Mosul and the smaller towns tended to look towards the cities of Syria, particularly Aleppo, with which they had a long history of economic interaction. With their overwhelmingly Sunni populations, a certain affinity existed between the Syrian and northern Iraqi towns in their overall lifestyle and religious affiliation. Baghdad, in contrast, was far less homogeneous, since the Sunni population, although concentrated in particular parts of the old city,[4] was flanked by ancient and well-established Shi'i, Christian and Jewish quarters.[5] This pattern of sectarian co-residence tended to be reproduced when the city expanded under the mandate and monarchy, although a few 'secular'

---

4. Hanna Batatu, in his *The Old Social Classes and the Revolutionary Movements of Iraq; A Study of Iraq's Old Landed and Commercial Classes, and of its Communists, Baathists and Free Officers* (Princeton, 1978), p.18, lists the principal pre-modern quarters of Baghdad and their main ethnic and sectarian composition.

5. Although this should not be taken too literally. The population figures for the quarters of Aleppo at the end of the nineteenth century in Kamil al-Ghazzi, *Nahr al-Dhahab fi Tarikh Halab* [The Stream of Gold in the History of Aleppo] (3 vols.,

or 'mixed' quarters such as Alwiyah and Karrada inhabited primarily by the educated elites, also came into being at the same time.

Since the Ottoman Empire was a Sunni institution, the local Sunni elite, many of whom were actually Arabized Turks[6] or Arabized Kurds, constituted the notability in late Ottoman times and served as intermediaries between the Ottomans and the local population. It was the Sunnis who made use of whatever governmental educational facilities were provided (which were considerably increased towards the end of the nineteenth century) and were thus able to consolidate their positions in the expanding local administration. The corollary of this was that the Shi'is, for reasons which will shortly be discussed, were never substantially involved in the Ottoman civil or military administration, were not numbered among the 'notables' and did not, generally, send their children to the government schools.

At the beginning of the twentieth century, members of the Sunni Arab bureaucratic and military elite were influenced by the ideas of Arab nationalism current at the time in the Arab provinces of the Ottoman Empire.[7] In the course of the First World War, some of them transferred their loyalties from the Ottoman state to the British sponsored Arab Revolt, and served in the Hijaz Army or in the Arab kingdom of Syria between 1918 and 1920. Many of these individuals, including Jafar al-Askari, Nuri al-Said, Yasin al-Hashimi, Naji Suwaidi and Sati al-Husri, became leading politicians, soldiers or administrators in the kingdom of Iraq between 1920 and 1958.

In addition to this essentially secular group, whose fortunes rose with the establishment of the monarchy and the new state of Iraq, there was another important segment of the Sunni urban population whose changing situation, perhaps because it was not so visible, has not received so much attention. In all the towns in the Sunni area there was a substantial lower middle class which,

---

Aleppo, 1926) show that many of them included members of several different sects. Although such detailed figures do not exist for Baghdad, it is probable that the quarters were less rigidly divided than has been assumed. See also Heinz Gaube and Eugen Wirth, *Aleppo: Historische und geographische Beitrage zur baulichen Gestaltung, zur sozialen Organisation und zur wirtschaftlichen Dynamik einer vorderasiatischen fernhandelsmetropole* [Aleppo: Historical and Geographical Studies on the Built Environment, the Social Organisation and the Economic Dynamics of a Near Eastern Long Distance Trading Metropolis] (Wiesbaden, 1984).

6. A similar phenomenon is observable among the Aleppine notables.

7. Cf. Philip Khoury's *Urban Notables and Arab Nationalism: The Politics of Damascus 1860–1920* (Cambridge, 1983).

although potentially upwardly mobile, remained committed to a way of life that was partly traditional, encompassing the values of the 'Muslim family,' the mosque and female segregation, but which was also attracted to such 'modern' goals as secular education, economic development and national independence. This class saw no contradiction in pursuing both these sets of objectives simultaneously. Little is known about its historical role, beyond the fact that many, but not all, of its members came to constitute the main bulwark of support for pan-Arab nationalism, and were also vehemently anti-communist. Of course, some had also become more thoroughly secularized or 'westernized,' and supported more liberal political tendencies.

THE SHI'IS

Apart from the Shi'i residents of Baghdad and the holy cities of Karbala and Najaf, the great bulk of Iraqi Shi'is lived in the rural area south of Baghdad, where they worked as sharecroppers on the great estates which had been created during the period of the mandate and monarchy. These cultivators were the descendants of nomadic and semi-nomadic tribesmen who had converted to Shi'ism and settled in the area in the course of the previous 200 years.[8] There were few educational facilities in the countryside until comparatively recent times, and this, combined with grinding poverty and low life expectancy,[9] meant that the rural poor had few chances to improve their lot. In addition, perhaps influenced by the fact that there was no well developed network of religious institutions in the area,[10] their Shi'ism, or their Islamicism, seems to have been worn fairly lightly.

When migration to Baghdad began in earnest in the late 1940s,

8. For further details see Hanna Batatu, 'Shi'i Organizations in Iraq: Al-Da'wah al-Islamiyah and al-Mujahidin' in J. R. I. Cole and Nikki Keddie, eds., *Shi'ism and Social Protest* (New York and London, 1986), pp.179–200.
9. In 1953 a British physician, Professor Michael Critchley, described the Iraqi fellah as 'a living pathological specimen' and estimated average life expectancy at between thirty-five and thrity-nine years, quoted in Ronay Gabbay, *Communism and Agrarian Reform in Iraq* (London, 1978), p.29.
10. See Batatu, 'Shi'i Organizations,' pp.184–85, who writes that 'in the overwhelmingly Shi'i rural districts of the provinces of Basra, Karbala, Diwaniyah, Hilla, 'Amarah, Muntafiq and Kut, where more than forty-nine per cent of the total rural population of Iraq lived, there were in 1947 [the year of the first accurate census] only thirty-nine religious institutions, or, to put it differently, there was on the average only one religious institution for every 37,000 persons.'

the bulk of the migrants were from Kut and Amara, the poorest parts of the rural south. Most of them were illiterate, superstitious rather than religious, with little or no contact, either emotional or intellectual, with institutionalized or 'high' Shi'ism. As is well known, the parts of the city in which these poor migrants settled became some of the principal recruiting grounds for the Iraqi Communist Party in the course of the 1940s and 1950s.[11]

Before the First World War, Hanna Batatu tells us, the Shi'is formed about a fifth of the population of the city of Baghdad; there were some 30,000 Shi'is and 53,000 Jews out of a population of about 150,000. It is difficult to assess their social stratification, but it seems that few of the former were men of real substance. In 1936, for example, only three out of thirty-nine *sarrafs* [money changers] listed in the *Iraqi Directory* were Shi'is, and in 1935–36 there were only two Shi'is on the eighteen-member administrative committee of the Baghdad Chamber of Commerce. It was only after the expulsion of almost all the Jews from Baghdad in the early 1950s that the Shi'is of the city began to become of major economic significance; by 1957–58 there were fourteen Shi'is on the same eighteen-member committee.[12]

The less well-to-do among the Shi'i urban community of Baghdad (and Basra) were traditionally involved in the retail and wholesale trades and in service industries. The virtual exclusion of the Shi'is from government service and their relatively low participation in the new Ottoman educational system meant that even later, under the less avowedly discriminatory conditions of the mandate and monarchy,[13] they were initially either not appropriately qualified, or simply not inclined, to take up government employment. In time, however, particularly with the spread of education in the 1930s, 1940s and 1950s—in the major urban centres, but also in the smaller country towns—Shi'i representation in government employment at all levels became a closer reflection of the numerical strength of the sect in the population as a whole, especially after the Revolution of 1958.

11. See Hanna Batatu, 'Iraq's Underground Shi'a Movements: Characteristics, Causes and Prospects' in *Middle East Journal*, vol.35 (1981), pp.578–94.
12. Batatu, *Old Social Classes*, pp.248, 271; cf. the same author's 'Iraq's Shi'a: their Political Role and the Process of their Integration into Society' in Barbara Stowasser, ed., *The Islamic Impulse* (Georgetown and London, 1987), pp.204–13.
13. Although it is clear that the Shi'is were discriminated against by the Ottomans, it is obviously difficult to document this accurately.

In their religious observances many of these urban Shi'is continued to be committed to their traditional way of life, with strict adherence to Islamic ordinances and, in particular, to patriarchal values. Like their Sunni counterparts they also combined their commitment to this value system with a desire for progress and development, but unlike them they were not much attracted to Arab nationalism, with its strongly Sunni overtones. Their own political aspirations were centred much more on the idea of Iraq than on the idea of the Arab nation, which partly explains the attraction of communism for the more secular-minded members of this class. In addition, many Baghdadi Shi'is lived in relative proximity to the recent arrivals from the countryside, whose numbers and whose visible economic deprivation must also have heightened the social awareness of their urban co-religionists.

Here it may be appropriate to interject an important consideration which applies as much to the class of 'urban Shi'is' we have just described as to their Sunni counterparts. The struggle for national independence under the mandate and monarchy, which came to engulf all but a very few privileged members of Iraqi society, was by definition embedded in an essentially secular way of thinking, whether its roots were socialist or nationalist. Almost inevitably, one effect of this experience on many of those involved was that they themselves became partly secularized, although, as we have stressed, they simultaneously retained a deeply rooted feeling for much of the Islamic cultural and social value system in which they had grown up.

A significant by-product of this was that within the new parameters of the nation state such people gradually came to feel more conscious of their identity as 'Iraqis' than as 'Sunnis' or 'Shi'is.' This gathered increasing momentum after the Revolution of 1958, and in an important sense sectarian barriers began, if not to disappear, at least to become of less pressing political and social significance. Examples of this 'melting pot' tendency are the huge demonstrations against the Portsmouth Agreement in 1948 and in favour of Abd al-Karim Qasim in 1959, and the fact that it was the Shi'is of Kadhimayn who were among the most active of those who rushed onto the streets of Baghdad to defend Qasim's government, which was almost entirely composed of Sunnis, in the terrible days of February 1963.

A small but vital component of the Shi'i population are the inhabitants of the Holy Cities of Twelver Shi'ism, the *atabat*, Najaf,

Karbala, and (to a lesser extent) the Baghdad suburb of Kadhimayn. Najaf, where the tomb of Ali ibn Abi Talib is located, was the preferred burial place of pious Twelver Shi'is, to which corpses were brought for interment from all over the Shi'i world. In Ottoman times, and until comparatively recently, when the functions of the *atabat* were increasingly taken over by Qum, these cities were the world centres of this sect of Islam, housing its chief shrines, the residences of its senior clergy, and theological colleges which served Shi'ism in Iran, Iraq, Lebanon and the Indian subcontinent. The permanent inhabitants of the *atabat* were long established urban dwellers, who were engaged in the religious occupations and/or in the wholesale and retail trades, particularly in the commercialization of agricultural produce but also in the sale of luxury commodities, such as carpets. Most of the main religious leaders, the *maraji al-taqlid*, were Persian, as were many of the other inhabitants of the *atabat*. It was here that what we may call 'high' Shi'ism was practised, where the most elaborate versions of the main religious festivals were enacted.

The Ottomans had not been closely involved with the administration of the Holy Cities, and this, combined with the generally separate existence of the Shi'is that has already been described, meant that the communities of Karbala and Najaf generally had fairly little contact with the Ottoman state. Some of the clergy of the *atabat* played a vital role in *Persian* national politics at the end of the nineteenth century, beginning with the famous *fatwa* [finding based on religious jurisprudence] against tobacco by Ayatollah Muhammad al-Yazdi in 1890, and later participated on both sides in the Constitutional Revolution; some groups supported the provisions of ulema participation, and others opposed the idea of a constitution altogether on the grounds that such an innovation was western inspired.

Similarly, many of the Shi'i clergy had been profoundly opposed to the secularizing ideology of the Young Turks, but rallied to the Ottoman side as soon as the British invaded Iraq at the beginning of the First World War, declaring a *jihad* against the invaders in November 1914. The Holy Cities appear to have been almost completely unaffected, or at least unmoved, by the Sharifian propaganda urging the Arabs to join with the British in throwing off the Ottoman yoke.[14] After the war, the clergy set themselves at the

14. See Pierre Martin, 'Le clergé chiite en Irak hier et aujourd'hui' in *Maghreb/Mashreq*, no. 115 (1986), pp. 29–52.

forefront of the opposition to Britain, playing a vital role in the Iraqi Revolution of 1920. They continued to function as a major obstacle to the creation of the Iraqi state under British mandate until June 1923, when the British and Iraqi authorities deported a number of leading ayatullahs to Iran, including Muhammad Mahdi al-Khalisi, as a result of their refusal to withdraw *fatwas* against Shi'i participation in the Iraqi elections.[15] After this the senior clergy tended to play a quietist role and did not substantially involve themselves in Iraqi politics for several decades, partly, no doubt, influenced by the knowledge that they could expect little moral or material support from the new and more secular government in Teheran. This vigorous initial resistance to the Iraqi state and its British sponsors was symptomatic of the clergy's general inclination to stand on the side of 'Islam' against 'the infidels' and, as their support of the Ottomans against the British a few years earlier had shown, had nothing to do with the largely Sunni composition of the mandatory government.

Apart from these deportations, which certainly served their purpose at the time, most Iraqi governments under the mandate and monarchy continued the Ottoman tradition of a fair degree of circumspection in their dealings with the Holy Cities. Increasingly, the cities' relative distinctness served to consolidate the growing gulf between their 'traditional learned population' on the one hand, and the rural Shi'is and the migrants to Baghdad on the other.[16] The Shi'i hierarchy made little or no attempt to incorporate their rural or poor migrant co-religionists institutionally, in the sense that the hierarchy founded hardly any schools or mosques either in the slums or in the rural areas, and showed little concern for the inhabitants' material or spiritual welfare. For their part, the migrants did not hesitate to take state employment or send their children to state schools if they were in a position to do so, thus increasing their own and their children's political and social awareness, and, as often as not, their secularization.

In the latter years of the monarchy this gulf between the bulk of the Shi'i population and their nominal religious leaders widened further, partly because of the political and social processes which have already been described, but also because of the more general

15. For an account of the expulsions see Peter Sluglett, *Britain in Iraq 1914–1932* (London, 1976), chapter 3.

16. This should not be taken as inferring cause and effect; there is no suggestion that they had been in close touch with them before.

secularizing tendencies of the inter- and post-war periods. Secular ideologies became more attractive, or at least more obviously 'relevant' to everyday concerns, and government employment became more prestigious. At the same time, the prestige of the religious profession seems to have undergone a considerable decline. The falling rolls in the theological colleges of Najaf were paralleled by a similar phenomenon in Iran, where 'a comparison of the [numbers of] madrasahs of Tehran between. . .1960 and 1975 shows that the . . .city lost. . .9 out of 32 madrasahs over the. . .period.'[17]

By the 1950s the Shi'i clergy had become deeply concerned at what they saw as the increasing threat posed by secularism and, in particular, at the spectre of Communism and atheism.[18] Of course, these sentiments were shared by the British and the government in Baghdad, and a certain convergence of interests is observable; in the course of a meeting with the eminent *mujtahid* [Shi'i scholar of jurisprudence] Shaykh Muhammad al-Husain Kashif al-Ghita' in Najaf in October 1953, the British Ambassador, Sir John Troutbeck, inveighed, to an obviously sympathetic listener, against the 'dark propaganda [thriving today] in this very city which is a centre of Islam and holiness.'[19] These fears naturally increased after the Revolution of 1958, which was led and implemented by a group whose political views, however contradictory in other ways, were unmistakably secularist in tone. In April 1960 Muhammad al-Hakim and Murtada al-Yasin issued *fatwas* against membership of, or support for, the Communist Party, and Kashif al-Ghita issued a *fatwa* 'execrating communism' in the autumn of the same year.[20]

In an attempt to stem the rising tide of secularism, a number of religious parties were founded in the late 1950s, most notably *al-Dawa al-Islamiya* [The Islamic Call], whose moving spirits were the ayatollahs Muhsin al-Hakim and Baqr al-Sadr. These movements were directed particularly against Communism; Baathism, which is also secular, probably had too insignificant a following at the time

17. These statistics are quoted in Batatu, 'Iraq's Underground Shia Movements,' p.581, from Fadhil Jamali, 'The Theological Colleges of Najaf' in *Muslim World*, vol.50 (1960). There were 6,000 students in Najaf in 1918, and 1,954 in 1957. See also Shahrough Akhavi, *Religion and Politics in Contemporary Iran: Clergy-State Relations in the Pahlavi Period* (Albany, NY, 1980), p.129.
18. See Batatu, 'Shi'i Organisations,' p.190.
19. Batatu, *Old Social Classes*, p.694.
20. Akhavi, *Religion and Politics*, p.98; see also Chibli Mallat, 'Religious militancy in contemporary Iraq: Muhammad Baqr as-Sadr and the Sunni-Shia paradigm' in *Third World Quarterly* vol.10 (1988), pp.683–98.

to be viewed as a major threat to 'Islam.' In the late 1950s and early 1960s, Baqr al-Sadr, one of the leading Shi'i intellectuals of the second part of the twentieth century, published two important books, *Falsafatuna* [Our Philosophy] and *Iqtisaduna* [Our Economic System], both of which were primarily attempts to refute Marxist philosophy and economics, and to lay the foundations for an Islamic polity, which, it should be emphasized, he was at pains to set out in terms which would be attractive to both Sunnis and Shi'is.[21] Both books enjoyed considerable popularity, went into a number of editions and were translated into Persian. Al-Sadr's thought and writings are considered to have provided significant intellectual substance for much of the subsequent ideology of the Iranian Revolution and of the Islamic Republican regime.

DEVELOPMENTS SINCE 1958

After 1958, and particularly after 1968, the Iraqi state changed very fundamentally. It developed great coercive powers, and a degree of autonomy from the rest of society, underpinned as it was by massive oil revenues and an efficient and wide-ranging military, police and security apparatus. It became increasingly unwilling to tolerate independent centres of power, whether emanating from individuals within or outside the Baath party, 'allied' political parties,[22] national-ethnic independence movements, such as those sponsored by the various Kurdish forces, or from Islamic movements supported by the Muslim Brotherhood (never particularly powerful in Iraq), or the Shi'i clergy.

In the 1970s and 1980s the principal obstacles to the Baath's political monopoly were the Kurds and the Shi'i clergy. The Communists, once the Baath's most formidable foes, had been substantially weakened first by allowing themselves to be absorbed as allies in the National Patriotic Front in 1973, and then by being

---

21. For a discussion of al-Sadr's writings see ibid., where Mallat points out that this more universalist discourse gave way to a particularist Shi'i discourse by 1979. In one slightly misleading feature of an otherwise excellent study, Mallat seems to equate a 'government composed of Sunni Muslims' with a 'Sunni government,' though there is no necessary relation between the two.

22. The Iraq Communist Party, for example, which joined the Baath in the National Progressive Front in 1973. Subsequently, it had to pursue a policy of unconditional support for the Baath, but was severely suppressed in the late 1970s. Cf. also the token Kurdish Progressive Party which continued to put up candidates for the National Assembly, a rubber-stamping institution without real power.

crushed at the end of the 1970s when the Baath once more unleashed its fury upon them. As we noted earlier, the Kurds had little room in which to manoeuvre after they lost the support of the Shah in 1975, although they were able to regroup after he fell in 1979.[23] By 1975, therefore, having nationalized the Iraqi Petroleum Company, neutralized the Communists and defeated the Kurds, the only major area over which the Baath did not exercise more or less total control was the Shi'i religious hierarchy. It is interesting here not only to investigate whether the policies pursued by the Baath towards its Shi'i opponents furthered integration, in the sense of contributing to the process of state formation, but also to inquire whether the gradual weakening of sectarian differences and antagonisms which we noted for the 1950s and 1960s continued or was halted.

THE BAATH AND THE SHI'IS

It may be worth reiterating at this point that although Baathism is indeed secular in its outlook, the nationalist tradition from which it derives is essentially Sunni, in the sense that the idea of Arab unity necessarily implies unification with an overwhelmingly Sunni Arab world. In consequence, for this and other reasons that have already been mentioned, the Baath has traditionally found most of its recruits among the Sunni lower middle classes, from Mosul, Baghdad and the smaller towns of the Sunni triangle. In spite of the general truth of this assertion, it so happened that, for a brief period at the very beginning of the spread of Baathism in Iraq, many of the early leaders were Shi'is, largely because the first Secretary-General of the party, Fuad al-Rikabi, was a Shi'i. After his departure in 1960, however, no Shi'is held positions of importance in the party until 1974. Only four members of the twenty-two man Revolutionary Command Council in September 1977 were Shi'is, and three of the four lost their lives in the great purge of July 1979. In broad terms, committed Shi'i Baathists have almost certainly been more attracted to the movement's social policies than to its nationalist ideology.

At the end of 1976, relations between the Baath and the Shi'i

---

23. One reason for the Iraqi attack on Iran in 1980 was that the Iranian Revolution had indirectly reopened the Kurdish 'problem,' which the Baath were to show themselves determined to 'solve' by a policy little short of genocide.

hierarchy began to show signs of strain. Dissatisfaction at the poor harvests of 1975 and 1976 (partly caused by disputes between Iraq and Syria over the distribution of Euphrates water) produced protest demonstrations on the road between Karbala and Najaf in February 1977. These ended in confrontations with the army in the course of which several arrests were made and a number of people killed. In the 'trials' which followed, eight Shi'i dignitaries were executed, an unprecedentedly audacious affront. This incident proved to be the beginning of a systematic and vicious attack on the religious hierarchy, which culminated in the arrest and execution of Muhammad Baqr al-Sadr and his sister, Bint Huda, in April 1980. In the course of this campaign, Ayatollah Khomeini, who had been living in exile in Najaf since 1964, was expelled from Iraq in October 1978.

Of course, the severity with which Shi'i dissidents were treated in the period before the Iranian Revolution gives no real indication of the strength of 'Shi'i opposition' in the Holy Cities, or, indeed, elsewhere. It was more indicative of the regime's absolute determination not to permit the formation of the smallest pocket of dissent either there or anywhere else in the country. In consequence, it is extremely difficult to make any but the most tentative assessment of the extent of Shi'i opposition as a phenomenon, and in particular of the appeal of such parties as *al-Dawa* outside the traditional religious centres, particularly in the Shi'i agglomerations in Baghdad.

Whatever the actual strength of the Shi'i movement may have been, the acquiescence which the bulk of the Shi'i population showed in the course of the war with Iran seems to demonstrate that the majority of Shi'is, who constituted most of the ordinary soldiers, did not identify either with the Islamic Republic of Iran or with the pro-Iranian clergy in Karbala and Najaf; most Iraqi Shi'is proved to be Iraqis, Arabs and Shi'is, in that order.[24] In this respect both the Iraqi and Iranian regimes seem to have misjudged the nature of Shi'i feeling in Iraq and underestimated its patriotic content. The Iranian leadership seems not to have been aware of the

24. Comments, such as the one that follows, give rise to a certain scepticism: 'La résurgence du facteur religieux comme base d'inspiration d'un projet politique pour la première fois depuis le début du siècle ... est un fait remarquable qui traduit des tensions nées des bouleversements considérables des dernières décennies.' Pierre Martin, 'Les chiites d'Irak: une majorité dominée à la recherche de son destin' in *Peuples Méditerranéens*, no.40, July–September 1987, pp.127–69.

great gulf that continued to exist between the masses of ordinary Iraqi Shi'is and the high clergy in the Holy Cities,[25] while, for its part, the Iraqi regime seems to have overestimated the emotional impact of the Iranian Revolution upon the population of al-Thawra and other Shi'i quarters in the capital and elsewhere.

As we have seen, Saddam Hussein had begun to suppress the Shi'i movement long before the Iranian Revolution. He did this with the same kind of thoroughness and vindictiveness which he applied to the extirpation of any other potential or real opposition forces, throwing the full weight of the state and its coercive apparatus against the movement[26] and the dissident clergy.[27] Naturally, the Shi'i movement was persecuted more vigorously during the Iran–Iraq war, when every Iraqi Shi'i came to be seen as a potential enemy sympathizer. The movement was crushed and its leaders forced into exile with the rest of the opposition forces.

Having suppressed, eliminated or weakened all the opposition, Saddam Husain could claim to be in charge of a unified country. This led him to be portrayed as the leader who forged a divided Iraq into a nation state, successfully weakening or destroying tribal, sectarian or ethnic forms of identity. This may have been done brutally, the argument runs, but he succeeded where others failed. But was this really the case? Did his rule not, in fact, have the opposite effect, slowing down the process of nation formation and integration and blocking the sectarian and ethnic fusion which had begun to take place earlier?

One paramount factor which must be taken into account is that the mass of the population, whatever its sectarian affiliation, was effectively excluded from participation at all levels, a situation which led to a profound feeling of alienation from the state. The rulers of Iraq in this period came to consist of an extremely limited group, most of whom were either relatives of the President or his closest and most trusted personal friends. The authoritarian nature of the state, with its massive personality cult and the absence of an independent judiciary, responsible executive or representative

---

25. During Khumaini's stay in Najaf his contacts seem to have been largely confined to the clergy elite with little awareness of the wider Shi'i world within Iraq.

26. Including the law: membership of *al-Dawa* became punishable by death.

27. Typically, Saddam Hussein combined the use of force with attempts at incorporation, co-opting some of the Shi'i clergy—like the Najafi, Shaikh Haidar al-Marjani—who began to glorify him and justify his rule. See Mallat, 'Religious militancy.'

legislature, also meant that the population as a whole was deprived of its civil and human rights. Even the Baath Party was left with little influence on the way the country came to be run, and became transformed into an organization with the sole mission of eulogizing the president and endorsing or saluting his actions.

Under such circumstances, where the law does not protect the individual, where access to the state and its resources cannot normally be obtained on an individual basis but only through a network of patronage, and where the state is seen as a potential threat to any kind of individual liberty, citizens take refuge in family, kinship, regional and sectarian connections.[28] This has led not to national integration but to particularism and to the fragmentation of society, a state of affairs which cannot simply be attributed to the war with Iran. The *laqab* [an individual's tribal or regional name] once again became important and many Iraqis became acutely aware not only of being Sunnis or Shi'is but also of their regional and tribal origins. In such circumstances, individuals seek support, protection and influence through family, sectarian and regional connections, and attempt to create new social networks, or recreate old ones, to assist them to advance or safeguard their interests within the state bureaucracy, and to gain access to positions, contracts or preferential treatment.

Hence, despite all declarations to the contrary, in the decades examined in this essay the regime exercised a divisive rather than unifying influence. This was because it crushed all democratic institutions, however embryonic they may have been, and thus destroyed the basic preconditions for national integration. Only when democratic liberties and human rights are guaranteed, and when the individual can exercise the responsibilities of a citizen rather than be forced to rely on membership of a particular group, will a country like Iraq be unified and its sectarian and other divisions wither away.

---

28. For an excellent sociological discussion of this phenomenon, see Sami Zubaida, 'The nation state in the Middle East' in Sami Zubaida, *Islam, the People and the State* (London, 1989), pp.121–182.

The Iran-Iraq War and the Iraqi State

Charles Tripp

The capacity of Iraq to survive nearly eight years of war with Iran raises a number of questions regarding the nature, the causes and the effects of this success. It also raises the question of what exactly is meant by 'Iraq' in such a context. In outward form, it would seem that the state of Iraq proved, through the test of war, to have had a greater degree of definition and to have possessed stronger foundations as a territorial organization of power than had been suspected prior to the war. Led by Saddam Hussein, the government which started the war remained more or less intact, as did the administrative structure of the state. In spite of massive casualties, the armed forces expanded during the years of war and, if anything, improved in quality during that time. Apart from the rebellion in some areas of Kurdistan and isolated acts of violence by the Shi'a based al-Dawa organization, there was no evidence of significant popular disaffection with the government, despite the increasingly onerous nature of its demands. On the contrary, the government was able to organize the population on an unprecedented scale in order to counter the Iranian military threat. In general, this was successful and the territorial integrity of the Iraqi state was maintained.

The question which arises, therefore, is whether the Iraqi state itself was similarly strengthened, not simply as an organization of power, but, crucially, as an authoritative institutional expression of collective interests. There are two features to note in this connection. The first is that while one could see the fact of resistance to Iran and of mass obedience to the government's directives, the motives of the Iraqis themselves cannot be easily ascertained. There was no voice in Iraq independent of the control of the government. That which is now in the common domain was a product of a government strategy to safeguard its own power, as well as to maintain the war effort against Iran. Consequently, it is impossible to disentangle real motive from projected myth. However, the way in which the myth was presented is in itself of significance. This is because it underlined and was used to support the second feature of Iraqi politics during the war: the strengthening of the autocracy of Saddam Hussein.

Whilst Saddam Hussein utilized all the images appropriate to the collective organization of power, he made certain that both in symbolic terms and in reality such an organization, indeed the definition of such a collectivity, should only find expression in his person, not in the impersonal office which he occupied. The reinforcement of so exclusive a claim to personal power would seem to suggest that it is perhaps not the foundations of the state which were strengthened during the war, but the rule of one man, Saddam Hussein. The fact that he was so apparently successful in using both the structures and myths of state power should not disguise the solitary nature of the endeavour.

Nevertheless, it raises the question of the degree to which the organization of power, whatever its public rationale, corresponds to a system of greater indigenous material and moral significance than the forms of the European state which appear to characterize the dispensation of power in Iraq. Where the implications of the latter do not seriously impede or contradict the former, they can prove to be valuable amplifiers of the power of the autocrat. Equally, in using these instruments, particularly under the stress of war, it is possible that processes will have been set in motion, appropriate to the rationale and the transformations associated with the structure of the state, which may ultimately undermine so individual a claim to rule.

Patrimonialism and its Implications

Quite apart from the ubiquitous and unforeseeable workings of chance, success in politics generally results from the capacity to pursue a course which is regarded as both fitting and practical by those whom it affects. This consideration embraces not simply those who are required to obey the policies in question, but also those whose task it is to carry them out. Success of this kind had been a very obvious part of Saddam Hussein's eleven-year rise to absolute power in Iraq, culminating in his assumption of the presidency in 1979. As important as the notorious *tarhib wa-targhib* [terror and enticement, or stick and carrot] formula, was his knowledge not only of the proper recipients, but also of the channels through which punishment and reward should be doled out. In this respect, Saddam Hussein's relative advantage was that he placed no reliance whatsoever on either institutions or ideologies as sufficient guarantors of men's loyalties and political behaviour. Whilst others might have seen institutions as having an autonomous existence, defined by certain rules which, in turn, determined the relations between those who staffed them, Saddam Hussein seemed to have little faith in the intangible and abstract compulsions of formal procedures. He might—and often did—use the organizations in question and their respective rationales as a way of justifying and extending his own power. Equally, he was content to use such devices insofar as they became the focus of others' beliefs and activities. Quite apart from anything else, this placed a certain restraint on their imagination and action. However, Saddam Hussein himself had no intention of becoming beholden to such insubstantial entities.[1] Instead, he relied increasingly on the informal mechanisms of socially accepted patronage to reinforce and indeed to justify his growing power.

The fact that Saddam Hussein was so successful in erecting a system of power largely based on this patrimonial principle, indicates its continued efficacy in the society and politics of Iraq. Given the various histories of the peoples who inhabit the country, as well as the record of the development of the formal institutions of the Iraqi state, this is perhaps scarcely surprising. However, where Saddam Hussein—and indeed others before him—was markedly successful, was in combining the social efficacy of the networks of patronage denoted by the term *al-intisab*, with the administrative organization of power inherent in the formal structure of the state.

From this perspective, the offices of state have come to be regarded as so many prizes to be captured on one's own behalf, and on that of the network of clients who depend upon all prominent

---

1. A vivid example of this can be seen in his address to party officials: 'Since the earliest days of the revolution, various writers used the epithet "strong man" when writing about me. I did not want my colleagues to read those articles, because I was worried about the effect it might have on them especially since—officially—I was only No. 2. However, thank God, those circumstances have now passed'. *Al-Thawra* 23 August 1986 (5).

individuals. The normative expectations associated with the idea of *al-intisab* [lit. 'membership' or 'affiliation', but also signifying kinship and linkage, as well as suitability or appropriateness] sustain such networks. Under this heading, the more generally understood logic of patron-client relations comes into play, with the weak serving the strong in exchange for protection and reward. The relationship benefits both parties, since the greater the entourage of the patron, the greater his prestige and the wider the circle of his power and influence. This, in turn, amplifies the capacity of the weaker client and enhances his own standing. In order to be taken on as a client, an element of personal trust is necessary. In the first place, this might be founded on kinship, clan and tribal ties. Here the expectations vested in the patron would be that much greater, as would the augmentation of his authority for being seen to help so generously those whom it was felt 'natural' or fitting that he should help. However, beyond these family circles, reassurance of the kind necessary for trust and expectations to develop might also be afforded by common provincial, sectarian or ethnic origin.[2]

From this perspective, the power and resources available through control of the administrative machinery of the state, are not regarded as being for the common good of the unknown and possibly mistrusted other inhabitants of the state as a whole. Rather, they are deemed to be primarily for the benefit of these informal, but highly resilient and efficacious client groupings. Their very cohesion depends upon the manifest ability of the patron to acquire and to share the fruits of office with his followers. Failure to do so means social disgrace and political oblivion, as clients defect to someone who can more successfully protect and advance the interests of those who pledge their service to him. Saddam Hussein was able to prevent this from happening, not simply through the physical elimination of potential rivals, but also through the placating and cultivation of those whose support made the exercise of absolute power both worthwhile and possible.

The implications of the sustained operation of such a system are various. Most importantly, in this context, has been the vicious circle which it established in regard to the operation of the formal institutions of the state. Clearly, the resilience of such a social mechanism as that associated with *al-intisab* is both cause and

---

2. N.T. Al-Hasso, *Administrative politics in the Middle East: the case of monarchical Iraq 1920–1958* (PhD Thesis, University of Texas at Austin, 1976) pp. 60–65.

effect of the lack of faith among much of the Iraqi population, including the political leadership, in the authority or efficacy of the impersonal institution of the Iraqi state. If people already believe that the power to reward and to punish lies in the hands of networks based on family trust, or common provincial and/or sectarian origins, they will seek to operate the logic of such a system to their own advantage. In doing so, they further strengthen the very principles of efficacy and authority which sustain these networks, and consequently assist in the degradation of the normative framework of the institutions of the state. By this means, one can see how the foundations of such patrimonially based systems of power tend to reproduce themselves, despite the elaboration of formal institutional structures and despite the apparent contradiction with the public justification for the exercise of power.

Further important political outcomes of such a system of power have been the reinforcement of a sense of communal privilege and the tendency towards autocracy. The sense of communal privilege may not be explicit, but it has been implicit in the whole system of trust and mutual favour denoted by *al-intisab*, and the way in which this has taken over the machinery of the state. To admit that other principles might govern the allocation of power in the state would be to acquiesce in the dismantling of the networks which guarantee the advancement of those already entrenched. Given the history of the foundation of the Iraqi state and its subsequent development, those best placed to benefit from such a dispensation of power have come disproportionately from the clans and families of the Sunni Arabs. To suggest another principle for the organization of power—such as democracy, nationalism or constitutionalism—might be to suggest the theoretical equality of all inhabitants of the Iraqi state. This would leave the twenty per cent who were Sunni Arab in a position where they might be ruled by someone from the remaining eighty per cent. He could be, therefore, in theory at least, a Shi'i, a Kurd, a Christian, a Jew, a Turkoman, a Sabean or a Yazidi. Quite apart from the specific prejudices which colour one group's views of the others, such a development would turn the political world upside down. It would automatically exclude most Sunni Arabs from the networks of kinship and communal trust emanating from the new holders of power.

Saddam Hussein used this system to good effect. He observed its conventions and played upon the fears and hopes which it encourages. He may have propagated the myth of Iraqi nationalism and national identity, but he did not let it determine the pattern of his appointments to positions of real power in the state. Whilst he frequently appointed people who were not Sunni Arabs to positions of relative prominence in the public hierarchy of the state, the inner circle of those with substantial delegated power remained almost exclusively Sunni Arabs, largely drawn from the clans of Saddam Hussein's tribe, the Al Bu Nasir.[3] Parallel to the formal, institutional structures and hierarchies of the state, there existed another structure, governed by the rules of patronage, in which the power and rank of each was determined by their position in relation to Saddam Hussein himself. Naturally, the overlap is close, not least because Saddam Hussein, after all, heads most of the formal organs of the state itself. However, it is the informal, clan-based hierarchy which is the true repository of power and authority. Unsung in the public propaganda of the regime, but implicit in its very organization, this is the order which Saddam Hussein could only have disrupted at his peril, even had he wanted to.

Conversely, as long as he maintained the proprieties, he was assured of a large measure of support from the wider circles of the Sunni Arabs. In addition, all those who benefitted from his patronage, or believed themselves in a position where their social connections would allow them to do so, whatever their sectarian or ethnic origins, have helped to maintain a system with which they are familiar. This generalized fear of being forced to deal with the unfamiliar, unknown personnel of an alternative dispensation was a significant reinforcement for autocracy under Saddam Hussein, but also under his predecessors. The powerful Sunni Arab leader who could dispense favours and who stood at the apex of a pyramid of patronage, might be resented for any number of reasons, but could be relied upon not to overturn the whole system. As long as such a leader existed, there was always a chance of advancement. Above all, however, there was little chance that another community could monopolize the power and resources which were regarded as rightfully belonging to the Sunni Arab inheritors of the Ottoman Empire's successor states.[4]

---

3. See A. Baram, 'The ruling élite in Ba'thi Iraq 1968—86; the changing features of a collective profile', *International Journal of Middle East Studies* 21 (1989) pp. 476–493; *The Economist* 29 September 1990.

4. H. Batatu, *The old social classes and the revolutionary movements of Iraq* (Princeton University Press, 1978), pp. 13–16.

Iraqi Autocracy and War with Iran

A feature of autocratic rule is the desire for authority, control and order through the manipulation of the beliefs of the population concerning the rightness, uniqueness and indispensability of the ruler, without relying for this on any form of institutional solidity that might eventually challenge that authority or call the leader to account. To invest an institution with authority and to give it the licence to act upon that authority, is to create a potential base of opposition. Autocracy is, therefore, in many respects the antithesis of the institutional and, above all, impersonal order suggested by the Western idea of the state. Yet, at the same time, it is clear that the autocrat, no less than any other ruler, has need of organizations that will amplify his power, extending surveillance and control throughout the population he intends to govern, maintaining thereby an order that does not threaten his hold on power. These were the considerations which apparently underpinned Saddam Hussein's progressive domination of both the Party and the administrative structure of the state in Iraq.

This domination was facilitated by his ability to assemble around himself an inner core of men whose loyalty was to him personally, either because they were members of his family, of his provincial community or because they had proved their personal loyalty during the long years of association with him in the conspiracies of the Baath. They owed their position neither to their official rank in the institutions of the state, nor to their position within the ideological vehicle of the Party. They did not, therefore, represent any principle of impersonal authority. On the contrary, they were placed in positions of seniority in both organizations precisely because of their pre-existing relationship with the person of Saddam Hussein. It was this which they had chiefly in common and, therefore, it allowed Saddam Hussein to control in a particularly effective way their activities, even if he was perforce obliged to delegate some of his own powers to them.[5]

The cohesion of this inner core allowed Saddam Hussein progressively to dominate the Party and, through the insertion of Party cadres, to dominate the apparatus of the state. The provincial governorates, the principal ministries, the intelligence and security services, the judiciary and the armed forces were either in the

---

5. 'Document: La Nomenklatura Irakienne', *Les Cahiers de l'Orient*, 8/9, 1987/88.

hands of men whose main allegiance was to Saddam Hussein, or were dominated by Party bureaux which were themselves the creation of Saddam Hussein. When, in July 1979, he finally persuaded his uncle the President to stand aside, he himself became President of the Republic, Chairman of the RCC, Secretary General of the Baath and Commander-in-Chief of the armed forces. In addition, he presided over the Cabinet, the Office of Financial Supervision, the Planning Council, the Intelligence Directorate and, whenever necessary, the Revolutionary Tribunal. He was, therefore, in a strong position to purge all organs of the state and Party of the few remaining figures of authority who had shown themselves to be lukewarm to the prospect of Saddam Hussein's personal ascendancy. The spate of executions of senior officials in both party and state administrations which accompanied his assumption of absolute power demonstrated not only his absolute ruthlessness, but also his inability as an autocrat to compromise with those who might adhere to principles of rule and of order other than those dictated by Saddam Hussein himself.

At the same time, a personality cult of truly impressive proportions was in the making, in which Saddam Hussein was portrayed as the only figure who could unite the various communal identities existing within the Iraqi population. On a symbolic level, this meant appealing to the various communities by presenting himself as one of them and, therefore, as uniquely qualified to apprehend their true interests. Saddam Hussein was variously portrayed masquerading as a Kurd, as a Shi'i tribesman from the lower Euphrates, a Bedouin sheikh and, even more ambitiously, as a descendant of the Caliph Ali ibn Abi Talib. This campaign appears to have been due less to some desire for an abstract national unity—to the principles of which Saddam Hussein himself might have been held accountable. Rather, it seems to have been designed to persuade people of all the other communities of Iraq—however they defined their communal identity—that Saddam Hussein was their rightful leader. Whatever their identities, he had their true interests at heart, he was the source of all benefits and, therefore, it was to him that they should give their unquestioning obedience. Not only did he intend thereby to derive from these people the kind of support he had enjoyed among the clans of the Sunni Arab northwest, but he was also determined to displace their own communal leaders in the affections of their people. He had to establish that it was not only prudent to obey him, but fitting to do so as well. There was, in addition, a second reason why, in 1980, Saddam Hussein should have sought to stress the unity of the Iraqi people under his command, and to project himself as their sole authoritative leader.

The rapid deterioration of relations with Iran since the revolution of 1979 had left the Iraqi state potentially vulnerable in two respects: firstly, the Kurds might have thought once more of exploiting Iraqi-Iranian enmity in order to carve out a degree of autonomy from the control of central government in Baghdad; secondly, there was considerable fear in Iraq that significant numbers of Iraq's Shi'i majority might take inspiration and encouragement from the Islamic Republic in Iran and rise against the Iraqi government. Potentially, therefore, there existed two disaffected communities within the territory of the Iraqi state which, if mobilized to seek political power appropriate to their particular communities, would mean the dismemberment of that state, or, at the very least, a radical reshaping of the political order. In a speech in February 1980, Saddam Hussein, unusually, gave voice to this fear, declaring that unless the inhabitants of Iraq demonstrated their loyalty to a specifically Iraqi state, the country would be divided into three 'mini-states': one Arab-Sunni, one Arab-Shi'i and one Kurdish.[6] It was in this regard that increasing stress was to be placed on the common history and common interests of those who occupied the territory of Iraq.

Saddam Hussein had long been associated with those in the Baath who believed that if the Iraqi government were to dedicate the resources at their disposal to the creation of a pan-Arab state, and thus neglect the non-Arab inhabitants of Iraq, this might destroy both the Party and the state. This had been evident in his attempts to resolve the problem of Kurdish separatism in the early 1970s. However, it was clearly a delicate task, if conducted from within a Party whose raison d'être was apparently the creation of an Arab state coterminous with the territory inhabited by the Arab nation. It was also dangerous for a Sunni Arab ruler, whose chief constituency lay among the Sunni Arabs who saw him as their champion, if necessary against the other communities inhabiting Iraq. As his influence grew during the 1970s, however, it was noticeable that the government gave increasing encouragement to the idea that all Iraqis were the cultural heirs to the great

---

6. BBC/SWB/ME 12 February 1980 (A/2-3).

civilizations of Mesopotamia. Sumerian, Babylonian and Assyrian themes were stressed in much of the government sponsored art and architecture of those years. Amongst many of the Arab nationalists of the Baath there was evidently some unease, but the rise of Saddam Hussein to a position of political dominance allowed him to be bolder in his assertion of a specifically Iraqi collective identity. As he was to declare in 1979:

> As along as we place Iraq at the core of the Arab nation, we are not afraid that strengthening Iraqi identification would occur at the expense of the Arab nation, much as we talk, with great pride, of Iraq's present, past and future.[7]

The coincidence of his assumption of the Presidency and the growing threat of the Iranian revolution to Iraq's social cohesion and territorial integrity led to an increasingly explicit attempt to inculcate a belief in the moral value of Iraq's territory amongst its inhabitants. Thus, in his effort to transfrom the Baath into a party of mass mobilization, open to general membership, Saddam Hussein stated that 'The new organizational structure of the Party includes all Iraqis who believe in Iraqi soil'.[8] In May 1980, during the mass expulsions of thousands of Iraqi Shi'is who had even the most tenuous family links with Iran, or who simply bore a name of Persian origin, Saddam Hussein declared: 'Those who do not love Iraq and are not ready to shed blood in the defence of Iraqi territory and dignity, must leave Iraq'.[9]

As relations with Iran deteriorated to a point where open conflict seemed highly probable, these themes were repeated with much emphasis by Saddam Hussein. It is true that, at the same time, he was careful to allude to the Arab identity of Iraq, as well. Clearly, in a struggle with the Iranians, where the crucial question was the loyalty of the Iranians' Arab Shi'i co-sectarians in Iraq, this was as important as the stress on a specifically Iraqi identity. Two other factors appear also to have played a part. Saddam Hussein was simultaneously making irredentist noises about the need to 'liberate' the Arab-speaking inhabitants of the Iranian province of Khuzestan. He was also seeking pan-Arab approval for his defiance of

---

7. A. Baram, 'Culture in the service of wataniyya', *Asian and African Studies*, 17 (1983), p. 266.
8. A. Baram, 'The June 1980 elections to the National Assembly in Iraq', *Orient*, September 1981, p. 393.
9. BBC/SWB/ME 5 May 1980 (A/9).

Iran, hoping thereby to extend Iraq's, and thus his own influence throughout the anxious Arab states of the Gulf, as well as in the Arab world generally.

Saddam Hussein's attempt to establish himself as undisputed master of the Iraqi state had led in the first instance to his successful domination of the apparatus of the state. It had also led him to stress the identity of all Iraqis, their supposed common history and purpose, and his own unique qualifications to represent and to further that purpose. At the same time, as a means of giving definition to the Iraqi community that was held to underpin this sense of identity and to legitimate its submission to a unitary state apparatus, the territoriality of the Iraqi state was emphasized. In September 1980, all three elements led Saddam Hussein to order the Iraqi armed forces to invade Iran. War had come to seem not only an appropriate activity, but also perhaps the only possible activity that, if successfully conducted, would finally legitimate Saddam Hussein's exclusive claim to rule Iraq.

The rapid and decisive humbling of Iran seemed to have been intended to achieve three objectives pertinent to the cohesion of Iraqi society under the domination of Saddam Hussein. Firstly, it would inhibit the crystallization of communal disaffection among either the Shi'i or the Kurds, by demonstrating that it would be useless to look to Iran for aid. Secondly, it would enhance the authority of Saddam Hussein in the Arab world, thereby satisfying not only a Sunni Arab and Baathist constituency in Iraq, but also greatly promoting the influence of Iraq and of Saddam Hussein in the region. Thirdly, and equally importantly, it was intended to wring territorial concessions from Iran.

The latter point is of considerable significance, since it relates both to the territorial definition of the Iraqi state and to the obligations which Saddam Hussein appeared to have assumed in claiming the right to rule the state. In 1975 he had been the principal architect of the Algiers Agreement which, in the face of Iran's overwhelming military might and its persistent aid to the Kurdish rebellion, surrendered Iraq's claim to territorial sovereignty over the whole of the Shatt al-Arab waterway which runs between Iraq and Iran at the head of the Gulf. Since this made no difference to the actual use by Iraqi vessels of the waterway, but did stipulate that, thenceforth, they would have to fly the Iranian flag if they crossed the median line that constituted the new frontier between the two states, the shame of this surrender was largely symbolic. It was no less keenly felt, for all that. Saddam Hussein's determination to use war as a means of reasserting Iraq's territorial sovereignty seems to have been due to the belief that failure to do so would seriously weaken his own authority, since it would weaken his claim to be the sole competent defender of the territorial integrity of Iraq. Consequently, his ability to restore the 'lost honour of Great Iraq', by forcing the Iranian government to acknowledge Iraqi territorial sovereignty, was to be the measure of his success as guardian and ruler of the Iraqi state.

The interesting feature of this aspect of the conflict was that it represented a synthesis, or apparent hybridization, of two different principles of state power, originating in two different state traditions. On the one hand, there was the 'state of Iraq' organized by Saddam Hussein as his own personal following—the obedience of all Iraqis in a patrimonial system of power constituted the moral foundation of the state, the pattern of beliefs which allowed his reach and command to extend to the four corners of his domain. This was *al-sulta* ['power', but also, interestingly and significantly, 'authority' and 'sovereignty'] which ensured that his will would be obeyed. It had been constructed on the basis of all the many networks of reward and punishment which had bound people to him precisely because he was so obviously in a position to promote or harm their interests, as well as those of their own followings. Regional powers made their appearance as rivals for the loyalties and support of the circles which Saddam Hussein had assembled. Their prestige could only be won at the expense of Saddam Hussein. Conversely, as their power was seen to wane, so the reach of Saddam Hussein could be extended.[10] The competition was, therefore, seen as a contest between rival leaders to extend their respective followings.

Interestingly, in 1980, the abstract question of territorial sovereignty over a waterway (and over some small areas of land), and not over people or populations, became the token and symbol of this competition. Precisely because of the relative insignificance of the material value of the physical areas in dispute, it was the moral or normative aspects of the territorial state which appeared thereby to be emphasized. That is, Saddam Hussein had decided to make

10. Saddam Hussein on 20 July 1980: 'An Iraqi ruler who bows to Khomeini or to anyone else will be trampled upon by the Iraqis...we are not the kind of people to bow to Khomeini. He has wagered to bend us and we have wagered to bend him. We will see who will bend the other' BBC/SWB/ME 24 July 1980 (A/12).

this issue a test of his own authority within Iraq—as President of the territorial state of Iraq—and in relation to the rulers in Tehran. It is unlikely that many in Iraq knew or cared where Iraqi sovereignty began and Iranian sovereignty ended in the waters of the Shatt al-Arab.

However, once Saddam Hussein had decided to make the extensions of formal Iraqi territorial sovereignty a test of his own power relative to that of the government in Iran, few in Iraq could be in much doubt about what was at stake in the conflict. At this stage, before the full gravity of the situation had become apparent, this was clearly a struggle for relative regional prestige and influence between Saddam Hussein and Khomeini. Were Saddam Hussein to fail in his bid to compel the Iranian ruler to acknowledge Iraq's, and thus his own ascendancy, the population of Iraq might not transfer their allegiance to Khomeini. However, significant numbers of them might well transfer their allegiance away from Saddam Hussein and towards a domestic rival who could protect their standing, as well as their material interests more effectively. In this respect, it was not the Shi'a whom Saddam Hussein had most to fear, but the Sunni Arab clans who had hitherto benefited from his patronage and basked in the glow of his ascendancy.

WAR AND THE STATE IN IRAQ

War is an activity which to some extent both defines and tests the state. The latter idea has given rise to a rather suspect school of thought which claims to see in the fact of successful prosecution of war proof of the moral superiority of the victorious community, defined as the state and the nation which is believed to find its proper expression in the state. Nevertheless, leaving aside the sinister overtones of such speculation, there is a sense in which a state at war is being tested on the three levels that constitute its definition: as an organization of power, capable of exercising its power through the use of violence; as an 'ethical community' whose members have a sense of their own identity and who actively participate in the violent protection or extension of certain commonly defined interests; as a territorial unit capable both of being maintained in the face of attack and the definition of which has entered into the imagination of its inhabitants in the belief that this territory is worth defending with their lives.

In examining the relationship of war to the state, therefore, one will be examining the ways in which the strategies required for the conduct of successful war may have consequences for the three areas central to the definition of the state. The consequences of these policies may be the reinforcement of the foundations of the state in the moral perspective of its inhabitants, as well as its strengthening as a political unit able to withstand external attack. Nevertheless, success of this kind may be a hollow one for the architects of victory, since their very strategies may set in motion processes among their subjects which would throw into doubt their right to continue in the exercise of power. The endeavour by Saddam Hussein in Iraq to ensure that his strategies for strengthening the outward forms of the state in its war with Iran should not erode his own autocratic power forms the subject of the following pages. That is, the degree to which the conduct of a prolonged war forced him to attend to the definition and foundation of the Iraqi state, whilst at the same time his own preoccupation with the exercise of highly personalized power led him to seek to avoid becoming beholden to the obligations of impersonal, collective authority that underly such a conception of the state.

The Instruments of Violence

In Iraq, under the pressure of the war, considerable transformations had necessarily to take place within the organization of the armed forces. Not only were they expanded to nearly one million men (four times their peacetime strength), but the earlier methods of ensuring their complete obedience to the leadership no longer seemed so advisable. The ubiquity of Baathist commissars in all units, the appointment of officers whose chief qualification was loyalty to Saddam Hussein, rather than military competence, the rapid rotation of officers to ensure that they formed no bonds of solidarity either with each other or with the men under their command, the confusion of lines of command and the denial of any independent initiative to local commanders—these had been the techniques whereby loyalty, or at least absence of effective conspiracy had been assured.

The lacklustre performance of the armed forces in the early years of the war and the realization after 1982 that the Iraqi government would have to organize an effective defence if it was to hold back the Iranian onslaught, necessitated considerable changes. A crucial component of that defence was to be the increasing professionalization of the military. This entailed the encouragement and promotion of competent officers, the establishment of clear lines of command, the effective delegation of authority based on rank, the reduction in the role of the Baathist political officers and the enhancement of unit solidarity. In short, attention was paid to the establishment of an institutional order within the armed forces, unparalleled in any of the other organs of the Iraqi state.

The structual, institutional solidity, as well as the moral element, the *esprit de corps*, which Saddam Hussein found himself compelled to encourage in the armed forces, were dictated by the urgent need to defeat the forces of Iran on the battlefield. Whilst there was little doubt that this was the common aim of Saddam Hussein and of much of the Sunni Arab dominated—but by no means exclusively either Sunni or Arab—officer corps, there clearly existed a suspicion that this did not necessarily imply the total, uncritical commitment to Saddam Hussein that he demanded of all the organizations of power in Iraq. At times of stress, the perennial fear surfaced that relative institutional independence might encourage army officers to see in their immediate superiors, or amongst their colleagues, individuals more fitted than Saddam Hussein to supervize the war effort. This was particularly in evidence when Saddam Hussein's strategic judgement and personal intervention interfered with the conduct of operations and threatened to bring about disaster on the battlefield. The military set-backs of 1982 and of the first half of 1986 witnessed precisely such a development, probably with good reason.[11]

Consequently, whilst obliged to grant the armed forces a measure of independent initiative and to routinize their internal organization, Saddam Hussein sought to ensure his personal control in a manner similar to that in which he attempted to retain control over all the principal organs of the state. The prowess of the armed forces was regularly extolled as evidence of Saddam Hussein's military genius and unparalleled strategic vision; in victory, they were called the 'Army of Saddam Hussein'; the idea was maintained that there was something exceptional in carrying out the commands of Saddam Hussein, since only in this way were the armed forces truly serving the people of Iraq.[12]

11. See S. Chubin and C. Tripp, *Iran and Iraq at war* (London, 1988), pp. 89–90, 118–9.
12. See, for instance, the special number of *al-Thawra* 6 January 1987, published to coincide with Army Day, its headline reading 'The army of Saddam Hussein is the army of great victory'.

At the same time, Saddam Hussein was careful to ensure that key positions of command were held only by those who owed him personal loyalty, preferably as kinsmen. His first cousin and brother-in-law, the late General Adnan Khairallah Tulfah, was the Minister of Defence, deputy Commander-in-Chief and overall commander of the Southern Region. Another first cousin, Ali Hasan al-Majid, headed the Military Bureau of the Baath and was placed in overall command of the Northern Region in order to supervize the campaign against the Kurdish insurgents during 1988. The most prominent of the serving generals, Mahir Abd al-Rashid, was allied to Saddam Hussein by marriage and commanded the Army Corps fighting on the crucial Basra/Fau front. The commanding officer of the Air Force, Hamid Shaban al-Takriti, was a member of Saddam Hussein's provincial community and of his tribal clan. The same applied to Hussein Kamil al-Majid al- Takriti, who commanded the divisions of the Presidential Guard and of the Baghdad garrison, and who cemented his alliance with Saddam Hussein by marrying one of the latter's daughters. In this way, it was clearly hoped by Saddam Hussein that the links of blood and clan loyalty would counteract any tendency within the armed forces to make use of the relative autonomy they had been granted during the war to question the capacity and the right of the 'imperative leader' to command absolute, unconditional obedience.

The Question of Community and Differentiation

The problems that may arise with particular piquancy in regard to the armed forces, may also apply to some degree to the inhabitants of the state as a whole. It is in the interest of those who rule the state and who conduct the war, to insist upon the particularity and community of those who inhabit the territory of the state. Underlying all the rationales for sacrifice in war lies the idea that in risking personal extinction, the individual is helping to protect a collective reality that has prior claim on his loyalty, since it incorporates a set of values that give meaning to his collective existence.[13] This is all

13. See Ben Anderson on the importance of timelessness/historical continuity in defining the bonds which constitute a feeling of national community, B. Anderson, *Imagined communities* (London, 1986), pp. 28–40. Saddam Hussein seemed to echo these concerns in his speech of 22 April 1987 to air force officers, when he said: 'This generation, to which we belong, will pass and a new generation will come after us, pursuing the same course, because this course...was not intended to be for only

the more important in an age when the successful organization of force depends upon the ability to transform, through mass mobilization, large numbers of individual subjects into an army. Visible in all these efforts is the attempt to convince those who are mobilized that they share a history as an identifiable community, that they share values which mark them off from others and that they share with those who are commanding them to fight, a common concern for a benign order, guaranteed by the territorial integrity of the state, but now threatened by the activities of the enemy.

These themes were much in evidence in Iraq during the war. At the 9th Baath Party Regional Congress in July 1982, it was decided that

> For the first time in many centuries, Iraqi nationalism [sic] becomes the prime bond for all the children of this people, and a symbol of which the Iraqis are so proud that they are ready even for martyrdom. Equally, this deep, strong and creative Iraqi nationalism has for the first time been linked to the Arab nationalist bond, constituting a living and abundant tributary of it and a steel base guarding it against the evil of enemies and covetous forces'.[14]

Precisely in order to communicate the fact that Iraq's geographical territory was coterminous with a moral community, Saddam Hussein was to state in 1987 that 'others must remember that Iraq is not simply a geographical entity, but is now also a will. This state of affairs exists and the matter is now at an end. There is no force capable of reversing it'.[15]

The war years are full of exhortations by Saddam Hussein, his associates and the Iraqi media which all convey the message that Iraq as a whole was worth defending. That is, the territorial state was represented as having a moral value, in the sense that its physical existence and the integrity of its borders were portrayed as being necessary conditions for the security of all. This was clearly intended to mean not simply the physical security of its inhabitants, but also the values which made life worthwhile. An example of the genre should suffice to give the flavour, but more importantly also to illustrate the kinds of themes which the leadership seemed

ten, twenty or thirty years...all must remember that Iraq holds fast to this spirit and will continue to do so for hundreds of years to come', Saddam Hussein, *Al-muallafat al-kamila*, Part 15, 1986–87 (Baghdad, 1987–90), pp. 295–6.

14. The Arab Baath Socialist Party, Iraq *The central report of the ninth regional congress June 1982* tr. SARTEC, Lausanne, C.H. (Baghdad, January 1983), p. 40.

15. Saddam Hussein, *op. cit.*, Part 15, 1986–87, p. 295.

determined to communicate. In a speech by Saddam Hussein to the 1st Army Corps on 28 May 1987, he declared:

> How do you give expression to your life? Defending it is defending what? Defending your blood...your free will...defending the present and the future, your home and the laws, whether your home is in Jisan or in Baghdad. The enemy, if he were to reach Jisan and find no man there capable of confronting him, would then reach al-Kut. And if all the men were only to be found in Baghdad, he would attack Baghdad as well... Because defence of the homeland in its remotest parts, is the defence of it all, of every home, of every compatriot, of the present and the future.[16]

It is, of course, impossible to measure the effects on the Iraqis of Saddam Hussein's campaign to elaborate a myth of Iraqi nationalism. The organization of the successful defence of Iraq during the years following the disasters of 1982 may have been influenced by the government's relentless attempt to persuade the Iraqis of the essential otherness of the Iranian enemy and of their common plight as victims of Iran's historical enmity. In doing so, it was noticeable, however, that the Iraqi authorities were not content simply to stress the uniqueness and continuity of the Iraqis as a distinct people, although this was certainly the most prominent of the arguments used. Often simultaneously, other images and themes were deployed which appeared to be aimed at the various communities inhabiting Iraq.

Thus, in exhorting his troops to fight in 1987, Saddam Hussein was to appeal not simply to Iraqi patriotism, but also to the sense of Arab national duty:

> Do not believe that your sacrifices in the difficult march of your revolution, particularly your sacrifices in the Qadisiya battle are only a defence of Iraqi territory, although this deserves sacrifices and martyrdom. These sacrifices are more than this: they are for the future of the Arab nation, as well as for the future of Iraq.[17]

This was an important theme to stress, in view of the suspicion with which many Iraqi Sunni Arabs have regarded the idea of Iraqi nationalism. Precisely because the widespread acceptance of the

---

16. Saddam Hussein, *op. cit.*, Part 15, 1986–87, p. 359.
17. BBC/SWB/ME 7 May 1987 (A/9). The war had come to be called 'Saddam's Qadisiya'. Qadisiya was the name of the battle in 636 A.D. when the Arab Islamic armies had defeated the armies of the Sassanian Empire, thus opening up Persia to conversion to Islam.

idea of an Iraqi nation would, at best, make them no more than the equals of their non-Sunni and non-Arab compatriots, adherence by the government to such a principle would indicate a radical shift of power within Iraq. Ostensible adherence to Arab nationalism, however, ensures Sunni dominance.

In encouraging popular commitment to a war against a professedly Islamic republic, the Islamic aspects of the community of Iraqis were also stressed. For the first time, therefore, the Baath Congress devoted itself to lengthy discussion of Islam. Taking as its cue Saddam Hussein's statement that 'We are not neutral between belief and unbelief. We are believers', the Congress stated that:

> The Party does not call for the creation of a religious state, but for a state based on patriotic links within the framework of one country, and based on pan-Arab links throughout the great Arab homeland. Such a state should be inspired by Islam as a mission and a revolution.[18]

The chief purpose appears to have been to convince the Iraqi Muslims, especially the Shi'i, that the Iranian leaders' claim to speak authoritatively in the name of Islam itself was a sham. Consequently, the speeches of the war years are full of passages denouncing Khomeini and his supporters as bogus Muslims. They are accused of being 'Magians' [Zoroastrians], working hand in hand with the Jews, in an attempt to further the imperialist designs of Persia. Given the history of Islam, especially in Mesopotamia, the twin themes of Arabism and Islam could be felicitously combined with the accusation that the Iranian forces were no more than 'Shu'ubists'.[19] Saddam Hussein now denounced the Iranian regime for using the cover of religion to assert their fundamental hostility to the Arab nation:

> The Arabs are a religious nation, charged with the task of conveying to the peoples of the world the religion's message ... especially that of Islam ... It is the Arab man who correctly understands religion

18. O. Bengio, 'Iraq', in C. Legum, H. Shaked and D. Dishon, eds., *Middle East contemporary survey 1982–1983* (London, 1985), p. 624; Arab Baath Socialist Party, *The central report of the ninth regional congress*, pp. 245–283.

19. The Shu'ubiya was a movement under the Abbasid Empire which was centred largely among that Empire's Persian-speaking subjects. It was mainly a literary and cultural movement which challenged the Arabs' claim to primacy within the Islamic dispensation and championed the cause of non-Arab, especially Persian, cultures.

more than any other non-Arab pretender . . . The Shu'ubi movement's anti-Arab activity through religion will surface when the Arabs abandon their bright leading role and also when the Arabs play their bright leading role. In the first case, the Shu'ubis will fill the vacuum and in the second they will move to resist the tide and the leading role of the Arabs.[20]

Taking their cue from the President, books appeared such as Dr Faruq Umar's *Mabahith fi al-haraka al-Shu'ubiya* [Studies in the Shu'ubi Movement]. Ostensibly a historical study of the Shu'ubiya under the Abbasids, this had a clear contemporary purpose, as the author explicitly stated in the Conclusion:

> A common feature of all the various religio-political movements that emerged in Persia was their hostility to the Arabs and to the latter's Arab, Islamic Caliphate. In all these movements, the Shu'ubiya played its part . . . It is clear that the roots of the Khomeinism which Iran is presently experiencing lie in this. The research has demonstrated that it is influenced by Magian-Batini-Shu'ubi trends in its values, strategies and goals.[21]

Whatever the images of the community used to stiffen the morale of the Iraqis in the war, they shared two common features. The first was that of the essentially foreign nature of the Iranians, whether as non-Iraqis, non-Arabs, non-Arab Muslims, or even as non-Muslims. Only the first of these corresponded to a specific attempt to inculcate loyalty to a territorial Iraqi state. In a war against Iran, where the victory of the latter could be portrayed as a potential disaster for the values associated with these other communities, images such as these might have been thought equally effective, however tenuous a hold the notion of loyalty to an Iraqi nation-state might be. The second common feature was, of course, the centrality of the person of Saddam Hussein, as an Iraqi, an Arab and a Muslim, the symbol and true guarantor of the values associated with these identities, as well as of the Baathi revolution. Combining in his person the qualities and interests associated with all the various peoples of Iraq, it was Saddam Hussein who most truly represented them and to whom they were tied by a personal bond of loyalty and service.[22]

20. Saddam Hussein, *Religious political movements and those disguised with religion* [in English] (Baghdad, 1987), pp. 8, 14.
21. Faruq Umar, *Mabahith fi al-haraka al-Shu'ubiya* (Baghdad, 1986), p. 161.
22. It was significant that the 'referenda' and demonstrations of support,

As Saddam Hussein is reported to have said to his Cabinet in late 1980:

> We know of no other place on earth where people, old and young, the very families of martyrs, face Saddam Hussein and tell him that those they lost were a 'sacrifice to you'. They do not utter such words merely because the person they address is actually Saddam Hussein. No. What they want to express to him, and to the Revolution through him, is that what they say and feel represents the essence of the prevailing new spirit of the Iraqis.

He proceeded to spoil the relatively selfless tone of the above by adding, somewhat disingenuously:

> Now we may wonder what makes an old father, or a widow of a martyr, say to us: 'What is important is (not the person we lost but) that you should be alive and well and keep yourself in good health?'[23]

The Legitimation of Rule

Saddam Hussein's prime consideration was that he should not find himself under an obligation as ruler to those who, in obeying his commands, so greatly extended his reach and power. This concern had underpinned the structure whereby he had sought to delegate a measure of non-threatening power to the armed forces. It had also been evident in his handling and presentation of the myths of Iraqi national identity. For instance, in the elaboration of these myths of Sumerian, Assyrian or Babylonian antecedents for Iraq as a whole, it often seemed that the parts played by the absolute rulers, such as Hammurabi, Sargon or Nebuchadnezzar, were being stressed as much as, if not more than the other achievements of these civilizations.

Similarly, whilst talking of democracy, openness and participation, it was evident that Saddam Hussein had two principal objects in mind. The first was that not he, but those to whom he delegated a measure of power should be accountable for their activities. His idea of accountability was that they should answer to him, but with the forms of popular backing granted by such organizations as the National Assembly. The second intention was to make it clear that participation should mean participating in common obedience to him as:

> organized particularly in 1982, were generally referred to as being evidence of the Iraqi people giving to Saddam Hussein the *baya*—the traditional Arab-Islamic oath of homage to the person of the ruler.

the Leader-Necessity...the man who at a certain stage represents the aspirations and basic interests of the Party and the people. Therefore it is in the interest of the Party and the people to preserve this (Necessity) and adhere to it in a sincere and genuine manner and within the context of democratic practice, collective leadership and sound and genuine Party-related and national relations... Rejecting such a (Necessity) or leaving its strategic line is not an individual stance or special interpretation. Rather, it is an act aimed at inflicting direct and deliberate damage on the basic aspirations and interests of the Party and the people.[24]

There was evidently not much space here for the people themselves to participate in the definition of their own interests, except by giving unqualified support to Saddam Hussein.

When Saddam Hussein felt compelled to talk about the virtues of law and legality, it was clear from his description of the process which he seemed to believe was open and democratic, that his was to be the final word. The function of everyone else—legal experts, ministers, members of the RCC—was simply to give him their advice, in the manner of the absolute monarch. He would then make his decision, on the basis of this counsel and of what he considered to be correct.[25] By this means, as he stated in an earlier interview, he would ensure that the rule of law would not be equated with unthinking respect for existing legislation. He went on to say that the person who had the capacity [*al-iqtidar*] to do so, must use it to legislate and enforce conformity with the law. His guiding principle should be the ideals of the revolution because they correspond with the fundamental interests of the people. Saddam Hussein was thereby carving out for himself a crucial position as law giver and legal arbiter. He himself should be the sole legal innovator and the people would participate simply through their devotion to him, since he embodied and was aware of their true interests.[26]

The very confidence with which he set out the qualities of his own supreme leadership and the relationship between that and the dispensation of power in Iraq, indicate the degree to which he conceived of the state itself as an emanation of his own person. It may also have been possible that, in doing so, he felt that he was basing

23. *President Saddam Hussein addresses the cabinet on conflict with Iran*, tr. N.A. Mudhaffer (Baghdad, 1981), pp. 27, 28.
24. Arab Baath Socialist Party, *The central report of the ninth regional congress*, pp. 39–40.
25. See Saddam Hussein's speech at a conference to discuss legislation and the drafting of laws on 14 December 1987, Saddam Hussein, *Al-muallafat*, Part 16,

his claims on a more indigenous conception of the state which was both more comprehensible and more readily accepted among those on whose obedience he ultimately depended. Although constant reference was made to 'the people' and to their true interests, it was clear that these were only to find their proper definition in the person of Saddam Hussein himself. His was to be the will which animated the organs of the state and supervized their performance; the community of all Iraqis was to find expression in common devotion to Saddam Hussein himself, who was the symbol and epitome of the historical myth which linked them to the glorious past of 'Great Iraq'. It was he, after all, who saw himself as the leader produced by historical necessity to liberate, unify and defend a single people, for too long unaware of their common interests. War and the nature of his revelatory leadership, he proclaimed, had changed this:

> The people have bestowed their trust in the regime and in the leadership of the regime step by step. The people have discovered that the leadership is in their interest and they have given their allegiance to it. This is the allegiance they have demonstrated by spilling their blood in the battle of Qadisiya.[27]

CONCLUSION

In many respects, the nature of the autocracy which Saddam Hussein established in Iraq seems to be the very antithesis of the principle of power and authority embodied in the formal structure and rationale of the Iraqi state. The definition of power is individual, not collective. The claim to the right to rule is personal, not institutional. It is maintained, in the last analysis, by personal and private networks of trust, not by organized, public alliances or coalitions. Yet at the same time, it is evident that Saddam Hussein found the European model of the state, as structure of power and as collective myth, of some utility in the reinforcement and amplification of his own control. This appears to have served him well in the war with Iran. It also served the interests of most of the inhabitants of Iraq, if those interests could be taken to include a desire not to be subject to the rulings of the Iranian government, however perceived. Whether such a coincidence of interests exists on any other level, remains to be seen. In some respects, it would be considerably to the advantage of Saddam Hussein if such a definition

1987–88, pp. 299–301.

of collective identity and of common interest had failed to crystallize around anything more positive than simply resistance to the armed forces of Iran.

In view of the nature of the Iranian threat, very few sections of the Iraqi population had any reason to welcome an Iranian victory. On the contrary, whilst it would have meant the end of Saddam Hussein's rule in Baghdad, it would also have meant domination by people who are regarded as foreigners by whatever definitions of community exist amongst the peoples of Iraq. Such a victory also raised the spectre of the intercommunal conflict that has frequently been associated with the collapse of effective power at the centre. These social cataclysms were apparently deemed too high a price to pay. The effect of this process was to extend the circle of those who implicitly obeyed the commands of the 'imperative and indispensable' leader, greatly contributing to the war effort by their obedience, but also enhancing thereby the retinue and reach of the autocrat. Although the principles would seem to be wholly different, there does not appear to have been any serious conflict between the European *forms* of state organization and the more locally derived perceptions of how power can and should be organized. Personal service of the leader, whether through a desire to preserve communal or even family advantage, or through an acknowledgement that he and his clan's protection are necessary to stave off a worse evil, has less to do with the legitimacy of the state than with the perceived efficacy of a given dispensation of power The nature of the war with Iran tended to reinforce such perceptions in Iraq.

These developments have given an appearance of solidity to the state, but it may be merely the product of expediency caused by the unusual circumstances of the war. Had the state been strengthened as an impersonal organization of power, founded on collectively accepted principles of authority and maintained by the rule of law, it would have set a limit on the degree to which Saddam Hussein could maintain so self-centred and personal a style of rule after the ending of the war. Consequently, it appears to have been the intention of Saddam Hussein that no such crystallization of impersonal, institutionalized authority should take place. The organization of power had been useful to him in a multitude of ways. However, the possibility that these organizations should in some sense become autonomous was seen as the real danger. After the ending of the war, it was noticeable, therefore, that Saddam

26. *Al-Thawra* 23 August 1986 (5).

Hussein did his utmost to disrupt the 'institutional memory' which might have formed the basis of self-sustaining, and thus self-willed, institutions. This was particularly visible in the armed forces. As far as his own immediate survival was concerned, it may also have been particularly necessary in that sphere of the state's organization of power.

The impressive edifice of power which Saddam Hussein constructed in Iraq depends ultimately upon his own capacity to service it and to keep it subject to his will. As developments during the years following the end of the war with Iran showed, this is an undertaking fraught with risks, hazardous not only for those inside Iraq, but also for those who find themselves drawn into the strategies by which Saddam Hussein seeks to maintain this edifice. It also suggests that it will only be as long-lived as he himself. This does not mean that the state as an administration or as a territorial entity will vanish, unless his passing is accompanied by a series of regional developments that would mobilize sufficient force and ambition to encompass the territorial partition of Iraq. More probable, is the emergence of another leader and another clan well placed—possibly because of the position they already occupy within it—to take over the state administration and use it in the service of their power. A sense of community is at work, but it is of a community that does not appear to correspond to a political community of Iraqis. Despite the images projected by the Iraqi government during the war and despite the mobilization of much of the Iraqi people in a common war effort, there is as yet little evidence that such a conception has emerged, let alone that it acts as an organizing principle of power or as the impersonal collectivity that justifies the tenure of office. In its absence, the question of the moral foundations of the Iraqi state must remain in doubt.

27. *Al-Thawra* 23 August 1986 (4).

Iraq: Environmental, Resource and Development Issues

Peter Beaumont

INTRODUCTION

Following the Gulf War the economy of Iraq was severely damaged through the bombing of its infrastructure by the Western nations. In particular transport facilities such as bridges were demolished making the movement of all goods difficult. Estimates made in April 1991 suggested that over eighty road bridges had been destroyed through bombing by allied forces. Services, especially water and power, were also disrupted. Almost all the electricity generating stations received direct hits, with the result that in July 1991 power generation in Iraq was at a level of twenty-five per cent of the pre-War output. Even this was only achieved by cannibalizing equipment from many sources and working with safety levels which would not be tolerated in the Western world. The sheer devastation in the electricity industry is hard to conceive, but estimates suggested that it would cost around $12 billion fully to restore the damaged facilities. Petroleum installations and all other industries which were thought of as being of strategic importance were often severely damaged or completely destroyed as well. Any recovery process will be slow and will require massive capital investment.

In the rural areas the war caused little direct damage, but even there the impact was considerable owing to the disruption to the transport infrastructure. Crops proved more difficult to market and crucial inputs like fuel and fertilizers were in short supply. Even more worrying problems are likely to be caused by the destruction of veterinary laboratories in which animal vaccines were produced and stored. In the summer of 1991 irrigation was difficult in a number of areas owing to the lack of fuel/electricity and the breakdown of machinery for which spare parts could not be obtained.

The biggest problems being faced by Iraq were food shortages and health difficulties. The inability to export oil has meant that there was insufficient foreign exchange to import the necessary foodstuffs, particularly staples like wheat. The general disruption in the country in early 1991 meant that many crops were not planted or that key aspects of the agricultural cycle were neglected or omitted. As a consequence yields and total output were low, and so certain foods in which Iraq is normally self-sufficient, like most fruits and vegetables, became short in supply and their costs rose sharply. To some extent this might have been caused by hoarding and profit maximization by middle men, although many workers in the field indicated that the shortages were real. Like everything else though conditions varied markedly from one place to another.

The current health difficulties in Iraq are the result of a combination of factors—one of which is growing food shortages. More important were the high summer temperatures and the fact that the season normally produces problems such as summer diarrhoea. In 1991 it was greatly intensified by the lack of adequate clean water resources. The problem here is a very varied one. In some parts water supplies were operating as normal. However, elsewhere key parts of the distribution system were destroyed meaning that hundreds or even thousands of customers were denied any further water supply. In urban areas the results were chaotic as few other water sources are available. The problem was compounded by the fact that sewage disposal facilities, which are still extremely primitive in many cities in Iraq, broke down or were destroyed as well. Untreated sewage is a common sight in many streets and large pools of it accumulate in low-lying areas. Under such conditions the potential for disease is very high.

Over the last thirty years the economy of Iraq has benefitted from large capital investments. Western propaganda would have us believe that all of the vast oil revenues were spent on military hardware. Whilst it is true that a high proportion of the available resources have been utilized in this way it would be wrong to think that little else has happened. Indeed, very large sums have been invested in infrastructures dealing with transport, communications, electricity, water and sewage. Industry has also benefitted greatly from the creation of a range of factories which have been constructed to lessen dependence on imported goods.

Apart from the petroleum industry there has been very little large scale industrialization in Iraq. Of that which exists most is located in the Baghdad region and only dates from the late 1950s and early 1960s. The first industries were concerned with food processing, light engineering and textiles. During the 1970s more varied industrial development took place, though most of it remains relatively small in scale. This industrialization was given high priority in the National Economic Plan (1976–1980). This priority was to have been maintained in the 1981–85 Plan, but the war with Iran meant that the hope of any continued ordered development had to be shelved.

Since the early 1980s Iraq has been a country at war and as a result the industrialization and infrastructure development which has taken place has been in those areas which have, even indirectly, strengthened the overall war effort. For example, electronic communications systems in Iraq were, before the recent Gulf war, of a very high standard. Similarly the major road systems were capable of carrying heavy loads under almost all weather conditions. Electricity was widely available and the service reasonably reliable.

What has happened in Iraq during the late 1970s and 1980s has been a very uneven form of development. The military have gained access to expensive weapon systems, almost as sophisticated as any in the world, but at the same time rural areas, especially in the north and west, have been neglected. As a result the disparity in development levels between Baghdad and the peripheral areas has been greatly intensified over the last two decades.

In the 1986–90 five year plan the emphasis was placed on improving and extending infrastructure facilities and social services. This included power generation and distribution, water supply and sewerage, housing, health and education. Although most investment still went into the oil industry there was a growing attempt towards lessening Iraq's dependence upon oil. The industrial base has been broadened and there was a move towards agricultural self-sufficiency. Whether this latter aim is a sensible one is a matter of dispute. Considerable encouragement has also been given to the private sector in an attempt to speed up the diversification of the economy. One of the areas which has benefitted from massive investment over the last two decades has been water supply to the cities, towns and larger villages. Throughout the country over 200 major plants and more than 1,000 minor works have been constructed. This has ensured that good quality drinking water is widely available throughout Iraq; at least in the larger centres. By way of contrast sewage treatment has remained at a low level and it was not unusual for some of the larger centres to dump their wastes into the nearest water course with only minimal treatment.

ENVIRONMENT

Topographically Iraq consists of a lowland corridor, tilted downwards from north-west to south-east, in which the major rivers of the Euphrates and Tigris flow. To the west of the rivers the ground rises to the plateau lands of Syria, Jordan and Saudi Arabia, while to the north-east are the foothills of the Zagros Mountains. Over one-third of the area of Iraq lies below 300 metres above sea level and it is only in the extreme north-east where the Zagros mountains rise in excess of 2,000 metres.

The drainage of the country is dominated by the rivers Euphrates and Tigris, both of which have their sources in eastern Turkey. Within Iraq today the Euphrates receives no significant tributaries with perennial flows. However, there is clear evidence in south-west Iraq, in the form of a series of major dry wadis, that significant runoff did occur from the Arabian plateau at some former period. In contrast the Tigris possesses four large tributaries which drain the high Zagros mountains to the east. These are from north to south— the Great Zab; the Little Zab; the Adhaim and the Diyala.

Iraq experiences a Mediterranean type of climate which is somewhat modified by the distance from the sea.[1] Almost all of the rainfall occurs in the winter months and is associated with eastwards moving depressions. On being forced to cross the Zagros Mountains the air in the depressions has to rise producing high precipitation totals. In the highest parts of these mountains this winter precipitation often falls as snow. During the summer months much of the country does not receive any precipitation at all. Not surprisingly, therefore, Iraq is dominated by desertic conditions, with most areas to the south and west of the Euphrates receiving less than 100 mm/year. To the north and west of the Tigris precipitation increases in a series of parallel bands correlated with increasing relief in the Zagros foothills. Even in these foothills, though, there are few areas which receive more than 500 mm/year.

1. P. Beaumont, G.H. Blake and J.M. Wagstaff, *The Middle East—a geographical study*, (London, 1988), 623 pages.

Summer temperatures are everywhere high. In the riverine lowlands mean daily July temperatures commonly reach 33° or 34°C., while maximum temperatures can reach the high forties on a regular basis. In winter the mean daily January temperatures reveal more variations with a range from about 7°C. to 13°C. At this time of year the warmest temperatures are found at the head of the Gulf. During the winter months temperatures can fall suddenly as a result of outbursts of very cold air from central Asia. These outbursts do, on the whole, tend to be short lived. Given these seasonal variations most of the country experiences mean annual temperature ranges in excess of 20°C., with the extreme north-west recording values in excess of 25°C.

In Iraq four major vegetation zones can be identified which correlate well with climatic zones and water availability. The densest vegetation is found in the forest zone of the Zagros mountains in the north and west of the country. The oak is the dominant species and is found on land between 500 and 2,000 metres. Many other plants exist in this woodland and the region has always been widely used for grazing. As a result of these human pressures over the years the forest has been severely degraded, especially around the settlements which exist in this zone. Above the forest the vegetation becomes less continuous until a true arctic-alpine flora is found above 2,700 metres.

Below the forests, as the precipitation falls to less than 500 mm/year, the trees are replaced by shrubs and then by grasslands. This zone forms a broad sweep from the point where the Euphrates enters Iraq along to the foothills of the Zagros mountains to the east. In the wetter areas dense vegetation persists but as precipitation totals decline the grasses become sparse and xerophytic species become more common. Where precipitation totals are below 200 mm/year true desert vegetation is found. This consists largely of low, widely separated, shrubby perennial species and annual grasses whose density varies according to local rainfall conditions.

Iraq is also unusual in having zones of fairly dense vegetation along the river valleys and especially along the Tigris. These plants, which are fed by the shallow water-table, are dominated by poplar, tamarisk and willow, but many other shrubby species are also present. Further downstream as the water-table becomes closer to the ground surface marshes are developed in the low-lying areas. These too have their characteristic vegetation communities.

SOCIAL AND ECONOMIC CHANGE

Iraq, like most other Middle Eastern countries, has experienced a rapid population increase during the twentieth century. In 1900 the population of the country was estimated at about two million. By 1920 it had risen to three million and to 4.8 million by 1947.[2] From then on population growth increased markedly to give a population total of 8.2 million in 1965 and 17.6 million in 1988. Projections suggest a population of 26.5 million in the year 2000 and 43.8 million in 2020.[3] This latter figure represents an eightfold growth since 1950.

The distribution of population in Iraq is far from even. As a generalization it can be said that the districts with the highest population densities are concentrated to the east of the Tigris River and immediately adjacent to it. This, of course, reflects water availability in terms of rainfall or irrigation water. Along the Euphrates only a limited number of districts, such as Karbala, Hilla, Nasiriya and Basra have relatively high population concentrations. The norm here is for very low densities indeed.

Inevitably it has been population growth which has dominated the development of especially the rural areas, where pressure on the available cultivable land has been considerable. Since the Second World War the other major trend has been the urbanization of the population. This has affected many parts of the country in a spatial sense. As far as population structure has been concerned this migration has been markedly age and gender selective. Most of the people who have moved to the cities have been in the age range eighteen to thirty-five and the vast majority have been male. In the initial stages these young males maintained close contact with their villages and small towns, often returning on a regular basis, and certainly remitting at least a part of their earnings back to these centres. However, with time the wives and children often move to join their husbands in the urban centres, leaving an ageing population behind in the rural areas.

By the late 1980s (1988) it was estimated that sixty-eight per cent of people lived in urban settlements. Prior to the 1930s it would seem that the urban percentage had remained relatively

2. R.I. Lawless, 'Iraq: changing population patterns', in J. I. Clarke and W. B. Fisher eds., *Populations of the Middle East and North Africa*, (London, 1972), pp. 97-127.

3. Population Reference Bureau, Inc., *World Population Data Sheet, 1988*, (Washington D.C., 1988).

constant at about twenty-five per cent.[4] Although much of this urban growth has been achieved by migration from rural areas, it is important to realize that most villages have larger populations, and, therefore, more pressure on their available land resources than they had thirty or forty years ago. It is only in the more isolated villages on extremely marginal lands where rural populations have actually fallen in absolute terms.

Despite the rapid urbanization which has occurred in recent years there have still been pronounced labour shortages in key areas like teaching and low-level commerce. This caused a large influx of foreign migrant workers, particularly from Egypt and Jordan. Almost all of these workers left the country in late 1990 as a result of the invasion of Kuwait and it seems unlikely that many will go back until the Iraqi economy has returned to some form of normality.

Iraq has experienced political tensions as a result of the racial and religious differences which exist within the country. In the north the Kurds have always sought political autonomy and on many occasions there have been conflicts between government forces and Kurdish militia. This long continued unrest has meant that the north of Iraq, outside of the oil-field zones, has been an area which has received less than its fair share of development funds. What development there has been is concentrated in the urban areas where central government control has been greatest. Rural areas especially have been neglected.

Much the same pattern can be observed in the south-east of Iraq where the population is largely Shi'i and has close connections with Iran. The economy of this part of the country was disrupted in the war with Iran and the regional centre, Basra, severely damaged. Rural areas here, as in the north, have lagged behind in terms of infrastructure provision. Eight years of warfare with Iran also meant that agricultural systems were neglected and inevitably decayed.

PETROLEUM

One of the reasons for the rapid economic growth of Iraq over the last forty years has been the availability of large capital sums for investment provided by oil revenues. Oil was first discovered in

---

4. M.S. Hasan 'Growth and structure of Iraq's population 1867-1947', *Bulletin of Oxford University*, 1958, 20, pp. 339–50.

Iraq at Kirkuk in 1927 by the Turkish Petroleum Company. Two years later the company changed its name to the Iraq Petroleum Company and subsequently gained further concessions west of the Tigris and in south Iraq. The Mosul Petroleum Company and the Basra Petroleum Company respectively were established to exploit these fields. Production began from the Ain Zaleh field in 1952 and from the Zubair field in 1951. Later new fields were brought into production at Batma in the north and Rumaila in the south.

Given the remote nature of the large Kirkuk oil field production was unable to commence until pipelines were constructed to the Mediterranean coast at Haifa and Tripoli. When the establishment of the state of Israel closed the pipeline to Haifa a new line was constructed to Tripoli and in 1952 a pipeline was constructed to Banyas. With the instability of the Lebanon in the 1970s Iraq decided to go ahead with a new outlet from the Kirkuk field to Dortyol on the Mediterranean coast of Turkey. This had the advantage of not passing through Syrian territory. In future the importance of this route seems likely to grow. Output from the fields of the Basra Petroleum Company was transported initially to al-Fau on the Gulf and later to a deep water terminal at Khor al-Amaya.

With the advent of the war with Iran Iraq's oil exports were severely disrupted. The Gulf oil export terminals had to be closed owing to damage and the Syrian pipeline to the Mediterranean coast was closed on orders from Damascus. This meant that the only oil exports which could be maintained by Iraq were at a rate of 600,000 barrels/day via the pipeline to Dortyol on the Mediterranean coast of Turkey. This pipeline, which crossed only Turkish and Iraqi territory, had been devised primarily for such strategic circumstances. As the long war with Iran progressed Iraq increased the output of the Turkish pipeline system to more than one million barrels per day. Road tankers were also able to move between 60,000 and 80,000 barrels per day to Turkish ports on the Mediterranean as well as across the desert to Aqaba in Jordan. One of the keys to Iraq's continued war effort in the mid-1980s was the construction of a new pipeline through Saudi Arabia to Yanbo on the Red Sea coast which was completed in 1985. During the first phase of its operation this pipeline had a capacity of 500,000 barrels per day. Transfer of petroleum within certain parts of the country was also now possible through an expanding internal grid system.

Oil production in Iraq showed a steady increase from the late 1950s until the late 1970s, when it peaked at around 170 million tonnes per annum. Since then with the advent of the Iran-Iraq war, and more recently with the Gulf War, production has been severely curtailed. However, as far as Iraq was concerned the really important spur to development took place in the 1970s as a result of soaring oil prices. Between 1970 and 1979 oil production in Iraq rose by only 2.2 times, yet its oil revenues increased by forty-one times (Figure 1). At their peak annual oil revenues were in excess of $25,000 million. This money provided the means to develop the military machine of Iraq as well as to greatly improve the economic infrastructure of the nation.

As far as proven petroleum reserves (1985 values) are concerned Iraq is ranked fourth in the region after Saudi Arabia, Kuwait and Iran, with 5,900 million tonnes. Equally important, though, is the question of just how much oil remains to be discovered in the Middle East region. Such estimates are, at best, only informed guesses. However, work by the United States Geological Survey[5] suggests that Iraq is the country with the greatest potential for future petroleum discoveries, with predicted values considerably greater than those for Saudi Arabia (Table 1). If these estimates are basically correct it means that Iraq is likely to have abundant oil revenues available to it for many decades into the future. This will mean that the pace of development can be maintained at a high level.

AGRICULTURE

The cultivated area of Iraq is approximately 5.45 million hectares, or about 12.4 per cent of the total area of the country. Agricultural land in Iraq is clearly divided into two categories. In the foothills of the Zagros and in the larger intermontane valleys rain-fed cultivation is possible. Here the limiting factors are the steepness of slopes and the nature of the soils which are present. However, in the more favoured regions cultivation over considerable areas is possible. In the drier parts of the alluvial lowlands arable cultivation can only be carried out with irrigation water from the Euphrates

5. C. D. Masters, H. D. Klemme and A. B. Coury, *Assessment of undiscovered conventionally recoverable petroleum resources of the Arabian-Iranian basin*, United States Geological Survey Circular, No. 881, 12 pages.

and Tigris rivers. In Iraq about 2.54 million hectares are irrigated currently.[6] This represents 46.6 per cent of all cultivated land and shows just how important this aspect of agricultural production is for the country as a whole.

In terms of the area covered the cereal crops dominate the pattern of cultivation, but vegetables, fruits and industrial crops all make a significant contribution to the economy[7] (Table 2). The wheat crop alone covers at least twenty per cent of the total cultivated area and in some years can be appreciably higher than this figure. Wheat and barley together usually account for about forty per cent of the total arable area. The main areas of wheat production are found in the north and west of Iraq. Highest production levels occur in the administrative units of Nineveh, Arbil and Sulaimaniya.

Vegetables are grown around all the villages and towns, especially with the aid of irrigation. In recent years vegetable and fruit production has increased for both local use and also to supply the lucrative markets of the Gulf. Very important date production is located along the lower Tigris and the Shatt al-Arab, although production suffered greatly as a result of the long-lasting Iran-Iraq war.

In the more isolated parts of the Zagros Mountains traditional cultivation methods still prevail, but nearly everywhere else mechanization of farming activities has progressed steadily. In the late 1960s there were about 10,000 tractors in use. This figure had risen to 20,000 in the mid-1970s and estimates for 1989 suggest that approximately 43,000 were being employed. The use of chemical fertilizers has also increased for the production of high value crops. Between 1970 and 1980 total consumption of fertilizers increased from 17,000 tonnes to 77,000 tonnes. However, fertilizer use in Iraq, compared with other Middle Eastern countries still remains relatively low.

Nowhere is the impact of population growth seen more clearly than in the production and consumption of staple crops. For example, with wheat Iraq was self-sufficient until the late 1960s. Since then wheat imports have increased steadily until by the mid-1980s they were in excess of 2 million tonnes per annum. Indeed, in the

6. FAO, *Production Yearbook 1989*, (Rome, 1990), 346 pages.
7. H. W. Okerman and S. G. Samano, 'The agricultural development of Iraq', in P. Beaumont and K. S. McLachlan eds., *Agricultural development in the Middle East*, (London, 1985), pp. 189–207.

period 1983–87 Iraq's import of wheat has averaged about four times its indigenous production levels.[8]

This increasing dependency of Iraq on imported wheat needs to be set against what happened in the early period after the Second World War. In the mid-1940s the wheat area in Iraq was around one million hectares. This grew steadily from 1950 onwards reaching almost 1.7 million hectares by the early 1970s. Subsequent disruption through wars and economic uncertainties has led to much more variable figures for the area of wheat cultivation. Average cultivated areas for wheat by the late 1980s were certainly less than they had been in the late 1960s. On the other hand wheat yields have shown a significant rise since the mid-1940s. At this time average yields were approximately 500 kg/ha. By the late 1980s they were averaging between 700 and 1,000 kg/ha. Interestingly these latter figures are still below the yields achieved by neighbouring countries such as Syria and Iran. In the case of Iraq it seems that the increased cropped area and increased yields were able to satisfy domestic needs for wheat until the late 1960s. From then onwards, however, the increasing population growth rate was such that ever larger amounts of foreign wheat had to be imported. At the moment this situation seems likely to deteriorate still further as the government does not seem to have a coherent policy with regard to food production.

WATER RESOURCES

The key to understanding the agriculture of lowland Iraq is provided by the rivers Euphrates and Tigris. In lowland Iraq the precipitation is so low, less than 150 mm/yr, that cultivation is only possible with irrigation from the two major rivers. Problems do occur, however, as both these rivers are trans-boundary rivers, with their head-waters in adjacent countries (Figure 2). Up to the present day Iraq has been by far the largest user of the water of these two rivers, but over the last few years the upstream countries, Syria and Turkey, have begun to utilize greater amounts of the available waters. It seems inevitable that this trend will continue in the future.

Superimposed on this is the whole question of the impact of

---

8. P. Beaumont, 'Wheat production and the growing food crisis in the Middle East', *Food Policy*, 1989, 14, pp. 378–84.

global warming. Although there is still no accurate way of assessing the likely results with any precision, most models suggest that temperatures over the Middle East could rise by as much as 4°C over the next century.[9] Assuming that precipitation totals do not change it seems likely that evapotranspiration amounts will increase, and this will mean that water flows in the rivers will decline. Perhaps equally important will be the fact that irrigation volumes for all crops will have to be increased to cope with the increased evapotranspiration totals. Therefore, a given volume of water will be able to irrigate fewer crops. At the moment all these estimates are imprecise and will probably remain so for at least the next decade. However, the direction of the trend is not really in dispute and so any planning authority which does not take global warming into account is asking for trouble in the future.

The River Euphrates rises in eastern Turkey in mountains reaching to more than 3,000 metres, where precipitation totals often surpass 1000mm/annum. As most of this precipitation occurs in winter it falls as snow and remains in the mountains until the spring snow-melt of April and May. Following this period of maximum flow the river level declines throughout the hot summer period to reach a minimum flow in August and September (Fig. 3). After leaving Turkey the River Euphrates flows into Syria, where it receives water from a tributary, the River Khabur. Calculations have shown that approximately eighty-eight per cent of the total flow of the Euphrates is generated in Turkey and a further twelve per cent in Syria. The net contribution of Iraq to the flow of the river is zero in normal years.

This then is one of the major problems as Turkey claims that as the waters are generated within its boundaries, the waters belongs to Turkey and can be used for whatever it wishes. The volume of water in the river Euphrates varies from year to year, dependent upon climatic conditions. In recent times flows have varied from about 17,000 to 44,000 million m³/yr, with an average flow at Hit in Iraq of around 32,000 million m³/yr.[10]

The Tigris river also rises in the mountains of eastern Turkey, but this river differs significantly from the Euphrates in so far as it

9. P. Beaumont, 'Water scarcity as a limiting factor to development in the Middle East', in A. V. Lorca, and M. Rosario de Andres, eds., *Obstaculos al Desarrollo en al Mediterraneo Oriental*, (Madrid, 1990), pp. 91–9.
10. P. Beaumont, 'The Euphrates River—an international problem of water resources development', *Environmental Conservation*, vol. 5, 1978, no. 1, pp. 35–44.

also receives the waters from four major tributaries from the Zagros mountains. As with the Euphrates a large proportion of the total flow of the river is generated outside Iraq in either Turkey or Iran. At Mosul in northern Iraq the mean annual flow of the Tigris is about 23,000 million m³. The major tributaries draining from the Zagros Mountains of Iran and Iraq contribute a further 29,500 million m³/yr, to provide a total annual flow of 52,555 million m³. This, it will be noted, is about sixty-four per cent greater than the flow of the Euphrates River.

In the most optimistic scenario, assuming that Turkey, Syria and Iran do not use significant quantities of the waters of the two rivers, Iraq receives a water flow from the Euphrates and Tigris rivers totalling 84,500 million m³/yr. This figure is very similar to the total flow of the River Nile in Egypt. From now on it seems inevitable that this figure will decline as both Syria and Turkey continue to develop irrigation projects. At the moment it will be the Euphrates River which will see the greatest reduction in flow, as fewer developments are currently planned in the head waters of the Tigris and its tributaries. Indeed, even in the future the Tigris flow looks to be relatively assured as a major portion of the flow is generated in Iraq.

In Turkey plans are already going ahead to develop large irrigation projects close to the southern border of the country using waters from the Euphrates River. For these projects water will be abstracted from the newly completed Atatürk dam. With the first stages of the development it is proposed to pump water through the Urfa tunnel before distributing it by canals to the various irrigation schemes. Other irrigation projects will follow until by the early years of the twenty-first century approximately 1.1 million hectares of land will be being irrigated. Assuming field irrigation rates of between 5,000 and 10,000 cubic metres per hectare, which are probably quite low estimates, the amount of water needed will be between 5,500 and 11,000 million cubic metres per annum. Extra evaporation opportunities from the reservoirs behind the dams on the Euphrates are also likely to consume an extra 1,000 million cubic metres per year. Taken together this implies that the river flow from Turkey is likely to be depleted by between 6,000 and 12,000 million cubic metres per year. With the completion of the Atatürk Dam in 1990 Turkey has pledged that it will not let the flow of the Euphrates fall below an average value of 500 cubic metres per second. However, this represents an annual flow of only

15,768 million cubic metres per year, which is well below the uncontrolled flow leaving Turkey of around 28,400 million cubic metres per year.

Controversy about the use of the waters of the Euphrates has been going on for a number of years and as yet no agreement has been reached between the riparian countries. Detailed talks between Turkey, Syria and Iraq took place in June 1990 when Iraq put forward two demands. The first was that Turkey should increase the flow of water in the Euphrates from 500 cubic metres a second to 700 cubic metres per second and secondly that a formula should be devised for the allocation of the waters of the Euphrates. Turkey's response was that as Iraq had already agreed with Syria to take fifty-eight per cent of the 500 cubic metres a second flow which it was guaranteeing no more water was required. Turkey also proposed that the three countries should map all the cultivable areas in the basin and work out how much water would be required to irrigate them. The plan also emphasized the need for all countries to utilize irrigation systems which needed the minimum amount of water for their operation. Both Syria and Iraq rejected this proposal as they felt that the real issue was the distribution of the flow of the Euphrates and they did not want to be drawn into new areas of discussion. Iraq's position was that the Euphrates is an international river and that Iraq had 'acquired rights' for the use of water for irrigation over many hundreds and even thousands of years. It claimed that the only water which could be discussed for allocation amongst the three countries was that remaining after all the 'acquired rights' had been satisfied. Not surprisingly Turkey would not have anything to do with this idea. The position, therefore, remains unsolved with Turkey continuing to maintain a flow of only 500 cubic metres per second.

Syria too has ambitious plans for irrigation development fed by waters from its own dam on the Euphrates at Tabqa, as well as projects using the waters of the River Khabur. In total as many as one million hectares of new land may be irrigated compared with the situation prior to 1970. New schemes have already been constructed, but as yet these projects do not appear to have been as successful as the government originally hoped.[11] Final completion

---

11. I. R. Manners and T. Sagafi-Mejad, 'Agricultural development in Syria', in P. Beaumont and K. S. McLachlan eds., *Agricultural development in the Middle East*, (London, 1985), pp. 255–78.

of these schemes does not seem likely before the beginning of the next century. However, the likely water demand from them will be between 5,000 and 10,000 million cubic metres per year.

As far as Iraq is concerned the proposed irrigation projects for Turkey and Syria, together with evaporation losses from the various reservoirs, means that the flow of the Euphrates at Hit in Iraq may well be reduced by 11,000 to 22,000 million cubic metres per year (Table 3). When it is remembered that the average flow of the river is only 32,000 million cubic metres per year the seriousness of the situation for Iraq becomes obvious. Effectively the flow of the Euphrates could be reduced to less than half its normal value by the early years of the twenty-first century at a time when Iraq would be proposing a large expansion of its own irrigation network.

The position in the Tigris is not quite as critical as that on the Euphrates. As part of its huge South-East Anatolia project Turkey is to develop 600,000 hectares of irrigated land using water from the Tigris. However, Turkey only generates about forty-five per cent of the total flow of the river and so the maximum amount it can abstract is much more limited than is the case on the Euphrates.

The position has, however, been recently complicated by the fact that Syria, whose border reaches the Tigris in southern Turkey, has approached the Turkish government with a view to diverting water from the Tigris into the Euphrates. If this were to go ahead it would obviously reduce the flow of water available to Iraq still further, unless larger quantities of water were released by the Syrians down the Euphrates.

Detailed figures of irrigation along the rivers Euphrates and Tigris in Iraq are very difficult to obtain owing to the lack of detailed government statistics over the last decade since the war with Iran began. Statistics published in the early 1970s[12] suggested that water withdrawals from the Euphrates in Iraq between Hit and Hindiya rose from 8,641 million cubic metres per year in the 1940s to 16,368 million cubic metres per year in the 1960s. Government estimates from the mid-1980s suggested that use at that time was about 18,100 million cubic metres per year. However, compared with the earlier 1960 values these figures do seem rather low. Similar estimates for the Tigris put irrigation use at 21,800 million cubic metres per year.

12. K. Ubell, 'Iraq's water resources', *Nature and Resources*, 1971, 7, no. 2, pp. 3–9.

Whatever the reality or otherwise of these figures it can be stated that every 100,000 hectares of newly irrigated land will require between 500 million and 1,000 million cubic metres of water each year. For some time the Iraq government has talked of expanding the irrigated area of the country by as much as 1.5 million hectares. This implies, of course, extra water demand amounting to between 7,500 and 15,000 million cubic metres each year.

What is obvious is that the Euphrates River is not capable of supplying these water demands, but some unused water may be available from the Tigris. Indeed, since the 1960s there have been plans for diverting flood water from the Tigris into the Euphrates via the Thartar depression. However, studies showed that water quality would be seriously compromised by the high salinity soils over which the water would have to flow. Nevertheless the idea of diversion of excess waters from the Tigris to the Euphrates basin remains a sound one and is indeed a view highly favoured by the Turkish government as a solution to the problems of the Euphrates basin as a whole.

Another possibility worth further study is to use less water per unit area for crop production. At the moment irrigation methods in the Tigris-Euphrates lowlands are not very sophisticated and water application rates could be substantially reduced with better water application systems. The only drawback here is that these methods would require considerable capital investment for their implementation.

Water is, therefore, one of the keys to the future of the Iraqi economy. As population numbers rise the demands for water for domestic, industrial and agricultural use will increase as well. As far as domestic use is concerned there will also be a rise in per capita use as standards of living of, in particular, urban dwellers increase. Currently at least eighty per cent of all water consumption in Iraq is used for irrigation purposes. This means that extra water can always be supplied for industrial and domestic purposes by diverting water away from agricultural usage. The actual amounts that would be required are quite small compared with the huge volume used by agriculture.

The question must be posed though as to whether it is in Iraq's long term interests to try to continue with extensive irrigated agriculture which is so wasteful of water. Iraq is a rich country as a result of its oil revenues and would be perfectly capable of importing its food needs. Such a policy would have the great merit of permitting the scarce water resources to be utilized for higher value uses such as industry.[13] At this moment though the government appears committed to a policy of food self-sufficiency because of strategic reasons at whatever costs. In the future the lack of available water will mean that this policy will have to be reviewed and, hopefully, rescinded.

CONCLUSION

At the moment Iraq is a country about which it is extremely difficult to make predictions of the future. To a great extent there is a planning and development blight which will not be lifted until the United Nations has decided just what reparations Iraq will have to pay to Kuwait. Recent discussions would suggest that the agreed figure may be as high as thirty per cent of the total oil revenues of Iraq in the immediate future. Until the figure is finally settled and agreed by all the parties concerned Iraq will not be permitted to resume its oil exports. This means that the work of rebuilding the Iraqi infrastructure will be delayed until that time. Already it has become clear that the inability to obtain vital spare parts has meant that utilities like electricity and water supply have not been able to be fully restored even though the war damage may have been relatively minor.

Given these facts it seems inevitable that it will be many months or even years with regards to certain facets of the economy, before Iraq returns to the level of services it enjoyed prior to the recent Gulf war. Already there have been severe food shortages and food prices have risen rapidly. Inflation too is reaching disturbing levels. Just how bad the situation is likely to become is difficult to estimate because it is largely controlled by countries other than Iraq, and in particular the United States of America. What seems obvious though is that the level of economic growth in the country seems destined to, at best, stagnate and at worst to show a serious decline over the next twelve months.

The resilience of the Iraqi economy should not, however, be underestimated. Given adequate capital investment in key areas there is no reason to doubt that a major new growth phase could be initiated fuelled by capital from oil revenues. Here the critical factor is the price of oil which can be obtained on the world market. This

13. P. Beaumont, *Environmental management and development in drylands* (London, 1989), 505 pages.

will determine the volume of the revenues which are available, but whatever the price of oil the amount of money accruing to Iraq will remain considerable.

It is interesting to note that prior to the Gulf war of 1991 Iraq looked set for a period of sustained economic growth between 1990 and 1995 following the cease-fire with Iran, with oil revenues predicted to rise from around $15,400 million in 1990 to $23,500 million in 1995. The dependence upon oil as an export earner still continues to be worrying for the economy as a whole and in the last years of the 1980s non-oil exports contributed only about three per cent of all export earnings. There seems little chance of this situation changing in the near future, though there is considerable potential for industrial development geared to reducing import demands. This may well turn out to be labour rather than capital intensive but even so could make a substantial contribution to the economy. Once the oil fields and related facilities have been repaired it would seem likely that Iraq could return to a production total of around three million barrels a day without too much difficulty. As domestic consumption is only of the order of 500 barrels per day, this means that exports can be at least 2.5 million barrels per day. With this high export potential the future of the Iraqi economy in the long-term seems assured.

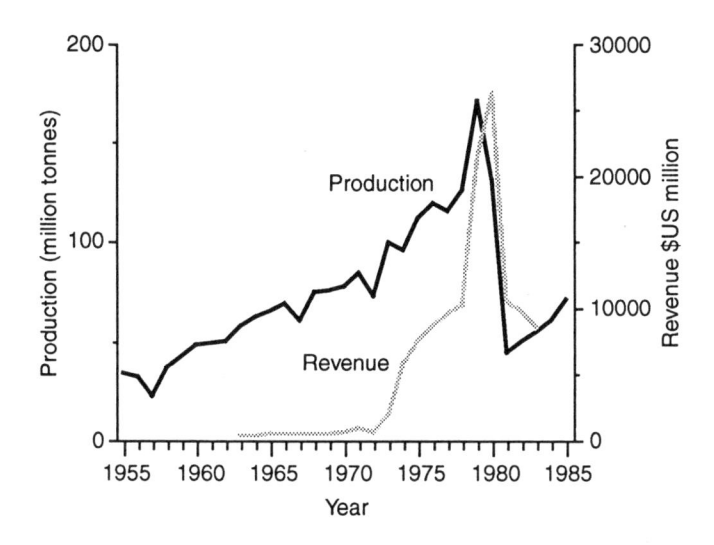

Fig. 1 Oil Production and Oil Revenues

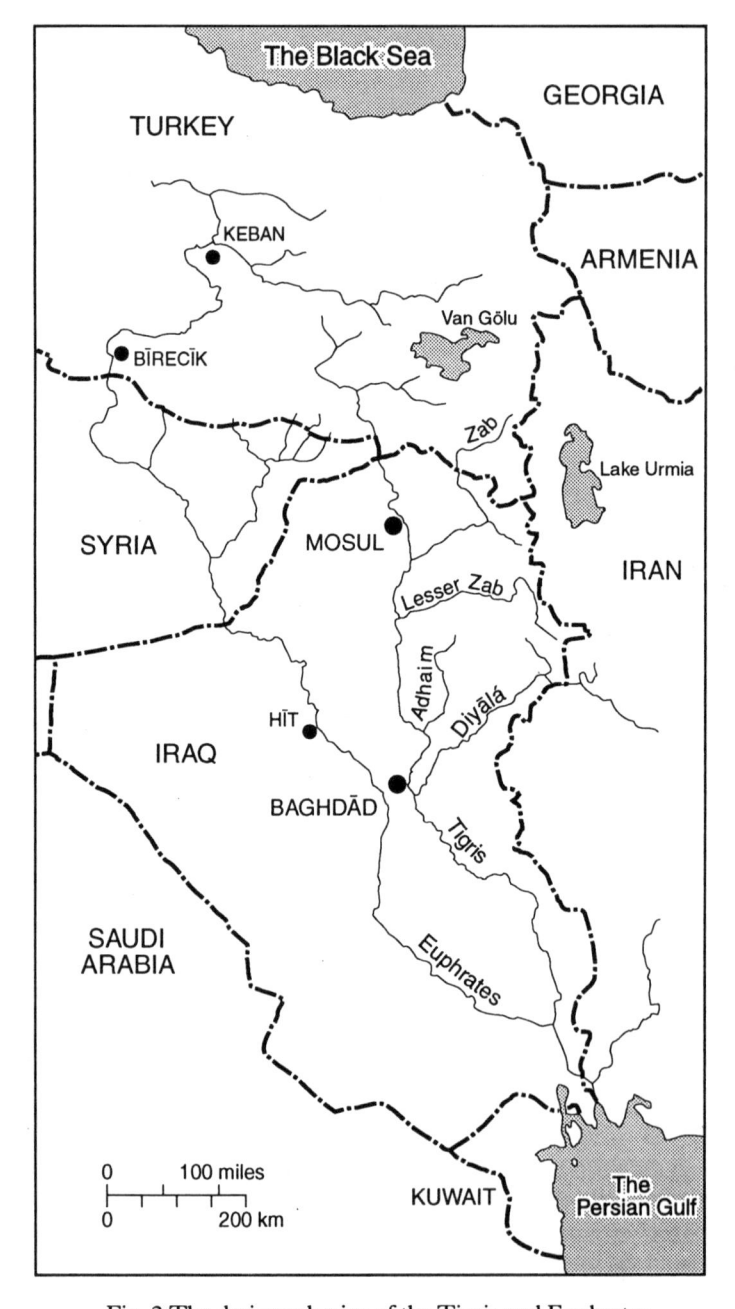

Fig. 2 The drainage basins of the Tigris and Euphrates

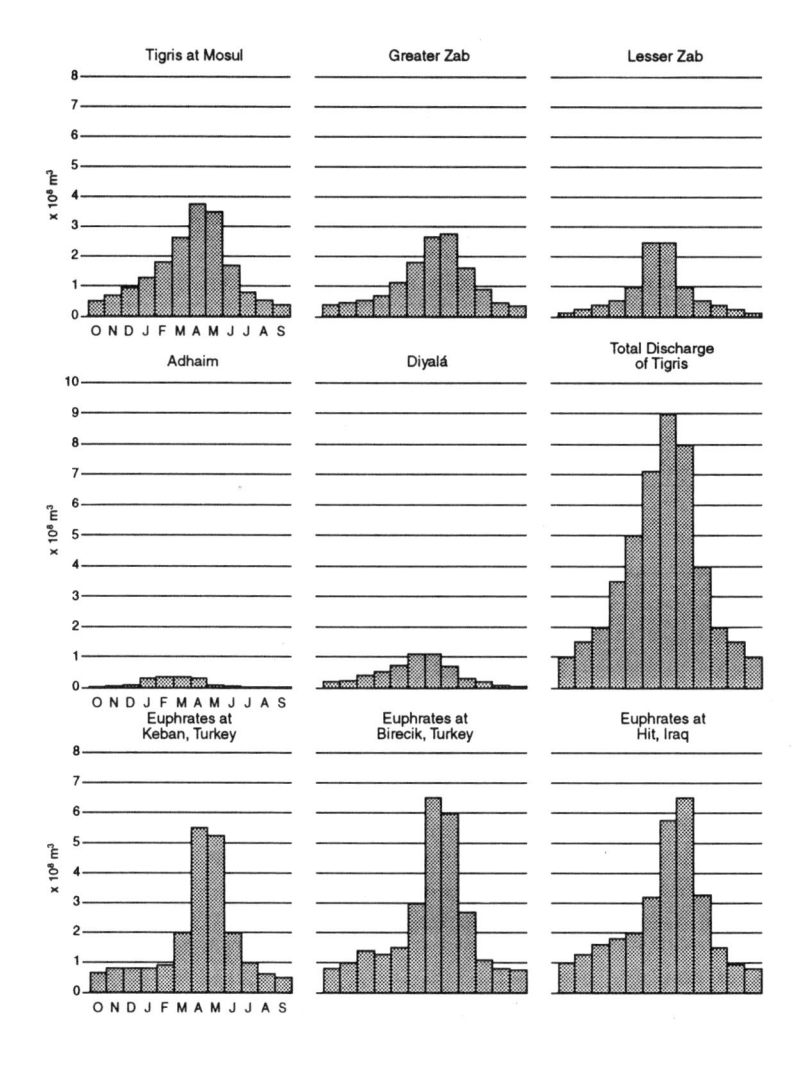

Fig. 3 Selected regime hydrographs of the Tigris and Euphrates rivers

Table 1 Assessment of undiscovered conventionally recoverable petroleum resources of the Arabian–Iranian basin by country (billion tonnes).

	Low	High	Mean
Saudi Arabia	3.27	15.14	7.78
Iran	1.50	6.82	3.55
Iraq	4.37	20.46	10.64
UAE	0.27	1.77	0.96
Kuwait	0.27	1.23	0.55
Oman	0.14	0.55	0.27
Total	9.82	45.98	23.74

Note: The probability of more than the low value is 95 per cent. Similarly the probability of more than the high value is 5 per cent.

Source: Masters C.D. *et al.*, 1982

Table 2 Major crops – area under cultivation in Iraq – hectares (thousand)

	1979–81	1987	1988	1989
Cereals				
Wheat	1,215	859	1,041	(500)
Barley	858	972	1,314	(700)
Rice	56	70	50	(55)
Industrial Crops				
Seed Cotton	13	17	12	(14)
Tobacco	11	9	2	(2)
Linseed	2	1	1	(1)
Sesame	11	17	18	(20)
Sugar Cane	4	2	1	(2)
Sunflower	12	11	12	(12)
Vegetables and fruits				
Dry onion	15	13	13	(14)
Tomato	34	42	35	(40)
Water melons	40	42	35	(40)
Cucumber	28	39	33	(37)
Egg plants	7	14	12	(12)
Cantaloups & other melons	19	32	27	(38)
Grapes	56	(57)	(57)	(57)

Note: ( ) = estimates

Table 3 Potential water use in the Tigris-Euphrates watershed

River	million cubic metres per annum
Euphrates	
Mean discharge at Hit (Iraq)	31,820
Turkey	
Evaporation from reservoirs	1,000 (max)
Potential water withdrawals for irrigation	5,500–11,000
Syria	
Evaporation from reservoirs above Tabqa Dam	630 (max)
Potential water withdrawal for irrigation	5,000–10,000
Iraq	
Current water use (1980s)	18,100
Evaporation from reservoir above Al Haditha Dam	602 (max)
Predicted total water use as a result of schemes actually built, under construction or planned	Minimum 30,832 Maximum 41,332
Tigris	
Mean discharge in Iraq	52,555
Turkey	
Evaporation from reservoirs	500 (max)
Potential water withdrawals for irrigation	3,000–6,000
Iraq	
Evaporation from reservoirs	1,000 (max)
Current water use (1980s)	21,800
Potential water withdrawal for irrigation (for 1.5 million ha)	7,500–15,000
Potential total water use as a result of schemes actually built, under construction or planned	Minimum 33,800 Maximum 44,300

Iraq and its Oil: Sixty-five Years of Ambition and Frustration

Michel Chatelus

The history of the state and the history of oil are closely linked in Iraq. Throughout the century the various stages of the country's development have been punctuated by frustrations, ambitions and disputes in the oil sector. Even before the birth of the state oil influenced its existence, its status and its future borders. It would become both an economic reality of major significance and a symbol of the struggle for independence. No doubt more than anywhere else, the history of oil in Iraq is a political history, characterized by almost incessant dispute with the concessionaire companies, with the countries through which the oil is transported, and with other oil producers, notably those in OPEC.

Most leaders have displayed an oil militancy most probably based on the initial frustrations surrounding the conditions of the award of concessions. Most frequently at the vanguard of the struggle against the major companies[1] and in favour of the recovery of national riches, Iraq actually paid very dearly for the priority it gave to politics and for its lack of realism concerning the conditions of the international market. Its politics of confrontation cost a great deal in loss of revenue and delays in development investment, whilst its main competitors obtained effective control over their oil

---

1. The major companies referred to here are the seven largest companies who organized and controlled the oil market between the twenties and the end of the sixties: i.e. five American companies: Standard Oil of New Jersey (Exxon), Mobil Oil, Gulf Oil, Standard Oil of California (Chevron), Texaco; the British company B.P. and the Anglo-Dutch Shell. An eighth company might also be included: the Compagnie Française des Pétroles. These major companies are also known as the 'seven sisters' or 'the cartel'.

wealth at the same time as Iraq and without loss of resources. Today, with almost ten per cent of world reserves, Iraq is potentially the second largest oil power in the world; it would, therefore, be useful to attempt to explain the present and the future by analysing the past.

FIFTY YEARS OF DISPUTES OVER 'ARAB OIL TO THE ARABS'

From the Beginnings to the 1950s: the IPC Monopoly

When establishing the facts of Iraqi oil history, it is essential to consider the Ottoman heritage, which takes us back to the end of the nineteenth century, when the European powers were competing to extend their influence in the Arab provinces of the Turkish Empire and in Persia.[2] The presence of oil, known since ancient times, was confirmed by the identification of small deposits and by refining with the primitive techniques of the 1870s, but oil was not yet a significant issue. The award of a concession to the Deutsche Bank for the construction of a railway line to Baghdad opened the era of conflicts of interest amongst the Europeans, an era in which oil would gradually occupy an increasingly important place. Indeed, the Deutsche Bank was soon awarded preferential rights over any oil discovered on either side of the planned track. British and German groups came into conflict, finally creating the TPC (Turkish Petroleum Company) in 1912, uniting Turkish and German interests, the Royal Dutch Shell Company and the British interests of the (Anglo-Persian) d'Arcy group. The mediator of the operation, Gulbenkian, obtained a share in return for services rendered. The treaty confirmed a previous arrangement, which was later to play an important part under the 'red line accord', in which each of the participants ruled out holding any oil interests in the Ottoman Empire, except through the intermediary of the IPC.[3] In June 1914 the promise of a concession was made by the Turkish Grand Vizier.

But the war interrupted proceedings. The armistice of Mudros, which put an end to hostilities between the Western allies and the Ottoman Empire on 30 October 1918, saw the British army firmly

2. There are many works analysing this period. See, for example Issawi, Longrigg, Sampson (French translation 1972).
3. Penrose is very informative on subsequent developments and the very many analyses of the situation in Iraq.

established in Mesopotamia. Germany was excluded from the region and France was able to claim its assets in the form of reparations. The diplomatic imbroglio surrounding the reorganization of the region was considerable. In the Sykes-Picot agreement, Great Britain had recognized France's 'rights' over the vilayet of Mosul, by extending those over Syria; it also supported the Arab revolt by promising an Arab Kingdom; and it promised the Jews the creation of a national homeland in Palestine. In addition, the Turkish national recovery reintroduced a partner to the scene, who had been isolated too quickly. The British were primarily interested in Mesopotamia, for its potential oil wealth, but above all for its strategic position on the major imperial axis: the route to India.

In the initial attempts to dismember the Ottoman Empire, Russia would have received certain territories. But the 1917 revolution removed it from the game (it was, moreover, Russian revolutionaries who revealed the secret contents of Franco-Anglo-Russian discussions on the division of the Middle East). The French ended by renouncing the vilayet of Mosul—not without some ill-humour— and the English resisted the Turkish state's strong pressure to regain it, thus creating a 'unified' Iraq under British mandate. Created by the San Remo accord of 1920, the new state would not see its borders fixed until 1925, following numerous disputes, frequently bloody, between Arabs, Turks and Assyrians. Great Britain placed Emir Faisal on the throne and in 1922 imposed a treaty on him establishing the mandate over Iraq, which, nevertheless, also recognized the desire for independence.

From the TPC to the IPC

The war had confirmed that mechanization and the decisive role of transport would henceforth make oil the key to every conflict. Europe was well aware of the inconvenience of an almost exclusive dependence on American oil or on oil controlled by the United States. The Iranian discoveries (1910) reinforced the attraction of Mesopotamia, an extension of Iranian sites. The TPC then re-emerged, adapted itself to the new conditions and became the IPC (Iraq Petroleum Company) in 1929, entering a permanently tense relationship with the 'host state', which lasted for almost half a century.

After the war the German parts of the TPC were transferred to the CFP (Compagnie Française des Pétroles, later Total), an enterprise partly funded with public capital. After many negotiations between 1920 and 1928, the IPC's definitive shareholding was formed and the company's mode of operation established. It was a true multinational before the term existed. In addition to Gulbenkian (who received five per cent of shares), the company comprised four shareholders, with 23.5 per cent of capital each: Royal-Dutch Shell; what later became British Petroleum (BP), (half of which was owned by the British admiralty), the Near East Development Corporation, uniting the American companies which had made a forced entry into the red line (of eleven at the beginning only two were left at the end: Exxon and Mobil), and finally the CFP. The IPC was thus the prototype of the 'consortium' which would later proliferate in the region. The basic rule of operation was the absence of refining and distribution activity, except in Iraq; the IPC delivered its crude oil to the mother companies in proportion to their IPC shareholding. One of the major inconveniences of a structure of this nature for the host country is the possible divergence of interests between the member companies; certain companies, rich in crude oil because they were also producing elsewhere, tended to limit production, thus preserving reserves, whilst others who were 'thirsty for crude oil' (as was the case with the CFP) wanted to produce as much as possible. For a long time Iraq paid the price in terms of production stagnation for the fact that BP, Shell and Mobil preferred to produce elsewhere. The needs of the CFP were never sufficient to reverse the trend.

Contrary to the commitments made at San Remo, the Iraqis were refused a twenty per cent share in the IPC. American pressure to refuse was particularly insistent, whilst the French and the British appeared more accommodating. This exclusion was sharply denounced by the Iraqi political classes. It is the origin of Iraq's deep-seated frustration with the IPC and provides one explanation for the conflictual nature of subsequent relations between Iraq and the company; accusations of double-dealing and of bad faith were often made by Iraq to its omnipotent concessionaire.

A first *concession treaty* was concluded between the IPC and the government in 1925. Like the other countries in the region, and in contrast to what was happening in Latin America, it was not inscribed within the framework of general legislation on the oil deposits, but was the result of a government decision.[4] The duration

4. Cf. Issawi, p. 194.

(seventy-five years) was a compromise between the ninety years demanded by the IPC and the thirty years proposed by Iraq. A royalty of four gold shillings would be paid by the IPC for every tonne produced. The concession covered the entire country, but after thirty-two months the IPC had to choose a group of plots—532 km^2 in total—the other plots might then be awarded by the government to the IPC or to other companies.

After the 1928 accord between the companies on the issue of the 'red line', a new treaty was negotiated and signed in 1931. The IPC then absorbed an Italian-British company (the BOD) which had not been able to finance research on the concessions it had acquired; its concession was then increased to almost 87,000 km^2. Two sister companies with capital divided in the same way as the IPC were formed: the MPC (Mosul Petroleum Company) in 1932 and the BPC (Basra Petroleum Company) in 1938. With the concessions they were awarded, the IPC now controlled Iraqi territory in its entirety. The 1931 contract increased taxes on planned exploitation and led the IPC to construct an oil pipeline to the Mediterranean.

The first discovery of oil which could be exploited was made in Kirkuk in 1927 (this explains the desire of the American companies to finalize the 1928 accord on the final structure of the IPC). The first exports date back to 1934; they reached 4 mt in 1935, with the government collecting around one million pounds in revenue. Exports were made via the small oil pipeline which had been constructed between the enormous field at Kirkuk and the ports of Haifa (Palestine) and Tripoli (Lebanon).

A variety of grievances fed permanent tension between Iraq and the IPC over the next twenty-five years, until a crisis was reached in 1961. The Iraqis' basic complaint, which justified their accusations against the IPC, was the near stagnation of production, followed by an increase which was very much slower than that of its neighbours, Iran and Kuwait in particular (cf. Table 1). From 1935 to 1949 production rarely exceeded 100,000 barrels/day.[5] It only reached 140,000 b/d in 1950, at a time when Kuwait, which had only been producing since 1946, had exceeded 350,000 b/d. In 1960 the Kuwaiti consortium (B.P. and Gulf) produced 1,691

---

5. Volumes of production are expressed in tonnes or in barrels/day (b/d). This latter form is the most common and we prefer to use it too. One tonne = 7.4 barrels, one million b/d = 50 million tonnes/year.

million b/d, while the IPC produced 977,000 b/d. The Iraqis also accused the IPC of not making the necessary investments in oil pipelines (despite the Kirkuk Banyas oil pipeline (in Syria) opened in 1952 and the installations in the Gulf, export capacity remained small), of not training Iraqi technicians, of neglecting research and exploration in their huge concession and of refusing to apply the 'gold shilling' clause in the calculation of taxes.

In fact, at the heart of the problem was the abundance of oil and the many opportunities which were offered to Shell (present in Iran and in many consortia) to BP, (powerful in Kuwait and Iran), and to Mobil (present in Kuwait, and which, with Exxon had become a partner in Aramco in Saudi Arabia). Only the CFP wanted to increase production and export.

An important change took place during the period: the generalization in the Middle East of a practice established in Latin America—the division of profits on a fifty-fifty basis (the famous 'fifty-fifty'). Initially applied by Aramco in the region, it was applied in Iraq by the IPC after an accord in 1952, made retroactive to 1 January 1951. In 1953 Iraqi revenues represented eight times those of 1950 and had reached $150 million. It should be noted that this improvement was not the result of any particular Iraqi action.

Oil and the Revolution: Open Confrontation with the IPC

To 'law 80'

The revolution of 14 July 1958 which overthrew the monarchy which had been close to the British and brought General Qasim to power could not accommodate itself to the long-term oil status quo. The oil question had agitated opinion for a long time and a revolutionary government was able to take certain initiatives. Until now, although relations with the IPC had always been difficult, a split had been avoided: 'at no point did the negotiations pose a serious threat to the position of the company in the country'.[6]

At the beginning Qasim adopted a prudent stance, since he needed the oil revenue. The example of Iran, deprived of all exports in 1952, testified to the oil companies' capacity for retaliation. The IPC argued for the doubling of its production between

---
6. Penrose, p. 257.

1957 and 1959, which implied that it had anticipated increases in capacity, and set up various investment projects. An assassination attempt against Qasim in October 1959 (which the IPC was suspected of instigating) brought about a clear hardening of the Iraqi position. Furthermore, the IPC reproached Iraq for penalizing its oil by imposing extremely high taxes on exports from the Gulf ports; Iraqi oil was thus no longer competitive with the other crude oils of the Gulf. In the midst of negotiations the BPC reduced its exports by a third to restore them to the contracted minimum. This measure was regarded as outright provocation by the Iraqis, all the more so because it meant for Iraq and all the oil in the Middle East a reduction in the posted price (according to which profits are calculated) in August 1961. The first fall occurred in February. The major companies justified these falls by the surplus in world production.

The resumption of negotiations in August 1960 took place in an extremely tense climate. The Iraqis presented numerous claims, reiterating grievances accumulated since 1925. The IPC was ready to give way on many points, but remained inflexible on anything which challenged the concessions, because it feared that such tendencies would spread to other states. The 'taboo' questions concerned the participation of Iraq in the company's capital, the modification of the rules dividing profits and the government's ability to select unexplored zones which the IPC had to return.

The split came on 11 October 1961. December saw the enactment of the famous 'law no. 80' which withdrew 99.5 per cent of the IPC's concession, leaving it with only those oil wells already in production. The law created an irreversible situation; no subsequent Iraqi government would contemplate questioning it. All subsequent negotiations would have to take place within the framework of the law, and this itself was 'non-negotiable'. It would be twelve years before the IPC accepted it.

From 1961 to 1972 the situation was effectively frozen. Whilst production was increasing considerably in the region as a whole, Iraq had the meanest share. Indeed the companies, who had at their disposal vast quantities of crude oil, used every conceivable pretext to justify limiting production. The remarks attributed by Anthony Sampson to Exxon's negotiator are revealing: 'any country which makes things too difficult for the companies provides the ideal pretext for reduction. Sometimes they have aided our reductions by breaking a contractual accord, as was the case in Iraq: then we can "pack the whole thing in".[7] Most observers draw attention to the inability of the major companies to understand the resentment of the producing countries at the time, and their ' "dinosaur-like" and unrelenting defence of the status quo'.[8]

Opening up to the outside and friendship with France.
Iraq progressively established a mechanism to allow it to develop the areas it had regained and to implement its own oil policies. In 1964 the Iraqi National Oil Company (INOC) was created, which had to wait for law no. 97 of August 1967 before it was granted a real company structure and was given the right to embark on 'joint ventures' and to sign service agreements with foreign companies.

Despite the threat of a boycott called for by the IPC, the Compagnie Publique Françcaise ERAP (later ELF) was the first to become involved in November 1967. The importance of this agreement is twofold. On the one hand it constituted a recognition of the situation created by law no. 80, and on the other hand it profoundly changed relations between the state producer and the company, with the state obtaining the necessary decision-making powers and revenues.

It is also possible to observe that after the objective convergence of interests between the CFP and Iraq, the choice of a French enterprise (at the time when President de Gaulle's stand during the war of June 1967 had made France the only 'imperialist power it is possible to associate with'), marked a new stage in the privileged relations between France and Iraq. Despite the friction with ERAP, these relations were strengthened, becoming a de facto alliance from 1972 (with the visit of Saddam Hussein to Paris) until the end of the eighties.[9] Agreements of the same kind were signed with Petrobas (Brazil) and a public Indian company in particular. Relations were also strengthened with the USSR at the same time,

7. Sampson, p. 181.
8. Sampson, p. 160.
9. In an interview in *Le Monde* before his visit to France, Saddam Hussein insisted on the special nature of relations between Iraq and France. Penrose, p. 433. In a propaganda leaflet from the Arab Baath Socialist Party, 1974, the party justified the practice of differentiating between various kinds of imperialism, according a particular place to France and Japan. The party's decision to give France a privileged position at the time of nationalization in 1972 is described as 'very significant', p. 94. Penrose (p. 434) points out that the privileged treatment reserved for France in oil matters was not necessarily very advantageous. For example, in 1974 it was charged almost the same price as its rivals for the Kirkuk oil drilled by the CFP.

providing for a massive supply of material and expertise which would be paid for with oil. A comprehensive political and economic agreement was signed in Baghdad on 9 April 1972, allying the two countries for fifteen years. In the oil sector a new mechanism was established to accelerate oil production in the southern oil-fields, notably Rumeila.

The Final Phase: Nationalization.

At a time when Iraq was stuck in a confrontation which was costing it a great deal in lost revenues and delayed projects (certainly $2 billion were lost between 1962 and 1970),[10] the world oil scene suddenly came to life in 1970. For various reasons a serious restriction in oil supply was felt, whereas demand increased[11], and the producing countries (in particular those which had been united in OPEC since 1960) took advantage of this to impose negotiations on the companies, with particular reference to prices and taxation; these resulted in the Treaties of Teheran (February 1971) and Tripoli (April 1971). Iraq had to embark on negotiations to determine the particular mode of enforcement of the Treaty of Tripoli. But demand was growing in the country for the nationalization of the IPC. Difficult discussions opened at the beginning of 1972 and according to a scenario already described, the climate deteriorated further with the fall in Mediterranean exports. This was justified by the IPC in terms of too high costs, but it was regarded as insufferable blackmail by Iraq. The Iraqis remained intransigent in their refusal to award any compensation for concessions confiscated under law 80. On 1 June 1972 Iraq nationalized the IPC (but not the BPC which was extracting oil from the fields of the south).

Disputes between Iraq and the IPC were settled by a treaty in February 1973. The BPC remained the property of the IPC and was committed to raise production from 35 million tonnes/ annum in 1973 to 80 mt in 1980. The two parties implemented a system of financial compensation for their respective debts. After the October War, Iraq nationalized the American and Dutch shares (sixty per cent Shell) in the BPC and Partex's five per cent (Gulbenkian). Having refused any participation agreement of the kind negotiated

10. Figure cited by Agnes Chevalier in *Economie Prospective Internationale*, 3rd quarter, 1982, p. 145.
11. See for example J.M. Chevalier, Chapter 2.

by Saudi Arabia and the Gulf States, Iraq proceeded to nationalize the entire BPC in December 1975. And so, the stormy relationship between Iraq and the IPC, which had begun with the 1925 concession, finally ended after fifty years. The era of sovereign oil politics began. Often 'ahead', Iraq had hardly put its fight to good use. Too often a strong independence, together with a feeling of frustration and injustice, led to a position of militancy, which was not particularly effective economically.

The decision-making process frequently appeared hesitant, even chaotic, mixing dogmatism and pragmatism in the preparatory phases, and then a brutal decision was taken, without sufficient evaluation of the consequences.

Iraq always found itself in a very isolated position in its struggle against the IPC, disputes with its neighbours and partners were frequent, and it has never been the 'pioneer' along a road which others followed. Law 80 marginalized Iraq for twelve years and the events of 1972–1975 reflect the general conditions of the time and were not part of a specific policy.

INDEPENDENT OIL POLICY, OR HOW TO ESCAPE THE DESTINY OF A MAJOR OIL POWER

Iraq began the new era with the potential, the means and the ambition to become a major oil power. Twice between 1975 and 1980 and then in 1989–1990, it seemed that it would have to rise to the ranks of 'major power' in OPEC, initiator of important decisions, and it was predicted that it would become a new industrial country, the first in the region. Twice a miscalculated and mismanaged international political challenge led to a catastrophe, deflecting it from its destiny. Iraq never had any great influence within OPEC (paradoxically, except in July 1990); and if it had production capacities which would allow it quickly to regain its 1979 level, no one could have envisaged that mid 1991 would be the day of reckoning.

Iraq's ambition is to gain a place corresponding to its potential and its needs

Iraq, which had drawn attention to the political weapon which oil can constitute during the 1973 crisis, believed that its role and the sacrifices it had made in the past were not recognised by its partners. Thus the Party stated: 'it was the Socialist Baath Party which invented the slogan 'Arab Oil to the Arabs', and the nationalization of 1 June 1972 was the first coup carried out by the Arab people on imperialism since the defeat of June 1967. This was also the first scent of triumph for the Arabs for a long time'.[12] Thus it was only right that Iraq should be allowed to increase its production, if necessary to the detriment of those neighbouring countries which had profited from the semi-quarantine imposed by the IPC and had become great producers.

According to the Iraqis their reserves, estimated at thirty-five billion barrels, half of those of Iran, were in reality far greater; this low estimate was a consequence of the shortcomings of the IPC. In 1978 its reserves, which had not been re-evaluated, put Iraq in seventh place in the world, just behind Libya and far behind Kuwait and Iran.

Many experts shared Iraq's doubts and between 1988 and 1989 it is possible to observe a general re-evaluation of most of the great Middle Eastern producers' reserves, with a far higher re-evaluation for Iraq than for the others. Certainly the 'political' nature of these proceedings undermine their credibility to some extent, but the best established publications[13] today credit Iraq with 100 billion barrels of reserves, which would put the country in second place world-wide, after Saudi Arabia and in front of Kuwait (94.5 billions) and Iran (92.9), whilst Libya is thought to have only 22.8 billion barrels. For as long as these re-evaluations were not made, it was difficult for Iraq to justify its demands for production using its 'reserves' as an argument.

In 1975, after various revisions the government gave the INOC the task of producing 4 mb/d by 1981. Whilst pretending to limit its production below its capacities 'in order not to place our oil capital in the Western banks',[14] Iraq in fact increased production as far as its production and export capacities would allow. In 1979 it reached 3.4 mb/d (cf. Table 1), that is 137 per cent more than in 1972, whilst OPEC as a whole increased its production by only fourteen per cent, and Kuwait's reduced by twenty-four per cent. That of Iran, which was approaching 6 mb/d between 1972 and 1978, was reduced by almost a half in 1979. In 1979 Iraq was the second largest OPEC producer, and the second largest exporter

12. *Revolutionary Iraq*, p. 89.
13. Cf. B.P. *Statistical Review of World Energy*, 1990
14. Tayih Abd al-Karim, minister of oil in 1978, cited by *Arab Oil and Gas Directory*, 1979–1980

world-wide. Its main clients were in Europe; Japan bought more from it than its allies in 'the East' (cf. Table 3). In order to realize its ambitions Iraq encountered the very difficult problem of the geographical outlets for its oil. Access to the sea (Gulf) is both physically complex and above all subject to the de facto control of Iran and Kuwait. As we know, the oil pipeline question arose at a very early stage in the tense relations with the IPC. The only viable solution was to increase pipes and destinations and to ensure that they remained in use by a policy of good relations with the transit countries. This was easier said than done. The Kirkuk-Banyas (Syria) and Tripoli (Lebanon) link had a capacity of 1.2 mb/d.[15] But a conflict with Syria led to its closure from 1976 to 1979 and then again in 1982 following Iranian pressure on Syria. With Turkey Iraq negotiated the construction of a pipeline which completely bypassed Syria, emerging near Iskanderun and running to Dortyol. Completed in 1977, this pipeline had a capacity of 700,000 b/d, later taken to one mb/d (a second parallel line was inaugurated in 1987). A 'strategic' pipeline capable of transporting oil in both directions, according to the terminal in use, linked the oil-fields of the north with those of the south: Haditha-Rumeila Fau.

The fact that Iraq is geographically enclosed is certainly one of the major obstacles to an independent oil policy and it made the policies of confrontation and power struggles which the country frequently adopted towards its neighbours particularly costly. One might also imagine that such power politics are explained by the desire definitively to gain control over the geographical outlets; but until now Iraq has always failed to gain the control to which it aspires.

On the eve of its entry into the war with Iran (22 September 1980), Iraq was one of the 'major' oil powers, whose importance seemed set to grow. The first years of the war led to a fall in production and exports, notably due to the routes out of the country; from April 1982 onwards the only usable one was the Turkish route. In 1985 a pipeline (500,000 b/d) was joined to that of Petroline in Saudi Arabia and in 1987 the Turkish line was doubled, carrying the entire export capacity of approximately 2, 200,000 b/d. With the prolonging of the war and increasing financial difficulties, the only oil policy was henceforth to produce and export as much as possible.

15. *Middle East Yearbook*, 1986, p. 116.

Iraq, OPEC (and OAPEC)

A founder member of OPEC and host to the conference at which the organization was created (of which the five initial members were Saudi Arabia, Iraq, Iran, Kuwait and Venezuela), Iraq has always had an ambiguous attitude towards the organization. Indeed it accused OPEC of first being under the thumb of the Iranians and the Saudis and then after 1979 of being under the tutelage of Saudi Arabia, which did not hesitate to flood the market on several occasions in order to lower the price of oil and to regain its share of the market.

Iraq, together with Algeria and Libya, were generally regarded as the 'clan of hard men' of OPEC, frequently violently opposed to Saudi policies applied towards the allies of the peninsula. Indeed, Iraq's oil situation immediately placed it in a position of contradiction, which was highlighted by its anxiety to combine militancy with the pursuit of its national interests in the strictest sense of the term. Traditionally the distinction is made amongst oil exporting countries between 'long-term producing' countries and 'short term producing' countries. The former have significant production capacities and reserves with a small population and limited investments. These countries (Saudi Arabia, United Arab Emirates, Kuwait, Qatar, but also Libya to some extent) attempt to maximize the economic value of their oil resources through abundant production, leading to moderate prices. Thus they safeguard their future markets (which would be jeopardized by too high prices, since demand is reduced and substitutes encouraged) and the increased volume of their exports ensure important revenue. This revenue frequently exceeds their needs and is placed in the Western economy, which they have no interest in seeing suffer from too high oil prices. This was the situation of the 'countries with a surplus' in the seventies.

Short-term producing countries have limited reserves and capacities, dense population and immediate need of the revenue. It is in their interest to limit production, leading to high prices, bringing them revenue while using their reserves sparingly. The long-term consequences of high prices hardly concern them. In OPEC Algeria, Indonesia, Nigeria, the Gabon, Ecuador and to some extent Venezuela belong to this group.

In some respects Iraq and Iran belong to the first group (reserves, capacities) and in others (population, military and economic needs) they find themselves alongside the supporters of high prices and production controls. Iraq's position was therefore often out of step with that of OPEC; an automatic radicalism was combined with the refusal to apply the decisions of the organization when they did not suit the country, which frequently led to its isolation. Iraq accused OPEC of not really having supported it in its conflicts with the IPC (after the nationalization of 1972, for example, OPEC recommended that its members refuse an increase in their production to compensate for the purchases which the IPC had refused to make from Iraq, but Iran refused to comply).

Iraq played a limited role in the decisions to raise prices in October and December 1973. Generally Iraq had little influence throughout the period of great change 1971–1973, when the Saudis and the Iranians were the real instigators of policy, notably seventy per cent then 127 per cent rises which led to the first oil crisis.

In 1977–1978 Iraq was accused by a number of its partners of consenting to discounts or privileged conditions to ensure exports at any price, at a time when the excessive level of the official price had led to a drop in demand. Observers note Iraq's capacity to remain intransigent on principle, closely to follow developments in the market whilst playing on quality differentials and on quarterly revisions of its price lists (in 1975 when the Middle East's production fell by ten per cent Iraq succeeded in increasing its own by seventeen per cent) .[16]

Relations with OAPEC (Organization of Arab Petroleum Exporting Countries, created in 1968) were also charged with ambiguity. The spearhead of the political use of the 'oil weapon' in October 1973, Iraq presented such radical proposals (for example the nationalization of all American interests in the Arab world) that they were rejected by all other members. For this reason Iraq would paradoxically become the only Arab producer not to implement the oil embargo called for by the OAPEC.

Iraq and the Quotas

It rapidly became clear to OPEC after 1973 that it would not be possible to maintain very high oil prices, incorporating a high tax element, without limiting production. Until the end of the seventies demand continued to rise (except in 1974–1975) and Saudi Arabia

16. Cf. Penrose, p. 518.

maintained the equilibrium whenever necessary by adjusting production. The question became crucial from 1981 on, when the fall in world demand for oil and the height of production from non-OPEC countries combined to stimulate very high prices. It was then necessary to consider limiting production and to divide the limitations between member countries; the issue of quotas was born.

In March 1982 the first allocation of quotas was decided, for a global OPEC level of 18 mb/d (when production had exceeded 30 mb/d in 1979) (cf. Table 6). Iraq and Iran, at war, were each allocated 1.2 mb/d, a very low figure, but one which reflected the fall in their export capacity, due to the conflict between them. Iran explicitly refused its quota and decided to go it alone, i.e. to sell as much as it was possible to export by gradually reducing prices. Iraq's attitude was more subtle, foreshadowing its future behaviour. It accepted the quota, but as it explained in 1985 when it refused the same quota, it was only because it could not produce any more than this anyway and because it wanted to show a spirit of solidarity without actually feeling constrained. At bottom Iraq accepted the principle of quotas, but objected to the bases upon which they were calculated, which gave too much weight to previous production, reserves and capacities. Iraq believed that the sacrifices it had made in the struggle to obtain oil for the Arabs, the under-estimation of its reserves by the IPC, and the low levels of production chosen by the company, had placed it in an unfavourable position faced with these criteria.[17] It argued that it was necessary to place greater emphasis on demographic criteria, on a country's need to finance development and on the effective needs of the country. Quotas should not be permitted to certain states, just to accumulate investments abroad, when others lacked vital resources. Iraq believed it was quite justified in refusing quotas if it did not approve of the logic behind their calculation.

Gradually, with the prolonging of the war, the major issue became that of parity with Iran (obviously for entirely political reasons). Iraq became all the more insistent on this point from 1983, when Iran was allocated a far higher quota than its own (2.4 mb/d as opposed to 1.2 mb/d in 1983). This discrimination was repeated in 1984 (2.3 mb/d for Iran, 1.2 mb/d for Iraq). From 1985 onwards

---

17. For the functioning and weighting of various criteria, see *PIW*, 10 November 1986.

Iraq was 'exempted' from quotas (estimated Iraqi production was added to the OPEC ceiling), or refused the quotas it was allocated. The OPEC conference in November 1988 (three months after the cease-fire) adopted the principle of parity and granted Iran and Iraq a quota of 2.64 mb/d. This principle was retained in 1989 and for the first half of 1990 (the quota was then 3.14 mb/d for each country, which exceeded their effective production of 1989). In August 1990 quotas were suspended until the return of a 'normal' situation. In February 1991 Iraqi production was estimated at 75,000 b/d.

On the eve of the invasion of Kuwait in June and July 1990, Iraq seemed to be exercising an influence within OPEC which it had hitherto been unable to achieve. It vehemently denounced those countries which encouraged very low oil prices by greatly exceeding their quotas; this referred to the UAE and to Kuwait. Iraq and Iran united in obtaining OPEC's support for high prices (the 'target' price rose from $18 to $21 per barrel) when North Sea 'Brent', which might serve as a reference point, was unable to get $16 on 6 July. Even if it was unable to impose its ultimate aim (a target price of $25) Iraq appeared to be the victor of the confrontation. Indeed it had laid down the law to Saudi Arabia and Kuwait (according to an American journalist the latter had come round because 'when you have a pistol at your head, you have to agree'[18]). Striking up a tactical alliance with Iran and imposing a solution to suit its own interests, for the second time in fifteen years Iraq was in the process of becoming one of the great world oil powers and the major regional power. But on 2 August 1990, with the invasion of Kuwait, Iraq sabotaged its own ambitions.

IRAQI OIL POTENTIAL: THE PRESENT SITUATION AND OUTLOOK FOR THE FUTURE

Reserves, Capacities and Areas of Production

The present figure for Iraqi reserves is 100 billion barrels, i.e. more than 13 billion tonnes. Probably this figure, necessarily an approximation, is too low, given the Iraqi tendency to underestimate the rates of recovering known reserves, and given the fact that the very promising areas (for example the extension of the Zagros mountains in Iraq, near some very important Iranian reserves) have not yet been prospected to any great extent. Some extreme estimates

18. *Le Monde*, 28 July 1990.

go as high as 280 billion barrels.[19] Limiting ourselves to the well-established estimates, Iraq possesses ten per cent of world reserves and thirteen per cent of OPEC reserves. In seizing Kuwait Iraq was trying to control almost a fifth (nineteen per cent) of world reserves; it is not possible, however, to confirm that this was the main aim of the operation. Iraq's gas resources are far more modest; with 2.4 per cent of world reserves it possesses five times less than Iran's known gas reserves.

Current production derives almost equally from the 'old' fields of the north, where the giant oil field at Kirkuk is of major importance (production capacity was estimated at 1.3 mb/d in 1990), and the more recently developed deposits of the south, whose potential is still partly unknown. The Rumeila oil field is almost equal in capacity to that of Kirkuk. New discoveries have been made mainly in the south (Zubair 250 000 b/d possible by the year 2000), West Qurna (a potential 400 000 b/d by the year 2000) and Majnun, very close to the south-eastern border with Iran (a potential 400,000 b/d by 2000)[20]. Before it invaded Kuwait it seemed possible that by the end of the century Iraq would have a production capacity of five million b/d, at the cost of an investment of more than $10 billion.

Following the war an optimistic assessment would be a return to the capacity of 1990 by 1995 (3.3 mb/d) and it would be utopian to think that it could reach four million b/d by the year 2000.

Estimates of the investment necessary are all the more difficult because no one knows the exact extent of the destruction. Some interesting indications of the amount required (before the war) were, however, provided by the INOC; it would be necessary to invest $15,000 to $17,000 to increase reserves by one b/d. This prospect led the government in February 1990 to return to an idea from 1980, implying a real volte-face in Iraqi policy. It called on foreign companies to invest in the development of oil in the country. Excluding prospecting and evaluation, the companies were asked to invest in development and in setting up operations, payment being made in crude oil. Initial reactions from the companies seem to have been very reserved, but these actions betrayed Iraq's oil ambitions, its financial distress and its concern to tackle the international oil market pragmatically. In any case the Kuwait war did not allow the experiment to progress very far.

19. Aad (1990), p. 6.
20. *Ibid.*, p. 20

The Insoluble Problem of the Export Routes

We know how important the question of export routes is for Iraq, the only major producer at the mercy of the good will of its neighbours. In successive stages oil pipelines to the Mediterranean via Syria, then Turkey, then Saudi Arabia and the Red Sea were constructed, whilst the Gulf terminals suffered a rather difficult situation. Theoretically the established capacity was 5,430 mb/d (cf. Table 5), but all these installations have never been in operation at the same time. During the course of the war with Iran the Turkish outlet proved to be invaluable, together with the Saudi link, but in 1991 Iraq has at its disposal practically no method of exporting its oil, with the exception of a few hundred thousand barrels/day via the Gulf ports. The re-opening of the Mediterranean routes, which were hardly touched by destruction, depends above all on developments in the political arena, allowing the operation of the Turkish routes to be resumed and, more problematically, the Syrian and Saudi routes too.

The Purchasers of Iraqi oil

Iraq has always preferred contracts with states and long-term treaties over playing the market place. The part of the principal purchasers is therefore determined by both geographical factors (the Mediterranean outlets make Iraqi oil attractive to the Europeans), political factors and the variable importance of trends in the market. (cf. Table 3).

In 1960 France, the FRG, Italy and the United Kingdom took more than sixty per cent of Iraqi exports (albeit 'IPC oil'). The OECD as a whole bought ninety-four per cent. In 1973 Great Britain and Germany stopped buying almost entirely, leaving the Italians and the French buying forty per cent of Iraqi sales. The OECD share was fixed at around two-thirds, with a somewhat more stable percentage subsequently. In 1980 France was Iraq's largest Western client by far, followed by Japan, whilst Italy's share fell. At the end of 1981 Iraq's reduced exports were much less concentrated, France never again rose above twelve per cent, whilst, together with Italy and Spain, it constituted the nucleus of the European clientele. In 1988-1989 the United States, with almost twenty per cent, became Iraq's largest client, followed by Japan, while the share of each of the 'three Europeans' hardly reached five per cent. Any resumption of Iraqi exports would therefore require a significant attempt at commercialization (or preferential prices).

Oil: Iraq's Export Monoculture

Iraq is one of the oil countries 'with potential', in which it is hoped that the resources procured by their crude oil will be the foundation of a rapidly growing diversified and balanced economy, with industrial and agricultural development gradually allowing a reduction in their dependence on oil. The efforts of 'revolutionary Iraq' during the sixties and above all the seventies have frequently been the subject of positive analysis on the part of observers, who would otherwise criticise Iraqi policies. Today we are forced to note the total failure of this diversification, reflected in the country's inability to export any goods other than oil and the weakness of the productive sector outside activities linked to rearmament. Without discussing the 'Iraqi model' it is necessary briefly to examine this persistent oil monoculture.

Iraq's oil revenues (cf. Table 7) stagnated between $500 million and $1 billion until 1972. Between 1972 and 1978 they amounted to between $8 and $10 billion, rising to almost $25 billion in 1979-1980. Between 1974 and 1980 Iraq's accumulated surplus exceeded $30 billion. Thus Iraq was accumulating reserves and selling them, just like the oil markets it so decried. Everything changed from 1980 onwards when oil revenues oscillated around $10 billion, Iraq got into considerable debt, having exhausted its reserves (doubtless since 1982). The guarantee which the potential oil seemed to present no doubt played a decisive role in the renewal of loans to Iraq by its Western suppliers (clearly, there were no considerations of this kind in the quasi-enforced loans from the countries of the peninsula).

The absence of any official statistics for almost fifteen years[21] does not allow us to pronounce on the capacity which the Iraqi economy has acquired to satisfy national needs, but we do have a useful indication of the degree of dependency: the share of oil in total exports. Since 1974 this figure has reached or exceeded ninety-nine per cent

---

21. Most of the statistics provided by the IMF for example, were interrupted in 1977. In some cases (foreign trade) figures are available until 1982 (cf. *International Financial Statistics*).

(once it fell to 98.6 per cent). Iraq is and will remain more dependent on oil for its resources and its foreign currency than any other OPEC country, for whom the average ratio has fallen from ninety-five per cent in 1974 to 77.5 per cent in 1989.[22]

SOME FINAL OBSERVATIONS

It seems that the analysis of oil policy allows us a better comprehension of certain important tendencies in Iraq's general policies and its understanding of international relations.

Its oil policies reflect a permanent frustration towards the companies (and towards the Western imperialism which they embodied), towards the rival OPEC producers and towards the neighbouring states who controlled transit. Combining militancy, pragmatism, errors of execution and above all of timing, they reflect both a remarkable continuity of aims and perspectives and an inability to take the action necessary to achieve its aims under the right conditions.

Oil provided the resources for impressive militarization. It has also been able a powerful motif of recourse to violence (the control of the oil outlets, the attraction of the reserves in Iranian Khuzistan and Kuwait), even though it is not possible to reduce the two last conflicts to mere oil wars. In any case Iraq is in a position of absolute dependence on oil in order to exchange its resources for foreign currency.

Traditionally privileged political and economic alliances between France and Iraq have their origins in the convergence of interests between the CFP and Iraq at the time of the IPC. Great Britain on the other hand, pillar of the IPC, for a long time embodied imperialism and was held responsible for the losses forced on Iran and Kuwait in the fifties and sixties.

On two occasions in sixty-five years, at the end of the seventies and in 1988–1989 Iraq was poised to succeed to the rank of a 'major' oil power and a major regional power. Twice the country ruined its own ambitions.

Whatever its tendency to persevere with strategic and tactical errors, Iraq nevertheless has an oil potential of enormous dimensions, which always opens up the possibility of saving the day, given

---

22. For detailed lists and comparisons, see OPEC *Annual Statistical Bulletin*, 1989.

effective policies and taking international realities into account. Iraqi policy is often capable of worse, but thanks to its oil, the worst is never quite the end.

BIBLIOGRAPHY

1. Abi Aad N. (1991) *Oil production and export capacities in the Gulf.* Observatoire Mediterranéen de l'Energie, June 1991, (1990) *OPEC Production Capacity consumption and export prospects for the year 2003*. Presented at the 4th annual conference on Middle East Strategy to the year 2003, Nicosia, October 1990.
2. Arab Baath Socialist Party, *Revolutionary Iraq 1968-1973*, (Baghdad, January 1974).
3. B.P. *Statistical Review of World Energy*, Annual.
4. Centre Arabe de recherche pétroliäre, *Arab oil and gas Directory*, (Paris), annual publication.
5. Chevalier J.M., *Le nouvel enjeu pétrolier*, (Calmann Levy, Paris, 1973.)
6. *Economie Prospective Internationale: Les grands auteurs de la scène énergétique mondiale*, 3rd quarter 1982.
7. IMF. *International Financial Statistics*—retrospective annual number (1950-1989).
8. Issawi C. (1982) *An Economic History of the Middle East and North Africa*, (New York, Columbia University Press,).
9. Longrigg S. (1988) *Oil in the Middle East*, 3rd edition, (Oxford University Press,).
10. *Middle East Yearbook*, annual.
11. OPEC. *Annual Statistical Bulletin*
12. Penrose E. and E. F. (1978), *Iraq, International relations and national development*, (London, Arthur Benn, 1978).
13. *Petroleum Intelligence Weekly*, weekly publication.
14. Sampson, A (1976) *Les 7 soeurs*, Alain Moreau, (Paris 1976), English edition, *The seven sisters* (1975).

Table 1 Iraqi oil production from the beginning to 1989

Year	production 1000 b/d	accumulated production 1000 barrels	percentage of annual change	Year	production 1000 b/d	accumulated production 1000 barrels	percentage of annual change
1928	2.7	988		1959	856.9	2,394,613	17.2
1929	3.0	2,083	11.1	1960	972.2	2,750,438	13.5
1930	2.0	2,813	−33.3	1961	1,007.1	3,118,030	3.6
1931	2.0	3,543	0.0	1962	1,009.2	3,486,388	0.2
1932	1.4	4,056	−30.0	1963	1,161.9	3,910,481	15.1
1933	1.6	4,640	14.3	1964	1,255.2	4,369,885	8.0
1934	16.5	10,662	931.3	1965	1,312.6	4,848,984	4.6
1935	78.1	39,169	373.3	1966	1,392.2	5,357,137	6.1
1936	85.7	70,535	9.7	1967	1,228.1	5,805,393	−11.8
1937	92.4	104,261	7.8	1968	1,503.3	6,355,601	22.4
1938	91.5	137,658	−1.0	1969	1,521.2	6,910,839	1.2
1939	85.5	168,866	−6.6	1970	1,548.6	7,476,078	1.8
1940	55.9	189,325	−34.6	1971	1,694.1	8,094,424	9.4
1941	36.3	202,575	−35.1	1972	1,465.5	8,630,797	−13.5

Table 1. (cont.)

Year	production 1000 b/d	accumulated production 1000 barrels	percentage of annual change	Year	production 1000 b/d	accumulated production 1000 barrels	percentage of annual change
1942	55.7	222,905	53.4	1973	2,018.1	9,367,404	37.7
1943	79.3	251,850	42.4	1974	1,970.6	10,086,673	-2.4
1944	92.5	285,705	16.6	1975	2,261.7	10,912,193	14.8
1945	100.1	322,241	8.2	1976	2,415.4	11,796,236	6.8
1946	101.8	359,398	1.7	1977	2,348.2	12,653,333	-2.8
1947	103.0	396,993	1.2	1978	2,562.0	13,588,475	9.1
1948	76.6	425,029	-25.6	1979	3,476.9	14,857,555	35.7
1949	90.6	458,098	18.3	1980	2,646.4	15,826,155	-23.9
1950	139.6	509,052	54.1	1981	897.4	16,153,707	-66.1
1951	180.8	575,044	29.5	1982	1,012.1	16,523,117	12.8
1952	389.0	717,418	115.2	1983	1,098.8	16,924,174	8.6
1953	581.4	929,629	49.5	1984	1,221.3	17,371,178	11.2
1954	636.2	1,161,842	9.4	1985	1,404.4	17,883,768	15.0
1955	697.0	1,416,247	9.6	1986	1,876.5	18,568,702	33.6
1956	641.0	1,650,853	-8.0	1987	2,358.7	19,429,617	25.7
1957	449.5	1,814,920	-29.9	1988	2,739.8	20,432,398	16.2
1958	731.3	2,081,845	62.7	1989	2,785.8	21,449,210	1.7

Sources: Direct communications to the Secretariat and Secondary Sources. OPEC *Annual Statistical bulletin 1990*.

Table 2 The development of oil production in OPEC member countries, 1960–1989 (mb/d)

	1960	1961	1962	1963	1964	1965	1966	1967	1968	1969
Algeria (1)	181.1	330.9	436.9	504.3	557.8	558.7	718.7	825.7	904.2	946.4
Ecuador	7.5	8.0	7.0	6.8	7.6	7.8	7.3	6.2	5.0	4.4
Gabon	15.4	14.9	16.4	17.7	21.0	24.9	28.6	69.0	91.9	99.8
Indonesia	409.6	424.3	453.4	444.0	456.6	480.6	464.6	505.4	600.7	742.3
I.R. Iran	1,067.7	1,202.2	1,334.5	1,491.3	1,710.7	1,908.3	2,131.8	2,603.2	2,839.8	3,375.8
Iraq	972.2	1,007.1	1,009.2	1,161.9	1,255.2	1,312.6	1,392.2	1,228.1	1,503.3	1,521.2
Kuwait (2)	1,691.8	1,735.0	1,957.8	2,096.3	2,301.0	2,360.3	2,484.1	2,499.8	2,613.5	2,773.4
S. P. Libyan A.J.	—	18.2	182.3	441.8	862.4	1,218.8	1,501.1	1,740.5	2,602.1	3,109.1
Nigeria	17.4	46.0	67.5	76.5	120.2	274.2	417.6	319.1	141.3	540.3
Qatar	174.6	177.2	186.2	191.5	215.3	232.6	291.3	323.6	339.5	355.5
Saudi Arabia	1,313.5	1,480.1	1,642.9	1,786.0	1,896.5	2,205.3	2,601.8	2,805.0	3,042.9	3,216.2
United Arab Emirates	—	—	14.2	48.2	186.8	282.2	360.0	382.1	496.6	627.8
Venezuela	2,846.1	2,919.9	3,199.8	3,247.9	3,392.8	3,472.9	3,371.1	3,542.1	3,604.8	3,594.1
TOTAL OPEC	8,696.9	9,363.8	10,508.1	11,514.2	12,983.9	14,339.2	15,770.2	16,849.8	18,785.6	20,906.3

Table 2 (cont.)

	1980	1981	1982	1983	1984	1985	1986	1987	1988	1989
Algeria	1,019.9	797.8	704.5	660.9	695.4	672.4	673.9	648.2	650.7	727.3
Ecuador	204.1	211.0	198.3	237.5	256.1	280.6	256.5	180.9	300.8	278.9
Gabon	174.5	151.4	155.1	155.4	157.4	171.7	164.7	154.5	157.0	204.3
Indonesia	1,575.7	1,604.2	1,324.8	1,245.3	1,280.1	1,181.5	1,256.8	1,158.1	1,177.5	1,231.0
I.R. Iran	1,467.3	1,315.9	2,391.3	2,441.7	2,032.4	2,192.3	2,037.1	2,297.6	2,305.4	2,814.1
Iraq	2,646.4	897.4	1,012.1	1,098.8	1,221.3	1,404.4	1,876.5	2,358.7	2,739.8	2,785.8
Kuwait	1,663.7	1,129.7	824.3	1,054.1	1,163.0	936.3	1,237.7	971.6	1,396.5	1,463.5
S. P. Libyan A.J.	1,831.6	1,217.8	1,136.0	1,104.9	984.6	1,023.7	1,308.0	972.5	1,029.8	1,129.2
Nigeria	2,058.0	1,439.6	1,287.0	1,235.5	1,388.0	1,498.9	1,466.6	1,323.0	1,367.6	1,716.3
Qatar	471.4	415.2	332.0	269.0	325.3	290.1	313.6	291.4	319.4	320.2
Saudi Arabia	9,900.5	9,808.0	6,483.0	4,539.4	4,079.1	3,175.0	4,784.2	3,975.2	5,086.3	5,064.5
United Arab Emirates	1,701.9	1,502.3	1,248.8	1,149.0	1,069.0	1,056.8	1,308.9	1,417.7	1,509.5	1,857.8
Venezuela	2,165.0	2,108.3	1,895.0	1,800.8	1,695.5	1,564.0	1,648.5	1,575.5	1,578.1	1,747.4
TOTAL OPEC	26,880.0	22,598.6	18,992.2	16,992.3	16,347.2	15,447.7	18,333.1	17,324.8	19,618.5	21,340.3

Notes: (1) Prior to 1978, including condensate production.
(2) Including production from Neutral Zone.

Sources: Direct communications to the Secretariat
Twentieth Century Petroleum Statistics, De Golyer and MacNaughton
Petroleum Intelligence Weekly.
Weekly Petroleum Argus.
OPEC Annual Statistical bulletin 1989.

Table 3 The main buyers of Iraqi crude oil 1960–1989 (percentage of Iraqi exports according to destination)

	1960	1973	1980	1985	1989
France	17.3	20.8	19.3	12.2	5.0
FRG	10.1	1.9	2.4	0.6	n.d.
Italy	17.7	21.4	9.8	8.9	4.4
Spain	–	–	5.2	11.2	4.7
UK	15.9	3.0	3.3	1.1	1.5
Western Europe as whole	–	–	53.1	62.4	38.4
US	–	–	1.5	5.1	19.4
Japan	8.2	0.4	13.2	6.4	9.5
OECD	93.8	66.7	69.2	73.7	65.4

Table 4 Purchases of Iraqi crude oil by France (mb/d) 1976–1989

Year	French purchases	Iraqi Exports	Year	French purchases	Iraqi Exports
1976	342.3	2,241	1983	39	725.4
1977	372.3	2,167	1984	76	856
1978	419.3	2,384	1985	133	1,085.4
1979	499.3	3,275	1986	120	1,395.5
1980	475	2,459	1987	131.6	1,717
1981	46.6	697.4	1988	121.2	2,095
1982	30.1	811.4	1989	115.4	2,260

Sources: OPEC *Annual Statistical Review*, various years.

Table 5 Iraqi oil export outlets and the situation in 1991

Date brought into service	Route	Length km	Capacity 1000 b/d	Present situation (Mid 1991)
1952	Kirkuk-Banyas	890	700	Closed since 1982
1960	Kirkuk-Tripoli	855	500	Closed since 1982
1975	Haditha-Rumeila Fau	760	980	Damaged
1977	Kirkuk-Dortyol (Turkey no. 1)	920	1,000	Theoretically operational, closed by Turkey
1985	IPSA 1 linked to the Saudi Petroline to Yanbo Red Sea	640	500	Pumping stations destroyed, closed by Saudi Arabia
1989	IPSA 2 to the Red Sea	740	1,150	
Total oil pipelines			5,430	Hardly any capacity
Gulf terminals			1,300	Destroyed, the Port of Basra can export 300000 b/d
By lorry to Akaba (Jordan)			100	Usable

Sources: Observatoire Médierranéen de l'Energie: Oil production and export capacities on the Gulf: Post war situation and prospects to 2000 (Sophia Antipolis, June 1991).

Table 6 Iraq and the OPEC quotas (mb/d)

Date	OPEC ceiling	Iraqi quota	Iranian quota
March 1982	18	1.2 (1)	1.2
March 1983	17.5	1.2	2.4
March 1984	16	1.2	2.3
Dec. 1986	15.06 plus Iraqi production	– (2)	2.36
1st 1/2 1987	15.8	1.466	2.255
2nd 1/2 1987	16.6	1.540	2.369
1st 1/2 1988	15.006 plus Iraqi production	– (3)	2.36
1st 1/2 1989	18.5	2.64	2.64
4th 1/4 1989	20.5	2.92	2.92
1st 1/2 1990	22.08	3.140	3.140
August 1990	abolition of quotas until the end of the war		

Notes: (1) Iraq would not accept 1.2 except during the period where the war prevented it from producing more.
(2) Iraq was placed "outside the quotas" and in the calculations of production OPEC was credited with 2/3 of Iranian production, i.e. 1.56 mb/d.
(3) Iraq refused any quotas which did not place it in a position of equality with Iran.

Table 7 Iraqi oil revenues (Value of oil exports in millions of dollars)

Year	Sum	Year	Sum	Year	Sum
1950	18.8	1975	8,227	1983	7,816
1955	206	1976	9,201	1984	9,354
1960	455	1977	9,560	1985	10,685
1965	660	1978	10,913	1986	6,905
1970	780	1979	21,382	1987	11,416
1972	1,027	1980	26,296	1988	10,952
1973	1,842	1981	10,422	1989	14,500
1974	6,534	1982	10,096		

Source: OPEC *Annual Statistical Bulletin,* 1989

The Development of Agrarian Policies since 1958

Habib Ishow

In Iraq, as in the other countries of the Middle East, relations between the central power and the peasantry are essentially relations of conflict, since the government is traditionally made up of and controlled by townsmen who behave towards their rural communities in the manner of contemptuous conquerors and oppressors.

Thus, relations between the peasantry and central power are determined above all by opposing interests. And for this reason they have evolved into relations of force. Whenever the state is weakened its influence is limited to the large towns and their immediate surroundings; the overwhelming majority of rural communities then become autonomous. On the other hand, as soon as the state grows stronger again it attempts to regain control of the rural communities through the imposition of numerous taxes. Since the 1950s, thanks to modern technological progress and to the means of coercion the state has in its power, this control has become quite formidable. It extends throughout the peasantry and has a direct influence on agrarian activity and structures. There is thus an unyielding antagonism between the rural world and the central power, an antagonism which is further reinforced by the existence of numerous rural communities inhabiting their own areas, each with its own language, culture and religion, its own history and particular ethnic identity. The most important, in descending order, are the Arab[1], Kurdish, Chaldean and Turkoman communities.

---

1. Arabs in Iraq are for the most part Assyro-Chaldeans and Christians who converted to Islam, becoming arabophones through religion, following the Arab conquest of Mesopotamia under the banner of Islam during the first half of the seventh century of the Christian era. The religious and legal system, which taxed the Assyro-Chaldeans heavily and subjected them to a particularly vexatious and

On the eve of the 1958 revolution agrarian structures were characterized by the pronounced concentration of landed property in the hands of a small privileged group and by the lack of land for the vast majority of peasants. This imbalance was the result of more than a century of state intervention in this domain. Indeed at this time eighty-five per cent of a total 253,000 landowners owned only seven per cent of a total of 8 million hectares of agricultural land, with almost twenty-nine per cent holding less than one hectare per family, that is to say they owned less than the minimum land required to sustain life.[2] To this mass of small landowners should be added the 1.5 million landless peasants who worked in the agricultural sector as share-croppers or day-labourers.[3]

By contrast, less than two per cent of landowners possessed sixty-nine per cent of agricultural land.[4] In the south of the country two shaikhs owned more than 250,000 hectares each.[5] The inequality of agrarian structures, for the most part the result of land reforms,[6] was one of the factors which periodically stirred up the peasantry under the Hashimite monarchy.

Since 1958, when the monarchy was overthrown, state intervention on a massive scale has led to great changes in agricultural structures. Agricultural policies since that time have been characterized by two phases: the first covers the years from 1958 to 1980, the second was introduced at the end of 1980.

THE FIRST PHASE: 1958–1980: THE ERA OF IDEOLOGY AND IMPROVIZATION

Following the overthrow of the Hashimite monarchy on 14 July 1958 by General Abd al-Karim Qasim's army, the country's new

oppressive social status, encouraged most of them to convert to Islam to escape the discriminatory system instituted towards them by the new conquerors of the country in all spheres of life.

2. Ministry of Agriculture (Iraq), *Dalil al-qita al-zirai fi al-Iraq li-amay 1968–1969* (Guide to the agricultural sector in Iraq for the years 1968–1969), Baghdad, Ministry of Agriculture, Diwan General Administration, Department of Agricultural Economy, publication no. 7 November 1970, p. 11.

3. Abd al-Sahib Alwan, *Dirasat fi al-islah al-zirai*. (Studies on agrarian reform), Baghdad, Matba'at al-Aswaq al-Tijariya, 1961, p. 150.

4. Ministry of Agriculture (Iraq), *op. cit.*, p. 11.

5. D. Warriner, *Land reform and development in the Middle East*, (Oxford University Press, 1962, 2nd edn.), pp. 141–2.

6. H. Ishow, 'Le statut foncier, la paysannerie et le pouvoir politique en Irak depuis 1921', *Revue de l'Occident Musulman et de la Méditerranée*, 34, 1982, pp. 105–18.

leaders, the military and its civilian allies had no agricultural policies appropriate to the rural world. They had virtually no knowledge about anything which concerned the peasantry—its social and political structures, its mentality, its living conditions, the organization and functioning of its economy and above all the administration of the ownership of its lands. Nevertheless, for chiefly political and ideological, and less so for economic and social reasons, the country's new leaders improvised policies which would profoundly alter agricultural structures.

On a political level, the leaders sought allies in order to consolidate their position against a possible coalition of forces favourable to the old order. Indeed, the agricultural policy of the military and its allies had a double objective. On the one hand it wanted to destroy feudalism in the Iraqi countryside, regarded as the main pillar of the monarchy, the ally of imperialism in the country and the cause of all Iraq's ills. Consequently the elimination of the great landowners was considered to be a priority. As General Qasim asserted in a declaration, it was in order to achieve this objective[7] that law no. 30 on agricultural reform was promulgated, in great haste, on 30 September 1958, two and a half months after the military coup d'état of 14 July of the same year. On the other hand, the new leaders' enactment of general agricultural reform and its use as a political measure was also intended to apply pressure on the sympathies of the peasants, who at the time formed the majority of the population, by creating a class of small landowners who would support them. Finally, the military hoped that these policies would help to legitimize their power in public opinion, giving them a benevolent leading role in the affairs of the country.

On an ideological level all the succeeding governments in Baghdad during this period invoked socialism under various guises, which formed the official ideology. In this respect, during the early years of General Qasim's régime the Iraqi Communist Party played a very important role in the agricultural sector, thanks to favourable political circumstances. On the external level Iraq strengthened its links of friendship with the Soviet Union through the conclusion of an accord of economic and technological cooperation, signed on 9 March 1959. Internally Ibrahim Kubba, Minister for Agricultural Reform, a Marxist, though not affiliated to the

7. M. Khadduri, *Republican Iraq, a study in Iraqi politics since the revolution of 1958*, (Oxford University Press, 1969), p. 152.

Communist Party, allowed members of the Party to occupy key posts in his ministry and thus to control its activities. Thanks to this privileged position, inspired by the Soviet model in this area, the Iraqi Communist Party implemented a double strategy. On the one hand it accelerated the expropriation of land which exceeded limits fixed by law. On the other hand as far as possible it hampered and restricted the distribution of these lands to the peasants in the form of private property, since the distribution of the land went against its ideology, the aim of which was the collectivization of land and its cultivation within the framework of collective cooperatives.[8]

The Arif brothers, Abd al-Salam and Abd al-Rahman, who governed the country from 1963 to 1966 and from 1966 to 1968 respectively, effected no important changes to the agricultural policies defined by General Qasim's régime.

By contrast, the Baathists, who took power following the two military coups on 17 and 30 July 1968, set about strengthening the state's grip on the rural world. Indeed, from this date onwards the central power intensified its control on the principal resources of the country which included agricultural resources, in order to integrate them within a planned economy and apply 'socialism' to the entire Iraqi economy.

In the agricultural sector the political report of the eighth Baath Party Congress held in Baghdad in January 1974 clearly underlined the authorities' intention in the following terms:

> New production yields and new traditions have appeared in the place of the old ones which are gradually fading. However, current forms of rural property, despite the progress which they represent over ancient feudal and capitalist types, are not yet socialist. We must rapidly take the political, legislative and economic measures necessary to expand the socialist sector according to three forms; state farms, collective farms and cooperatives, in order to form a predominant and developed sector on all levels. Equally, we must increase our efforts to spread the socialist culture amongst the ranks of the peasantry.[9]

---

8. D. Warriner, *Land reform in principle and practice*, (Oxford, 1969), p. 81. See also: E. and E.F. Penrose, *Iraq, international relations and national development*, (London, 1978), p. 247; R. Gabbay, *Communism and agrarian reform in Iraq*, (London, 1978), p. 77.

9. Baath Party, *L'Iraq révolutionnaire 1968–1973. Rapport politique adopté par le 8e congrès régional du parti ba'thiste*. Baghdad, January 1974, printed September 1976 in Milan, p. 110.

In accordance with its political and ideological objectives, the central power therefore intervened excessively in the agricultural sector throughout this period, with the enactment of three agricultural laws in 1958, 1970 and 1975.

The Agrarian Reform of 1958

The agrarian reform Law No. 30 of 30 September 1958 applied to various aspects of Iraqi agriculture.[10] It limited the agricultural property owned by one person or granted to one person by virtue of the *tapu* or *lazma*[11] to 250 hectares of irrigated land or to 500 hectares of dry land. Where one landowner owned both irrigated land and dry cultivated lands, one hectare of the former category of land was considered to be worth two hectares of the latter (article 1).

In order to avoid fraud the law excluded the *waqf* (the religious charitable institution) from inheritance or association. This is because in the past landowners had often used the institution of the *waqf* to protect their lands from the frequent and arbitrary confiscation effected by the central authorities.

Likewise, land in excess of the limits authorized by the law could not be transferred to or divided amongst heirs, spouses or relatives. The landowner affected by this limitation had to choose which land he would prefer to retain, within the limits outlined above.

However, the law allowed for three exceptions which escaped the fixed ceiling of the provisions of the first article (art. 3). The first concerned societies or associations whose aim was to increase the amount of land cultivated or to develop the national economy by establishing breeding or agricultural production projects. This exception was significant in that it allowed large landowners to form societies or associations with a view to retaining their lands in full, which was both contrary to social justice and to the spirit of the agricultural reform. The second exception protected the creditor who had acquired his agricultural property in place of the

10. M.S. Hasan, *Dirasat fi al-iqtisad al-'Iraqi* (Studies on the Iraqi economy), (Beirut, 1966), pp. 383–404.

11. The title of *tapu* was established by the Ottoman land law of 1858, whilst that of *lazma* was a new form of land status, established by laws 50 and 51 in 1932. In principle these two statutes accorded the beneficiaries nothing but the right of tenure of the lands awarded them, the right of ownership belonged to the state. But in practice the tenants of the *tapu* or *lazma* had all the rights derived from private ownership; they could dispose of the land and its fruits, and had the right to sell and to pass it on to their heirs.

reimbursement of debts, following the sale of the property by the authorities in execution of a judgement pronounced against a debtor who was unable to pay his debts. This exception, too, reinforced the position of the major landowners, since many of them had recently acquired all or part of their property by forcing those peasants who were overwhelmed by debts to sell their land. Finally, the third exception concerned private individuals who were permitted to possess lands in excess of the legal limits if the excess was the result of an inheritance or a donation. These exceptions highlight the true intent of the political powers in this sphere. In reality they wanted to limit as far as possible the effects of this law, to make allowances for the interests of their allies and their sympathizers from the privileged social classes.

Two remarks might be made on the provisions of the agricultural law concerning the limits set on the land owned by one person. Firstly it should be noted that the landowner was recognized by the law (art. 1) This recognition was not fortuitous. It expressed the desire of the new leaders to create a relatively large class of landowners. The military which overthrew the régime in 1958 was not against landowners. But the limit set by the law was too high. It did not permit the retrieval of enough agricultural land for redistribution amongst the landless and small peasants. A marked disparity remained, too, between large and small landowners. Once again this illustrates the influence of the large landowners on General Qasim's government.

Nor did the law take into consideration direct and indirect means of enforcement. Above all, it did not settle the serious problem of absenteeism. Indeed, this was not even mentioned. This practice led to the abandonment of lands and also involved excessive transfers of revenue from the countryside to the city. The rural world was disadvantaged to a considerable degree, since it was deprived of the investment necessary to improve agricultural production. The chiefs of the tribes, leading citizens, influential politicians and major businessmen in the towns were thus able to continue to exploit their lands using share-croppers or day-labourers, thus maintaining the property rent.

Consequently, as in the past, most agricultural land remained in the hands of non-farmers, with all the trying problems which this entailed for the peasants and for the development of Iraqi agriculture.

Expropriation principally affected the very large landowners.

Indeed, the total number of owners affected by the law was only 3,277.[12] Those owners whose lands had been expropriated under article one of the agricultural law of 1958 had a right to compensation (art. 6). This applied to all expropriated lands which were owned as private property, or by virtue of *tapu* or *lazma*. Compensation was also awarded for buildings, fittings, motor pumps, agricultural machinery and fruit trees on the expropriated land. Generally, compensation was paid in the form of public treasury bonds issued at a tax of three per cent interest per year, for a period of twenty years if the total did not exceed 10,000 dinars,[13] or forty years for sums in excess of this. The Ministry of Agrarian Reform valued the total amount of compensation paid at 131.5 million dinars, not including buildings, fittings and agricultural machinery.[14]

It is clear from the principle of expropriation that the authors of the military coup of 1958 confirmed the rights of the major landowners to the lands they had usurped from the peasants under previous legislation, in particular the Ottoman law of 1858 and the Iraqi law of 1932. Precisely these two laws had allowed the concentration of land in the hands of a small privileged group, who robbed the peasants of their rights by various fraudulent means, the application of pressure or through intimidation. The agricultural reform of 1958 not only failed to correct these abuses, but actually recognized the rights of the large landowners to the lands they had usurped, as a consequence of which it provided for the issue of large sums of money by way of compensation for expropriation.

The advantages accorded to the large landowners by the agrarian reform of 1958 may be explained by the interests and social origins of the authors of the 1958 coup d'état. Indeed it is interesting to note that most of the new leaders had a direct interest in the agrarian policy they implemented. The organization of free officers was essentially comprised of sons of well-to-do Muslim and conservative families; of the fifteen members of which it was comprised, five owned vast amounts of land and four came from commercial

---

12. Ministry of Information, *L'économie de l'Iraq. Développement et perspectives 1958-1976-1980*, Baghdad, printed in Madrid 1977, p. 49.

13. The Iraqi dinar is divided into 1000 fils. It was worth one pound sterling or U.S.$2.8 in the 1950s. This became $3.38 during the 1970s. On 1 January 1989 it was worth $3.21 (official exchange rate) or approximately 16 francs.

14. Abd al-Wahhab M. Dahiri, *Al-siyasa al-zira'iya, Iqtisadiyat al-islah al-zira'i*. (Agrarian policy; the economy of the agrarian reform), (Baghdad, 1976), p. 282.

families. Likewise, General Qasim's first government included thirteen ministers, of which three were major landowners and six were businessmen, four of whom who owned important lands.[15] Thus, many of the new leaders belonged to a privileged group of the old order. And their legislation in the agricultural domain naturally protected their own fundamental interests.

The agrarian reform of 1958 stipulated that expropriated lands and the State lands should be distributed in plots to landless and small peasants, enabling each of them to own property varying between 7.5 and fifteen hectares of irrigated land or between 15 and 30 hectares of dry land (art. 11), according to region and type of cultivation. The beneficiaries of the agrarian reform had to fulfil the following conditions: They had to be of Iraqi nationality and of age. They had to be farmers by profession. They were not allowed to own more than 15 hectares of irrigated land or 30 hectares of dry land. Priority was given in the first place to the distribution of land to those who were effectively farming the land in the capacity of share-croppers, in an association or as owner, and in the second place to those with large families or who were least provided for amongst the inhabitants of a region (art. 12). The new owners had to pay for their plot of land and for existing trees, buildings, fittings, agricultural machinery, motor pumps, in so far as their plot benefited from them. This price was determined by the valuation commission of the Ministry for Agricultural Reform. The total sum was to be paid in equal annual instalments for a period of twenty years (art. 14). But because many beneficiaries experienced difficulties in paying the instalments, the conditions of payment were modified in the amendment of 31 December 1964. From this date onwards beneficiaries had only to pay half of the value of their plot of land in annual instalments over a period of forty years.

The agrarian law also organized production links between the peasants and land owners. These links had evolved under the monarchy in a manner which strongly disadvantaged the peasants. The latter, originally co-proprietors of lands in the vast majority of cases, had been transformed progressively into share-croppers or day-labourers, subject to harsh economic and social conditions. Law no. 28 of 1933 on the rights and duties of farmers had

15. H. Batatu, *The old social classes and the revolutionary movements of Iraq*, (Princeton University Press, 1978), pp. 778–82.

reduced the peasants to the status of bondsmen. Share-croppers in debt were obliged by this law to continue to work on the lands of their master until all the debts which they had contracted with him or his manager had been repaid. Since most of them were incapable of repaying their debts they remained under the power of their master indefinitely. It is for this reason that the new leaders had to improve or at least attempt to improve the social and economic conditions of the peasants in order to obtain their support.

For these various reasons the agrarian law of 1958 also regulated relations between the peasants and landowners in three main areas:

1) the conditions of contract for share-cropping

2) the respective obligations of share-croppers and owners

3) the division of produce between the relevant parties.

The owner's share ranged from thirty-five to forty-five per cent of the harvest, if he was also owner of the means of irrigation and responsible for administration. In contrast, the share-cropper's share was in the order of sixty-five per cent, from which in general the seeds which the owner advanced on the harvest at the beginning of the agricultural season had to be deducted. The share-cropper's share came to around fifty per cent of the harvest. All things considered, the new system for the division of the harvest was fairer and certainly more favourable to the share-cropper than that of the old order.

The Supreme Committee for Agrarian Reform could modify the percentages of the parties concerned on a regional basis if the circumstances and general interest required (art. 41). Any legal disputes which arose between the contracting parties were settled by the commission for conflicts established in every sub-prefecture (*qada*) or chief town (*nahiya*) where a reconciliation tribunal was established.

A number of observations may be made on the organization of relations between the share-croppers and the owners. First of all, although it was an improvement over the old system, the length of the share-cropping contract—three years—remained too short. This hardly encouraged share-croppers to invest in their plot of land with a view to improving and augmenting production. This was above all true for irrigated lands in general and for central and southern areas in particular. It was principally for this reason that the share-croppers cultivated only those plots which were immediately profitable. The share-cropping contract therefore remained precarious and its effects detrimental to the progress of agriculture. The agrarian reform also took no measures to award fair compensation to protect the rights of share-croppers who had made improvements to their plot of land. The inadequacies of the agrarian law in this area therefore prejudiced the development of agriculture. For under such conditions share-croppers were not encouraged to make improvements, such as the digging and maintenance of irrigation canals, drainage or other work necessary to improve the soil or increase production.

Finally, the agrarian reform of 1958 did not organize relations between share-croppers and the owners in the orchards and other plantations. Thus, the share-croppers who worked there remained subject to the harsh conditions of a traditional and unfair system of production. The most direct consequence of this loophole in the law was the neglect of the orchards and palm-groves, and in many cases their abandonment. The fact that the law did not regulate the relations between these two categories of people in this sector may once again be chiefly explained by the influence of the important families and politicians on the government. Owning vast lands, such families naturally had a direct interest in maintaining the traditional system of share-cropping.

The Agrarian Reform of 1970

Following the supervening political changes of July 1968, a new law on agrarian reform, no. 117, was promulgated in 1970, repealing that of 1958 for essentially political reasons.[16] From this date onwards this new general law governed various aspects of agriculture.

Its fundamental objectives remained the same as the preceding law, although it contained certain modifications. The first of these concerned the reduction of large agricultural properties, the limits of which varied between 250 and 500 hectares for dry cultivated land and between 10 and 150 hectares for irrigated land, according to the quality of the land, rainfall conditions in each region, and according to irrigation methods and types of cultivation. In addition, landowners no longer had the right to choose which land they wanted to retain (art.3). The agrarian reform of 1970 provided for

16. Superior Agricultural Council, *Majmuat tashriat al-qita al-zirai* (Collection of legislation in the agricultural sector) (Baghdad, 1977), pp. 137–86.

two exceptions to the authorized limits to the amount of land which one person was allowed to own. In the first case it created a sizable reserve to the advantage of lands planted with date-palms and other fruit trees for a minimum of five years, comprising 160 trees per hectare. These properties were not subject to the reform, and were therefore permitted to exceed the maximum authorized limits (art. 2). Situated primarily in the irrigated area of the Mesopotamian plain, they included the best land in this region. How might this exception be explained? The official account declares that the agrarian law of 1970 encouraged palm-grove and orchard owners to develop these lands and thus to preserve national resources.[17] But this explanation is inadequate on two counts. Firstly it applies to all agricultural land. These constitute national resources whether they are planted with fruit trees or whether cereals, vegetables and industrial plants are grown on them. Agriculture in these various branches develops to the extent to which all owners are encouraged and aided. This explanation does not account for the retention of the huge disparities between landowners, since one of the fundamental objectives of the agrarian reform was the creation of greater equality between the various classes of landowners, and in particular the liberation of peasants from the grip of the great land-owning nobility. In addition orchards and palm-groves have far greater yields than cereal-growing lands, for example, which allow their owners to make greater profits. In any case this exception is in complete contradiction to the spirit of the 1970 agrarian law. The most plausible reason for this exception rests on the fact that the owners of the orchards and palm-groves exercised significant pressure on the new leaders, with a view to protecting their wealth from the effects of the agrarian reform. Moreover, many of the leaders themselves owned large amounts of land.[18] It was rumoured, for example, that the former President of the Republic, Ahmad Hasan al-Bakr, who ruled Iraq from 1968 to 1979, had become a large landowner, owning in particular vast areas of orchards and palm-groves. This would be entirely in keeping with the tradition whereby the central power makes discretionary awards of important land to politicians to the detriment of the peasants.

In the second place the agrarian law of 1970, like that of 1958, allowed the ownership of land in excess of the authorized limits if it

17. *Ibid.*
18. Batatu, *op. cit.*, pp. 1086–9.

had been obtained through an inheritance or by donation. The second modification applied to the right to compensation for expropriated land. The agrarian law of 1970 now abolished this right. This abolition was justified by the fact that the ownership of land belonged to the state (art. 49). Logically, therefore, the state could not and did not have to pay compensation for that which had been legally returned to it. In reality, this aspect of the agrarian law was wrongly inspired by the Muslim law of the period during which the country was conquered by the Arabs under the banner of Islam in the first half of the seventh century AD. The new conquerors of Mesopotamia had deprived the peasants of their right to own the land that they cultivated, by confiscating this property for their own profit, regarding the peasants as mere grantees of the lands they farmed and subjecting them to heavy land and other taxes.

The 1970 agrarian reform was applied retrospectively, annulling the balance of compensation due for the expropriations under the law of 1958. The state did award some compensation, but only for the value of the trees, buildings, fittings, agricultural machinery and motor-pumps found on the expropriated land (art. 8), compensation which was actually derisory in the majority of cases.

The third modification referred to the distribution of the lands of agrarian reform. The expropriated lands were normally to be given to landless peasants and small landowners. Alongside this distribution to individuals, the law of 1970 also introduced the principle of the collective distribution of lands, in keeping with the ideological radicalization of the political régime under the influence of the Baath Party and its development towards a collective system of lands and their cultivation.

Likewise, the law of 1970 contained certain changes to the sizes of the plots distributed to the peasants, according to their geographical location, their fertility and types of cultivation. These plots varied between 25 and 50 hectares in dry lands and one to 15 hectares in irrigated lands.

It should be noted at this point that all the lands distributed in this way were regarded as having been granted to the beneficiaries of the agrarian reform by virtue of *tapu* and were registered as such (art. 23). This provision also applied to the lands distributed to the peasants within the framework of the agrarian law of 1958. Thus, the beneficiaries of the first reform, who had acquired the right to private ownership of their plot in accordance with the law, now found themselves

Agrarian Policies since 1958 183

subject to the rule of the *tapu* imposed by the new law. Henceforth beneficiaries no longer had the right of tenure or usufruct on their lands. The state was the owner of the distributed lands.

This development towards the grip of the state on agricultural land was extremely serious, for instead of consolidating the status of the peasantry and the land, it placed them in a precarious position, which was neither in the interest of the farmers, nor in the interest of society as a whole.

The Agrarian Reform of 1975

This reform solely concerned Kurdistan. It had not been possible to apply the agrarian reforms of 1958 and 1970 to the mountainous region, because of the war between Mullah Mustafa Barzani's Kurds and the Iraqi government between September 1961 and March 1975. The Kurds were actively supported by Iran, mainly because of its differences with Iraq, in particular on the subject of the navigation of the Shatt al-Arab, an important internal navigation route for both countries. The Treaty of Algiers of 6 March 1975, concluded between the Shah of Iran and the Iraqi Vice President, Saddam Hussein, following the mediation of Algerian President Boumedienne, led to a provisional reconciliation between the two countries.[19] Having obtained what it wanted by this accord, in particular the right to use the Shatt al-Arab, Iran had no major reason for continuing its aid to the Kurds against Baghdad. This change in Iran's attitude led to the collapse of Mullah Mustafa Barzani's military movement, allowing the Iraqi army to occupy the mountainous region. Following this enforced pacification, on 25 May 1975 the Revolutionary Council promulgated law no. 90 on agrarian reform in the 'autonomous region of Kurdistan'.[20]

This law took into account the characteristics of the region, its geographical location and the agricultural lands available in relation to the density of the population, since there are far fewer areas which can be cultivated in this region than in the rest of the country because of the geographical features.

The law of 1975 frequently referred back to the agrarian law of 1970. Consequently, though no specific reference was made to them, both these laws applied to the so-called autonomous region

19. E. and E.F. Penrose, *op. cit.*, pp. 372–3.
20. Superior Agricultural Council, *op. cit.*, pp. 187–91.

of Kurdistan, comprised of the provinces of Sulaimaniya, Arbil and Dohuk. This law is characterized by three features. Firstly, with regard to the ceiling authorized by the law of 1970, that of 1975 reduced the limits of the land which one person was allowed to ow˙ or which was granted to one person by virtue of the *tapu* or *lazma*. These limits varied between 75 and 125 hectares of dry cultivated land and between 10 and 30 hectares of orchards and irrigated land (art. 2), depending on the rainfall, methods of irrigation, type of cultivation and plantation. Land which exceeded the limits fixed by the law were expropriated (art. 2). Likewise, contrary to the law of 1970, these provisions applied to both inherited land and land acquired by donation (art. 3). Expropriated lands became the property of the state. The law also considered that water sources formed part of the national wealth. These too were expropriated and their ownership transferred to the state (art. 7).

The agrarian law of 1975 also gave great powers to the Ministry of Agrarian Reform, powers which were greater in this region than in the rest of the country. Thus it 'could expropriate all agricultural land or orchards judged necessary for the creation of large agricultural units' (art. 5). The expression 'large agricultural units' here refers to state farms, agricultural cooperatives and collective agricultural cooperatives.

Finally, since official ideology had evolved very clearly towards the collectivization of land, most expropriated lands were to be collectively distributed to peasants with a view to creating large units of production. These were of three types: state farms, collective agricultural cooperatives and agricultural cooperatives of peasants, each of whom had an individual plot awarded under the agrarian reform. But the law privileged the first two categories which were considered to be the two advanced socialist forms of production. The third category was not favoured by the authorities, for it was regarded as maintaining the peasant mentality which remained attached to the ownership of the land and to individual cultivation. Thus, according to official ideology, this category of peasants had to disappear.

One might make three observations on the agrarian reform of 1975. In the first place, this reform was generally speaking far more rigid and restrictive than those of 1958 and 1970. These conditions may be chiefly explained by the effects of the war in this region between Mullah Mustafa Barzani's Kurds and the Iraqi government. In the second place, the agrarian reform of 1975 introduced an important difference with regard to that of 1970. This difference referred to orchards. The 1970 agrarian law had made a major exception by excluding palm-groves and orchards from the limits on agricultural property (art. 2c.), but the 1975 law fixed authorized ceilings on orchards owned by a single person in the autonomous region of Kurdistan. The same principle, with variations according to local circumstances, ought to have been applied throughout the country in order to avoid contradictions which had serious effects. We must not forget that this region is inhabited solely by Kurds and Assyro-Chaldeans. By not respecting the principle of equality between its citizens, the agrarian law of 1975 submitted the inhabitants of this region to serious discrimination.

Finally, the third observation concerns drinking water sources. The 1975 agrarian law nationalized all natural sources of water in the region and transferred their ownership to the state (art. 7). This provision appears excessive in the Iraqi context, since the state would henceforth be able to use the water from the sources as it pleased, without taking necessary account of the wishes and interests of the inhabitants. This could be very prejudicial for the latter, given the fact that they did not have any legal institution capable of contesting or negotiating the state's projects and decisions, or which might constitute a counterbalance to the desires of the central powers with a view to defending the interests of the local communities. The municipalities had no power—even the mayors were nominated by the government.

To grasp the full significance of article 7 of this law it is enough to understand that the entire social and economic life of the villages is organized around the water sources. The inequalities introduced in this organization therefore posed a serious threat to the social and economic structures of the villages concerned.[21]

The land subjected to expropriation under the above three agrarian laws was estimated at three million hectares,[22] of which 2,609,800 hectares were expropriated between 1958 and 1976 and their ownership transferred to the state. During this period 1,890,930 hectares

21. To comprehend the full destructive and harmful effects of the state's excessive intervention in the socio-economic structures of the rural communities, see H. Ishow's study, 'Structures sociales et système d'irrigation d'Araden, village assyrochaldéen au nord de l'Irak', in André de Reparaz, ed., *L'eau et les hommes en Méditerranée*. Centre National de la Recherche Scientifique, 1987), pp. 236–52.

22. Khitab al-Ani, *Jughrafiyat al-Iraq al-ziraiya*. (Agricultural geography of Iraq), (Cairo, 1972), p. 99.

were redistributed to 222,925 peasants.[23] These last two figures were 2,440,750 hectares and 264,800 beneficiaries respectively at the end of 1981[24]. But in fact these figures bear no relation to reality, for the numbers of withdrawals were large. Many beneficiaries abandoned their plot of land and left the country for the towns where they hoped to find better living conditions.

The administration of the lands withheld by the state was and is ensured by the Ministry of Agriculture and Agrarian Reform, which rents the lands to private farmers as far as they can be found, under share-cropping contracts, which is not always easy in the Iraqi context.

Generally speaking the farming of those lands which were the subject of agrarian reforms was organized within the framework of agricultural cooperatives[25] conforming to national developmental plans and to the government's directives. The peasant beneficiaries were organized by the general union of agricultural cooperatives in a pyramidal structure and controlled by the central authorities. Parallel to these provisions, from 1959 onwards state farms were created in cooperation with the Soviet Union, in accordance with the economic and technological accord concluded between Iraq and the Soviet Union on 16 March 1959.

If one considers the 210,000 hectares of state farms, the 2,440 750 hectares of the cooperative sector and the lands administered directly by the Ministry of Agriculture and Agrarian Reform, then at the end of this first phase the state controlled around fifty per cent of agricultural land.[26] In reality, the state legally controlled almost all agricultural lands, since law no. 53 transferred ownership of 99.2 per cent (7,974,000 hectares) of lands used for agricultural purposes to the state, leaving only 0.8 per cent (64,500 hectares) in private hands, thus depriving the peasants of their fundamental

23. Central Statistical Organization, *Annual abstract of statistics 1976*. Baghdad, Ministry of Planning, 1976, pp. 111–12.
24. *Idem., Statistical Pocket Book*, p. 25.
25. There are two categories of cooperative in Iraq:- agricultural cooperatives, called locals, composed mainly of beneficiaries of agrarian reforms, who farm their plots individually; and collective agricultural cooperatives, essentially formed of allottees of the agrarian reforms. The members collectively farm the cooperatives' resources on the basis of collective ownership of the lands and the other means of production.
26. The lands used for agriculture are estimated to be around 8 million hectares of a total of 12 million hectares of cultivatable land. However, cultivated land annually is around 2.5 to 3 million hectares.

rights.[27] In addition, from 1970 onwards the state imposed a monopoly on the commercialization of all agricultural products, creating public offices for the purpose. It also controlled the purchase and sales of agricultural materials and the credit system.

This group of measures led to a so-called 'socialist avant-garde' model controlled by the state. But at this level the bureaucracy established on a country-wide scale ceased to function. It failed for a number of reasons, including the absence of serious prior studies on the subject of the rural world, the lack of financial and technological means, political insecurity and instability, policies which were inappropriate in the context of the country and, above all, lack of interest on the part of the peasants.

THE SECOND PHASE: CHANGES TO AGRARIAN POLICIES IN THE FACE OF NECESSITY

Since Iraq earned sufficient oil revenue, its leaders were able wantonly to sacrifice agriculture and the peasantry to ideological and political considerations. But from 1980 onwards the failure of agrarian policies, combined with difficulties in other sectors of the economy, increasing military expenditure incurred in the Iran-Iraq war (1980–1988), and engendered by the decrease in oil revenue which essentially stemmed from the war, led those in power to put in place a new agrarian policy completely in contradiction to its predecessor. This policy aimed to privatize the public or socialist agricultural sector. Indeed, from 1980 onwards the government called on the private sector to invest in agriculture in order to improve yields and increase production. To this end it signed many contracts of tenancy with Iraqis and foreigners, acting individually or within the framework of private societies to farm state lands and those abandoned by the beneficiaries of the agrarian reforms.

These contracts are regulated by law no. 35 of 1983. The contracts are signed for a period which may vary from five to twenty years and relate to large-scale farming. Each farm extends over many hundreds, even thousands of hectares. Between 1983 and 1987 the government signed 1,473 contracts of this kind, comprising 220,500 hectares.[28] This last figure exceeded 1,180,000 hec-

27. Superior Agricultural Council, *op. cit.*, pp. 211–7. See also Abd al-Wahhab M. al-Dahiri, *op. cit.*, p. 175.
28. Isam al-Khafaji, 'Al-iqtisad al-iraqi bad al-harb maa Iran'. (The Iraqi

tares at the end of 1989.[29] Likewise, to make economies and to make existing units of production profitable, the government abolished those agricultural cooperatives and state farms which were unprofitable. Thus, agricultural cooperatives numbered 1,935 units in 1978 and 713 in 1988. The peasants, former members of the cooperatives, are henceforth free to farm their plot of land as they see fit. What is more significant is that the collective cooperatives, which were to constitute the socialist model, developing according to official ideology, have for the most part been eliminated. Of seventy-nine cooperatives comprising 7,569 members in 1978, only seven cooperatives with 138 members remained in 1988.[30]

The state farms have been subjected to the same treatment. On 17 May 1987 the Minister of Agriculture declared in Baghdad that 'state farms must be sold or rented'.[31] State farms, 210,000 hectares in 1979, had shrunk to 52,925 hectares by 1986.[32] In principle, this new policy should lead to the disappearance of the entire agricultural sector controlled by the state.

The contracts refer primarily to irrigated lands situated near large towns where market garden produce and fruit trees are grown, since these products have greater yields than cereals and are easier to sell on the market. Such products are grown to satisfy the needs of the comfortable urban middle classes with relatively high spending power. Thus the capital invested in the lands is quickly made profitable and appreciable short and medium-term profits may be drawn.

It is also interesting to note the recourse to foreign manpower in the farming of the lands which are the subject of tenancy contracts. Until 2 August 1990, the date of Iraq's invasion of Kuwait and the serious crisis which followed it, most agricultural workers were Egyptian immigrants. These were thought at the time to number 440,000, according to the estimates of the Egyptian Centre for

economy after the war with Iran). Beirut, *Arab Strategic Thought*, 32, April 1990, p. 212. See also *Middle East Economic Digest* (MEED), London, vol. 28, 2, 13–19 January 1984, p. 14.

29. MEED, vol 34, 5, February 1990, p. 20.

30. Central Statistical Organization, *Annual abstracts of statistics 1978*, p. 83. See also idem., 1988, p. 125.

31. MEED, vol 31, 21, 23–29 May 1987, p. 14.

32. *Ibid.*, pp. 14 and 18. See also Majid Faraj Samal, 'Adwa ala waq mazari al-dawla wa subul tatwiriha'. (Explanation of the situation of state farms and means of development), *al-Iqtisadi* 9, 2, July 1979, p. 57.

Statistics.[33] Because salaries and the standard of living were higher, Iraqi peasants preferred to migrate to the towns where they took part in the tertiary sector in particular, in such activities as small itinerant businesses, caretaking and employment in restoration work etc.

The main beneficiaries of the new agricultural policy are, as formerly under the Hashimite monarchy: rich townspeople, merchants and businessmen able to invest in agriculture; politicians, high functionaries and retired officers. This privileged group has a complex social network and applies significant pressure on the government in which, moreover, it has influential representatives, with a view to obtaining many advantages: to sell freely their products; import machinery and equipment necessary for their farms; to gain credit under advantageous terms; and to facilitate the functioning of their affairs in sectors other than agriculture, etc.

In the long term it is highly probable that the central power will increasingly encourage the development of the private agricultural sector, for the following reasons. Firstly, the failure of government intervention in the agricultural sector bears witness to the inability of the government and its bureaucracy correctly to administer the sector to enable it to become prosperous. The lack of financial resources has also led the central power to conceive a more realistic policy. The state simply could not continue to subsidize unprofitable farms (state farms and cooperatives) indefinitely on the basis of ideology and senseless policies. The consequences of the Iran–Iraq war (1980–1988), the critical situation into which Iraq was plunged following the occupation of Kuwait on 2 August 1990, and the war which brought it into opposition with the Allies in January and February 1991, will weigh heavily on the Iraqi economy for a long time to come. Beyond this, the failure of agricultural policies in the countries of the Middle East and North Africa (Syria, Egypt, Tunisia, Algeria) and in the countries of Eastern Europe and the Soviet Union is hardly an incentive for the Iraqi leaders to persist in their erroneous ideological and political desire to control or apply socialism to the agricultural sector. Finally, it is possible to observe the emergence from within the political class and its allies of a privileged group whose aim is to become wealthy. This social group, which dominates the state, is seeking to develop its activities in the agricultural sector as much as in other sectors. In this context the following

33. Isam al-Khafaji, *op. cit.*, p. 213.

example illustrates this development very well. The Maktab Khalid group, based in Baghdad, deals in various affairs in the public and civil sectors, including the construction of roads and military bases. This group has become very rich, thanks in particular to its network of contacts. Indeed, one of its members is married to a close relative of the former Minister of Defence, Adnan Khairallah al-Tulfah, who is the cousin and brother-in-law of Saddam Hussein. He owns large agricultural lands in the Rashidiya region on the Tigris, a region highly valued by the rich inhabitants of Baghdad.[34] He represents the privileged social class partly created by the political power since 1958.

In the agricultural sector it is possible to observe a resurgence of major landowners, who had not disappeared since agricultural laws authorized the possession of vast lands. If one considers the agricultural policies of successive governments, past and present, it is clear that the political leaders—both foreign and national—and their allies have always tried to appropriate the country's cultivatable land for themselves to the detriment of the peasants.

It is interesting to conclude this account with the following figures, which serve as an excellent illustration for the failure of agricultural policies since 1958. They refer in particular to agricultural production, which has steadily decreased since 1958 (see Table 1).

Comparing the figures in this table it is clear that only the production of rice has increased somewhat compared to its 1957 level; however it has decreased markedly from that of 1967. In general, the production of all three cereals has decreased steadily during the period concerned. In 1957 Iraq produced 4 hundredweight of cereals per inhabitant, in 1987 only one hundredweight. The country's population numbered 6,340,000 and 16,335,000 respectively.[35] To meet the level of production of 1957 in relation to the population Iraq would have had to produce 6.6 million tonnes of cereals in 1987. But that year only 1.6 million tonnes were produced, a deficit of five million tonnes. The policy of the privatization of the socialist agricultural sector, embarked upon from 1980 onwards, has not brought with it the anticipated results for two

34. R. Springbord, 'Infitah, agrarian transformation, and elite consolidation in contemporary Iraq', *The Middle East Journal*, vol, 40, 1, Winter 1986, pp. 44–5.
35. Central Bureau of Statistics, *Statistical abstract 1961*. (Baghdad, 1962), p. 102. See also: *Annual abstract of statistics 1988*, p. 40; Nations Unies, *Annuaire demographique 1988*, (New York, 1990),vol. 40, p. 166.

main reasons. Firstly, because it is an agricultural sector oriented towards speculative farming. And secondly because the country has been plunged into a crisis following the wars undertaken since 1980 by the Iraqi government. Under these conditions it is difficult for rural communities to prosper and for agriculture to develop. Because of the increasing agricultural deficit the country is obliged to import considerable quantities of food products in order to satisfy the needs of its population. In 1988 and 1989 Iraq imported $2.5 billion worth of food per year.[36] Only oil revenues make these imports possible, saving the population from famine. The part that oil plays in the country's exports illustrates this reality very well. For example, it was 98.1 per cent in 1978, 99.5 per cent in 1980 and 96.1 per cent in 1986.[37]

This excessive dependence of the Iraqi economy on oil makes the country particularly vulnerable, as was shown by the Iran-Iraq war of 1980 to 1988 and the commercial embargo imposed on Iraq on 6 August 1990 by resolution 661 of the United Nations Security Council, following the occupation of Kuwait on 2 August of the same year. In summer 1991, deprived of oil revenues, boycotted on a commercial level by the community of nations, with insufficient agricultural production, Iraq was in a drastic situation, the direct result of the imprudence and reckless policies of its leaders. Its population was threatened by real famine, despite the potential importance of its agricultural resources.

Thus the central power, through its excessive intervention in the agricultural sector and its general policies based on violence, seems to be the main cause of the inequalities of agricultural structures, the destruction of the rural communities and the decline in agricultural production.

36. FAO, *Annuaire FAO du commerce 1989*, (Rome, 1990), p. 43.
37. *Le pétrole et le gaz arabes*, Paris, vol. XVII, 402, 16 December 1985, p. 34, vol. XIX, 440, 16 July 1987, p. 14.

Table 1 The development of the production of corn, barley and rice between 1957 and 1987 (thousands of tonnes)

Products	1957	1967	1977	1980	1987
corn	1,118	866	695.7	975.6	722.2
barley	1,305	860	457.7	682.4	742.9
rice	147	311	199.2	166.9	195.9
Total	2,570	2,037	1,352.6	1,824.9	1,661

Note: These three cereals take up more than 90 per cent of cultivated land annually in Iraq and constitute the basic food of the population.

Sources: Abd al-Wahhab M. al-Dahiri, *Al-tahlil al-iqtisadi li-amaliyat al-intaj al-zirai* (*Economic Analysis of the process of agricultural production*).
Central Statistical Organization, *Annual Abstract of Statistics*, 1978, p. 58. See also *ibid.*, *Statistical pocket book*, p. 15, Annual Abstract of Statistics 1988, p. 104.

The Distribution of National Income in Iraq, with Particular Reference to the Development of Policies Applied by the State

Aziz Alkazaz

INTRODUCTION

Rather than limiting an examination of the changes in national income and its distribution to a statistical description, it is useful to present a dynamic analysis which incorporates all the determinants of this development, that is which includes extra-economic factors and the state development policy which was applied. Changes to the political system and to the legal framework, relations with the western superpowers and conflicts with neighbouring states all play a significant role here. Changes in economic and social structures only become clear in the context of longer periods of time. For this reason we will examine the various stages and periods which Iraqi economic development has undergone: during the reign of the monarchy (up to 1958) and in the first fifteen years of the Republic the Iraqi economy was grossly distorted and burdened by political instability. Only after the nationalization of the oil sector (1972–1973) did a quantitatively and qualitatively different upturn begin, which continued until 1980. Development in the 1980s took place during the Iran-Iraq war which influenced all sectors of economic and social policy. In the brief period between the two Gulf wars (1988–1990) Iraq experienced the beginnings of far-reaching economic and administrative reforms (liberalization), which were unfortunately interrupted by the outbreak of the Kuwait crisis (August 1990). However, it is still possible that the attempts at reform (constitutional reform, decentralization of the administration, multi-party system, wider application of the principles of the market economy etc.) will be resumed when the economic blockade has been lifted and conditions have been normalized.

Many scholars of Iraq and those with an interest in politics were influenced by the policy of the systematic demonization of the figure of Saddam Hussein, which had certain operative objectives within the context of military conflicts. To some extent we are all victims of this extraordinary focussing. I have attempted to free myself from these chains and to examine the development from a regional perspective.

Definition of Development

Development, along with social security, is a central objective of Iraqi society. These twin objectives are to be sought in a national (Iraqi) as well as a regional (Arab) context. Well-designed national and regional development interact closely and promote each other. In the same way development and security are interdependent; each is vital for the achievement of the other. There is a need to distinguish between growth and development. 'Growth' is a mere increase in real national income (or income per capita) which can take place within the circular flow of the economy, that is its social and political institutions and its technological capabilities and demographic realities. 'Development' on the other hand is growth of a size and continuity which cannot materialize without important structural changes occurring previously or concurrently in the technological, social, and political frameworks, in addition to the economic framework itself. Hence it follows that a number of demands must be satisfied before it can be said that development is occurring or has occurred:[1]

> (1) Rise in the level of economic performance, that is rise in productivity and increase in the national product, within a sectoral pattern which is balanced as far as possible, and where manufacturing industry occupies a prominent position and is associated with the acquisition of the values of discipline, rationality, inventiveness and scientific causality. Furthermore, the performance must be continually high, not a seasonal or accidental

[1]. Y.A. Sayigh, *The Arab economy: past performance and future prospects* (Oxford University Press, 1982).

occurrence, and it must be the result of society's abilities and efforts, and not the activity of 'enclave sectors' that are weakly integrated with the national economy (like the activities of foreign companies in oil production and export in the framework of the traditional concessions system);

(2) Provision of an expanded volume and improved quality of goods and services to satisfy the basic needs of the population— these needs to be understood in a dynamic context whereby the level or quantity of the needs rises and their coverage widens as they become increasingly satisfied; in other words, the satisfaction of one generation of needs leads to the emergence of another, more sophisticated generation;

(3) Provision of distinctly wider opportunities for productive employment and the reduction of unemployment, whether open or disguised, and the mobilization of a very large proportion of manpower resources. Special attention should be paid to the employment of an increasing number of women. This should be attempted both because of its social and human significance, and because of the purchasing power that employment can put in the hands of the population;

(4) Correction of the pattern of income distribution within the country, by raising the income floor for the mass of the population, widening the base of ownership of productive assets, and reallocating the burden of development and of state services and institutions in such a manner as to increase the absolute and relative contribution of those who have the financial ability to carry a larger share;

(5) Parallel with income distribution at the national level, the narrowing of the 'development gap' among Arab countries— that is, narrowing the wide differentials in economic capabilities and performance, which in turn would speed the advances in productivity and expand the national product in the less developed countries. This would have positive effects on the Iraqi economy and security;

(6) Developing the capability of the social, cultural and political environment so that it may provide the economy with the ideas, knowledge, skills, attitudes and institutions necessary for the efficient operation of the economy and for continuity in the improvement of the economy's performance;

(7) Achievement of a wide measure of popular participation in

the process of development and in the social, economic and political decisions related to the formulation of development strategies and policies and the allocation and use of resources. The principle underlying this specification is that there can be no profound commitment to development and the tasks associated with it without participation both in the design and the rewards of development;

(8) Achieving the widest possible measure of collective (regional) self-reliance in development—not in the sense of isolationist autarky, but in the sense of the acquisition by the Arab region as a whole of greater productive capability and its success in the mobilization of its human and material resources and in the upgrading of the quality of these resources. Underlying and accompanying this demand is the need to improve the position of the Arabs in the world economy and its pattern of division of labour; the need to remove the state of excessive dependency on the advanced industrial countries and their transnational corporations with all the exploitativeness, imbalance and inefficiency that the dependency carries with it.

The achievement of an acceptable degree of national and regional security is an essential objective, worthy of effort and sacrifice, and that security requires a solid economic base which cannot be ensured without development that meets the demands listed above. Likewise, the safeguarding of developmental gains calls for the achievement of secutity in the face of Israel imperialist incursions and continued threats. Security in the present context is not restricted to the narrow confines of strategic/political/military security—important as this is—but extends to include the liberation of the Iraqis and other Arabs from ignorance, poverty, disease and internal insecurity; the liberation of Iraqi and Arab society from its dependency on foreign economic power and cultural domination; and the promotion of dynamism and creativeness in the society.

NATIONAL INCOME AND ITS DISTRIBUTION BEFORE THE REVOLUTION ON JULY 1968

In the 1950s and 1960s, and actually until the nationalization of the oil sector, the levels, distribution and use of national income were unsatisfactory in several respects. This may be attributed in the first instance to distorted economic structures and the economic policies applied by the state, as well as to political instability (in the 1960s). Because of the interference of the armed forces in domestic politics there were numerous coup attempts and disruptions to the management of the developmental process during the 1960s.

The Distorted Structure of the Economy

The extent of the distortion of the structure of the economy and its incompatibility with development is reflected amongst other things in the contributions of individual sectors to the gross domestic product (GDP) and in the structural weaknesses of these sectors:

(1) A disproportionately large expansion of the service industries at the cost of productive areas, associated with the inflation of the state administrative apparatus and with the increases in defence expenditure.

(2) The two most important sectors were oil production and agriculture. They alone accounted for more than fifty per cent of GDP. But it was in these very sectors that the state's opportunities for managing development policies and the possibilities for prognosis and predictions were extremely limited. Oil production lay in the hands of foreign concerns (owners of the Iraq Petroleum Company, IPC) and was determined primarily by the business interests of these concerns and by developments on the world market. Agricultural production was highly dependent on the weather. Thus, the contribution of these two major sectors to the GDP was subject to considerable fluctuations.

(3) As we have said, the oil sector was in the ownership of foreign concerns, forming an 'enclave' in an otherwise backward national economy. Less than one per cent of the country's workers were employed in this sector. So it was able to make only a very small contribution to employment and education or to the direct creation of income for the people (in the form of salaries and wages). The foreign oil companies were not interested in developing refineries and other 'downstream operations' in the country. The government had failed to establish a national petrochemical industry. Thus, the Iraqi economy was robbed of the opportunity to establish the beneficial effects of the backward, lateral and forward linkages usually associated with the existence of a 'leading sector'.

(4) Agriculture remained characterized by low yields per hectare, by low productivity and by semi-feudal ownership and production arrangements. Amongst other things, this led to agriculture making no contribution of any significance to the acquisition of capital or to the industrialization of the country. The fact that agriculture employed more than half of the workers, yet contributed less than twenty-five per cent to real national income, was one of the reasons for the extremely uneven distribution of income and wealth. The observed decrease in the relative contribution of agriculture to GDP should not be attributed to the increased expansion of national industry, but to the expansion of the service sector, in particular the expansion of the state administration and the increase in defence expenditure.

(5) In last place was industry. Its contribution to real national income may have increased from five per cent (1953) to fourteen per cent (1969), but was still low. It employed less than ten per cent of the country's workers and was characterized by low productivity. Its structural characteristics were:

(a) By far the majority of 'industrial concerns' were very small and technically under-developed workshops with fewer than ten employees each. Of the 27,635 firms which existed in 1966, 26,310, or ninety-five per cent, were small or tiny workshops. The remaining five per cent (1,325) were medium-sized and large firms, which employed twice as many workers as the small firms.

(b) With the exception of the few firms engaged in cement production, oil refining, electricity production and technical repairs, most were part of the consumer goods industry. In 1966 the consumer goods industry's share of the entire production value of all medium and large sized firms was seventy-one per cent.

(c) There was too great a dependence on the import of machinery, mechanical plant, replacement parts and semi-finished products.

(d) Limited technical know-how: in the 1960s in the medium and large sized firms only one per cent of those employed were technicians, and only forty-four per cent were trained workers, while forty-six per cent were untrained workers.

(e) Geographically, industry was concentrated in only five provincial capitals (Baghdad, Basra, Mosul, Karbala and Kirkuk) which had the most basic of infrastructures at their disposal, in contrast to the other parts of the country. In 1966 eighty-four per cent of all medium and large firms were concentrated in these five towns, fifty-six per cent of which were in Baghdad.

The state's industrialization policies remained unsuccessful until the end of the 1960s. Although the first legal basis for the promotion of private industry had already been created in 1925, the private sector was unable to make any major contribution to the industrialization of the country, since that class of the population with capital was mainly interested in trade, in investing in land, in short-term profits and speculative deals. The state sector was unable to undertake the task given the dominant political conditions of the time. The state Industrial Bank founded in 1940 and the Development Board created in 1950 could provide little impetus. The bank had a small capital, its bank borrowings were limited to a few existing firms. Although seventy per cent of oil income was legally ear-marked for the financing of development projects, the number of investments actually carried out in the industrial sector at the end of the 1960s was very small. The Development Board's first investment programme (1952–1956) contained no industrial projects whatsoever. In the national development plan (1956–1961) only fourteen per cent of all planned investments was allocated to the industrial sector, i.e. only the tiny sum of 32 million ID. After the overthrow of the British-dominated monarchy and the proclamation of the republic (1958) the establishment of a national industry was given top priority and thirty per cent of all investments of the development plan of 1962–1966 were set aside for the industrial sector, but because of the power struggle and domestic instability very important projects could not be carried out. In the end only sixteen per cent of those investments actually carried out were allocated to the industrial sector.

(6) Inadequate employment policies: At the end of the 1960s there was no systematic state employment policy in Iraq. The high official and hidden unemployment rate was largely determined by the system. The oil sector was able to contribute only very little to employment, because of its capital intensity. The

effects on employment of state expenditure were limited. Generally, the effects on employment of the income multiplier were very small, and this may be attributed to the following factors:

(a) weak connections between state services and domestic industry;

(b) the extreme openness of the economic system to the outside and the failure of trade policies oriented towards investment on the one hand and the country's limited production capacities on the other, led to a large proportion of created income flowing abroad (imports). Thus the multiplier-accelerator mechanism could not contribute a great deal to the construction of new domestic production capacities or to employment.

To relieve the unemployment problem an increasing number of high school and university graduates had to be employed by the state. In this way the (still uneven) distribution of income was shifted in favour of the state employees, whose productivity decreased further. Their number increased seventeen-fold between 1950 and 1970.

In the 1960s the percentage of the total population in employment was, at twenty-eight per cent, far lower than in the developed countries, which was not only attributable to the distorted economic structure but also to the non-inclusion of most women in the national economic production process. This aspect relates to the basic question of women's liberation. Of those employed (a total of 2.5 million at the time) fifty-three per cent were concentrated in agriculture, thirty-three per cent in the service industry, whilst only nine per cent were employed in industry, electricity and the building sector (cf. Tables 1 and 2).

(7) An extraordinarily high degree of dependence on foreign trade: we refer here to foreign trade, oil income and the capital flow abroad associated with the profits and imports of the foreign oil companies. The volume of foreign trade (import and export) totalled an average of sixty-one per cent of domestic income and fifty-three per cent of GDP in the years between 1960 and 1968. This was even higher than the figures in developing countries such as Egypt, Kenya and Bolivia, let alone the industrial countries. Exports were not diversified and ninety-four per cent of them consisted of crude oil, four per cent of

other raw materials and two per cent of agrarian and industrial products. This reflects the many problems of a 'monoculture'. The Iraqi economy was far more tightly bound to western countries in foreign trade than the neighbouring Arab countries. The foreign oil companies (the IPC group) transferred immense sums of money abroad every year, consisting of profits, salaries, wages and the costs of imported goods. The capital transferred abroad increased from 95 million ID (1960) to 157 million ID (1968) and represented an average of sixteen per cent of domestic income. The most important sources for the financing of investments in Iraq were:

(a) taxes and levies from foreign oil companies;

(b) the oil companies' investments in the oil sector;

(c) credits from the oil companies and foreign governments;

(d) domestic savings. This shows the extent to which the entire economic development was dependent on the foreign oil companies, because domestic savings and loans from abroad were small.

Levels of Income and Income Distribution

Against the background of the distorted economic structure described above and the domestic political instability in the 1960s, the growth of the Iraqi economy remained subject to considerable fluctuations until the beginning of the 1970s. As Table 3 shows, the average annual growth rate of GDP slowed from 8.15 per cent in the period 1958–1961 to 4.57 per cent in 1961–1964 and then again to 3.28 per cent in 1965–1969. Correspondingly, the growth rate in gross national product, GNP, decreased from 8.53 per cent to 4.95 per cent and 3.28 per cent. Given the small bases and the dominant position of crude oil exports, growth rates were far too low. Within the space of a whole decade real national income increased from 456 million ID in 1960 by seventy-one per cent to 780 million ID in 1969. At the same time its growth rate fluctuated between -6.7 per cent and +15.0 per cent. The increase in per capita income was even smaller. It rose from 66 ID in 1960 by only twenty-nine per cent to 85 ID in 1969 (cf. Table 4). Its annual growth rate fluctuated between -9.7 per cent and +11.5 per cent.

In 1969, despite its oil wealth Iraq found itself with a per capita income of 85 ID (approx. US$255), low when compared to the international situation and still in the group of poorer developing countries. Two basic trends were particularly relevant: (1) state consumption rose far faster than all other macro-economic variables, (2) the growth of national economic savings and gross investments was far below that of national economic (state and private) consumption, which had a negative effect on the development of the national income.

In fact this negative course could be observed until 1972–73, i.e. until the successful nationalization of the oil sector. In the twenty years between 1953 and 1973 real GDP rose (in 1969 prices) from 406 to 1,360 million ID, with an average annual growth rate of six per cent. The two leading sectors oil and agriculture lay above the average, all other sectors below it (cf. Table 5). It may be further ascertained that the general growth between 1964 and 1973 was far weaker than that between 1953 and 1964, and that this slowing down of growth was associated with the following factors: stagnation of production and prices in the oil sector, in agriculture a delay in the execution of agrarian reform due to political instability, inadequate planning and bad weather conditions. The decrease in the goods producing sector's (except oil) share of GDP with an increase in the service sector's share meant that the dependence of the total economy on oil exports increased. This unfavourable change in structure was reflected amongst other things in the stagnation of goods exports (except oil) and a continuous increase in imports. In agrarian trade Iraq changed from a net exporter to a net importer.

In the distribution of income there were huge differences between businessmen's incomes (profits) on the one hand and the income of the dependent employees (salaries and wages) on the other. As Table 6 shows, an average seventy per cent of national income went to businessmen and thirty per cent to employees. The uneven distribution of income was also manifested in the great differences within the two groups. The 'businessman' group included merchants and owners of service, agricultural and industrial undertakings. Statistically the group also included the numerous small share-croppers who did not earn a living wage, and the great landowners and land agents who acquired an average sixty-two per cent of harvest yields.

Further striking differences existed within the industrial sector because of its specific structure. In 1967 in Iraq there was a total of

26,932 'industrial firms', of which 25,549 or ninety-five per cent were small workshops with less than ten workers each and 1,383 or five per cent were medium or large firms. In the former 63,498 workers and 30,232 owners were employed, in the latter 89,024 workers and only 902 owners. The workshops were underdeveloped and made little money. Their share of the net product of the industrial sector came to only twenty-five per cent, whilst the remaining seventy-five per cent went to medium and large firms. The industrial sector's unfavourable structure was reflected in relative incomes. The average annual income of the owner of a workshop was only 577 ID in comparison to 79,000 ID for the owner of a medium or large firm. The average annual wages of a worker in a small workshop was only 77 ID (about 770 DM) compared to 266 ID (2,660 DM) in the medium and large firms.

To provide deeper insight into the distribution of income the group 'dependent employees' is sub-divided into five sub-groups. Calculations give very different levels of income for the five sub-groups shown in Table 6. The following facts were established from these calculations:

(1) The small group of employees of the foreign oil companies (IPC) stood at the tip of the income hierarchy by a long way. In the year 1969 for example, an employee in this sector earned an average of about 851 ID, compared with only 83 ID for an employee in the small workshops, and compared with a per capita income in the total population of 90 ID.

(2) Those groups which profited the most from the economic and social order were the state civil servants and employees. The average annual income of a state employee rose by sixty-four per cent between 1960 and 1969 compared with a growth in national income of twelve per cent to eighteen per cent, which reflected a significant shift in income distribution in its favour. We should also take into account the many perks which state employees were given, including cheap land and mortgages, discounts in transport costs, free use of state public transport, old age pension provision and the promotion of civil servants' cooperative societies etc.

(3) Similar statements may be made about the growing number of state pensioners (civilians and military) who claimed a disproportionately large share of the national budget. Between 1953 and 1969 the number of pensioners increased only fivefold

from 15,373 to 83,108, while the cost of their pensions rose sixteenfold from 1.21 to 18.72 million ID. Thus, in 1969 for example, this group, which represented just 0.9 per cent of the population, claimed more than 2.2 per cent of national income.

(4) Workers in the small workshops were severely disadvantaged. Their average annual income of 85 ID was the lowest.

(5) Far below the level of income of the above groups lay the mass of the sharecroppers and agricultural workers. The average annual income of such a farming family was c. 60 ID, although deviations from the average were often considerable. Farmers had profited a little from the first agrarian reform (1958), but due to certain economic and political developments the growth in their income remained far behind that of other population groups.

All in all it is possible to say that in the decade under consideration (1960–1969) the distribution of income shifted in favour of the town-dwelling classes, who were characterized by low productivity and high consumption. Increases in income were modest and did not allow the accumulation of the required investment capital. The uneven income distribution led to disproportionately large increases in national economic consumption (in particular state consumption) with which neither domestic production nor the development of state services could keep pace. All these factors contributed to the fact that productive investments and therefore the growth of the Iraqi economy remained low. It was a kind of vicious circle of under-development which had to be broken before the fight against under-development might be begun.

IMPROVEMENTS IN THE 1970S UNDER THE NEW BAATH REGIME

The Creation of the Necessary Domestic and Foreign Policies

In order to be able to carry out structural comparisons and to ensure the continuity of the development process, certain prerequisites had first to be established regarding domestic and foreign policy. These included:

(1) An end to subversive activities of rival parties within the armed forces and therefore an end to the interference of the

army in domestic politics. Members of the armed forces received training in the new constitution of 1970, and were included in the execution of development projects such as road construction, the building of settlements and irrigation canals, literacy campaigns, harvesting etc.

(2) The intensification of the Kurdish problem due to the solution established in the manifesto of 11 March 1970, i.e. the establishment of a system of self-government in the areas where Kurds were in the majority. The solution rested on the following principles: the recognition of the national rights of the Kurdish people and the anchoring of these rights in the constitution of the country, recognition of the Kurdish language as an official language and a language of education in the autonomous region, the guarantee of all cultural rights and the establishment of a university in Sulaimaniya and a Kurdish Academy, the establishment of a system of self-government with a legislative and executive council, and the decentralization of the Iraqi state administration, amnesty for all Kurds who had taken part in unrest, the nomination of a Kurd to the position of Vice President of the Republic, the inclusion of five Kurds in the Council of State in Baghdad (instead of the previous two) and increased economic development in the Kurdish regions. On the other side the requirements were the renouncement of separatism and the preservation of the territorial integrity of the Republic, the handing over of all heavy weapons to the central government, and the requirement that the tapping and development of all natural resources (including oil) should remain in the hands of the central government. This solution did not satisfy all Kurdish demands, but it improved their situation considerably, especially when compared with the neighbouring countries of Iran and Turkey. Conditions would have been further improved given political stability and the use of oil revenue for civil development projects. But Iraq's political opponents (USA, Israel, Iran) tried to use the Kurdish problem to weaken Iraq and to prevent the development of its considerable potential. After the nationalization of the western oil companies (IPC group) in June 1972 US President Nixon and the Shah of Iran gave the CIA the task of providing Mullah Mustafa al-Barzani and his supporters with weapons and munitions to the value of $16 million (see *The Sunday Times* of 15 February 1976 and the *New York Times* of

26 January 1976). The solution outlined above was pushed through in 1974–5 despite the resistance of Mullah Mustafa al-Barzani.[2]

(3) The creation of a new economic and social order oriented towards development, and a corresponding change in the aims and priorities of state economic policy as regards industrialization and accelerated economic growth. For the elimination of absolute poverty and illiteracy is a prerequisite for true democratization.

(4) The overcoming of Iraq's regional isolation and the strengthening of its regional role. In the 1970s Iraq succeeded in improving its relations with most Arab states. The border problems with Jordan and Saudi Arabia were resolved. Relations with the Arab Gulf States were relaxed and gradually improved. The border conflict with Kuwait was not resolved, but it was pushed into the background. Iraq granted all poor Arab countries, such as Egypt, Yemen, Jordan, Morocco, Mauretania, Somalia, Sudan and Tunisia development aid. Only the relationship with Syria remained tense. As for non-Arab countries, relations with Turkey were systematically strengthened on the basis of mutual benefit. However, relations with Iran remained difficult, due to the Shatt al-Arab border dispute, political rivalry in the Gulf region, the Iranian occupation of the three Arab Gulf islands (1971) and superpower policies. Only during the relatively short period of 1975 to 1978 (after the signing of the so-called Algiers Accord of 1975) did Iraqi-Iranian relations become less tense, and this relaxation was one of the favourable political conditions for the boom in the whole region in the second half of the 1970s. After the fall of the Shah's regime and Khomeini's seizure of power in 1979 the conflict with Iran intensified dramatically. Iraq was trying to take a leading role amongst non-aligned states in the Third World, and it granted numerous African and Asian countries development aid (before 1980). Iraq tried to build up good co-operative relations with both the Soviet Union and the United States superpowers, without entering any relationship of dependence. This met with problems. The friendship treaty with the USSR of 1972 did not prevent Iraq from sharply

2. On the development of the Kurdish conflict see Sa'ad Jawad, 'Recent developments in the Kurdish issue', in *Iraq, the contemporary state*, edited by Tim Niblock (London, 1982), pp. 47–61.

condemning Soviet intervention in Afghanistan in 1979. And it criticized the American attempts at hegemony in the Gulf region and in the rest of the Near and Middle East just as sharply.

Restructuring the Economy

The 1970 Constitution

A new constitution was now drawn up which contained the basic ideas and long-term aims of the new political system. This took effect on 16 July 1970. It emphasizes the unity of the Iraqi people, which consists of two main nations; the Arab and Kurdish. It recognizes the national rights of the Kurdish people and all legitimate rights of other minorities within the framework of the unity of the Iraqi state (article 5, para. 6). Minority languages are officially recognized in the areas of religion, culture and the academic world. Kurdish is the official language in the autonomous region, alongside Arabic (art. 6). For the first time in modern Iraqi history institutions were recognized and promoted by the state which were concerned with research into and the development of the culture and cultural heritage of the ethnic and religious minorities. Islam, the religion of the majority, was regarded as the state religion (art. 4), although the religious freedom of all citizens and the rights of all religious minorities were fully recognized and protected (art. 25).

With regard to the economic and social order the Baath ideology was expressed as a constitutional duty: society consists of equal and responsible individuals who are bound together by social solidarity. It is the state's duty to develop such a classless society through revolutionary processes and with the aid of scientific knowledge. The right to work is guaranteed by the state and work is an honour and the sacred duty of every citizen (art. 31). The state guides and plans the national economy with the aim of (a) establishing an economic order based on social equality and (b) bringing about pan-Arab economic unity (art 12). Mineral resources and the basic means of production are the collective property of the people: the state uses them and invests them for the good of the whole nation (art 13). Private property is recognized and has a social function which is exercised within the framework of social aims and the state programme. Private business is recognized and is protected by law, provided that it does not conflict with general development plans. Private property may not be expropriated unless it is in the public interest and only if fair compensation is paid within the law. There is an upper limit on agricultural property and according to the conditions of the law of agrarian reform, anything above this limit is the property of the people (art. 16).

All basic rights and duties of citizens are anchored in the constitution (art. 19–36). The state is duty-bound to fight illiteracy and to ensure free education and training from primary school to university. The aim of education is the creation of a nationalist and patriotic progressive generation, proud of its nation and fatherland, which identifies with the legitimate rights of minorities and is against exploitation, imperialism, Zionism and reaction and which is committed to the realization of Arab unity, freedom and social justice (art. 28).

Any organization and activity which is aimed against this constitution, or which threatens national unity or which creates racist, religious or regional antagonism is forbidden (art. 36).

Naturally there was and is (as in every country on earth) a rather large gap between the constitution and reality. But it cannot be denied that the social and economic policies applied in many spheres were influenced by the spirit and the letter of the constitution.

The Basic Issue of Democracy, the Participation of the Population in the Political System and its Motivation

One of the most important questions which determines the success of development policy is the issue of how far the population identifies with the political system and participates in the decisions, and how far the system mobilizes the working population, preparing and motivating it for an increase in productivity. The ruling élite assumed that the western system of 'parliamentary liberalism' was not suitable for developing countries. The right social and economic conditions had to be created first. The battle against underdevelopment requires other forms of participation. They were concerned to build a different model which embraces specific elements such as an elected parliament, people's councils in local government, and participation in the workplace, involvement in mass organizations and the National Front.

In the beginning (1968) the new political system was not formally legitimized, for the Baath Party had come to power by means of a (bloodless) military coup, and, since the monarchy had been overthrown (1958), there had been no parliament in Iraq. The Baath Party took the view that their aims embodied the rights and aspirations of the Iraqi people and that this provided material legitimacy for the system. With the elimination of social disease and poverty, with the increase in the standard of living and education and the involvement of the population in mass organizations (unions, professional groups, youth associations, women's associations, student groups etc) and their decisions, the basis of the system could later be expanded in stages.

The legal basis for a parliamentary system was anchored in articles 46 to 55 of the constitution. According to this Parliament performs a legislative function alongside the Command of the Revolutionary Command Council (RCC). Parliament advises on the drawing up of laws which are proposed by the RCC, the State President or by at least a quarter of the representatives. Thus, a law may only be passed with the agreement of Parliament and the RCC. In the case of controversies between institutions, a joint sitting is held at which a two thirds majority decides. On 15 March 1980 the National Council (Parliament) law was enacted. Parliament consists of 250 representatives who are elected by the people by direct secret ballot. According to this law the Member of Parliament is to represent the whole nation. He may not at the same time be a board member of a private firm, except as a workers' representative, and he is not permitted directly or indirectly to receive business contracts from state establishments.

The first Parliament was elected on 20 June 1980. 840 candidates took part in the election in fifty-six constituencies. More than six million men and women were entitled to vote. Of the 250 members elected, sixteen were women. The elected representatives were members of the ruling Baath Party, the National Front, the Workers and Peasant Organizations as well as various professional associations. Naturally, Kurds, as part of the total population, also participated in the elections and famous Kurds such as, for example Ubaid al-Barzani (son of the Mullah Mustafa al-Barzani) were elected. At the beginning Parliament had very limited powers, but during the course of the 1980s, and especially after 1987, its powers were widened considerably. For example, it was even possible to bring about the fall of some ministers in votes of no confidence.

On 19 September 1980 the population of the three provinces of Arbil, Dohuk and Sulaimaniya held the first direct elections for the legislative council of the Kurdish autonomous region in Northern Iraq. 700,000 men and women took part in the elections in eleven constituencies. fifty of the 194 candidates were elected. The legislative council is responsible for the handling and enactment of only those laws which concern the autonomous region. The elections were overseen by eleven electoral committees, each of which included a representative of the Ministry of Justice (as Chairman), a representative of the Ministry for Local Administration, a representative of the Baath Party and a representative of the National Front. The establishment of the autonomous system in the north was an important step on the long path towards democratization, even if it did not fulfil all Kurdish demands. In comparison to the neighbouring countries of Turkey and Iran, the Kurds in Iraq were granted more rights.

The National Front was founded in 1973 and works on the basis of a 'Charter of National Action', which was publicly discussed in 1971–1972. This Front included the Baath Party, the Kurdish Parties, the Progressive Nationalists, the Independent Democrats and the Communist Party. However, the CP was later excluded. The highest executive organ of the Front was the 'Supreme Committee' made up of eighteen members, in which the above-named parties were represented in proportion to their size and their importance: the Baath Party had eight representatives, the Kurdish Democratic Party five, the CP three, the Progressive Nationalists one and the Independent Democrats one. All decisions had to be unanimous, following adequate discussion.

In the 'people's councils' system developed during the 1970s a 'people's council' was formed for every municipality and every district of a larger town. The council has certain planning and supervisory functions and works closely together with the relevant local administration. All community problems, needs, complaints, projects etc. affecting the inhabitants of the relevant municipality or district are discussed there and solutions devised.

Of course this 'system of democracy' has great loopholes. And of course the most important decisions remained centralized. Certainly the constitutional position of the State President was too strong. But despite all this we should not overlook the fact that workable approaches to problems were being devised, which might have been further developed under specific conditions. These conditions include domestic political stability and the repulsion of the numerous attempts at interference on the part of foreign powers. Without the two Gulf Wars and without the other acute regional conflicts, which affect the political situation in the country, the opportunities for democratization in Iraq would have been far greater.

Restructuring Individual Economic Sectors

In the first half of the 1970s all economic sectors were restructured to create the foundations for autocentric development. Specifically the aim was to create a public sector which was in a position to guide and influence the development of the economy as a whole. We should refer in particular to the nationalization of the oil sector and its integration into the rest of the national economy, the direct exploitation of other natural resources and the new agrarian reforms.

The oil sector was almost completely nationalized between 1972 and 1975. After the creation of a national oil drilling industry with Soviet and French aid (contracts with Elf/ERAP) the difficult negotiations with the IPC group began in 1972. The dispute, which lasted for fourteen years, was finally ended with the nationalization of the IPC plants in June 1972. The French were able to negotiate a favourable holding. In the contract signed on 28 February 1973 the IPC accepted the compensation offered of fifteen million tons (at a value of $350 million). It became the newly-founded Iraq Company for Oil Operations. During the fourth Arab-Israeli War in October 1973 the American, Dutch and Portuguese interests in the Basra Petroleum Co. were nationalized. At the end of 1975 the remaining fifty-seven per cent foreign share in this company was also nationalized. These measures had far-reaching consequences. For Iraq they meant a strengthening of political and economic independence, the possibility of more effective total economic planning, an improvement in the Terms of Trade and technology imports, and last but not least, improved opportunities for the development of the oil sector itself. On the other hand the IPC owners and the powers behind them could never forget that Iraq had nationalized their interests. They remained determined to regain control in the oil sector whenever possible. This is an important fact in the background to political opposition to 'the regime of Saddam Hussein' in the west. It involves extremely complicated problems for Iraq, since the country faces extremely powerful opponents.

Because of the nationalization of the old foreign companies and the elimination of the traditional system of concessions, whose origins are to be found in colonial times, the opportunities for domestic and international oil policies grew. On a domestic level these include increased exploration activities, boring and development of discovered oil fields, the construction of the necessary oil pipe lines and ports, the development of a national fleet of tankers, the construction of new refineries, the development of a marketing system for oil products and the execution of projects using associated gases as well as the development of energy and hydrocarbon-intensive industries, such as the petrochemical, iron, steel, aluminium and fertilizer industries etc. Major progress was made in all these sectors during the 1970s. Thus, due to increased searching for oil and developmental work the oil reserves with drilling potential were doubled and processing and export capacity was increased by 128 per cent to four million b/d. Of particular importance was the improvement in flexibility in the transport system. For the preceding decades Iraq had been dependent on the pipelines which joined its northern oil fields with the Mediterranean via Syria and the Lebanon. With the construction of a new pipeline (545 km long, carrying capacity: fifty million t/annum) the fields in the north and the south of the country were joined together and for the first time the opportunity was created to export oil via both the Mediterranean and via the Gulf. It was put into operation in March 1977. At the same time a 981 km long pipeline was built between the northern Iraqi oil fields and the Turkish Mediterranean port of Dortyol, and was put into operation in January 1977. These two new pipelines alone would be able to replace the old transport system in an emergency. The Iraqi oil ports in the Gulf were expanded and a new deep sea port (Mina al-Bakr) added, at which supertankers could also be serviced. The development of a national tanker fleet was also begun. Iraq, which had not owned a single tanker before 1972, owned eighteen tankers by 1979, with a total tonnage of 72.1 million t; it was also part of the Arab Maritime Petroleum Transport Co., which had thirty-two tankers at the beginning of 1978 with a total tonnage of 3.13 million t. Last but not least the construction of a modern and complex supply network within the country, supplying the consumer centres and ensuring cheaper transport than the railways and tankers previously used should also be mentioned.

The extraction of other mineral deposits was also taken over by the state, i.e. the traditional concessions were no longer granted to foreign companies. The 'State Organization for Minerals' played an important role here. It organized wide-ranging programmes involving geological studies, the drawing of maps and discovered various deposits of raw materials. It also contributed to the training of national qualified workers and executives. We refer here specifically to sulphur and phosphate. The important sulphur deposits found 45 km south of Mosul (since 1969) were mined and developed. A mine with a production capacity of one million t/year was constructed, after which installations were built to process the sulphur and produce sulphuric acid. Phosphate deposits in the Akkashat area (near the Syrian border) were also extracted and developed into an important industrial sector in a similar way. A modern fertilizer industry was built up on the basis of the mine constructed (capacity: 3.5 mt/year). The new industrial area was joined to the country's transport network by railway lines and new roads. All these projects were carried out in cooperation with foreign firms. But the situation differs from the old concession system in that the state is no longer degraded to the mere receiver of taxes, but now plays a leading role.

In agriculture some of the weaknesses of the first agrarian reform law of 1958 were first eliminated (1969). Then the second agrarian reform law no. 117 of 1970 came into effect. Its enactment led to a fundamental restructuring of agriculture. The new law aimed finally to destroy the political power of the large landowners, to liberate the new farmers and farm workers from exploitation and to improve their living standards, and to increase agricultural production. When fixing the limits on the amount of land it was possible to own and when distributing the land, various criteria were applied. These included the fertility of the soil, the type of irrigation, type of cultivation and position. The large landowner lost the right to compensation and the right to choose which lands he wanted to keep. That is to say, the agrarian reform authorities now determined such things. The agrarian reform land was distributed to the new farmers free of charge. In the first phases there were irritating 'socialist'-like experiments with cooperatives and state farms. Later these were relatively quickly abolished. All in all the process was carried out in a way that was not too dogmatic and the various forms of property were revised in favour of private property. Farmers were supported through the expansion of the infrastructure, the development of the soil, desalination projects, agricultural loans, advisory services and other complementary measures to promote agriculture.

For the northern Iraqi region, where the agrarian reform could not be enforced due to the conflict with the Kurds, a special agrarian reform took effect in 1975 (after the defeat of Barzani's supporters). In this law no. 90 of 1975 the amount of land any one person could own was set at a lower limit, due to the different types of irrigation and other economic and geographic circumstances. Thus, the estates to be redistributed could be increased. As early as 1 June 1976 633,645 dunums of land had been confiscated and distributed to 59,154 families in the provinces of Dohuk, Sulaimaniya and Arbil.

In total 10.8 million dunums were distributed to 300,000 landless families before 1988. There were 857 agricultural cooperatives with 376,329 members. In 1984 there were twenty-three large state farms with 188,000 hectares. But because of their low productivity, these state farms were privatized over the following years on President Saddam Hussein's instructions. Generally the tendency towards privatization increased during the 1980s. To this was added the beneficial effects of the newly operational dams and irrigation projects.

In the industrial sector state firms were reorganized and administrative reforms were carried out. New progressive employment laws and social security regulations were enforced and a new participation system for workers and employees introduced in larger firms. Existing firms were expanded and new branches of industry added. A 'mixed economy sector' was created, with the state and private investors contributing capital. Private businessmen were encouraged to start small and medium sized firms within the framework of the national development plans. Loans granted by the State Industry Bank to the private sector increased from two million ID in 1968 to 70 million ID in 1979. In 1979 this bank had a 16.3 million ID share in seventeen private industrial companies. During the period 1970–1975 839 million ID or twenty-eight per cent of all planned state investments were ear-marked for the industrial sector. Of this sum 629 million ID was actually invested. Sharp increases then followed during the development plan of 1976–1980. During this period 4.4 billion ID was invested in industry, and the value of industrial production doubled from 858 to 1800 million ID. New industrial zones were built in the south (Khor al-Zubair), in the west (Akkashat, al-Qaim) and in the north (Kirkuk, Mosul). Between 1968 and 1979 the state industrial sector achieved an average annual growth rate of twenty-one per cent. This was a quantitative and qualitative increase. Of course this relative progress was not easy to achieve given the complicated starting position. Old problems were overcome, but new problems arose as a result of the new system: high production costs, shortage of skilled workers, state subsidies which stretched the national budget, marketing problems etc.

In domestic and foreign trade restructuring policies followed three main objectives:

(1) the tightening of state control over foreign trade and over certain key areas of domestic trade;

(2) the structuring of foreign and domestic trade according to the requirements of development policies to be applied;

(3) the solution of the practical problems inherent in the domestic market.

The composition of imports was to be changed in favour of investment goods. To this end a series of state trade organizations was established. The annual import programme was determined together with the national investment plan. However, the regulation of prices and of the markets met with many difficulties, including the establishment of black markets. Management problems were also associated with the sharp increases in imports. Annual total imports had increased from 181 million ID in 1970 to four billion ID in 1980. It was only when the system was liberalized later that the problems decreased. Oil revenue made possible the subsidizing of food for the population and of raw materials and semi-finished products for national industries.

State services were given new emphases and priorities. The aim was an improvement in the infrastructure and the standard of living for the mass of the population. There was a scale of charges according to the income of the various population groups. Great emphasis was placed on narrowing the gap between town and countryside. The most urgent tasks were the opening up of rural areas by the provision of transport and their supply with electricity and water, the expansion of the public health sector, the fight against illiteracy and the expansion of the education and training sectors and the expansion of the public housing building programme. Yet despite all this what was actually achieved did not by any means meet what was required. For example; although many modern settlements were built, a shortage of housing was found in almost all larger towns. Increases in private income, immigration from rural areas and the immigration of foreign workers had increased demand for accommodation enormously. The country's total requirement for accommodation at the end of the 1970s was estimated to be 160,000 units per year, compared with the actual construction of 30,000 units annually. In contrast, achievements in the education and training sectors were remarkable.

The restructuring of the bank sector included, amongst other things, the merging of the five existing commercial banks to form one single commercial bank (Rafidain Bank), which later became the largest commercial bank in the Near East. The three state specialist banks (Agricultural Cooperative Bank, Industrial Bank and Real Estate Bank) were considerably expanded and provided with increased capital. The Central Bank was reorganized under the new law no. 64 which took effect on 1 June 1976, and took over new development tasks alongside its traditional duties (currency stability, the control of foreign exchange, bank supervision and the administration of state accounts etc.).

Changes in National Income Levels and in the Distribution of Income

In the 1970s, and especially during the second half of the 1970s, the Iraqi economy experienced an extremely dynamic growth. The restructuring of almost all economic sectors outlined above, the nationalization of oil and the increase in oil revenue made possible the elimination of many problematic areas and thus considerably improved the country's ability to invest.

Let us first examine the period 1973–1976: during this time the gross domestic fixed capital formation (GDFC) increased threefold from 269 to 873 million ID. The ratio of this GDFC to gross domestic product (GDP) doubled from 1.36 to two billion ID (cf. Tables 7 and 8). Nominal national income increased from 1,412 to 4,479 million ID. Correspondingly, per capita income rose more than threefold from 136 to 387 ID. Thus, national economic demand increased, and with it the domestic market expanded considerably. Imports increased from 270 to 1,151 million ID. They were fully financed by oil revenue, other export receipts and through economic savings. Capital goods made up more than fifty per cent of all imports. The participation of domestic private firms in many state development projects led to the accumulation of capital in private hands and the transformation of society. Already during this period the market began to play an increasingly important role.

The number of larger private industrial firms grew from 1,090 to 1,254, and the number of smaller private workshops from 26,377 to 37,669. The production value of the former rose from 67 to 162 million ID and that of the latter from 86 to 268 million ID. Development in the state industrial sector was even more impressive. In 1976 there were 225 state firms, compared with 185 in 1973. Their production value doubled from 224 to 428 million ID.

This growth may be attributed to the following factors:

(1) an improvement in the terms of trade and growth in real income;

(2) the increase in factors affecting domestic supplies, through imports;

(3) positive intersectoral effects;

(4) the government's determination to overcome the underdevelopment of the country using all possible means;

(5) the government's decision to accept low yields from its capital investments, and to prioritize the investment of oil revenue at home rather than abroad;

(6) the participation of the population in the development of the economy and in the improvement of their own standards of living;

(7) political stability.

The government was determined to accelerate the implementation of development projects. It devoted special attention to the elimination of problems in the building and construction industry, and the transport, public transport and communications sectors.

Even more progress was achieved in the second half of the 1970s. Within the framework of the national development plan of 1976–1980, planners expected an average growth rate in gross domestic product (GDP) of 16.6 per cent. Some of the growth rates achieved were higher than this figure. Comparing the figures for 1976 and 1980, we are presented with the following picture (cf. Table 9). The nominal GDP to market prices increased threefold from 5,236 to 15,825 million ID. In real terms (in constant prices from 1975) it grew from 4,751 to 7,284 million ID, i.e. by fifty-three per cent. The annual average growth rate of nominal GDP was 21.6 per cent during the period 1975–1980, real GDP was 12.8 per cent. Real per capita GDP rose from 413 to 550 ID, despite an increase in the Iraq population of nineteen per cent. On the other hand, the rate of inflation of 1979–80 was extraordinarily high due to the overheating of the economy, and the government was forced to take measures to depress the economy.

Remarkable changes in the structure of the economy could also be observed. With the formation of GDP to factor costs the contributions of industry, the building sector and services (trade, transport and communications) increased to a disproportionately large degree in absolute and relative terms, while the relative importance of agriculture decreased. During the period 1975–1979 real GDP to factor costs rose from 3,970 to 6,977 million ID. The contribution of industry to GDP rose from sixty-six to seventy per cent, that of the building sector from two to six per cent and that of the service industry from nine to thirteen per cent, while agriculture's share decreased from seven to five per cent (cf. Table 10). These were the sectors in which the development projects were concentrated.

Analysing the use of GDP to market prices (Table 11) it is interesting to note that in the second half of the 1970s (1975–1980) real gross plant investments as well as real national economic consumption doubled. The former increased from 1,219 to 2,305 million ID, whilst the latter rose from 2,267 to 4,471 million ID. Here the growth in state consumption was far greater than the growth in private consumption. There was a considerable room for manoeuvre for further increases in investment, especially if one considers the opportunities available to slow down the growth in state consumption.

The distribution of income shifted in favour of employers. As Table 12 shows, the proportion of income from business activities and wealth of GDP to market prices increased from sixty-nine per cent in 1975 to seventy-six per cent in 1980, while the proportion of salaries and wages decreased from twenty-one to eighteen per cent. The absolute growth in salaries and wages was considerable, from 839 to 2,802 million ID. In contrast, businessmen's profits had increased fourfold from 2,770 to 12,047 million ID. An atmosphere was therefore created in which a dynamic business class could have been further developed.

Generally the standard of living of the whole population increased considerably. The increase in consumption of the lower income groups was of particular significance. These groups were not only able to improve their living conditions materially, but from a social and cultural point of view too. A 'minimum wage act' was passed and in many cases exceeded. The average annual income of an industrial worker rose by 234 per cent from 250 to 834 ID between 1968 and 1979. In the years 1972 to 1978 alone consumer expenditure per person increased more than threefold, and expenditure on 'non-food items', such as personal hygiene, culture etc. increased in significance.

The improvement in living conditions of the mass of the population is not only to be attributed to the increase in disposable income and to consumer expenditure, but also to the increased (free) state services. We refer here primarily to the achievements in the areas of public health, training and education. The number of general hospitals rose by fifty per cent in the decade 1970–1980; and from the mid-1970s onwards the emphasis lay in the building of hospitals in rural areas. The expansion of basic health care led to patients increasingly being treated in health centres rather than specialist hospitals. At the beginning of the 1980s there were 249 main centres, 955 branch centres and 201 out-patient departments. By 1990 the number of main centres was to have been increased to 1,022 in order to provide blanket medical care in the rural areas too. In the specialist hospitals the capacity in the children's illnesses sector was expanded above all. Health provision for the population improved considerably: whilst there had been one doctor for every 3,320 inhabitants in 1970, the ratio had become 1:1,837 by 1980. In comparison to countries of the same income category, however, Iraq was still very far behind (Jordan, for example had one doctor for every 900 inhabitants). It should also be noted that the majority of doctors practised in the towns, leaving rural areas under-served. In order to relieve this situation, graduates of medical faculties had to work in the rural health service for one year. State health care could be claimed free of charge, except for in-patient treatment. The other points of emphasis in state health policy lay in the establishment of a safe drinking water supply, improvements in sewage and waste disposal, a decrease in air and water pollution and the establishment of a national pharmaceutical industry.

Similarly remarkable progress was seen in the education sector. From the school year 1970/71 to 1980/81 the number of elementary schools doubled from 5,617 to 11,280. A similar development was found in middle and high schools (from 921 to 1,891). Professional training, promoted more intensively since the 1970s, showed a remarkable increase in the number of training colleges, from forty-seven to 143. Furthermore the number and capacity of universities and colleges were considerably increased and their curricula reformed in view of the requirements of development policies. There were six universities for further education in Baghdad, Mosul, Basra and Sulaimaniya, as well as a technological university. These were complemented by several technical colleges, agricultural colleges and teacher training schools.

Through the introduction of compulsory schooling the government succeeded (1970–1980) in increasing enrolment figures from fifty-five to 100 per cent. The success of the education policies was seen above all in girls, where attendence rose from only thirty-four per cent (1970) to ninety-five per cent (1980). In the secondary sector (age groups twelve to seventeen) enrolment figures of sixty-five per cent for men and thirty-three per cent for women (1980) were a great improvement over those of 1970, when they had been twenty-seven per cent and twelve per cent respectively. The proportion of twenty to twenty-four year olds in further education rose from five to ten per cent. The number of female students also rose continually.

Last but not least, the achievements in employment policies should be referred to. Economic growth led to full employment between 1977 and 1980. A shortage of skilled and unskilled labour was only partly relieved by the employment of (more than two million, mainly Arab) foreigners. The immigration of workers from Arab countries (Egypt, Jordan, Morocco and others) was facilitated and encouraged. Arab guest workers were treated as equals to Iraqis in keeping with the government's pan-Arab orientation. There were qualitative differences in the employment policies in comparison to neighbouring the Gulf states.

All in all it is clear that important structural reforms were carried out in almost all economic sectors during the 1970s, that investment opportunities were improved with the systematic elimination of problems, that remarkable real growth rates were achieved in the production sector and in the service industry, and that the standard of living of the population as a whole was improved and the distribution of income corrected in favour of the middle and lower classes. Of course there were set-backs and failures in some sectors, and of course the increased oil revenue played an important role, but this does not allow us to dismiss the achievements of the new system. At the end of the 1970s Iraq had become the largest property market in the entire Near and Middle Eastern region. In the execution of the numerous development projects and the import of technology the government worked mainly with the western industrial states, but it also worked with the developing countries of the Third World (e.g. Brazil) too. There was a certain tendency to strengthen links with those western states (such as France) which pursued politics independent of the USA. The outlook for the future seemed bright and promised much. By and large the Iraqi population was optimistic. On a regional level Iraq played a specific regional role as an oil-rich country with pan-Arab orientation, which was qualitatively different from the role of the Gulf States. It granted North and South Yemen considerable development aid, and contributed a great deal to their later unification. It supported Jordan, the Sudan and Mauretania economically and militarily in order to repel negative, foreign influences. As a granter of aid it had its own development policies towards the poor Arab countries. Contacts with the conservative Gulf States which were under American-British influence, were pragmatic. In the sphere of international politics Iraq attempted to loosen its ties with Moscow as far as possible and to strengthen the line of independence from any pact in the Arab region and thereby to take on a leading role in the non-aligned movement. In this phase American pressure on Iraq was not great, for the USA was busy (alongside its engagement in Vietnam) in improving relations between Egypt and Israel (the preparation of the Camp David Treaty).

A Fundamental Change in Regional, Political and Strategic Conditions During the Eighties

In 1978/79 the regional, political and strategic constellation underwent a fundamental change. Egypt broke free from the Arab Front and, despite many warnings, signed a separate peace treaty with Israel. This had and still has wide-reaching consequences for the whole region, including a deep split in the Arab camp. Egypt was boycotted by most Arab states; its membership of the Arab league was suspended. In the attempts to re-establish the former equilibrium and the establishment of a 'northern front', Iraq's importance grew. Reflecting this new role, it hosted the Arab summit in 1978 in Baghdad. Iraq was determined to halt the further 'catastrophic disintegration' of the entire Arab front. Hardly had Iraq begun to overcome this extremely difficult task, a new front was opened on the Iranian border, with which it would be occupied for a long time: immediately after the fall of the Shah's regime (beginning 1979) the new rulers in Teheran began their campaign to 'export the Islamic revolution' to Iraq, i.e. they began to agitate to bring about the fall of the Iraqi political system. Iraq reacted strongly. This conflict escalated into a war which lasted for eight years. It really consisted of two wars: an Iraq-Iran war, 1980–1982, in which Iraq tried to obtain political advantages from its favourable military position, in particular regarding the reestablishment of Iraqi sovereignty over the Shatt al-Arab; and an Iran-Iraq war, 1982–1988, where the Khomeini regime (having repelled the Iraqi troops from its territory) tried to found an 'Islamic Republic' in its own image in that part of southern Iraq which it had conquered, and to extend its influence throughout the entire Near and Middle Eastern region. The superpowers would allow neither. They applied their arms export policies to the warring parties in careful doses, so that at the end of the day neither could win or lose. It was in the USA's and Israel's interest in particular that the war should be prolonged and the two countries (Iran and Iraq) weaken each other. The war also weakened OPEC internally. From 1982 onwards a continually decreasing trend is noticeable in oil prices, a trend which had far-reaching implications for the economic development of all regional states.

The Development of the Iraqi Economy during the 1980–1988 War

The eight-year war not only changed the political and economic situation in Iraq and Iran, but in the entire Near and Middle Eastern region. It changed the judicial conditions of the development process, led to the existence of contradictory alliances and axes, weakened regional organizations, created intervention opportunities for powers from outside the region, endangered the security and territorial integrity of the countries concerned, and made the co-existence of various social systems in the region difficult. Its economic consequences were many and varied:

(1) the destruction of a large part of the national wealth;

(2) the transfer of urgently needed workers from the civil sector to the front;

(3) the transfer of capital abroad and the emigration of skilled workers;

(4) the obstruction of achievements in training institutions;

(5) the poisoning of the investment climate for domestic and foreign investors;

(6) the neglect of agriculture;

(7) enormous increases in expenditure on defence and internal security at the cost of civil investments;

(8) increased inflation and black market problems;

(9) disruption to intra-regional cooperation;

(10) increasing mistrust of foreign workers and limitations on the regional mobility of workers.

For the period 1980–1985 alone war costs were estimated to be $417 billion. Iraqi losses were estimated at $176 billion, of which $94 billion represented defence expenses, $56 billion lost oil exports and $26 billion GNP (gross national product) losses. All these factors not only affected Iraq and Iran, but also the Gulf states and other countries of the Near East. The increase in defence and internal security expenditure in the whole region at the cost of civil sectors transformed the structure of the markets and decreased export opportunities for the western partner countries.

A further factor was the dramatic fall in oil prices and their purchasing power. The oil revenues of the eight Arab oil exporting countries, Algeria, Bahrain, Iraq, Kuwait, Libya, Qatar, Saudi Arabia and the UAE fell from $205 to $104 billion between 1980 and 1984, i.e. by almost fifty per cent. Added to this was the extremely painful oil price fall of 1986, when revenue fell by a further fifty per cent to $49 billion within a very short space of time. The purchasing power of the oil revenue also fell due to fluctuations in the dollar exchange rate, a rise in the cost of imported goods and a reduction in US interest rates. This transformed the balance of payments surplus of the above-mentioned countries (1980: $91 billion) into a deficit of $11.2 billion in 1986. The combined GDP of these countries fell between 1982 and 1986 from $338 to $262 billion. The government reacted with cuts in imports and to the budget. State expenditure, the main pillar of the economy, fell between 1980 and 1986 (by a third) from $137 to $99 billion. The EC states lost important market shares in the region. Many observers were surprised again and again: how could the western industrial states allow a war with such consequences and in such an inflammable region to be prolonged for eight years?[3]

In Iraq itself annual oil revenue fell from $26 to $12.5 billion from 1980 to 1985, and within another year (1986) to only $8 billion, despite the fact that the quantity of oil exported rose from 1.1 to 1.75 million barrels/day. As a result goods imports had to be cut by sixty per cent in the space of a year.

The effects of the war on the Iraqi oil sector and the countermeasures taken were generally of decisive importance. At the beginning of the war in September 1980 Iraq had a production and export capacity of more than 4 million b/d, with oil outlets in the Gulf and in the eastern Mediterranean, via Turkey and Syria. During the war the Iraqi Gulf ports were damaged and closed. Syria closed the Iraqi pipelines for political reasons on 10 April 1982. The result was an abrupt and painful fall in oil exports between 1979 and 1981 from 3.28 to 0.75 million b/d and of oil revenue from $21 billion to $10 billion. Nevertheless, Iraq refused to be discouraged. The protection of all oil installations was systematically strengthened. Not only were the damaged installations quickly repaired, but they were also expanded with the construction of new installations. Highest priority was given to energy and economic projects within the national development programme which had been made more flexible. Thus, the country's oil product supplies were safeguarded and some products were even exported via Turkey and Jordan. The capacity of the oil pipeline via Turkey was increased from 0.35 to 1.0 million b/d and then doubled through the construction of a similar parallel line. To this was added another important export outlet via Saudi Arabia, first through the construction of a connecting pipe between southern Iraqi oil fields and the Saudi East-West Pipeline (Petroline) which runs to Yanbo on the Red Sea, and later through the construction of an independent Iraqi oil pipeline parallel to Petroline with its own oil port, al-Mujizz. The 'time exchange deals' agreed with Saudi Arabia and Kuwait should also be mentioned. These allowed the export of 0.3 million b/d at Iraq's expense.

It was due to all these measures that Iraq was able to increase production and export during the war (and despite intensive

3.Aziz Alkazaz, 'The Middle East Economy since the 1980s' in *Aussenpolitik* (German Foreign Affairs Review), vol. 39, Quaterly Edition, no. 3/1988 pp. 252–264.

clashes and the continued blocking of its export via Syria). In the last year of the war (1988) Iraqi oil production was 2.72 million b/d, of which 2.4 million b/d were exported. The pre-war situation could not be re-established, but nevertheless annual oil revenues increased between 1986 and 1988 from $7 billion to $11 billion. Iraqi refinery capacity was considerably expanded thanks to the implementation of a number of projects. In 1988 it reached around 650,000 b/d, compared with only 100,000 b/d in 1968. It was planned to rise again to 800,000 b/d after the completion of the Musaiyab refinery, which was under construction. Several large projects were being prepared to use the associated natural gases, and in the petrochemical and fertilizer industries. In the north and the south of the country 'gas gathering systems' such as processing and liquefaction installations were constructed, which served domestic supplies and the export of gas. Annual gas production almost doubled between 1985 and 1989 to 11.84 billion m^3, and a gas pipe was built to supply Kuwait.[4]

THE DEVELOPMENT OF THE OTHER SECTORS OF THE ECONOMY

If we take the other sectors of the economy into account it is possible to establish that during the eight years of the war (1980–1988) around 6,000 development projects were implemented in Iraq. In 1968 1,298 new projects were embarked upon, of which 207 were in the industrial sector, 135 in agriculture and 209 in education and research.

A particularly significant obstacle was the continuing lack of hard currency, which may be attributed primarily to the effects of the war, obstruction to oil exports in any quantity and decreases in oil prices, as well as to high defence expenditure. The country's hard currency reserves, which had been some US$37 billion before the outbreak of the war were US$2 billion in 1987. After 1983 the government was forced to undertake debt conversion negotiations and to ask suppliers for credit. At the end of 1986 the Iraqi foreign debt was estimated to be about $50 billion. By the middle of 1989 it was $65 billion, of which $26 to $30 billion represented war subsidies from Gulf states, $2.8 billion was publicly

---

4. Cf. in detail Aziz Alkazaz, 'Die Ölstrategie des Saddam Husain', in *Bonner Energie-Report*, Bonn, no. 10/1990 and no. 11/1990.

guaranteed economic credits (to be paid back 1985–1990) and $6 billion was non-guaranteed supplier's credit. The largest creditor was Japan, with $3 billion, followed by Italy, the Federal Republic of Germany, France and Turkey. Debt servicing amounted to some $3 billion annually.

This significantly slowed down investment activity in both the public and the private sector. Annual gross capital formation in the public sector, for example, decreased from 5.1 billion ID in 1981 to 2.9 billion ID in 1988. Private capital formation decreased from 1.0 to 0.8 billion ID (cf. Table 13). In general total economic development was better in the second half of the 1980s than it had been in the first half. Real gross domestic product (GDP) at factor costs, which had decreased in the first half of the 1980s, rose between 1984 and 1988 from 11 to 14 billion ID. This growth was mainly attributable to the contributions of the goods-producing sectors (mining, industry, agriculture, building and construction, electricity, water) whilst service sectors declined (cf. Table 14). All in all, real national income and the real per capita income of the population was stagnant, even declined in the period between 1981 and 1988. Nominal national income rose from 10 to 15 billion ID and nominal per capita income rose from 736 to 832 ID, but inflation rates were too high (cf. Table 15).

Yet despite this, remarkable progress was made in many areas of the infrastructure, as well as in various economic sectors. Energy use (an indication of the degree of industrialization and the standard of living), which had risen by an average 16.5 per cent per annum between 1973 and 1979, and which had reached the order of 16 million tonnes of oil equivalent (TOE), had more than doubled by 1989 to 37 million TOE. In 1987 the country's electricity generating capacity was 8,538 MW and the aim was to double it by the year 2000 to 17,500 MW. Already at the beginning of 1988 ninety-five per cent of the total population had electricity, as millions of households were connected to the electricity supply under the 'rural electricity supply scheme'. Per capita use reached 1,450 kWh by 1987. During the period between 1984 and 1988 alone electricity use increased from 16,191 to 23,228 kWh as a result of the establishment of large power stations and dams. The development of alternative energy sources, including sun power, was also begun. The road network was fundamentally expanded and modernized, with the building of modern motorways, which connected Iraq to neighbouring countries. The same was true of the rail network. New international airports were built in Baghdad and Basra, with a third to be added in Mosul. In the telecommunications sector the number of telephone connections rose from 745,222 to 826,764 between 1985 and 1989 alone. Telephone density (connections per 100 inhabitants) rose to 4.8 in 1989. In the 1986–1990 development plan 750 million ID was earmarked for the installation of one million new telephone connections. The telecommunications system established included microwave connections, data transmission networks and terrestrial stations for news satellites.

Large sums were invested in the building of new settlements and in the modernization of existing towns, with a particular emphasis on the preservation of the cultural heritage. In order to absorb the influx of people moving to Baghdad and other conurbations the construction of satellite towns was begun. The plan to develop Baghdad was to give it a new urban structure and amenities which will carry it into the twenty-first century. Between 1979 and 1987 Amanat al-Asima (municipality) spent 3.2 billion ID on water and sewage, roads and new buildings. Other authorities spent a further one billion ID on roads and bridges, housing and a new airport. There are also expansion plans for other towns close to Baghdad: Rashidiya, Zubaidiya, Abu Ghraib and Nahrawan. New master plans have been completed for many cities including Samarra and Takrit, both of which are geared for population explosions (Samarra from 45,000 to 150,000 in the year 2000 and Takrit from 26,000 to 150,000). The government was and is keen to set up new communities to relieve the pressure on the main population centres. In the north new towns are to be built near Mosul, Arbil, Sulaimaniya and Dohuk. In the south, plans for building new towns near Basra, Amara, Nasiriya and Samawa were completed. Construction work on the new town near Basra (150,000 people) began in 1990.

Although it was possible to make a small number of improvements in the agricultural sector, the increase in agrarian production and the degree of self-sufficiency aimed at turned out to be a very complicated task. Despite the assurances of planners that 'food is a more valuable export than oil', and despite Saddam Hussein's words that 'agriculture is permanent oil', the planners had to comment that 'years of underinvestment and failure to follow through on policies have resulted in only a half-hearted exploitation of the agricultural potential'. About 1.5 million people left the land between 1973 and 1977 and had to be absorbed in the cities, an exodus which forced the government to hire farmers abroad, mainly from Egypt and Morocco.

By 1988 a total of 10.8 million dunums had been distributed to more than 300,000 families under the agrarian reform. There were 772 agricultural cooperatives with 360,498 members and a few large state farms. In view of their relatively low productivity and the slow progress made the state farms were abolished and private initiative encouraged. From 1984 onwards farmers were no longer required to be members of a cooperative or a state farm. The state began to concentrate on 'strategic projects' and to create more room for manoeuvre for private farmers who invested some 72 billion ID in the leased 220,000 hectares alone before 1988. Since 1983 they have been permitted to circumvent the state marketing system and to sell directly to private wholesalers. Farmers were given privileged access to necessities such as cars, lorries and building materials, as well as to cheap credit. Between 1980 and 1987 the agricultural bank granted favourable credits of a total of 570 million ID and improved its incentive system by implementing lower interest rates and longer credit periods, and introducing rural savings schemes and new systems of wealth protection. The state invested large sums in river control (dams) and irrigation projects as well as in land development, soil desalination and the construction of the infrastructure for private agrarian concerns. To solve the problem of salination the government devised integrated programmes: water supplies were regulated through river control and dam projects. The excess drainage water in all areas of central and southern Iraq was fed into the Gulf through a 'main outfall drain'. This had a beneficial effect on the Euphrates basin in particular. Numerous land development projects were implemented, embodying good long-term investments which will remain in effect for centuries. There were 135 irrigation projects, primarily in the Euphrates, Tigris and Shatt al-Arab regions. Before the middle of 1988 drainage systems for 875,000 hectates were installed, with further systems for 750,000 hectares planned.

By March 1984, more than 500,000 hectares of reclaimed land had been handed over as part of the programme to reclaim a total 4.4 million hectares. Between 1980 and 1985, work started and was completed on a number of large irrigation projects, including the Kirkuk scheme, Khalis, Hilla/Diwaniya, Ishaqi, Dalmaj, Basra/ Jassan and Abu Ghraib. North Jazira is part of an ID 820 million programme to irrigate 250,000 hectares of the Jazira plain in the north near Mosul. Water is provided by the Saddam (Mosul) Dam to feed sprinkler irrigation systems. The introduction of irrigation to rain-fed land is expected to lead to a five-fold increase in crop production. In 1988 work began on other big irrigation projects: East Jazira (building a canal to feed water to irrigation networks for 70,000 hectares), and South Jazira (135,000 hectares).

To prevent the resalination of its newly reclaimed lands and irrigation schemes, the government has initiated the main outfall drain (MOD) which aims to collect highly saline water from irrigation projects in the central and southern areas and drain it into the Gulf. MOD was expanded to a total 550 km, draining 1.6 million hectares of irrigated land at a maximum discharge capacity of 300 cubic metres a second. The 261 km Euphrates East Drain will flow into the MOD.

While recognizing the success of its reclamation programme, the government was also aware that the land should be properly cultivated, administered and maintained. Far-reaching changes and reforms were introduced. Many of the responsibilities of the Ministry of Agriculture were devoted to the private sector. The Ministry continued to offer subsidies and assistance in buying or hiring machinery and equipment, fertilizers and seeds, plus technical advice. It encourages wider private development of grain, industrial crops, poultry farms, red meat production, fisheries and fruit orchards. Incentives include marketing and pricing policies. Other priorities include redressing the balance in the countryside by bringing education, health, transport and communications, water and power into line with existing urban facilities.

All these measures improved living conditions for farmers and provided them with better opportunities to increase their incomes. On the other hand the increases in agricultural production were generally unsatisfactory and subject to fluctuations. If the average figures for 1979/1981 are represented by 100, the figure for agricultural production in 1989 was 136, plant production was 139, animal production 116 and fishing 154. Correspondingly it was necessary to spend US$3 billion a year on food imports, and this in an agriculturally rich country!

In the industrial sector the establishment of a diversified national industry was pursued as a main objective. Between 1975 and 1983 alone US$16 billion were invested in this sector. Further investments followed in the 1980s, albeit it at a slower pace. Outside oil production there were 640 larger industrial companies in 1988 in Iraq (definition: with more than thirty employees and plant worth more than 100,000 ID) with a total of 154,000 employees and a production value of 2.7 billion ID. Of these 142 were state firms with 126,000 employees and a production value of 2.2 billion ID. Alongside these were eleven mixed economy companies employing 9,000 people and 462 private companies with 17,000 employees.

Small industrial firms experienced a true expansion (these are in fact craftsmen's businesses each with less than 300 employees and operating capital of less than 100,000 ID). In the five years between 1984 and 1988 alone their number almost doubled from 21,000 to 40,000. Correspondingly total employment rose from 46,000 to 92,000 and production value from 462 to 1,777 million ID (cf. Table 16). This considerably improved the geographic distribution of the industrial firms, which had been concentrated in the Baghdad area in earlier decades.

Industrial production had more than doubled between 1976 and 1980, rising from 858 to 1,800 million ID. This was a quantitative and qualitative leap in Iraqi economic history. During the war with Iran industry was encouraged to manage capital surpluses with which to finance new investments in its own and other economic sectors, to replace imports and to meet an increasing proportion of domestic demand. Old and new problems and obstacles therefore had to be mastered (such as insufficient infrastructure, lack of technical expertise, insufficient investment in research and development, weak management). The state, which had previously also been involved in smaller companies, began to concentrate solely on larger capital-intensive projects, encouraging private initiative everywhere else. It offered various incentives to increase industrial production. These included the privatization of 'non-strategic' investments, the promotion of domestic and foreign (Arab) investments, and the intensification of quality control and competition. State and mixed economy firms could no longer rely on state subsidies, but were to be administered commercially and to focus on profitability. These moves towards reform led to productive increases and other positive results between 1987 and 1989.

Through massive investment, particularly in heavy industry and petrochemicals, modern industrial zones were established in Basra, Khor al-Zubair, al-Taji, al-Iskandariya, Samarra, al-Mishraq, al-Qaim, Baiji, Ramadi, Nasiriya, Najaf, Karbala and other parts of the country. This created new employment opportunities and sources of income in areas previously untouched by the industrialization policies. Established industrial complexes manufactured various petrochemical products, fertilizers, drugs, cleansing agents, iron and steel, agricultural machinery, aluminium, cement, glass, textiles, consumer goods etc. Industrial cooperation with neighbouring Arab countries was also encouraged. Baghdad became the headquarters of several regional organizations and joint enterprises. In August 1988 forty-seven state firms were offered for sale to the private sector. Previously, in April 1988, the law on the promotion of Arab investments had come into effect. It contained a number of incentives, including the following:

(a) permission for the foreign investor to hold majority capital;

(b) free transfer of profits abroad;

(c) the freeing of taxes and duties;

(d) protection from expropriation.

For foreign (Arab) investors lists were drawn up of concrete projects with detailed pre-investment studies. The list presented in 1989/90 encompassed 229 industrial projects with investment capital of around 234 million ID.

On the other hand industry continued to face both old and new problems: a lack of specialist employees and basic services, lack of hard currency, bureaucracy and the effects of the war with Iran. An increasing number of workers had to go to the front and were replaced by women in the factories (in some firms up to fifty per cent of the total staff). The Ministry for Industry had to set up numerous education and retraining courses and to offer additional incentives such as cheap homes, food and medical care.

Investments in the education and training sector were of particular significance for the standard of living and the quality of life. These fields expanded rapidly at all stages and have been designed to fulfil the objectives of developmental needs. For all citizens free education is provided. In the period 1980–1989 the number of kindergartens rose from 387 to 643 and children from 56,347 to 87,920, where the numbers of males and females were approximately equal.

The number of pupils in the primary schools rose from 2,612,332 to 3,168,563. The majority of these schools (6,837 from 8, 344) are mixed schools.

At the secondary level the number of schools rose from 1,891 to

2,615 and the number of their pupils from 950,142 to 986,983. Among these schools there were 589 mixed schools.

The number of vocational (commercial, technical and agricultural) schools rose from 143 to 287 and that of their students from 56, 835 to 147,942.

At the university level the number of students rose from 102,430 to 184,047, of which 62,008 were females. In 1989 there were eleven universities and three private colleges in Iraq. The number of students in Institutes of Technology reached 49,209. The need to develop a wider scientific base was behind the decision taken in August 1988 to set up a new university for engineering and sciences which specializes in high technology areas such as robotics, lasers and space studies. Some universities and institutes have done research on behalf of local companies in oil refining, oil products, sulphur and plastics as well as providing assistance to foreign contractors. Party loyalty is no longer necessarily the path to follow to get to the top. In order to alleviate the pressure on university places the government decided in 1987 to establish four new universities and to allow private universities and colleges.

The country has also witnessed wide changes in the field of health care. The number of hospital beds increased in the period 1968–1979 by fifty-two per cent and reached 26,652 in 1989. Besides the 252 hospitals there were (in 1989) 1,434 other health units and 142 Public Medical Clinics. There were 177 laboratories and 1,542 pharmacies. The number of doctors and dentists increased in the period 1968–1979 two and a quarter times and reached 10,312 in 1989, plus 35,022 paramedicals. In 1989 the ratio of doctors to the population was 1:1690 as compared to 1:4200 in 1968.

This expansion of education and health facilities not only improves the quality of human life but also adds to the productivity of the workers and employees.

INCOME DISTRIBUTION

All these measures and developments had positive effects on the standard of living and the income distribution in the country, although the state regional policy met with many difficulties and had only limited success.

Until 1975 it was difficult to isolate measures within the national development plans that were specially designed to foster regional development other than those prepared for the Kurdish area. Allocations had been at the national level and by sector and on a project-oriented basis within the sectors. Regional development was a function of the strength of the sector most widely represented in any given province. Geography and political decisions played an important role.

Industry apparently holds a favoured position within the development objectives. Yet industry was located firmly in the major urban centres and especially in the Baghdad and Basra regions. Outside these centres, industry created under the development plans has been small-scale (consumption industry). This concentration was supported by economic logic; the existence of large scale resources of power and water, skilled cadres, major markets etc. In the small towns and cities there were no traditional industries like craft centres for carpets, metalwork, jewellery, pottery or leather work which might act as foundations for the creation of modern industry. Iraqi planners were confronted, therefore, with these structural constraints.

Investment in the oil industry has shown a bias towards provincial areas in so far as oilfields and oil facilities are located around the Kirkuk, Mosul and Basra areas, and the oil industry is generally not labour-intensive. Pipelines, pumping stations, oil terminals, refineries and petrochemicals tended to benefit Baghdad as the administrative centre, as well as Kirkuk, Mosul and Basra-Zubair as the operational centres to the exclusion of other provinces. The pattern of investment in the petrochemical industry tends to reinforce the imbalances between the country's central axis through the riverine belt Basra to Baghdad and the outlying districts.

Nevertheless, a growing number of industries has been established in different provinces of the country: al-Mishraq (sulphur plants), Akkashat and al-Qaim (chemical industries) with the construction of a new town and a degree of genuine regional industrial development, Sammara, al-Khalis and Samawa (middle-scale industries), Nasiriya (aluminium industry).

What are the results of all these measures and developments as far as living standards and income distribution are concerned? One answer could be found in the household budget surveys which explore the consumption and expenditure patterns of the Iraqi household, its income and resources. They could measure the level of welfare and provide information about social, living and accommodation conditions as well as the level of public services.

We have to rely mainly on household budget surveys compiled by the Central Statistical Organization/Ministry of Planning. This organization carried out several surveys during the period 1971–1988. Surveys implemented in 1971/72, 1976, 1979 and 1984/85 were devoted to consumption and income. The 1988 survey included in addition to income and consumption the demographical situation of the families and the public services benefit to them.

The household budget survey of 1971 was taken on the basis of one and a half percentage per 1,000 of total households situated in the rural areas. The proportion was two per 1,000 in the urban areas. The number of households in the sample amounted to 1,000 and 1,600 in the rural and urban areas respectively. We refer here to two types of income: (a) cash income, (b) adjusted income which includes imputed rent and income in kind in addition to cash income. The household was the unit used to measure the inequality of income distribution. However, the debate continues as to whether it is the household or the individual that should be regarded as the basic unit of assessing income distribution. The households were classified according to fourteen income groups for both cash income and adjusted income.

The study highlights some important points:

(1) A greater disparity between top and bottom brackets for adjusted income as against cash income. The difference between top and bottom was in the ratio of 24:1 of cash income and 25:1 of adjusted income.

(2) Most households were concentrated in the centre of the distribution. For cash incomes, nearly fifty per cent of the units were found in the income groups 200–499 ID, and nearly sixty per cent in the income groups 200–599 ID of the adjusted income. The income group 300–399 ID includes the highest number of units in both cash and adjusted income.

(3) The national average amounted to 468 ID for cash income and 577 ID for adjusted income. The most common frequency in the distribution was around 200 and 300 ID and not much below the national average. The households lying below these averages accounted for seventy-six per cent in the cash income and sixty-seven per cent in the adjusted income.

(4) If we divide all households into equal groups, each containing ten per cent of all households we find that the highest ten per cent of households have cash incomes about fourteen times

those of the lowest ten per cent of the households, declining to only nine times in the adjusted income. The top fifty per cent of households get seventy-seven per cent of the total cash income and seventy-five per cent of the total adjusted income. This means that they get about three times the income of the lowest fifty per cent of the households.

(5) The distribution of income by individuals is more equal than that by households.

(6) The study of the urban-rural income distribution revealed that the average cash income of an urban household is 1.5 times that of a rural household (1.2 times in adjusted income). Out of the total adjusted income in the rural areas, only 7.3 per cent goes to the lowest twenty per cent of the households, while the top twenty per cent receives forty-two per cent. This distribution is more unequal in the urban areas. The lowest twenty per cent get 6.8 per cent and the top twenty per cent receive forty-three per cent of the total income.

(7) A comparison with other oil exporting countries (Iran, Libya, Indonesia, Mexico) revealed that the overall inequality (measured by the ratio of concentration) in these countries was greater than that in Iraq.

To compare the results of the surveys for the years 1971, 1979 and 1988 regarding expenditure:

In 1971 the expenditure of a representative urban household was 7.68 ID per month of which 48.2 per cent went to food stuffs, 10.2 per cent for clothes, 5.8 per cent for furniture and household commodities, 18.2 per cent for rent, fuel and energy, 6.1 per cent for transport and communications, 1.7 per cent for recreation, education and culture, 2.2 per cent for medical services and health care. The monthly expenditure rose then to 22.19 ID in 1979 and to 59.45 ID in 1988. The portion for food stuffs decreased in 1979 to 44 per cent and increased in 1988 to forty-nine per cent. The portion of rent, fuel and energy stood in 1979 at the sale level (18.2 per cent) but increased in 1988 to 21.7 per cent. The portion for recreation increased in 1979 to two per cent but decreased to 0.8 per cent in 1988. The portion for transport and communications decreased 1979–1988 from 8.6 per cent to 6.5 per cent which is an indication of improved infrastructure and services in the country.

In the rural areas the monthly expenditure of a representative household increased from 5.34 ID/1971 to 14.24 ID/1979 to 43.08

ID/1988. The portion for food stuffs first decreased from 64.7 per cent to 51.6 per cent and then increased to 54.5 per cent. The portion for clothes increased from 11.3 per cent to 14.8 per cent and then went down to 12.6 per cent. Furniture had a dramatic improvement from 3.6 per cent to 9.2 per cent and then decreased to 6.7 per cent. Rent, fuel and energy first decreased 7.9 per cent to 6.3 per cent and then increased sharply to 14.2 per cent. Transport and communications rose from three per cent to 7.5 per cent and decreased to 6.2 per cent. Here the rural household spent 2.67 ID in 1988 as compared with only 0.16 per cent in 1971 which indicates a significant improvement in provision of telephones and cars. Expenditure for medical services and health care rose from 1.8 per cent to two per cent and went back to 1.6 per cent. Expenditure for recreation, education and culture was in 1971 with only 0.03 ID or 0.6 per cent negligible, rose in 1979 to 0.22 ID or 1.5 per cent and reached in 1988 0.30 ID or 0.7 per cent.

How did the individual's income develop in urban and rural areas?

If we compare the figures of 1979 and 1988, the urban individual's income increased from 26.42 to 61.62 ID per month. The rural individual's income rose from 15.27 to 48.34 ID. The gap between urban and rural income narrowed. In 1979 the urban income was 1.73 times higher than the rural income, declining to 1.28 times in 1988. The monthly savings of an urban individual (household) decreased 1979–1988 from 4.23 to 2.17 ID whereas the rural individual could increase his monthly savings from 1.03 to 5.26 ID. This indicates a bigger improvement for the rural areas (higher prices for agricultural products). In both cases the components of the monthly income shifted significantly. The percentage of wages and salaries went down from forty-nine per cent to twenty-six per cent (urban) and from thirty-three per cent to sixteen per cent (rural) of the total income. That means a remarkable increase in the percentage of other sources of income (transferable income, hired ownership, economic activity) from fifty-one per cent to seventy-four per cent (urban) and from sixty-seven per cent to eighty-four per cent (rural).

THE BACKGROUND TO AND EFFECTS OF THE SECOND GULF WAR 1990/91

Before 2 August 1990 the bilateral Iraqi-Kuwaiti problems were essentially concerned with oil policies, Kuwaiti war subsidies and the disputed borders. In fact these problems were not new, but their quality changed completely in the context of the American-Iraqi conflict and the political and economic crisis of the Near and Middle Eastern region. This also explains why this bilateral conflict was so rapidly regionalized and internationalized.

The 'Irangate scandal' over secret American arms supplies to Iran (via Israel), the involvement of the Saudi arms dealer Adnan Khashogi, and the related occupation of the Iraqi port of Fao by Iranian troops (1986) had already signalled to Iraq the existence of American plans, the aim of which was to bring down the political system in Baghdad. At least these developments were interpreted by the Iraqi leadership as evidence of such plans. But, since it was still bound up in the war with Iran, Iraq was unable to respond.

The peace negotiations between Baghdad and Tehran which followed the end of the Iran-Iraq war in August 1988 were extremely difficult and lengthy. Iran was not prepared to make any substantial concessions. It became increasingly clear that American policy in the Near East was to prevent Iraq from realizing the fruits of its military victory and considerably to reduce its potential for power, a strategic objective which primarily serves Israeli interests (the maintenance of Israeli military superiority). There were indications that Israel itself would intervene if the USA were not to undertake the task. In reality the American congress decided on economic sanctions against Iraq in March 1990, i.e. a long time before 2 August 1990, and there was a systematic campaign against western firms who worked together with Iraq. Iraq viewed this campaign as 'the beginning of an economic blockade and as the preparation of the stage for a military blow, similar to the destruction of its nuclear reactor in 1981 by Israeli fighter aircraft'.

The Iraqi response to this challenge touched on three points:

(1) Israel and the Arab-Israeli conflict;
(2) the American presence in the Gulf region and
(3) the relationship between oil and politics.

President Saddam Hussein held the view that the military superiority of Israel, its intransigence in the peace negotiations and its expansionist tendencies (intensified by the immigration of large number of Soviet Jews) made necessary the construction of an Arab deterrent power. On 1 April 1990 he made it known that he had binary chemical weapons which could be employed in the case of an Israeli attack with weapons of mass destruction. With regard to the increased American presence in the Gulf, he accused the USA (in a speech at an Arab summit in February 1990 in Amman) of wanting to control Arab oil fields in order to determine oil policies, thereby increasing their ability to compete with Europe and Japan. After the Soviet troops had pulled out of neighbouring Afghanistan and after the end of the East-West conflict the presence of American warships in the Gulf could no longer be justified. It was said that it signified a considerable limitation of the sovereignty of the regional states, with Iraq in particular feeling threatened. Saddam Hussein called upon the Arab states to defend their sovereignty and to encourage the USA to leave the Gulf. He also emphasized again and again (for the last time on 16 July 1990) that the USA would use oil and oil income against Arab interests.

Against this background Saddam Hussein accused the Kuwaiti government of having worked with the USA to drain Iraq financially and to force the country to its knees economically. The exceeding of the agreed OPEC quotas and the associated price decrease led to losses which Iraq could not bear. In its memorandum to the Arab League on 15 July 1990 the Iraqi government estimated the Arab countries' losses to be US$500 billion for the period 1981–1990, of which $89 billion were Iraq's. In the three and a half years between 1987 and 1990 alone Iraqi losses amounted to $25 billion and with every dollar by which the price was lowered, Iraq lost one billion dollars a year. Kuwait's and the UAE's over-production, they claimed, had led to the oil price being forced down from $21 to $11 per barrel in the months of February to June 1990. Diplomatic attempts to change this course were unsuccessful. The economic war was seen as so dangerous because it strangled Iraq at a time when the country was confronted with particular challenges: the reconstruction of the towns and installations destroyed in the war, the satisfaction of its people's consumer expectations following eight years of deprivation related to the war, the servicing of high foreign debts and the undertaking of new development projects. For the period 1989–1993 Iraq needed at least $58 billion, of which $7 billion were for immediate projects in the infrastructure and petrochemical sectors, $30 billion for the reconstruction of the industrial sector and ports, $20 billion for the repayment of foreign debt and $one billion for the structural adaptation programme. But in contrast annual Iraqi oil income amounted to less than $15 billion, although Iraq could increase its

The Distribution of National Income 239

production and export capacity to more than 5 million barrels/ day (it remained within its OPEC quota of 3.1 million b/d). Between 1986 and 1989 Iraq experienced very little real economic growth. Growth rates in nominal gross domestic product lay far below the rates of inflation. Inflation remained a fundamental problem, weighing particularly heavily on those with contract-dependent income. In 1989 the government was forced to reintroduce price controls despite the liberalization begun in 1987 and to increase state subsidies for basic necessities. The salaries of state employees remained unchanged for nine years and were only raised in 1989 by an average of 25 Iraqi Dinars, burdening the state budget with an additional 600 million ID. Total state subsidies rose in 1989 to 235 million ID. Citizens pressed for foreign travel, but there was no hard currency available. Foreign guest worker transfers had to be reduced, which led to tensions with some of the Egyptians working in Iraq. To this was added increased competition for jobs following the discharge of numerous soldiers. The foreign value of the Iraqi currency sank so low that its exchange rate against the Kuwaiti Dinar reached 16:1, compared with 1:1 before the war.

All in all Iraq suffered greatly from the first Gulf War and its consequences. Alongside incalculable human victims, the war also swallowed enormous sums of money. Arms imports alone cost $102 billion. Interruptions to oil exports led to losses of the order of $106 billion. The Gulf states (Kuwait, UAE, Saudi Arabia) profited from the decrease in Iraqi oil exports and increased their exports and their market shares. The above mentioned sum of $106 billion practically flowed directly into their coffers. It is against this background that Iraq demanded reparations, especially since in the Gulf war it had defended not only itself, but all the Gulf states from Iranian expansionism (the export of the Islamic revolution). In particular Iraq demanded the remission of war subsidies and other contributions towards the financing of reconstruction, pointing to the example of the Marshall Plan for Europe after the Second World War. Iraq also took into account the requirements of the poor Arab countries (Egypt, Jordan, Mauritania, Morocco, Somalia, Sudan, Tunisia) when it suggested the creation of a new regional development fund. According to the Iraqi suggestion this fund would include any oil income which resulted from oil price increases above $25 a barrel.

When Kuwait refused to comply with Iraqi demands and

continued to work with the USA, Iraq played its 'historic card', claiming that Kuwait had been part of Iraq until 1913 and was only separated by the colonial power of England. Saddam Hussein accused the Kuwaiti government of having refused the Iraqi initiative of 1988 to fix the controversial border and of having built military and oil-industrial installations on Iraqi territory. In the process Iraqi oil to the value of $2.4 billion had been illegally lifted. The economic war and the intentional financial draining of Iraq were, they said, comparable to a military attack.

The invasion by Iraqi troops of Kuwait on 2 August 1990 was therefore (from the Iraqi perspective) a defensive measure. With the control of Kuwait and the threat to Israel with chemical weapons Iraq wanted to hold some form of security with which it could deter the USA from destroying the Iraqi power potential. But this did not succeed. The course and the results of the Second Gulf War are well-known. What effects did this war have on the Iraqi economy and society?

The war was concentrated not in Kuwait but on Iraqi territory. More than 110,000 air attacks were launched, for example, in which around 90,000 tons of bombs were dropped. Then there were ground battles. Iraqi society payed a high price in blood. According to the estimates of a Greenpeace study based on American military figures, 110,000 to 140,000 Iraqis were killed in allied air attacks (*On impact, modern warfare and the environment*: a case study of the Gulf War, by Arkin, Durrant and Cherni, London, May 1991). Several hundred thousand people were wounded, forced to flee or made homeless. The economic and social structure was almost totally destroyed. Air attacks disrupted electricity, water and fuel supplies, destroyed large parts of the communications system, the transport network and production plants. This had devastating effects on all areas of life in this modern society. With the cease-fire of 28 February 1991 the war was by no means at an end for Iraq. First, directly after the war, unrest broke out in the north and south of the country, and this, following the army's tough response, caused further comprehensive destruction and streams of refugees. Secondly, the UN embargo was continued. For medical supplies Iraq was forced to seek the help of international aid organizations which were able to cover less than ten per cent of the country's needs.

The allies' attacks were not only aimed at purely military targets, but at civilian installations too. The transport infrastructure, oil production and processing plants, energy creation and distribution, water supplies and the telecommunications network were entirely or partly destroyed, as were strategically important buildings and tens of thousands of private homes. Damage to these civil sectors was estimated by Arab regional institutions at around $200 billion. Oil export losses for one year amounted to $18 billion (at an assumed export of 2.8 million b/d at a price of $18/b). Concrete examples for the extent of the destruction (official figures): 99 of a total of 114 power stations, 134 bridges, three dams, 12 water regulators, 120 telephone exchanges, 43 radio and TV stations, 57 civil industrial companies, 46 of a total of 102 grain mills, 180 grain silos and cold storage depots, 14 shopping centres, 154 banks, 94 hospitals, 3,934 schools, 92 mosques and 10 churches. In the individual ministries' areas (number of destroyed units): public health 450, agriculture 1,595, industry 655, oil 34,534, trade 271, housing construction 602, finance 268.

In the meantime the Iraqis have succeeded in extensively rebuilding all these destroyed units. Reconstruction has been carried out without foreign help and under the conditions of the continuing UN embargo. By October 1992, for example, the following had been rebuilt: 76 of the 99 power stations, 122 of the 134 bridges, 112 of the 120 telephone exchanges, all the dams, all the grain mills, 154 of the 180 grain silos and cold storage depots, 39 of the 57 industrial companies, 3,136 of the 3,934 schools, all the mosques and churches. Eighty-five per cent of the infrastructure has been rebuilt. In addition, the production of cars and lorries and agricultural machines has begun.

However, these reconstruction achievements should not distract us from the fact that the economic situation of the country remains critical. Hyperinflation (1991: around 1,500 per cent) and the destruction of the currency (the smuggling in of counterfeit money by political opponents) have led to a drastic decrease in the middle class. In the lower income groups many households have fallen below the poverty level. Without the state distribution system, which may be judged as effective and fair, feeding the population would be far more difficult. According to American estimates more than 70,000 people died after the end of the war for lack of medicines and food.

Iraq was also confronted with considerable demands for reparations. Kuwait demanded $40 billion for destruction and for lost profits. Other states calculated their losses caused by the war at $35 billion. These were partially compensated for on an international level. We should also take into account the Iraqi foreign debt, which was $87 billion before the Second Gulf War, of which $44.5 billion represented war subsidies from the Gulf states. Even this brief outline shows that Iraq would not be in a position to pay full damages, even if it were allowed to produce oil in accordance with its previous OPEC quota (3.1 million b/d). In August 1991 the UN security council only agreed oil exports to the value of $1.6 billion for six months, the use of which it will determine: thirty per cent for the reparations fund, the covering of UN costs and the rest for the purchase of food and medicines. This was insufficient for Baghdad and was regarded as incompatible with the sovereignty of the country. The government feared the loss of control over the country's natural and financial resources, for, according to the UN security council's plan, a parallel authority (with foreign staff) should be established in the country to control oil exports and incomes (in a closed account) and oversee the import and distribution of goods. But by November 1992 no agreement had been reached. Iraq held the view that even with an annual income of $20 billion there was no room for reparations payments, for of this sum fifty per cent was necessary for indispensable civil imports, twenty-five per cent for debt servicing and twenty-five per cent for the repair of damages and developmental tasks. For this reason it applied for a five-year moratorium on reparations payments, an application which was, however, rejected. Against this background it has not been possible to ease the critical situation, despite the fact that reconstruction has been energetically pursued.

Table 1 Population and workforce (thousands) 1960–1969

Year	Total Population	Workforce	2:1 (per cent)	Unemployed
1960	6,925	1,944	28.1	47
1965	8,220	2,317	28.2	113
1969	9,432	2,680	28.2	121

Source: Ministry of Planning

The Distribution of National Income 243

Table 2 Average sectoral distribution of the Iraqi workforce during the decade 1960–1969

Economic sector	Contribution to GDP (per cent)	Proportion of workforce (per cent)
Agriculture	23.0	53.45
Industry	15.8	5.98
Electricity	1.8	0.54
Building	7.2	2.54
Transport, communications	9.9	5.56
Trade, banks	14.6	5.35
Other services	27.7	21.87
Total no. employed		95.87
Unemployed		4.13
All workers		100.00

Source: Calculated on the basis of data from the Iraqi Ministry of Planning.

Table 3 Growth rates of the most important macro-economic variables in Iraq during the period 1958–1969 (per cent)

	1958–61	1961–64	1965–69
Gross domestic product GDP	8.15	4.57	3.28
Gross national product GNP	8.53	4.95	3.28
National Income (Y)	8.90	4.70	3.40
Per capita income (y)	5.70	1.50	0.02
Private consumption (Cpr)	9.70	0.40	0.90
State Consumption (Cst)	14.70	10.90	7.90
Gross investment (I)	11.80	0.15	3.30
Savings (S)	10.80	0.50	4.50

Table 4 Real national income and per capita income 1960–1969 at 1966 prices.

Year	National income (mill ID)	per cent change	Per capita income ID	per cent change
1960	456.3	11.9	65.9	8.6
1961	518.5	13.6	72.6	10.2
1962	556.0	7.2	75.5	4.0
1963	536.6	−3.5	70.6	−6.5
1964	595.8	11.0	75.9	7.5
1965	685.3	15.0	84.6	11.5
1966	705.5	2.9	84.4	−0.2
1967	658.2	−6.7	76.2	9.7
1968	749.2	13.8	84.0	10.2
1969	780.0	4.1	84.7	0.8

Source: Ministry of Planning, Baghdad.

Table 5 Aggregate and sectoral real growth rates of the Iraqi economy (per cent)

	1954–73	1964–73
Overall GDP	6.03	4.72
Non-oil GDP	6.76	5.21
Non-oil, non-agricultural GDP	7.07	5.97
GDP in the agricultural sector	4.54	2.81
GDP in the mining and quarrying sector	4.68	3.80
GDP in the industrial sectors	6.68	7.21
GDP in the distribution sectors	6.86	3.96
GDP in the services sectors	8.96	6.54

Table 6 Average individual income of certain groups with contract-dependent income in Iraq during the decade 1960–1969 (ID)

Year	Civil Servants	Pensioners civilians and military	Employees of foreign oil companies	Employees of large industrial companies	Employees of small industrial companies	Per Capita income
1960	256	197	—	229	—	63
1961	301	181	970	237	—	68
1962	306	185	667	245	69	72
1963	317	194	655	259	72	69
1964	337	189	703	263	76	76
1965	340	199	725	268	90	81
1966	364	200	733	269	81	84
1967	380	213	755	282	85	83
1968	400	211	891	298	89	88
1969	419	225	851	314	83	90

Table 7 Iraq: Gross domestic fixed capital formation by economic sector at constant 1969 prices, 1953-1975 (million ID)

Sector	1953	1960	1968	1975(1)
Agriculture, forestry and fishing	12.6	13.8	17.0	45.5
Mining and quarrying	11.4	25.2	1.2	106.1
Manufacturing	12.6	10.4	36.8	195.8
Construction	1.7	1.6	1.7	28.9
Electricity and water	5.5	8.6	8.9	11.9
Transport, communication, and storage	22.6	28.3	20.2	90.3
Wholesale and retail trade	2.3	2.4	7.6	38.8
Banking and insurance	0.8	0.6	1.1	2.2
Ownership of dwellings	19.5	24.7	26.8	60.8
Public administration	3.1	3.5	4.7	52.2
Services	9.3	13.0	19.1	57.0
Total	101.4	132.1	145.1	689.5

Note: (1) Provisional.
Sources: Jawad Hashim, Hussein Omar, and Ali al-Munoufy, *Evaluation of Economic Growth in Iraq, 1950-1970*, vol. 1, *The Planning Experience* (Baghdad, Iraq: Ministry of Planning, 1970)
Jawad Hashim, *Fixed Capital Formation in Iraq: 1957-1970* (Baghdad, Iraq: Ministry of Planning, 1972)
Iraq, CSO, *Annual Abstract of Statistics 1974* (1957-1957-1970)
Iraq, CSO, *Annual Abstract of Statistics 1976*.

Table 8 Iraq: Gross domestic product by economic sector at constant 1969 Prices, 1953-1976 (million ID)

Sector	1953	1960	1969	1976
Agriculture, forestry and fishing	90.4	108.3	191.0	180.7
Oil extration	162.9	230.3	335.9	541.2
Other mining and quarrying	1.2	1.9	7.3	18.1
Manufacturing	24.9	60.1	103.0	228.5
Construction	14.2	25.6	38.5	248.3
Electricity, water and gas	1.4	4.0	16.8	35.2
Transport, communication and storage	27.0	44.0	69.1	156.6
Wholesale and retail trade	22.6	36.0	90.1	129.3
Banking, insurance and real estate	4.0	9.6	15.5	58.6
Ownership of dwellings	13.6	13.1	44.7	58.8
Public administration and defence	23.1	50.6	117.8	307.0
Services	21.3	42.2	80.0	32.4
GDP at factor cost	406.6	625.7	1,109.7	1,994.7

Sources: Jawad Hashim, Hussein Omar, and Ali al-Munoufy, *Evaluation of Economic Growth in Iraq, 1950-1970*, vol. 1, *The Planning Experience* (Baghdad, Iraq: Ministry of Planning, 1970), p. 286
IBRD, Economic and Social Data Bank
Iraq, CSO, *Annual Abstract of Statistics 1976*.

Table 9 Changes in gross domestic product (GDP) at market prices during the period 1975–1980

Year	Gross Domestic Product at market prices (million ID) prevailing prices	1975 prices	price components (1975 = 100)	In 1975 prices per inhabitants (ID)	Inhabitants (1975 = 100)
1975	4,022.4	4,022.4	100	362	100
1976	5,236.5	4,751.4	110	413	104
1977	6,042.1	4,908.8	123	408	108
1978	7,224.9	5,777.3	125	466	112
1979	11,390.9	7,135.2	160	557	115
1980	15,824.8	7,284.3	217	550	119

Change from previous year or average annual rate of increase (per cent)

| 1979 | +58 | +23.5 | +27.7 | +19.6 | +3.3 |
| 1980 | +38.9 | + 2.1 | +36.1 | − 1.1 | +3.3 |

Source: Federal Office of Statistics in Wiesbaden, Federal Republic of Germany, *Länderbericht Irak*, 1986.

Table 10 Gross Domestic Product (GDP) at factor costs 1975–1980 (million ID)

Year	GDP at factor costs	Agriculture forestry fishing	Goods producing trade	Including: processing industries	Mining, oil drilling	Building trade	Trade tourism transport communications	Other Areas(1)
at prevailing prices								
1975	3,970.5	297.3	2,635.2	238.5	2,287.7	91.3	352.5	685.5
1976	4,582.8	348.7	3,177.2	324.5	2,475.1	355.1	415.6	641.3
1977	5,858.3	498.4	4,046.5	488.6	3,114.9	415.6	589.6	723.7
1978	7,017.0	550.5	4,838.0	506.2	3,729.6	559.3	798.9	829.6
1979	11,167.2	611.8	8,410.1	628.6	6,749.9	993.8	1,211.7	933.6
1980	15,647.1	741.9	11,541.6	709.0	9,647.5	1,135.6	1,478.6	1,885.0
at 1975 prices								
1975	3,970.5	297.3	2,635.2	238.5	2,287.7	91.3	352.5	685.5
1976	4,673.6	337.6	3,242.4	309.9	2,713.9	197.2	394.0	699.6
1977	4,759.4	330.3	3,301.7	411.7	2,653.2	213.3	504.0	623.4
1978	5,590.2	339.2	3,905.8	419.0	3,185.0	263.1	657.0	688.2
1979	6,977.4	380.7	4,864.4	497.0	3,899.4	436.6	937.8	794.5
1980	7,202.5	389.6	4,491.8	528.8	3,426.0	498.9	1,001.1	1,320.0

Note: (1) Without assumed fees for banking services
Source: Federal Office of Statistics, Wiesbaden, Federal Republic of Germany, *Länderbericht Irak*, 1986.

Table 11 Use of Gross Domestic Product (GDP) at market prices between 1975 and 1981 (million ID)

Year	GDP at market prices	Private Use	State Use	Gross plant investment	Supply change	Last domestic use	Export of goods and services	Import of goods and services
at prevailing prices
1975	4,022	2,266	1,067		+150.8	3,485	2,329	1,792
1976	5,236	3,189	1,336		−301.8	4,223	2,491	1,479
1977	6,042	3,669	1,478		—	5,148	3,425	2,532
1978	7,224	4,947	1,573		−188.5	6,332	3,495	2,603
1979	11,390	6,598	2,714		−485.6	8,826	6,350	3,786
1980	15,842	8,571	3,471		−147.6	11,895	7,781	3,862
at 1975 prices
1975	4,022	1,042	1,224	1,218		3,485	2,329	1,792
1976	4,751	806	1,585	1,248		3,639	2,561	1,449
1977	4,908	1,169	1,745	1,327		4,242	2,427	1,760
1978	5,777	1,223	2,212	1,659		5,095	2,789	2,107
1979	7,135	1,507	2,990	1,536		6,034	3,656	2,555
1980	7,284	1,734	2,736	2,305		6,776	2,755	2,247
1981	4,056	1,976	1,979	2,973		6,928	942	3,815

Table 11. (cont.)

Year	GDP at market prices	Private Use	State Use	Gross plant investment	Supply change	Last domestic use	Export of goods and services	Import of goods and services
Change against previous year on average annual growth rate (per cent)									
1979	+23.5	+23.3	+35.2	− 7.4		+18.4	+31.1	+21.2
1980	+ 2.1	+15.1	− 8.5	+50.0		+12.3	−24.6	−12.0
1981	−44.3	+13.9	−27.7	+29.0		+ 2.3	−66.0	+70.0
1975/1981 Average	+ 0.1	+11.3	+ 8.3	+16.0		+12.1	−14.0	+13.4

Source: Federal Office of Statistics, Wiesbaden, Federal Republic of Germany, *Länderbericht Irak*, 1986.

Table 12 Distribution of Gross Domestic Product (GDP) at market prices 1975–82 (million ID)

Year	Income from dependent work	Income from business and wealth	Net domestic product at factor costs (col. 1 + col. 2)	Indirect Taxes	Subsidies	Deductions	Gross domestic product at market prices (col. 1 + col. 2) (col. 3 + col. 4 + col. 6 − col. 5)
1975	838	2,770	3,609	218	102	296	4,022
1976	956	3,830	4,787	254	131	326	5,236
1977	1,306	4,139	5,445	263	79	412	6,042
1978	1,651	4,919	6,570	277	69	446	7,224
1979	2,048	8,449	10,498	354	130	669	11,390
1980	2,802	12,046	14,848	504	327	789	15,824
1981	3,636	5,689	9,326	537	741	1,150	10,274
1982	4,664	7,364	12,029	545	479	633	12,728

Change against the previous year or average annual growth rate (per cent)

1980	+36.8	+42.6	+41.4	+42.3	+150	+19.3	+38.9
1981	+29.8	−53.0	−37.2	+ 6.5	+127	+44.1	−35.1
1982	+28.3	+29.4	+29.0	+ 1.4	− 35.3	−45.0	+23.9
1975/1982	+27.8	+15.0	+18.8	+14.0	+ 24.7	+11.4	+17.9

Source: Federal Office of Statistics, Wiesbaden, Federal Republic of Germany, *Länderbericht Irak*, 1986.

Table 13 Gross capital formation according to public and private sector, in prevailing prices 1981–1988 (million ID)

	1981	1982	1983	1984	1985	1986	1987	1988
Gross capital formation	5,099	5,697	4,713	4,433	4,301	3,859	3,658	2,899
Of which:								
Public sector	4,090	4,574	3,893	3,568	3,470	3,179	3,034	2,094
Private sector	1,009	1,123	820	865	831	680	624	805

Source: Ministry of Planning, Central Statistical Organization, *Annual Abstract of Statistics 1986 and 1989*.

Table 14 Gross Domestic Product (GDP) by economic activity at factor cost for the years 1984–1988, in constant prices of 1980 (million ID)

Activities	1988	1987	1986	1985	1984
Agriculture, forestry and fishery	884	860	937	1,001	852
Mining and quarrying	8,526	8,878	5,521	4,433	4,401
Manufacturing industry	755	942	722	759	679
Building and construction	557	813	846	944	1,087
Electricity and water	137	116	113	106	92
Commodity Activities	10,860	11,611	8,141	7,245	7,114
Transport, communication and storage	500	596	591	419	457
Wholesale & retail trade, hotels and others	723	1,025	999	1,016	1,025
Banking & Insurance	381	538	554	384	553
Distribution activities	1,604	2,161	2,145	1,820	2,036
Ownership of dwelling	296	298	305	313	336
Social & personal services	1,326	1,611	1,631	1,541	1,470
Services activities	1,623	1,909	1,936	1,854	1,807
Total	14,087	15,682	12,223	10,920	10,957

Source: Ministry of Planning, Central Statistical Organization, *Annual Abstract of Statistics 1989*.

Table 15 Gross Domestic Product (GDP), national income and per capita income in prevailing prices 1981–1988 (million ID)

	1981	1982	1983	1984	1985	1986	1987	1988
GDP at factor costs	11,261	12,554	12,461	14,551	15,012	14,652	17,600	17,035
GDP per capita of population (ID)	820	890	854	965	963	909	1,077	987
national income in per capita of population (ID)	10,065	10,031	10,620	12,407	12,799	12,494	15,311	14,704
	736	731	728	823	821	776	937	852

Source: Ministry of Planning, Central Statistical Organization, *Annual Abstract of Statistics 1986 and 1989*.

Table 16 Results of annual surveys for large industrial establishments for the years 1985–1988 (Value, wages and benefits in million ID)

Year	Sector	Value of sales	Value of input	Value of output	Benefits	Wages paid	Employees (000)	Number of establishments
1985	Socialist	1,918.5	815.16	1,801.04	28.8	242.2	146.7	242
	Mixed	211.5	106.63	197.22	3.3	16.3	9.8	10
	Private	275.0	170.84	252.33	3.8	34.2	21.8	558
	Total	2,405.0	1,092.63	2,250.59	35.9	292.7	178.3	810
1986	Socialist	1,999.3	767.2	1,844.1	30.3	257.7	151.0	236
	Mixed	197.4	80.6	162.3	3.9	17.3	10.1	11
	Private	254.6	153.1	229.1	2.6	33.1	20.9	550
	Total	2,451.3	1,000.9	2,235.5	36.8	308.1	182.0	797
1987	Socialist	1,841	763	1,705	36	195	116	173
	Mixed	194	90	161	3	17	8	10
	Co-operative	2	1	2	–	–	1	4
	Private	200	122	172	2	25	15	446
	Total	2,237	976	2,040	41	237	140	633
1988	Socialist	2,370	999	2,185	24	216	126	142
	Mixed	228	105	197	4	19	9	11
	Co-operative	14	10	16	–	2	2	25
	Private	294	184	266	2	28	17	462
	Total	2,906	1,298	2,664	30	265	154	640

Notes: Large industrial establishments are those employing thirty person or more and investing 100,000 ID or more. Table does not include figures of oil extraction activity. Production Value at approximate factor cost and sales at market prices.

Source: Ministry of Planning, Central Statistical Organization, *Annual Abstract of Statistics 1989.*

Egyptian Migrant Labour in Iraq: Economic Expediency and Socio-political Reality

Camillia Fawzi El-Solh

INTRODUCTION

Egyptian cultural, economic and political links with Iraq are not a novel phenomenon. Specifically with regard to the twentieth century, these links may be divided into three distinct periods: the first, from 1900 up to the 1940s, mainly involved an educated and skilled socio-economic stratum of Egyptians; the second, from the early 1950s to the late 1960s, can be said to have initiated the tide of temporary migration for employment; the third period from the early 1970s onwards is identified primarily with the contemporary large-scale migration of low-skilled migrant workers to Iraq.

Regarding the first period, little is known about the actual volume and motivation of Egyptians travelling to and from Iraq during the first two decades of this century. However, some information can be gleaned from writings on the region's socio-political history, from which one may conclude that the Egyptian presence in Iraq was at the time numerically relatively insignificant. Moreover, its impact was probably limited, in spite of the origin of some of these travellers in the social and political élite in Egypt.[1] By the 1930s, Egypt had begun officially to sponsor the secondment of Egyptian schoolteachers to Iraq.[2] This trend was influenced by both cultural and

---
1. See for example Abd al-Muti Hijazi, *Urubat Misr* (The Arabism of Egypt), (Beirut, 1979). The various biographies of Egyptian intellectual and political figures provide glimpses of such travel to and from Iraq during this period.
2. S.A. Messiha, 'The export of Egyptian school teachers', *Cairo Papers in Social Science*, American University in Cairo, 1983, vol. 3(4).

political considerations, leading, for example, to the establishment in 1942 of an office in Cairo for the organization of cultural cooperation between the two countries.[3]

The second period referred to above was more or less initiated by the 1952 Revolution in Egypt. The influence of Nasserism on Iraqi economic and social policies was reflected in the growing cooperation between the two governments, extending up to and to some extent beyond the 1958 Iraqi Revolution.[4] Egyptian government officials were seconded to serve in Iraq, mainly as teachers, but also as administrators, managers and high-level technicians.[5] Up to the 1960s, Egyptian migration to Iraq appears to have more or less followed the above pattern, i.e. to have been composed mainly of skilled and professional temporary migrants, though secondments were occasionally subject to the freeze and thaw of political relations between the two governments. Officially, this migration wave is estimated to have involved around 5,000 Egyptians.[6] This figure is plausible given that at this point in its development, Iraq did not feature among the capital-rich Arab labour importers. In fact, it was to some extent a net labour exporter due to the relatively limited absorptive capacity of its economy.[7]

The third period in the history of Egyptian migration to Iraq dates from the early 1970s, which initiated the contemporary migratory wave with its distinct characteristics and social and political ramifications. A first significant marker here is 1973, when the oil crisis and the subsequent development boom in the Arab region began to have an expansionary effect on the Iraqi economy. Among other things, this impact was reflected in the increasing number of Egyptians in Iraq, which by 1975 was officially estimated to have reached 30,000.[8] But as yet, Egyptian migrants consisted mainly of

3. N.B. Abd Allah, *Tatawwur fikrat al-qawmiya al-arabiya fi Misr* (The development of the idea of Arab nationalism in Egypt), (Cairo, 1975), pp. 88–9.
4. R. Wilson, 'Western, Soviet and Egyptian influences on Iraq's development planning', in T. Niblock, ed., *Iraq; the contemporary state*, (London, 1982), p. 229.
5. R.R. Sell, 'Gone for good? Egyptian migration processes in the Arab world', *Cairo Papers in Social Science*, Cairo, American University in Cairo, 1987, vol. 10(2); and S. Abdel Wahab Saleh, 'The brain drain in Egypt', *Cairo Papers in Social Science*, 1983, vol. 2(5).
6. Saddam Hussein, *Al-muallafat al-kamila* (complete works), (Baghdad, Ministry of Culture and Information, 1989), vol. 2, 1975–1977, p. 319.
7. J.S. Birks and C.A. Sinclair, *International migration and development in the Arab region*, (Geneva: ILO, 1980), p. 27.
8. Saddam Hussein, *op. cit.*, vol. 2, 1975–1977, p. 319.

professional and skilled personnel, reflecting the inadequate supply of trained indigenous labour in Iraq.[9]

The year 1975 is another significant marker during this period, initiating as it did a trend of what was to eventually become an avalanche of unskilled and semi-skilled Egyptian manual workers in search of employment opportunities. This was set in motion during talks between Saddam Hussein and Anwar Sadat at the 1974 Arab Summit Conference in Rabat, Morocco. The signing of a bilateral agreement between both countries the following year reiterated the aim of encouraging thousands of Egyptian *fallahin* (peasants) to migrate to Iraq. The first officially sponsored migrant group of 100 Egyptian rural families arrived in 1976, and was settled in a newly erected village some thirty-five miles east of Baghdad. Though the planned permanent settlement of many more such families was officially shelved after Egypt's separate peace treaty with Israel, this did not hinder the continuing large influx of Egyptian migrant workers into Iraq.[10]

The outbreak of the Iran–Iraq War in 1981 marks another important phase in the development of contemporary Egyptian migration to Iraq. It initiated a spiralling demand for replacement manpower, a development which the Egyptian government sought to capitalize on as a means of dealing with its economic problems. Again less skilled Egyptian manual labour was preponderant, with the category of higher educated Egyptian migrants remaining relatively underrepresented.[11] This was to some extent due to the preference of skilled Egyptians to secure financially more rewarding employment in the other Arab Gulf countries, in spite of the relative difficulty of gaining access to these labour markets. But it is also related to the employment of skilled Asian technicians as part of so-called turnkey projects, a trend in the Arab region also followed by Iraq.[12]

9. E. Penrose, 'Industrial policy and performance in Iraq', in A. Kelidar, ed., *The integration of modern Iraq*, (London, 1979), p. 163.

10. C.F. El-Solh, *Egyptian migrant peasants in Iraq; a case-study of the settlement community in Khalsa*, (unpublished Ph.D., University of London, 1984), p. 14.

11. S.E. Ibrahim, 'Oil, migration and the new Arab social order', in M.H. Kerr and E.S. Yassin, eds., *Rich and poor states in the Middle East: Egypt and the new Arab order*, (American University in Cairo, 1982), p. 31.

12. However, in contrast to other Arab labour-importing countries, most notably Saudi Arabia, Iraq's use of Asian labour is based primarily on economic considerations, rather than political/cultural calculations aimed at reducing the presence of non-indigenous Arab labour. See V. Robinson, 'Bridging the Gulf: the economic significance of South Asian migration to and from the Middle East', in R. King, ed., *Return migration and regional economic problems*, (London, 1986).

The mid-1980s are a fourth significant marker, characterized as they were by the repercussions of the war with Iran in terms of Iraq's dwindling foreign currency reserves, its rising foreign debt and the postponement/cancellation of an increasing number of development projects. These and other related factors came to have serious implications for the type and volume of employment opportunities open to Egyptian migrants. In turn this was expressed in social tensions which were beginning to affect relations between the host society and elements among the Egyptian migrant community in Iraq. Though the governments in both countries officially attempted to down-play these tensions, diplomatic endeavours could not paper over the fact that Egyptian labour migration to Iraq was confronting serious problems. The latter not surprisingly resurfaced following Iraq's invasion of Kuwait and the 1991 Allied-Iraqi Gulf War, when thousands of Egyptian migrants joined the exodus of those fleeing the area.

LIMITED INFORMATION AND THE PUZZLE OVER NUMBERS

The changing fortunes of Egyptian migrants in Iraq between the mid-1970s, when they were officially welcomed regardless of their socio-economic background, and did not seem to encounter any undue hostility on the part of the populace, and the late 1980s, when they were experiencing social and economic difficulties, reflects a complex interplay between a number of factors in both Egypt and Iraq. However, attempts to achieve a balanced analysis of these factors, and their implication for the status and roles of Egyptian migrants in Iraq, is to some extent hampered by the paucity of pertinent data in Iraq itself.[13] In fact, much of the rather

---

13. A. Izz al-Din, *Al-quwwa al-amila al-misriya al-wafida ila al-qutr al-iraqi: dirasa min manzur balad al-manshi* (Egyptian migrant labour in Iraq: a study from the point of view of the sending country), (Baghdad, 1982), which, however, provides unsubstantiated estimates of the number of Egyptians in Iraq. There are some unpublished papers, such as M.K. Ibrahim, 'Hawl tajribat al-iraq fi al-imala al-wafida' (Iraq's experience of migrant labour), submitted to the *Symposium on foreign manpower in the Arab Gulf region*, January 1983, as well as various reports issued by pertinent Iraqi ministries and government organizations. But these sources only contain general information on Egyptians in Iraq.

In fact, it is striking how little, if at all, the subject of Egyptian migration is dealt with even in the more recent English language books on Iraq. See e.g. F.W. Axelgard, ed., *Iraq in transition: a political, economic and strategic perspective*, (Boulder, Co., 1986).

limited information regarding this Egyptian migratory wave and its way of life in Iraq has to be gleaned from research on and in Egypt.[14] Though Arab media reports are also important sources of information, this generally requires the peeling away of political rhetoric in order to uncover a plausible rendition of facts.

An important aspect of this paucity of information is the actual number of Egyptians in Iraq. This point deserves particular mention, since the fluctuating pattern of this migrant labour movement, and specifically with regard to those originating from the lower social stratum in Egypt, eventually came to have important implications for the socio-economic status of Egyptians in Iraq.

As was documented during two recent conferences on Egyptian migration held in 1988 and 1990 respectively in Cairo, the actual number of Egyptian migrants continues to remain a puzzle in spite of increased research efforts in this field.[15] The wildly differing estimates presented during these meetings regarding the volume of Egyptian migration in the Arab region from the mid–1970s to the mid–1980s underlines this clearly. For example, the National Council in Egypt estimated that by the mid-1980s the number of Egyptian migrants in the Arab region had reached 1,217,000, while the Central Agency for Public Mobilization and Statistics (CAPMAS) and the Ministry of Foreign Affairs give figures of 1,578,000 and 1,976,000 respectively for the same period. Though these three official sources claim that around thirty per cent of Egyptian migrants in the Arab region were in Iraq, only the above mentioned Ministry explicitly indicates that its estimate does not include some one million Egyptians believed not to have registered with the Egyptian Consulate in Baghdad.[16]

Nor does the estimate provided by the Egyptian Ministry of

14. See for example S.I. Ibrahim and M. Abd al-Fadil, *Intiqal al- imala al-arabiya* (Arab labour mobility), (Beirut, Centre for Arab Unity Studies, 1983); and N. Fergany, *Sayan wara al-rizq* (In pursuit of livelihood), (Beirut: Centre for Arab Unity Studies, 1988).

15. *Al-mutamar al-iqlimi li-tanmiyat wa-istikhdam wa-hijrat al- quwwa al-bashariya* (The Regional Conference: development, employment and migration of human resources), Cairo: 5–7 December 1988; and *Mu tamar al-mukawwinat al-raisiya li-khassais al-quwwa al-amila fi harakat al-hijra wa-ikasatiha ala duwwal al-ifad wa duwwal al-istiqbal* (Conference on the main aspects of the manpower characteristics in the migratory process and their impact on the sending and receiving countries), Cairo: 3–5 March 1990. Both conferences were jointly organized by the Egyptian Central Agency for Public Mobilization and Statistics (CAPMAS), the ILO and the UNFPA.

16. M. Muhyi al-Din, *Taqdirat al-misriyin fi al-kharij: hal hunak farq?* (Estimates

Migration prove helpful, i.e. the very institution set up in 1981 to monitor the volume/direction of Egyptian migration for employment. This Ministry estimated that in 1984 some 3.5 million Egyptians were abroad, of which eighty per cent were believed to be in the Arab region, and updated this to 4.5 million for 1985.[17]

The puzzle over numbers is further complicated by the virtual lack of official data on migrant labour in Iraq itself. While the Iran-Iraq War (1980–1988) may explain the absence of up-to-date manpower statistics, it is doubtful that, were such data published, they would include a breakdown of expatriates by Arab national origin.[18] Officially, the Iraqi leadership perceives such differentiation to be contradictory to its political principle of equating Iraqi with non-Iraqi Arab citizens, as stipulated in the Iraqi labour law number 151 of 1970, as well as the Decree of the Revolutionary Council number 384 of 1977. Specifically in the case of Egyptians, the Iraqi leadership has claimed that the issue of numbers is irrelevant.[19]

The reality is that neither of the two countries involved has been keen to advertise the actual number of Egyptian migrants who have made their way to Iraq since the 1970s. The Egyptian authorities tend to refer to Article 52 in the 1971 Constitution, pertaining to the freedom of all Egyptians to leave the country unhindered, as the reason for inadequate statistics on the extent of migration for

of Egyptians abroad: are there differences?). Paper presented to the 1988 Migration Conference (see note 15 above), p. 7.

17. M. Muhyi al-Din, *op. cit.*, p. 6. However, A.M. Lesh writes, based on data obtained from the Egyptian Ministries of Foreign Affairs and Migration respectively, that the number of Egyptian migrants in 1985 was 3.5 million, a figure which appears more plausible. See A. Lesh, 'Egyptian labour migration', in I.M. Oweiss, ed., *The political economy of contemporary Egypt*, (Washington, Centre for Contemporary Arab Studies, 1990), p. 91.

18. Iraq is not unique in this respect. In fact, with the partial exception of pre-August 1990 Kuwait, none of the other Arab labour-importing countries publishes accurate data on its expatriate population due to political and/or cultural sensitivities. Pertinent information is generally based on an amalgamation of sources and projections. See I. Serageldin *et al.*, *Manpower and international labour migration in the Middle East and North Africa*, (Oxford University Press, 1983).

19. Saddam Hussein: '(They say) that the number of Egyptians in Iraq is around two million. Be this as it may. Whether there are two million or three or four or ten or five or one or half a million, they are in their country, and Baghdad is their Baghdad, just as Basra is their Basra', in *op. cit.*, vol. 18, 1988–1989, p. 515. See also the pamphlets published by the Iraqi Ministry of Culture and Information in 1980, *Al-muwatin al-arabi wa-tashriat al- thawra* (The Arab citizen and decrees of the revolution), and *Hurriyat intiqal quwwat al-imala al-arabiya ila al-Iraq* (Freedom of movement of Arab manpower to Iraq).

employment. In fact, this is also at least partly related to an unwritten policy to encourage the migration of unemployed—hence presumably potentially 'subversive'—elements in Egypt, for whom the Egyptian economy cannot provide any succour.[20] In the case of Iraq, apart from the fact that the dearth of data can be largely attributed to the official attitude towards published statistics, it is probably also due to the Iraqi authorities' avoidance of providing the opposition with concrete ammunition by which to propagate the view that importing Egyptian almost exclusively Sunni Muslim labour is demographically motivated. Either way, these governmental attitudes inadvertently encouraged less skilled Egyptian migrants in particular to avoid registering with their Consulate in Iraq, a pattern probably also related as much to their traditional mistrust of authority, as it is to their expectation of indifferent treatment at the hand of the bureaucrat. But it is this statistically invisible migrant who was eventually to become the main focus of social tensions between the Iraqi host society and the Egyptian migrant community.

It is probable that the number of Egyptian migrants in Iraq during the 1980s averaged between one and 1.5 million, but may have declined to around 900,000 by the second half of 1990.[21] This estimate takes account of the particular socio-economic characteristics of this migration wave, namely the preponderance of low-skilled manual labourers, which in turn implies a relatively high turnover rate. Thus, compared with other Arab labour-importing countries, the average migratory period in Iraq has tended to be of relatively shorter duration: i.e. 1.6 years compared with, for example, 3.2 years for Saudi Arabia and 4.7 years for Kuwait.[22]

IN SEARCH OF GREENER PASTURES

The mid-1970s is of particular significance to the pattern of contemporary Egyptian migration to Iraq, in that it marks the dramatic

---

20. The irony, as one source put it, is that the supporters of the government are more likely to migrate than opponents, notably the Islamic groups. See R.J. LaTowski, 'Egyptian labour abroad', *Merip Reports*, May 1984, p. 16.

21. International Labour Office, 'Migrant workers affected by the Gulf crisis', Report of the Director General, Third Supplementary Report, GB.249/15/7, ILO, Geneva, 15 January 1991.

22. H. Nassar, *Return migration*, Preliminary Report I/4, Cairo: CAPMAS, Labour Information System Project, 1990, p. 40.

upsurge in the number of less skilled Egyptians who came largely unhindered in search of employment. The term 'unhindered' encapsulates a crucial difference between Iraq and the other Arab labour-importing countries with regard to immigration policies. It also serves to explain why Iraq was to become a major country of destination for Egyptian migrant labour from the mid-1970s onwards.

The bilateral agreement concluded between the Iraqi and Egyptian governments in 1975 aimed at encouraging the permanent settlement of 'thousands' of Egyptian *fallahin* and their families in Iraq in order to cultivate its relatively under-exploited agricultural lands. However, though the first step, i.e. the settlement of 100 Egyptian peasant families in the newly erected village of Khalisah east of Baghdad, was implemented, the project itself came to a standstill in response to Anwar Sadat's trip to Jerusalem in 1977. It was officially shelved after the conclusion of the Camp David Treaty in 1979. A new settlement further east was instead handed over to Moroccans, whose migration to Iraq was sponsored under conditions similar to that of Khalisah's Egyptian peasant families.[23]

But these developments were not permitted to affect the situation of the Egyptian *fallahin* in Khalisah, and the settlement continued to be upheld as a show-piece of Arab labour mobility. The Iraqi leadership made a point of differentiating between its diplomatic relations with the Egyptian government, and the implementation of its pan-Arab political principles, which were also enshrined in the various addenda of the Charter of the Arab League.[24] This policy had implications for the influx of Egyptian migrants into Iraq, who continued to be exempt from the need to obtain entry visas and work contracts, or from having to have prepaid return fares before entering the country. Egyptians were not prohibited from bringing their families over, and no time limit was

---

23. See the Iraqi daily *Al-Jumhuriya* of 26 March 1981. Little is known about these Moroccan farmers and, to my knowledge, no study has been published on this settlement and its development. However, at the time of my fieldwork in the Khalisah settlement in Iraq during the winter of 1981/82, some officials familiar with this project indicated that it was economically not as successful as the Egyptian settlement, mainly—so their explanation ran—because many of these Moroccans were in reality urban and not agricultural labourers. The fact that some of the Moroccan settlers wore 'jeans' apparently reinforced this judgement. Rumours that a settlement further east would be settled with southern Somali agriculturalists could not be substantiated.

24. A.M. Gomaa, *The foundation of the league of Arab states*, (London, 1977).

set with regard to the duration of their stay in Iraq, even if they were unemployed. Moreover, they were permitted to apply for Iraqi citizenship. Few, if any, of these facilities were granted by the other Arab labour-importing countries (with the eventual and partial exception of Jordan).[25]

This unhindered entry not surprisingly encouraged the migration of a social stratum out of Egypt facing many difficulties in gaining access to the other Arab labour-importing countries, where restrictive immigration controls are the norm. Though publicly condemning Iraq and other Arab countries for orchestrating its expulsion from the Arab League in the aftermath of the Camp David accords, the Egyptian government was in fact quietly ignoring the reality that an increasing number of its citizens were making their way into Iraq, mainly by using Jordan as a transit route.

Thus, the typical Egyptian migrant in Iraq was male, in his twenties or early thirties, and illiterate or with little formal education. He originated predominantly from rural Egypt, and had generally not experienced the classic two-stage migration process, i.e. rural-urban-abroad. If married, he did not bring his family with him, and more often than not had to borrow the cost of his fare to Iraq. The primary motive in his decision to migrate was financial, i.e. to pay off debts and/or accumulate savings. Contrary to previous assumptions, this type of migrant was not necessarily unemployed back in Egypt, though very likely involved in low-status labour-intensive occupations, and more than likely underemployed if originating from the rural sector.

In Iraq, this typical Egyptian migrant worker was mainly employed in the agricultural and services sectors. He could also find employment in the construction and manufacturing industries where, at least during the boom years, his relatively low skill level did not present any undue handicap. His employment was subject to varying degrees of security, i.e. based (less frequently) on a written contract, or (more frequently) on precarious self-employment, or (even more frequently) on day-wage labour. With dwindling employment opportunities during the waning of the economic

25. But like other non-Iraqi Arabs, Egyptians are required to register with the *Maktab muwatinin al-arab* (Office for Arab Citizens).With regard to Iraqi citizenship, Palestinians are the only Arabs not permitted to apply, in order to maintain their political claim to Palestine. Moreover, Iraq does not permit dual citizenship, and expects claimants to give up their original national passports. For some documentation on Egyptian migrants in Jordan, see H. Nassar, *op. cit.*

boom, this typical migrant often faced unemployment and thus increasing hardship.[26]

CHANGING FORTUNES

A recent study on return migration to Egypt confirms the significant upsurge of migrants during the period 1981–1985, coinciding with Iraq's need for replacement manpower during its war with Iran. It also confirms the drop in this demand after the mid-1980s, signalling the end of the economic boom years in the Arab region, as well as the increasingly negative repercussions of the continuing Iran–Iraq war.

Thus, some thirty-eight per cent in the study's sample of return migrants to Egypt during the latter half of the 1980s were from Iraq. More specifically, around forty-nine per cent of all rural, and twenty-seven per cent of all urban returnees had been in Iraq. A breakdown by occupational categories indicates that forty-four per cent were agriculturalists, thirty-seven per cent were production workers, while the rest, nineteen per cent, were technical and professional employees.[27]

While such data reflect the reality that the search for employment opportunities in Iraq was becoming increasingly fraught with difficulties, they also indicate that the typical Egyptian migrant was not necessarily aware of this crucial fact. This was partly related to the Egyptian authorities' inadequate dissemination of realistic information concerning migration for employment. But it is also due to Iraq's continued policy of granting Egyptians entry without visa or work permit. Moreover, the average poorly educated prospective migrant was undoubtedly attracted by the relatively low cost of migrating for temporary employment to Iraq, as compared with the other Arab labour- importing countries, where agents' fees to secure entry visas and work permits, as well as the need for a *kafil* (local sponsor), could be prohibitive.

For lack of published research, indications of the changing fortunes befalling these typical Egyptian migrant workers can be traced through various media reports, which also indirectly shed light on their variable socio-economic status within Iraqi society. In fact, as

---

26. N. Fergany, 'Differentials in labour migration', Cairo Demographic Centre, Occasional Paper No. 4, (Cairo, 1987).
27. H. Nassar, *op. cit.*, pp. 31, 35–6.

early as 1983, i.e. when the first signs of the waning boom in the Arab region were appearing on the economic horizon, the Egyptian press took up the problem of Egyptian migration to Iraq by publicizing a recent Iraqi government decree regarding the curtailment of subsidy entitlements of public sector employees. This related to housing, marital and child allowances, as well as to financial incentives for serving in hardship areas. In effect, this meant that public sector salary levels fell on average by as much as fifty per cent. Moreover, the maximum amount which such employees were officially permitted to remit to their home countries was reduced from seventy-five per cent of salary inclusive of increments, to sixty per cent and eventually to fifty per cent of the basic salary only. As for expatriates employed in the private sector, the maximum amount of remittance fell from 1000 ID a year to 695 ID a year. Wide press coverage was also given to the long delays which remittances of Egyptian migrants in Iraq were being subjected to.[28]

Even the semi-official media in Egypt seized the opportunity to criticize the Egyptian authorities for shortcomings in the implementation of appropriate migration and manpower policies. The insinuation was that there was more concern with the negative implications of dwindling remittance levels for Egypt's balance of payments, than with the plight of Egyptian migrant workers, or even with the social and economic repercussions of this migratory trend for Egypt's development potential.[29] Such criticism was to resurface periodically over the following years, and served to initiate a public debate in Egypt on the social costs of migration, including its presumed correlation with an upsurge in the crime rate in Egyptian society.[30]

By September 1989, the Iraqi government had reduced the level of remittances even further. Skilled expatriates employed in the public/mixed sectors were now only able to remit a maximum of 480 ID a year, while the ceiling for the less skilled was reduced to 360ID a year. Those employed in the private sector fared even worse, for now they were only permitted to remit a maximum of

28. See the semi-official Egyptian weekly *Al-Ahram al-Iqtisadi* of 11 April 1983, no. 743; and of 25 April 1983, no. 746.
29. *Al-Ahram al-Iqtisadi* of 2 May 1983, no. 746; of 9 May 1983, no. 747; and of 23 May 1983, no. 749. It is estimated that the Egyptian migrants' remittances from Iraq averaged US$6 billion/year. See *Middle East International* (MEI) of 1 December 1989.
30. G. Amin, 'Migration, inflation and social mobility', in C. Tripp and R. Owen, eds., *Egypt under Mubarak*, (London, 1989); also a report on supposedly migration-related crimes in the London-based daily *Al-Sharq al-Awsat* of 26 November 1988.

240 ID a year.[31] Since Egyptian migrant labour was not only predominantly unskilled, but, by the late 1980s, was also mainly employed in the private sector, and given that remittances were subject to increasing delays (said in some cases to be over a year), these regulations caused much hardship to many Egyptian migrants trying to earn a living in Iraq.

But it was the news that there were 'suspiciously large' numbers of coffins of Egyptians arriving from Baghdad at Cairo Airport in November 1989, and the rumours that many of them had died under unexplained circumstances, which appear to have lifted the lid off the growing tensions between both countries. The ensuing media campaign in Egypt reached such a pitch that the Egyptian President felt compelled to warn the media against 'sensationalism'.[32] The response particularly of the Egyptian opposition to what came to be known as 'the story of the coffins' was more or less predictable, focusing as much on the plight of the migrants and their socio-economic status in both the home and host countries, as it did on the perceived shortcomings of social and economic policies.[33] However, it is the reaction of the official and semi-official Egyptian media, and the fact that the Iraqi government press broke its hitherto conspicuous silence on these matters, which are perhaps more revealing, not least because of the way such publicity became indicative of the increasing tensions underlying relations between the two countries.

The official Egyptian daily *Al-Akhbar*, responding to the swell of rumours, took up the coffins story on 14 November 1989. Apparently by coincidence, that same day Saddam Hussein summoned a number of Egyptian expatriates for a meeting in Baghdad, during which the issue of controversial Egyptian press reports was raised, and the special place of Egyptians in Iraq was reiterated.[34] Yet at the same time, Iraq began organizing additional flights (up to ten daily) in order to ferry Egyptian migrants back to Egypt. Seen in conjunction with the drastic fall in remittance levels and delays in money transfers, Iraq appeared to be unofficially signalling an end to this hitherto unencumbered labour migration.[35]

31. *Middle East Economic Digest* (MEED) of 22 September 1989. At the time, the official exchange rate stood at 1 US$ = approx. 3 ID.
32. *MEI* of 1 December 1989.
33. For pertinent examples of Egyptian opposition press reports see *Revue de la presse egyptienne*, no. 36–37, 1989. Published by the Centre d'Études et de Documentation Economique, Juridique et Sociale, Cairo.
34. See the official Iraqi daily *Al-Thawra* of 16 November 1989.
35. This is reported to have been publicly confirmed by the Iraqi Ambassador in

The Egyptian government initially down-played the crisis, with Husni Mubarak accusing 'hidden hands' of attempting to cause a breach in Egyptian/Iraqi relations, and hinting at a connection with the recently established Arab Cooperation Council (involving Egypt, Iraq, Jordan and Yemen).[36] By 20 November, there were reports that the problem of tardy remittances was being resolved.[37] However, on 29 November 1989, the official Egyptian daily *Al-Ahram* published a report implicitly criticizing Iraqis for their 'rough' treatment of Egyptian nationals, though it also made a point of praising the Iraqi leadership for its positive stance towards Egyptian migrant labour in the past.

The Egyptian Parliament took up the crisis which had befallen Egyptian labour migration in early December 1989. During the pertinent debates, government officials claimed that the number of Egyptians in Iraq had fallen from 1.6 million in 1987 to around 160,000 by late 1989, without, however, substantiating this figure.[38] An article in the semi-official Egyptian weekly *Al-Ahram al-Iqtisadi* during the same month more or less summed up public sentiment in Egypt by its title *al-karama wa al-rughba fi al-amal* (honour and the desire for work), implying that, for many Egyptians who had left in search of greener pastures, the actual gains from labour migration had fallen far short of anticipated results.[39] Official pronouncements by both governments notwithstanding, the 'golden era' of unhindered Egyptian labour migration to Iraq had more or less come to an end. A report in the Iraqi press concerning the migration of skilled Moroccan technicians to Iraq, and the encouragement of the Iraqi private sector to employ them, drove this point further home.[40]

The invasion of Kuwait, and the outbreak of the Allied-Gulf War in early 1991, set the seal on this process of changing fortunes. The rumours that Egyptians were facing difficulties in obtaining

Cairo. See *MEED* of 17 November 1989, and the London based daily *Al-Hayat* of 14 November 1989.

36. See the London based *Al-Qabas* of 24 November 1989. There were also insinuations that this crisis between Egypt and Iraq was due to some rapprochement between Egypt and Syria during this period, and that the Iraqi regime was bent on destabilizing Egypt's economy.

37. Iraq committed itself to transferring a first installment of US$ 50 million to Egypt. See *Al-Hayat* of 20 November 1989.

38. *Al-Hayat* of 6 December 1989.

39. *Al-Ahram al-Iqtisadi* of 18 December 1989, no. 1092.

40. *Al-Hayat* of 12 December 1989.

exit visas to leave Iraq, the international media coverage of the plight of refugees stranded in camps on the Iraqi–Jordan border, and of ordinary Egyptians carrying their salvaged belongings and desperate to secure transportation back to Egypt, all served to refocus public attention on the social and economic problems of labour migration to Iraq in particular, and the Arab region in general, and above all on the problem of return migrants whom the Egyptian labour market is largely unable to absorb.[41]

Mention needs to be made in this context of Egyptians said to have served in the Iraqi army during the Iran–Iraq War, an issue which was eventually to become another bone of contention between the two countries. Already in 1983, there were claims in the Egyptian press that some 17,000 Egyptians had been 'coerced' into fighting alongside Iraqi soldiers during the war with Iran, to the extent that some Egyptian migrants had found it expedient to 'flee' to Jordan.[42] These claims resurfaced during the crisis over the coffins at Cairo Airport in 1989, to which were added the further claim that there were 12,000 Egyptian prisoners of war still held by Iran, a point officially disputed by the Iraqi leadership.[43] What can be verified is that though Egypt supported Iraq during its war with Iran through the provision of arms, military equipment and training personnel, such aid did not include the official secondment of Egyptian soldiers to fight in the regular Iraqi army. Some psychological pressure was undoubtedly exerted on Egyptians to serve in *al-jaish al-shabi* (the popular army), apparently encouraging some to leave the country. But others did volunteer to serve as mercenaries, or in rear supply lines as cooks, cleaners, drivers and maintenance workers. In this they were no doubt attracted by higher wages compared with what they would have earned in low-status civilian jobs, given their relatively low skill levels.[44]

---

41. *Al-Ahram al-Iqtisadi* of 17 September 1990, no. 1131; and *The Guardian* of 29 January and 19 March 1991.The expulsion of Egyptians from Libya in 1985 due to a political crisis between the two countries, and the hardship this meant for the return migrants, has by all accounts not hindered a recent upsurge of Egyptian migrants seeking employment opportunities there. This reaffirms the political as well as economic difficulties faced by Egyptian manual labour in particular to secure employment in the Arab Gulf states, and as had been hoped for by the Egyptian government due to its stand during the 1991 Allied-Iraqi Gulf War. See *Al-Hayat* of 14 April 1991.
42. *Al-Ahram al-Iqtisadi* of 11 April 1983, no. 743.
43. *Al-Ahram al- Iqtisadi* of 4 December 1989, no. 1090.
44. R. LaTowski, *op. cit.*, p. 15; and R.R. Sell, *op. cit.*, p. 64.

PERMANENT SETTLERS OR TEMPORARY SOJOURNERS?

A harking back to the mid-1970s, when Khalisah's Egyptian peasant families were welcomed with much fanfare and publicity as part of the Iraqi government's officially proclaimed aim of dismantling barriers to labour mobility in the Arab region, serves to further illuminate the social status and economic roles of Egyptians in Iraq. It also serves to illustrate the changing fortunes befalling a migrant community which had initially encountered few impediments in securing temporary employment, a novel experience when set against labour migration trends in the Arab region.

As indicated earlier, the Iraqi leadership viewed the establishment of the Khalisah settlement as a pilot project. It was also economically expedient in that these Egyptian peasant families were regarded as the first of what at the time were expected to be many waves of migrant peasants come to cultivate Iraq's relatively under-exploited agricultural lands which, among other factors, had in the past been affected by the Iraqi peasantry's traditionally negative attitude towards manual labour, as well as by an upsurge in rural out-migration lured by more lucrative urban employment.[45]

For their part, the Egyptian settler families in Khalisah have tended to see themselves as pioneers, a conviction aptly captured by a pun in the Egyptian colloquial: *ijraat al-safar li al-iraq matkunsh khalsa illa fi al-khalsa* (travel to Iraq is not complete (i.e. *khalsa*) except in Khalisah). Moreover, few of the settler families were unfamiliar with the Iraqi President's pronouncement, to the effect that Egypt's *fallahin* were not migrants, and that the valleys of the Tigris and the Euphrates were as much their home as was the Nile valley.[46]

The incentives which these Egyptian peasants received in the form of subsidized travel, free housing and household furnishings, free plots of land which, in contrast to the agricultural policy implemented in Iraq at the time, they were allowed to cultivate as individual holdings, monthly allowances that were eventually extended beyond the decreed time limit, as well as exemption from land and

---

45. C.F. El-Solh, 'Egyptian migrant peasants in Iraq', pp. 10–12.
46. H. Badri, *Fallah Misr ala ard al-Iraq* (Egypt's peasant in Iraqi lands), (Baghdad, n.d.), p. 1. This is a journalistic account of the Khalisah settlement, based on interviews with some of the settler families, presumably during 1977.

income tax, are indicative of the Iraqi leadership's awareness that the Egyptian *fallah* of the early 1970s was not easily lured away from his land, however precarious the living it provided him and his family.[47] These incentives not only reduced the risk of migration, but not surprisingly also gave Khalisah's peasant settlers the feeling of being indispensable. This was no doubt a novel experience, considering that they were almost exclusively recruited from the class of subsistence peasants, i.e. were situated at the bottom of the rural social hierarchy back in Egypt.

Half a decade later—by the early 1980s—Khalisah's settlers had established a reputation as producers of high quality cash crops (mainly vegetables and animal fodder), for which there was much demand in the neighbouring area, and as far away as Baghdad. In fact, it was striking to what extent the settler families had taken advantage of the economic opportunities which had come their way after resettlement in Iraq. Though they would inevitably attempt to down-play their success as cultivators, partly out of fear of *ain al-hasud* (the evil eye), but mainly in order to encourage the Iraqi authorities' perception of them as impoverished agriculturalists in need of continued subsidies, as well as to discourage possible claims on their earnings by the Egyptian Consulate in Baghdad, in fact the majority of Khalisah's Egyptian inhabitants were enjoying a higher standard of living compared with their circumstances prior to migration.

The particulars of this economic success, and the wide-ranging implications this had for the division of labour within the settler family, for relations between settler households, be they kin or otherwise, and between the Egyptian peasants and the authorities supervising this settlement, can be traced elsewhere.[48] What is of interest here is the relationship between the settler families and the growing community of temporary Egyptian migrant workers living and working outside the Khalisah settlement, not least because it is indicative of the way of life of the majority of Egyptians in Iraq.

These *baladiyat* (i.e. from the same village/area of origin as the settler household) were kith or kin, or friends of the latter in Egypt.

---

47. Saddam Hussein *Social and Foreign Affairs in Iraq*, translated by K. Kishtainy, (London, 1979), p. 89.

48. For these and other related points in the Khalisah settlement see C.F. El-Solh, 'Egyptian migrant peasants in Iraq', *Arab Affairs*, 1988, vol. 1(7); and C.F. El-Solh, 'Egyptian peasant women in Iraq: adapting to migration', in A. Zegeye and S. Ishemo, eds., *Forced labour and migration*, (London, 1989).

Some were at one time lodgers in Khalisah, other visited regularly, or, if living in the vicinity, came to purchase ducks and geese (apparently not part of the Iraqi culinary taste), or *feteer meshaltet* (savoury pastry dripping with ghee) from a settler household. Either way, these temporary migrants took on the function of a human channel of communication between Egypt and Iraq, bringing news of events in the village of origin, and transporting messages and even consumer goods for the settler family back to Egypt.[49] Particularly relevant is the fact that, while the community of temporary Egyptian migrants outside the settlement served to psychologically shorten the geographical distance between home and host countries, it also inadvertently came to function as an impediment to the integration of these settlers into the wider society in Iraq, or at the very least to the encouragement of social contacts with Khalisah's Iraqi rural neighbours.

Many of these temporary migrants living and working in the vicinity of Khalisah were involved in the services sector, either as self-employed petty traders, or as waged workers in small establishments which were often Egyptian-owned. The Egyptian settler in Khalisah could thus obtain household necessities from an Egyptian grocer and meat from an Egyptian butcher, have his hair cut by an Egyptian barber, and his clothes sewn by an Egyptian tailor. It he wanted to avoid the settlement's coffee-shop, he could enjoy a *shisha* (water pipe) and a game of *tawlah* (backgammon) in one of the food kiosks strung along the nearby highway connecting Baghdad with Basra in the South, whose Egyptian ownership was advertised by such names as *falafil wadi al-Nil* (rissoles of the Nile valley). The settlement's mosque served as another meeting venue. Though it was also frequented by Iraqis, communal prayers did not necessarily initiate less formal social contacts between the host and migrant communities. Moreover, the Iraqi media inadvertently contributed to keeping the Egyptian settler family's links with the country of origin alive through its broadcasts of Egyptian films, serials and music. Closing their eyes to their physical surroundings, Egyptians in Iraq could almost believe they were back in the homeland.

These facts have had implications for prospects of permanent settlement in Iraq. Contrary to the Iraqi authorities' expectations,

---

49. These goods, sold at a profit in Egypt, also served to circumvent the ceiling on remittances. The *baladiyat* who transported them back to Egypt generally received a commission.

the majority of the Egyptian peasant families in Khalisah have tended to view their life in Iraq in more temporary terms, an attitude implicit in the continued reference to their life here as being *fi al-ghurba* (i.e. in a strange or foreign land). Among other things, this was also reflected in intra-settlement relationships, which tended to be based on short-term rather than on long-term reciprocity considerations. In spite of the cultural similarities between the two countries, the incentives provided by the Iraqi authorities, as well as the fact that the ebb and flow of diplomatic relations between Cairo and Baghdad were not permitted to interfere with the settlement, the home village in Egypt continued to function as *the* frame of reference against which achievements and social behaviour were measured. Life in Iraq was seen as a temporary sojourn, albeit of longer duration in order to accumulate the savings deemed necessary to ensure at the very least the social mobility of settler children out of the peasant stratum. Nonetheless, like every first generation of migrants, these Egyptian *fellahin* are not immune from the myth of return syndrome. Very probably it will be the future employment prospects for male settler children in particular, as well as the state of the economy in Egypt in general, which will decide whether this syndrome remains a myth or becomes reality.[50]

This pattern of unintended segregation, which already by the early 1980s was leading to the development of an almost separate community of working class Egyptian migrants within the host society, was more or less repeated across Iraq wherever sizeable numbers of Egyptian workers had settled. Though this does not imply that, for example, Egyptians engaged in petty trade activities did not cater for Iraqis, or that no inter-marriage was taking place, it did establish a pattern of self-sufficiency among a particular class of Egyptians elsewhere identified as the typical kind of migrants in Iraq. Their contacts with the host society came to be largely confined to dealings with Iraqi officials and employers. Not

50. C.F. El-Solh, 'Egyptian migrant peasants in Iraq'. The 1991 Gulf War obviously has implications for this myth of return syndrome. But any discussion must remain within the realm of speculation until more concrete information on Egyptian migrants, including those in the Khalisah settlement, can be obtained. However, if the current trend of Egyptian migrants streaming towards Libya is in any way indicative, then one can perhaps submit the tentative scenario that Egyptian workers may eventually make their way back to Iraq out of economic expediency. Contrary to the impression conveyed by the Egyptian media in particular, not all Egyptians left Iraq during the recent Allied-Iraqi War. Some remained for economic or family reasons, others because of irregularities in their travel papers.

surprisingly, this pattern of social and spatial separation also played a role in encouraging the so-called guest-worker syndrome.[51]

THE GUEST-WORKER SYNDROME

For skilled/professional Egyptian migrants, life in Iraq has been qualitatively different compared with that of their working class compatriots. Those of middle or upper middle class origin were more likely to have brought their families over with them, to live in the more up-market residential areas, to be working in relatively secure civil service or public sector jobs, and to have access to services and leisure time activities available to their Iraqi social peers. Though they were eventually subjected to repeated cuts in salary and increment levels, and to the erosion of their incomes due to rising inflation, they more or less shared this fate with Iraqis and other expatriates of their class. While they were undoubtedly affected by the progressively restrictive regulations concerning remittance transfers, they were probably better placed to cope compared with their less educated compatriots, who had difficulties with the now compulsory use of the banking system, having previously preferred to use their network of kith and kin to send money back and forth to Egypt.[52] Those among this educated Egyptian expatriate class who had come to Iraq during the 1970s were more likely to have social contacts with their Iraqi social peers than those who came over during the 1980s, i.e. when the economic tide in Iraq was turning, and when a shrinking labour market increased the level of competition over available employment opportunities. Either way, these skilled/professional Egyptian migrants in Iraq had little social contact with their working-class compatriots, no more than such vertical ties would have been the norm back in Egypt.

As mentioned earlier, the unhindered entry into Iraq facilitated the migration of a special stratum out of Egypt, which, due to its low skill and educational levels, faced difficulties in securing employment in most of the other Arab labour-importing countries observing stringent immigration controls.[53] During the economic boom

---

51. The term guest-worker is derived from the German Gastarbeiter, implicit in which is the association with low soco-economic status. Syndrome refers to the host society's tendency to use such migrant labour as a scapegoat for social and economic ills.
52. N. Fergany, *op. cit.*, p. 181.
53. This is not to imply that unskilled labour did not gain admission into some of

years of the late 1970s/early 1980s, and in particular after the outbreak of the Iran-Iraq War (1981), even unskilled Egyptian manual workers were in demand in Iraq. But the economic repercussions of the war, together with the restructuring of the Iraqi economy during the 1980s, had implications for the expatriate labour force in general, and for Egyptians in particular. These structural adjustments not only meant shrinking employment opportunities in Iraqi public sector enterprises, but also reduced job security in an expanding private sector.[54] This had particular implications for Egyptian migrants with less marketable skills, around eighty-five per cent of whom were estimated to be working in the private sector.[55] Those among them unable to secure employment in agriculture (also being restructured in favour of private ownership), or to generate self-employment (mainly as household help, but also in informal jobs such as street vending), or to obtain jobs in the petty trade activities of their compatriots, were particularly badly hit. Their situation became subject to further deterioration upon the demobilization of Iraqi soldier contingents after the end of the Iran-Iraq War in 1988. The subsequent swelling ranks of the unemployed depressed wage levels even further.

Thus, for the more typical Egyptian migrant workers—i.e. unable to afford, or unwilling to expend meagre savings for, the return fare to Egypt, either unemployed, dependent on casual day labour or poorly paid—life in Iraq was far removed from the image of greener pastures which had lured them to come and seek their fortune in the first place. Though there were no apparent restrictions on their continued stay, there was no safety net in terms of social security in Iraq to cushion them during periods of unemployment, other than the support network of compatriots very probably also experiencing hardship. Yet, to return to Egypt empty-handed, or without hard-earned savings due to delays in the transfer of remittances, was not necessarily an option. Many Egyptians were well aware that the likelihood of finding employment in Egypt could be expected to be frustrating, and few working-class migrants harboured any illusions that their plight would be accorded priority by

the other Arab labour-importing countries, though in very much restricted numbers. There is also some clandestine migration, e.g. remaining in Saudi Arabia after the pilgrimage. See R.J. LaTowski, *op. cit.*, p. 15.

54. K.A. Chaudhry, 'On the way to Market: economic liberalization and Iraq's invasion of Kuwait', in *Middle East Report* of May–June 1991.

55. *Al-Ahram al-Iqtisadi* of 4 December 1989, no. 1090.

the Egyptian authorities. Many continued to stay in Iraq in the hope that the end of the war with Iran would initiate another economic boom.

Equally frustrating to these Egyptian migrants was their growing subjection to the so-called guest-worker syndrome, reflected in the Iraqi public's tendency to attribute the negative behaviour of some Egyptians to the migrant community in general. This syndrome was largely encouraged by a number of interrelated factors, some of which will be singled out here.

To begin with, these typical Egyptian migrant workers in Iraq were largely confined to relatively low status jobs which indigenous workers were increasingly shunning. Their manner of dress would tend to set them even further apart, confirming as it did their social class origin in Egypt.[56] As single males unaccompanied by their families, and due to overcrowded living conditions, they would tend to congregate in coffee shops and food stalls (owned or run by Egyptians). In turn, this not only inadvertently reinforced their spatial segregation, but also heightened their social conspicuousness in the perception of the host society even further. The latter played no small part in the tendency to exaggerate the number of Egyptians in Iraq, and also contributed to their stereotyping as impoverished workers not averse to social deviance.

Assuming that at any one point in time during the 1970s and 1980s there were some one million Egyptians in Iraq, and given the fact that their exit from Egypt and entry into Iraq were seemingly uncontrolled, it would have been more than surprising had instances of social deviance not occurred. Undoubtedly, some destitute Egyptians did resort to petty crime in order to survive. But what is difficult to document, much less repudiate, is how widespread criminal activities among the Egyptian migrant community have actually been. This is not only due to the virtual silence of the official Iraqi media on the matter. It is also a result of the fact that Egyptian press reports have tended to down-play references to crimes committed by Egyptian migrants in Iraq in favour of speculative or sensationalist reports of crimes perpetrated against them.[57]

---

56. This applies particularly to Egyptian migrants of rural origin, who tend to continue to wear the traditional *jalabiya* (ankle-length loose gown) and turban headgear.

57. See for example *Al-Ahram al-Iqtisadi* of 4 December 1989, no. 1090, p. 29; and the official mouthpiece of the ruling party in Egypt *Mayo* of 27 November 1989.

It is the difficulty of realistically judging the negative behaviour and actions of some Egyptians, as well as appropriately evaluating the host society's reactions, which has inadvertently encouraged the negative stereotyping of Egyptian migrants in Iraq.

Whatever the reality may be, the fact remains that Egyptian migrant workers in Iraq have become associated with a variety of crimes, ranging from theft and forgery, to drugs, murder and prostitution.[58] Prostitution, being a particularly sensitive subject in Arab society, deserves some specific mention here, all the more since it also serves to throw some light on gender aspects of this migratory wave to Iraq. Various studies have confirmed that Egyptian labour migration to the Arab region tends to be biased towards males the lower down the socio-economic ladder one proceeds; i.e. that Egyptian women migrating for employment are for the most part from the more highly skilled and professional class.[59] Though, in contrast to the other Arab labour-importing countries, and very specifically Saudi Arabia, Iraq does not prohibit Arab women migrants from entering without the appropriate male chaperon, the fact remains that Egyptian migration to Iraq is similarly male biased. This is at least partly related to the fact that Iraqi women are employed in many economic sectors, a pattern officially encouraged during the 1970s, and which was to become an economic necessity during the war with Iran.[60] But another reason for this trend is related to the socio-economic origin of the vast majority of Egyptian migrants in Iraq. In other words, a social stratum in Egypt where, as elsewhere in the Arab world, women not under the supervision of male kin tend to be associated with socially suspect behaviour.[61] Since the majority of Egyptian migrants in Iraq could not afford to bring their families over, single Egyptian women, whose dress and mannerisms proclaim their membership in the low-income stratum, rightly or wrongly tend to find themselves under suspicion of immoral behaviour. This is indirectly confirmed by the

---

58. Of interest in this context is the different attitudes in Egypt and Iraq towards the punishment of crime. For example, there was much criticism in Egypt when Egyptians convicted of forgery received death sentences. The Egyptian government intervened to have these commuted to life imprisonment. *Middle East Journal*, vol. 40(4), p. 698.
59. N. Fergany, *op. cit.*, p. 175.
60. J. Crusoe, 'Economic outlook: guns and butter, phase two?', in F.W. Axelgard, *op. cit.*, p. 49.
61. R. Critchfield, *Shahhat: an Egyptian*, (Syracuse University Press, 1978); and N. El-Saadawi, *The hidden face of Eve: women in the Arab world*, (London, 1979).

fact that Iraqi families generally prefer to employ male Egyptians as household help. Thus, working-class Egyptian female migrants generally find employment as cleaners in offices and commercial or public sector enterprises mainly in Iraqi urban centres, where they too will tend to form socially and spatially separate groupings with their female compatriots.

The demobilization of Iraqis at the end of the Iran–Iraq War is another factor which indirectly served to further encourage the guest-worker syndrome. For example, Iraqi soldiers returning from the front now found themselves having to compete with Egyptian migrants over jobs in an increasingly recessionary labour market, where the customary prerogative of government and public sector employment had largely ceased to function as a safety net. They also found themselves being undercut in an expanding private sector, where Egyptians were accepting wages and salaries below the value of their marketable skills, and were also prepared to forego increments in order to hold on to their jobs. Moreover, many demobilized soldiers were faced with the fact of sisters, daughters, fiancées and even wives (believing they were widows) married to Egyptians. One verified incidence is perhaps symptomatic of the resentment which some demobilized soldiers understandably may have experienced. It concerns an Egyptian who managed to marry four Iraqi widows, all of whom apparently continued to receive their widows' allowance, thus absolving him from the necessity of seeking employment.[62]

This incident is of particular interest since it illustrates that, in contrast to previous years when relatively progressive legislation was enacted in order to raise women's social and economic status in Iraqi society, and polygamy was officially frowned upon (though it was never legally prohibited), it was now quietly encouraged in Iraq.[63] While this can be explained by the population losses suffered as a result of the Iran–Iraq War, and the subsequent demographic imbalance between the sexes, the encouragement of polygamy must also be viewed within the context of traditional male suspicion of female sexuality in Arab society.[64] The much vaunted Iraqi custom of not giving daughters in marriage to outsiders, in particular to non-Iraqis, has been shunted aside to accommodate this reality.

62. Personal communication from an Iraqi who met this Egyptian in Baghdad.
63. A. Rassam, 'Revolution within the revolution? Women and state in Iraq', in T. Niblock, *op. cit.*
64. F. Sabbah, *Women in the Muslim unconscious*, (New York, 1984).

It is mainly against this background that the incidence of coffins of Egyptians at Cairo Airport in November 1989 should be viewed. By all accounts, apart from natural causes, some of these and earlier deaths were apparently related to indiscriminate attacks on Egyptian migrants by demobilized Iraqi soldiers, to an explosion in a factory employing Egyptians, and to the panic reaction of the Iraqi security police finding itself confronted by what appeared to be rampaging Egyptians following an Egyptian football victory over Algeria.[65]

Much of the Egyptian opposition press chose to rally public opinion around these unexplained deaths, and to convey the impression that they were suspiciously frequent without, however, substantiating these claims. For its part, the Egyptian government initially chose to defuse the crisis by publicly reiterating that Iraq does not differentiate between its own and Egyptian citizens, and that these deaths were explainable.[66] This more or less echoed statements by the Iraqi leadership, who attempted to set these deaths within the context of the vast numbers of Egyptian migrants in Iraq, thus implying that they were to be more or less expected. This emerged during the previously mentioned meeting between Saddam Hussein and Egyptian expatriates in Iraq in November 1989, during which the Iraqi leader made a point of relating these deaths to the frequent road accidents in Iraq, as well as to the habit acquired by the Iraqi soldier during the years of war 'to fight with his fists instead of his tongue'.[67]

But none of these pronouncements could paper over the fact that the 'special relationship' officially propagated by both governments since the mid-1970s, and culminating in the proclamation of the Arab Cooperation Council, had turned distinctly sour. In particular the community of working-class Egyptian migrants in Iraq had become increasingly alienated, a feeling largely reciprocated by the host society. The repercussions of the Iraqi invasion of Kuwait and the subsequent 1991 Gulf War served to set the seal on a development which, in the realm of labour migration and economic cooperation in the Arab region, may be viewed as the saga of missed opportunities.

---

65. *Al-Hayat* of 17 November; *MEED* of 17 November and 24 November 1989; and *MEI* of 1 December 1989.
66. *Al-Hayat* of 18 December 1989.
67. Saddam Hussein, *op. cit.*, vol. 18, 1988–89, p. 516.

Egyptian Migrant Labour 281

CONCLUSION: AN INTERACTION OF FACTORS

The presence of Egyptians in Iraq, particularly from the mid-1970s onwards, has been subjected to the influence of a number of factors in the sending and the receiving countries respectively. The complex interaction between these factors has had far-reaching implications for the manner in which this migratory experience has come to be judged by both home and host societies.

With regard to Iraq, both the end of the economic boom in the Arab region by the first half of the 1980s, as well as the repercussions of the Iran-Iraq War during that same decade, have had important implications for the régime's ideologically motivated encouragement of Arab labour mobility. The economic expediency underlying the implementation of this ideological premise beginning with the 1970s, and which had favoured the almost unrestricted influx of Egyptians, began to be undermined by the Iraqi economy's increasing inability to absorb a largely unskilled migrant labour force. The restructuring of the Iraqi economy during the 1980s served to further widen the gap between political ideology and economic reality. The particular socio-economic characteristics of the vast majority of Egyptian migrants, in conjunction with the changing economic circumstances in Iraq, played no small part in encouraging the so-called guest-worker syndrome. Egyptian migrant labour has not only been cast in the role of scapegoat for social ills, but also came to function as a proxy for political opposition to the Iraqi régime. The latter's misconceived economic planning, for example the inadequate preparations for the absorption of demobilized Iraqi soldiers into the civilian economic sectors after the end of the war with Iran in 1988, inadvertently also played a part in fostering social tensions between the Egyptian migrant community and the Iraqi host society.

But the above factors also need to be understood in conjunction with developments in Egypt. Inasmuch as Iraq opened its doors to a class of Egyptian migrants encountering difficulties in gaining access to the labour markets of the other Arab labour-importing countries, this influx of largely unskilled workers was also encouraged by the laissez-faire migration policy implemented by the Egyptian authorities. The short-sightedness of such a laissez-faire attitude was further exposed by the inadequacy of medium- and long-term training and manpower policies in Egypt. In turn, this has had implications for return migration to Egypt, in the sense that, for lack of viable alternatives in their home country, Egyptian migrant workers felt compelled to hang on in Iraq even when it was becoming clear that the Iraqi economy was increasingly unable to provide them with a livelihood. The largely economically fed social tensions between the host society and the Egyptian migrant community in Iraq has been exploited by the Egyptian political opposition, who seized the opportunity to harangue the government over its migration and economic policies, but without necessarily offering much in the way of remedies for the social and economic problematics of Egyptian labour migration.

Underpinning all these factors is the subjection of Egyptian labour migration to the ebb and flow of political relations between Egypt and Iraq, a pattern in turn influenced by geopolitical regional as well as international considerations. The inter-Arab political alliances forged during the 1990–1991 Gulf crisis are but one aspect illustrating this reality.

If anything, this complex interaction of factors indicates that the circumstances under which Egyptians migrated to, and settled in, Iraq, and the eventual development of this migration process to the apparent detriment of both the host and the home societies, were wittingly or unwittingly fed by the economic mismanagement and political miscalculations of the governments in both countries. It is above all less skilled and poorly educated Egyptian migrant workers, seeking to escape the lack of economic opportunities in their home country, who have paid, and are continuing to pay, the price for these policy shortcomings.

Iraq as a Regional Power

Thomas Koszinowski

PREREQUISITES FOR IRAQ'S POSITION IN THE REGION

The position, importance and influence of a state within a certain group of other states depends on the range of factors such as the size of the country and its population, the geostrategic position of the country and the nature of its borders, resources, strength of industry, agricultural potential and military strength. The military power of a country is to a high degree dependent on all these factors. If certain conditions or factors are lacking, the military power will be negatively influenced. For example, the oil sheikhdoms of the Gulf are, in spite of their oil revenue, weak countries in military terms because their population is very small. A large population alone may be of minor importance if the country has not enough resources, as is true—to a certain extent—for Egypt. But even if a country's conditions are favourable for becoming a leading political power it needs more than such positive conditions, namely the political will to become a dominant power, e.g. a strong political leadership and an ideology which legitimate a policy pursuing such an aim.

With an area of about 440,000 square kilometres Iraq counts among the medium-sized states in the Middle East. On account of its central location it borders on a multitude of countries: Iran in the east, Turkey in the north, Syria and Jordan in the west and Saudi Arabia and Kuwait in the south. A considerable disadvantage is the very narrow access to the Gulf. Therefore, in its foreign trade it is dependent on the transit traffic through the adjacent countries. This contiguity to a large number of states and the partly unfavourably fixed boundaries are the cause of tensions and conflicts. The arbitrary definition of the frontiers by the former colonial power of Great Britain is considered unjust by Iraq, and nearly all past governments attempted to rectify the situation, thus repeatedly bringing about conflicts, especially with Iran and Kuwait.

In population Iraq holds a medium position. With approximately nineteen million inhabitants (1990) Iraq ranks fourth after Turkey, Egypt and Iran. Its population density of thirty-nine inhabitants per square kilometre is not as low as in the adjacent Arab oil producing countries. On the other hand, Iraq does not suffer overpopulation as Egypt or Iran where the population explosion inhibits development. The population is not very homogeneous in Iraq. It consists of three large groups classified according to ethnic or religious-denominational differences, respectively. The population is divided into the Sunni and Shi'i sects on the one hand, and into Arabs and Kurds on the other hand. The largest group is formed by the Shi'i (fifty-five to sixty per cent), the second largest by the Sunni Arabs (about twenty per cent), whereas the third group comprises the Kurds (approximately twenty per cent) who are predominantly Sunni but not Arab. The number of Christians is estimated at about three per cent. The differences between the individual groups again and again resulted in open conflicts and had a destabilizing effect on the country and impeded the Baghdad government in pursuing an expansive foreign policy in the area. The antagonism between the central government and the Kurds not only served neighbouring Iran as a pretext for intervening in the domestic affairs of Iraq, as did the religious kinship to the Shi'i it also gave rise to the expansionist moves of the Shi'i of the Iraqi régime against Iran.

Iraq disposes of large oil reserves, its share of world wide oil reserves amounting to 13,400 million tons or eleven per cent. Oil revenues were the foundation for an extremely forceful development in the second half of the 1970s after the increase of oil prices. In spite of the Gulf conflict, Iraq succeeded in implementing a large number of industrial projects, especially in the petrochemical field, and in considerably improving the infrastructure of the country. In contrast to most countries in the Middle East, Iraq also possesses substantial agricultural resources.

In conclusion one could say that a medium-sized population favourable to the economic potentialities of the country as well as vast oil reserves and advantageous agricultural conditions have endowed Iraq with excellent possibilities for development. While economic development in the rich oil producing countries is partially obstructed by too small a population, and in most other countries economic progress is limited by the lack of resources and the high growth of population (e.g. Egypt, Yemen, Jordan), the growing population and the economic conditions in Iraq combine in a dynamic pattern. Therefore, the economic power and political influence of Iraq will continue to increase in the future, irrespective of the political system in Baghdad. The influence of Iraq will become the larger, the more the government is successful in solving internal problems and in employing the national wealth for economic development. The natural riches and the resulting economic power are essential prerequisites for the political part the country and its government might be able and willing to play. In principle the natural conditions, the economic resources, and the size of the population represent the basis for the role of a regional power. Iraq has in nearly every respect ideal conditions to become a leading power in the region.

BETWEEN BAATH IDEOLOGY AND POLITICAL PRACTICE

Because of its central location and its wealth (formerly being based first of all on agriculture), Iraq was one of the earliest centres of civilization. In ancient times there existed on the territory of present Iraq the large empires of the Sumerians, Babylonians and Assyrians, later on Iraq with the capital of Baghdad became the centre of the Abbasid empire. Throughout the whole of history Iraq or the states ruling in Mesopotamia tried to gain ascendancy over the area of the Middle East. At one time Mesopotamia rivalled the empire in the Nile Valley, both empires alternating with each other in dominating the region. While the Nile Valley empire, however, never succeeded in controlling the whole of the Middle East, the ruling kingdoms in Mesopotamia repeatedly and over long periods of time gained ascendancy over the Nile Valley (Persians, Assyrians, Abbasids). After Iraq had lost political importance under Ottoman domination over several centuries, the foundation of the state of Iraq after the First World War prepared a new basis for an independent policy.

Since the end of the First World War and the formation of a new structure of states in the Middle East comprising in addition to Turkey and Iran the Arab states, Iraq has again developed a natural desire for hegemony. This ambition is directed at two different areas, firstly at the Gulf region with the Arab states on the west side of the Gulf and Iran on the east side, and secondly at the Arab states in the eastern area on the whole. As early as after the Second World War and the gaining of independence by the other Arab territories, Iraq endeavoured to seize adjacent Syria. As legitimation there served dynastic arguments (the rulers of Iraq and Jordan were sons of Sharif Husain of Mecca who aimed at the establishment of an Arab empire) on the one hand, and the arbitrariness of the boundaries and formation of states which had to be rectified, on the other. As in ancient times Iraq's drive for expansion in the Middle East met with similar efforts on the part of Egypt. On behalf of pan-Arabism both states were intent on extending their influence as far as possible. In the 1940s Prime Minister Nuri al-Said advanced a plan for a unified state including Syria. In the south Iraq looked for a wider access to the Gulf by raising a claim on the Emirate of Kuwait after it had been given independence by Britain in 1961. If the British government had not reacted instantly and sent troops to Kuwait the Emirate would have been incorporated into Iraqi territory. With the assumption of power by the Baath party in July 1968 Baath pan-Arabism became the official ideology. The most important objective of Baath ideology is the unification of all Arab states. Since the ruling Baath party in Iraq considers itself as solely legitimate, it believes itself qualified to bring about Arab unity.[1] This fundamental aim of the Baath party and the Iraqi government gathered momentum after Saddam Hussein's seizure of power in July 1979. In numerous speeches Saddam Hussein has stressed the significance of Arab unification and the part to be played by Iraq in this question. According to Saddam Hussein's understanding the Arab world is entitled to stand on a level with the leading powers on account of achievements such as the Arab contribution to medieval civilization on which European culture is based and on account of its economic potential thanks to the oil reserves which are vital to the western industrial nations. The united Arabs might—according to Saddam Hussein—play as important a role as the United States, Europe, the Soviet Union or Japan. 'We are called to influence the course of Arab policies effectively, in accordance with our conception. It will be extremely important and valuable for the future, if the Arabs show their ability to unite at least at a minimum level in politics and attitudes and thereby influence the process of international politics'.[2]

---

1. Since 1966 the Baath has been divided into two parties, one led by Damascus and the other by Baghdad.
2. Saddam Hussein, *Social and foreign affairs in Iraq* (London, 1979), p. 73.

In the opinion of the Iraqi Baath party and Saddam Hussein, modern Iraq is a direct successor of the great ancient empires of Mesopotamia, of the Sumerians, Babylonians and Assyrians, as well as of the Abbasid caliphs. The remembrance of the glorious past exerts a considerable influence on Saddam Hussein and his policy. The memory of these vast empires and their rulers like Hammurabi, Nebuchadnezzar or Harun al-Rashid points to Saddam Hussein's claim to a similar position of ascendancy in the area, at least over the Arab territories. He sees himself as a successor of these great rulers. In claiming the role of a leader of the Arabs the former Egyptian President, Nasser, is the great example for him.

In connection with Arab unity Israel and Zionism are for the Baath and for Saddam Hussein the arch enemy as Israel blocks its attainment. At the same time the Palestine question is a means to mobilize the Arab masses for his policy. The aim to Arab leadership always implies a certain responsibility for the Arab cause in the Palestine question. This was true of Nasser and his policy and Saddam Hussein too as his policy in the Kuwait crisis showed.

The ideological radicalism of the Baath leadership has had a direct influence on its domestic and foreign politics. This became clearly noticeable in the alignment with the Soviet Union (with whom a friendship treaty was concluded in 1972) and other Eastern bloc states. On the issue of Palestine the radicalism of the Iraqi leadership exceeded even that of Libya and Syria. Baghdad strongly rejected Resolution 242 and a peaceful settlement of the Arab-Israeli conflict, thus making itself the spokesman of the extremist forces amongst the Palestinians. The conservative and pro-western states in the Arab world were criticized as reactionary and agents of western imperialism, and their overthrow was pursued with the support of the local opposition movements. As a consequence of its extremely radical policy the Iraqi regime was driven into isolation within the Arab world.

Iraq's foreign relations were strained not only with the conservative countries but even with the so-called progressive states, Syria and Libya. The relationship with Damascus had been tense from the beginning, that is since the Baath party's seizure of power in Baghdad in 1968. The cause was the cooperation of the Iraqi Baath with the Aflaq wing overthrown in Damascus in 1966. Even after the assumption of power by Hafiz al-Asad in November 1970 who presented himself as pragmatic and ideologically less narrow-minded than his predecessor, Salah Jadid, there was no change in the relationship between the two Baath parties. The conflict was aggravated by differing attitudes towards the Middle East conflict. Whereas Syria in principle accepted Resolution 242 and thus a peaceful settlement of the Arab-Israeli confrontation, Iraq rejected both.

Sadat's journey to Jerusalem in November 1977 gave rise to a marked polarization within the Arab world and placed the Iraqi régime in a position to gain status as leaders of the radicals. However, at the conference in Tripoli at the beginning of December 1977 Iraq failed, because of Syrian opposition, to have its demand for total renunciation of a peaceful solution and sole reliance on violence accepted. Therefore, Iraq left the conference prematurely. The Front of Steadfastness and Resistance (*jabhat al-sumud wa al-tasaddi*), founded in Tripoli by Syria, Libya, Algeria, South Yemen and the PLO was not joined by Iraq which was thus isolated even from the ranks of the radical states.

During the course of the inter-Arab crisis caused by Sadat's policy (Camp David Accords of 1978 and Peace Treaty of 1979) Iraq was again able to lay more emphasis on its claim to a position of leadership. Since Egypt was no longer playing a role on the all-Arab political scene Iraq was necessarily given more weight. At the Boycott Conference in March 1979 organized by Saddam Hussein in Baghdad immediately after the conclusion of the Peace Treaty between Egypt and Israel the Iraqi leadership's demand for a general boycott of Egypt was largely accepted. When Saudi Arabia and Kuwait hesitated to support the boycott decision Iraqi media threatened violent measures so that both countries preferred to give in.[3] The Baghdad Boycott Conference against Egypt represented an enormous success for Saddam Hussein. Hardly ever before had Iraq exerted such substantial influence on the composition of all-Arab resolutions.

This success of the Iraqi leadership was not least a result of the temporary rapprochement between Baghdad and Damascus under the impetus of Egypt's withdrawal from the common Arab front. The announcement of Iraq and Syria to unite their states and the implementation of initial measures in this direction did not fail to have an effect on the neighbouring Arab states, especially on Saudi Arabia which was relatively isolated after Egypt's withdrawal. Iraq

3. Colin Legum, Haim Shaked, Daniel Dishon, eds., *Middle East Contemporary Survey* (MECS), 1978–79, pp. 219–222.

and Syria together had a combined economic and military potential which, in the case of unification, would have had a considerable effect on the whole region. The failure of the unity plan with Syria—apparently caused by Saddam Hussein—was not only a setback for the Baath ideology of Arab unity but in the long run a heavy burden for Iraqi policy especially during the war with Iran.

CHANGES IN INTERNATIONAL POLITICS AND IRAQ'S REACTION

Saddam Hussein'a success at the Baghdad Boycott Conference of March 1979 was not of long duration because of the developments in Iran. In connection with this priorities changed again: the Arab-Israeli confict over Palestine was pushed into the background by the necessity of warding off the dangers which might emanate from the Islamic revolution of Khomeini in Iran. The common threat from the east led to a shift in alliances and a rapprochement between Iraq and Saudi Arabia and other conservative countries, such as Jordan, which all feared the danger of the Islamic revolution of Khomeini and its influence on their own countries. Saddam Hussein's vision of a leadership of the Arabs thereby gained impetus, for now he regarded himself as the defender of the Arabs against the Persian peril. Inter-Arab conflicts had lost importance for him.

There were further dangers which Saddam Hussein saw in expansionist Soviet policy, apparent after the invasion of Afghanistan at the end of 1979. The strong engagement of the Soviet Union in South Yemen gave rise to fears that in a case of crisis Moscow might proceed there in a similar way as in Afghanistan and thus threaten the security of the whole Gulf area. Iraq's moving away from the Soviet Union which became visible in its voting on the Afghanistan question against the Soviet Union at the UN General Assembly in January 1980 was another prerequisite for a rapprochement between Iraq and the moderate Arab states, in particular Saudi Arabia and Jordan and later on Egypt. Saddam Hussein's idea was an Arab policy independent of both super powers. Therefore, he criticized both the pro-Soviet attitude of Syria and Libya to the issue of Afghanistan as well as the close military cooperation of Oman with the United States (US Air Force base on the island of Masira). Saddam Hussein's objective was to free the Arab world from dependence on the two blocs. The proposal to hold the non-aligned summit of 1982 in Baghdad was to stress the independent policy of Iraq. Saddam Hussein's view of the possibilities of a leading Iraqi role in Arab politics became clear from the 'Pan Arab Declaration' he published on 8 February 1980. According to this Declaration conflicts between Arab states were to be settled by peaceful means and in the case of foreign aggression all Arab states should declare their solidarity. Furthermore, the richer states should render economic aid to the poorer countries. Political differences were not to be of significance.[4]

The demand for a peaceful settlement of border conflicts in this declaration was not only aimed at the Arab countries but also at Iraq's eastern neighbour, Iran. Whereas Iraq has always maintained a relatively strong position against the Arab Gulf states, the relation to Iran was the reverse. In this case Iraq was in a weaker position. Since the withdrawal of Britain from the area east of Suez in 1971, the Shah of Iran tried to fill the political vacuum and claimed a dominant position on the Gulf. Evidence of this claim was the occupation of the three islands of Abu Musa, the Greater and Lesser Tumbs belonging to the sheikhdoms of Sharja and Ras al-Khaima, respectively, in December 1971. The claim to Bahrain the Shah was finally forced to renounce. The Iraqi government considered Iranian policy in the Gulf as a challenge and danger to the Arab nature of the Gulf. According to Saddam Hussein the responsibility of the Baath party for the Arab Gulf 'arises from their Pan-Arab principles and aims. Furthermore, Iraq, as the most important and advanced country in the area, and the one with the largest potential, must bear the heaviest burdens in protecting it against dangers and encroachment'.[5] On the other hand the Shah saw his policy and position in the area threatened by the socialist and pro-eastern attitude of Baghdad. A rivalry began to develop which increasingly strained relations between the two states. Both countries aimed at a dominant role, seeking control over the adjacent Arab Gulf territories or states and at the same time trying to weaken the rival's influence.

The weaker position of Iraq compared to Iran was not only the result of its lower population. More important was the fact that Iran was able to take advantage of Baghdad's internal problems with the

4. Text in MECS 1979–80 pp. 224–225.
5. The 1968 Revolution in Iraq. Experience and Prospects. *The Political Report of the Eighth Congress of the ABSP in Iraq, January 1974* (London, 1979), p. 133.

Kurds. Iranian arms support for the Kurdish insurgents against the central administration hindered the Baath regime in its expansionist drive. In March 1975 Saddam Hussein succeeded in reaching an agreement with the Shah (Treaty of Algiers) which ended Iranian support for the Kurds and thus ended the Kurdish war. A lasting improvement in relations with Iran, however, could not be achieved. After the overthrow of the Shah and the victory of Khomeini in 1979 bilateral relations deteriorated again. Khomeini, having lived in exile in Iraq for fifteen years, was well acquainted with the nature of Saddam Hussein's Baath regime. The overwhelming success of the Revolution and the drive to export it made Iraq with its mostly Shi'i population and the anti-religious policy of the Baath rule the immediate aim. Considering the longstanding brutal suppression of the Shi'i opposition in Iraq, Khomeini had every reason to expect the propaganda appeals to defeat Baath rule to fall on fertile ground.

Saddam Hussein and the Iraqi government recognized the deadly danger resulting from Khomeini's Islamic revolution. After the breakdown of the Shah's régime and the Iranian army—until then known to be the strongest in the area—they were intent on getting rid of the Iranian threat. The Islamic régime under Khomeini apparently not being willing to come to an understanding with the Baath in Baghdad, but, on the contrary, seeking its defeat, Saddam Hussein resolved to take the offensive. On 22 September 1980, Iraqi troops crossed the border into Iran. However, the hoped for success failed to materialize, the blitzkrieg Saddam Hussein had designed turned into a war which dragged on for eight years and ruined the country.

The war with Iran and the dependence on the financial aid of the oil rich Arab countries, Saudi Arabia and Kuwait, weakened the Iraqi position in the Gulf area. When Saudi Arabia and the other Gulf states founded the Gulf Cooperation Council (GCC) in May 1981 Iraq was excluded. Actually the military alliance of Saudi Arabia and the other Emirates was not only intended as a protection against a possible military attack by Iran but by Iraq also. The rulers in the Arabian peninsula had not forgotten that their countries has been the foremost target of Iraqi propaganda demanding the overthrow of their 'corrupt' and 'pro-western' régimes. Their support for Saddam Hussein and his Baath rule was not the result of sympathy but of fear of the much more dangerous revolution of Khomeini.

When Khomeini finally agreed to an armistice, Iraq could consider itself the victor on account of the use of missiles and the superiority of the Iraqi air force. Although Iran had not been defeated in the military sense because of its large territory and its three times larger population, Iraq had proved to be the stronger power. At the end of the war Iraq had emerged strengthened and had risen to be the most important military power in the area.

The Military Factor in Iraq's Policy

The Iraqi government under Saddam Hussein used the war with Iran to rebuild, expand and modernize the Iraqi army. After the ceasefire in August 1988, this policy was accelerated with the argument that Iraq had to be prepared for a new attack by Iran as long as the Islamic administration in Tehran did not conclude a peace treaty. Under this cover Iraq could obtain nearly every kind of arms it sought. The same was true for the development of its arms industry. On the eve of the Kuwait crisis and the allied war against Iraq the Iraqi army was considered to be the strongest in the Arab world and the world's fourth largest military force. According to the 'Military balance 1990–1991' of the IISS in London, Iraq had 995,000 men, 5,500 tanks (including 500 T-72S), 3,500 artillery pieces and 689 combat aircraft before the war. In comparison to the Iraqi armed forces Turkey had only 647,000 men, Iran 504,000, Egypt 450,000, Syria 404,000 and Israel 141,000. In tanks, Israel had 4,288, Syria 4,000, Turkey 3,714, Egypt 3,190 and Iran 500. The number of aircraft in the other countries was as follows: Syria 558, Israel 553, Egypt 475, Turkey 455 and Iran 185.

The sheer numbers of soldiers, tanks and aircraft are not the only indicator of military strength. Of importance also are the quality of the weapons and above all the training of the soldiers. In this case, too, Iraq could claim to have the best army as after eight years of war with Iran the Iraqi forces were reputed to be 'battle-hardened'. But at the same time there were some doubts about the real ability of Iraq's armed forces, especially the air force.[6]

Iraq's success in the war against Iran came only in the final six months when the morale of the Iranians suddenly cracked. A main reason for the change in the military situation was the successful

---

6. 'Doubt surrounds real ability of Iraq armed forces', *Financial Times*, 8 August 1990.

use of weapons of mass destruction (poisonous gas) and the missile attacks against Iranian towns, mainly Tehran. These weapons—gas and missiles—gave the Iraqi forces their mystique.[7]

This 'success' was the result of another aspect of Saddam Hussein's policy, that is the Iraqi arms industry. He knew as well as many other rulers of Third World countries that he was not really sovereign as long as he was dependent on arms deliveries from foreign countries such as the Soviet Union which had stopped deliveries at the beginning of the war with Iran. The building-up of the Iraqi arms industry took place with great determination and professionalism. Iraq tried to develop nearly every kind of weapon, but the main aim was to reach strategic balance with Israel. For this purpose Iraq needed its weapons of mass destruction, e.g. poisonous gas which is easy and cheap to produce. At a research centre at Salman Pak, twenty-five miles south east of Baghdad, Iraq developed more dangerous nerve agents such as tabun and sarin.[8]

At the same time a comprehensive programme was started to develop missiles in order to carry such weapons over long distances. With the 900 km-range al-Abbas and the 600 km-range al-Hussein Iraq developed missiles which could reach Israel and other important centres in the region.[9]

The most dangerous aspect of Iraq's military policy was the development of nuclear weapons. If Saddam Hussein had succeeded in building his own atomic bomb he would not only have become the great hero of the Arab masses, but Iraq would have represented the dominant power in the Near and Middle East. For the time being this programme has been halted as a result of the last war.

These ambitious weapon programmes proved that Saddam Hussein was striving for political predominance in the region. The fact that he actually used weapons such as poisonous gas against Iran and the Kurds shows clearly that he did not hesitate to apply every means available to gain political supremacy.

THE RETURN OF IRAQ INTO ARAB POLITICS

By the end of the war with Iran Iraq had become the major power

7. In March and April, 1988, Iraq hit Tehran with 150 missiles in the space of seven weeks, *Financial Times*, 8 August 1990.
8. Paul Abrahams, 'Spectre of Iraqi chemical warfare looms ambitious', *Financial Times*, 24 August 1990.
9. *Der Spiegel*, 15 January 1990.

in the Gulf area. Saddam Hussein had a free hand again to engage himself more intensively in Arab politics and to put forward his claim to a dominating role in the Arab world which he had already clearly defined before the outbreak of the war with Iran. It was Lebanon which presented itself as an ideal field of activity where, due to the existing power vacuum, the Arab states and Israel had been struggling for influence. Another reason why Saddam Hussein directed his particular interest to Lebanon was that it offered him the opportunity of setting bounds to his arch-rival, Syrian President Hafiz al-Asad, and to punish his pro-Iranian attitude during the Gulf war which he considered as treason to the common Arab cause. Saddam Hussein's objective was to prevent Syria from gaining control over Lebanon, because not only would Asad's position in the Arab world thus have been enhanced but his own endeavours for predominance in the area obstructed. Therefore, in the Lebanese civil war Saddam Hussein supported the anti-Syrian forces under the leadership of General Aoun with finance and arms. This resulted in a further escalation of fighting and pushed the possibility of a settlement of the conflict into the distant future. This policy, however, did not meet with the approval of the Arab world. Saddam Hussein's demand for the withdrawal of the Syrian troops from Lebanon had neither been supported by the Arab governments at the Casablanca summit in May 1989 nor had it been taken into consideration by the Lebanese delegation when negotiating the Treaty of Taif in October of the same year.

While Saddam Hussein was fighting against Syrian policy in Lebanon he was at the same time taking pains to improve his relationship with a number of other countries, Egypt, Jordan and Yemen, which had supported Iraq during the Gulf crisis. Egypt had already started to supply Iraq with arms and ammunition under Sadat, a fact that Saddam Hussein remembered. During the course of the war when more and more Iraqis had been enrolled into military service Egyptian migratory workers had helped to protect the Iraqi economy from collapse. Jordan had been no less important for Iraq as a majority of military and civil supplies had been imported through the port of Aqaba. King Hussein's unreserved support for Saddam Hussein helped secure his own future since a victory of Iran and the Islamic revolution could have threatened his rule as the fundamentalist forces in Jordan had been gaining influence, as the parliamentary elections of November 1989 had shown. Yemen was the only Arab country which had given direct military assistance by sending a battalion (about 3,000 men). This was much appreciated by Saddam Hussein as great moral support as he declared on the occasion of his visit to Sana in January 1989.

The confidence which had been established among Iraq and the other three states on account of their close cooperation formed the foundation for an intensification of the relationship. On 16 February 1989, King Hussein of Jordan, President Mubarak of Egypt, Ali Abd Allah Salih of Yemen and Saddam Hussein signed an agreement for the creation of the Arab Cooperation Council (ACC). According to the statutes the official aims of the ACC were economic cooperation and integration. It may be doubted, however, that political or military cooperation were excluded. If such aims were not aired officially, this is certainly due to consideration of the neighbouring countries. Israel would have regarded a close alliance between Egypt and Iraq as a breach of the Peace Treaty. At a press conference the Iraqi Foreign Minister Tariq Aziz declared that the ACC would prove to be an important element of stability in warding off the threat arising from Iran and Israel and that the defeat in the war and the formation of the ACC would be a lesson to Iran.[10]

Iraq at least was also pursuing political aims with the ACC. First of all, Iran, whose government refused to sign a peace treaty, was to be discouraged from resuming fighting. Syria, too, was to be even more isolated within the Arab world. Whereas Egypt did not rule out ACC admission of Syria in principle, it was vetoed by Iraq. Together with Egypt and the other two member states Iraq was now in a position to assume a firmer attitude towards the Gulf states in case certain claims were to be pursued. Iraq's relationship to the states of the Gulf Cooperation Council had been strained for several reasons. On the other hand Saudi Arabia could not but regard the rapprochement of Egypt and Iraq with the utmost distrust since it resulted in a marked shifting in power in favour of those two states. Even more dangerous in the view of the Saudi government must have appeared the entry of Yemen into the ACC. By this step Yemen not only escaped the pressure exerted by Riyadh but caused a possible threat to the Saudi régime through its more progressive—and in the case of North Yemen also more democratic—system. To a certain degree Saudi Arabia might have feared encirclement by the close alliance between Iraq and North Yemen.

10. *Jordan Times*, Amman, 12 February 1989.

The ACC could have had a favourable effect for those concerned if it had achieved economic integration of the member countries. As to the ACC as a political instrument it certainly served the purposes of Iraq best. Egypt expected an acceleration of its reintegration into the Arab League which had already been decided upon. Saddam Hussein, however, was pursuing far more comprehensive plans as became apparent in the later Kuwait crisis. He could hope to direct the ACC in accordance with his own objectives for he was by far the strongest personality and most capable of forcing his will on the others. This was especially true of King Hussein and President Ali Abd Allah Salih who to a certain degree were dependent upon Saddam Hussein. President Mubarak could not be compared with his predecessors Sadat and Nasser as a political leader, yet he did represent the most important Arab country and could not easily have been urged on to a political course incompatible with Egyptian interests.

In connection with its efforts to extend its influence in the Arab world the Iraqi government sought cooperation with other states on a bilateral basis. States in considerable economic and political difficulties and thus looking for help from other Arab countries, such as Sudan and Mauritania, were inclined to take Iraq's side. The Sudanese régime under al-Bashir obtained substantial military aid to fight the South Sudanese rebels, the SPLA. In exchange Sudan supported the Iraqi position on the inter-Arab level, as became evident later during the conflict over Kuwait. Mauritania was also granted generous aid by Iraq. It is said to have placed a test area for missiles at Iraq's disposal.

In the Arab-Israeli conflict Iraq had largely exercised restraint and displayed a moderate attitude during the Gulf war. Tariq Aziz had even indicated that Iraq might accept a peaceful settlement, thus completely reversing Iraqi statements before the Gulf crisis when Iraq had not even been prepared to accept UN Resolution 242.[11] At the end of the Gulf war Iraq changed again to an unyielding attitude and rejected a peaceful settlement. This was also noticeable in connection with the warnings against the mass immigration of Soviet Jews into Israel and their settlement in the occupied territories. Saddam Hussein had made himself the spokesman of the radical forces again, the end of this policy being to stress his claim to pan-Arab leadership.

11. MECS 1982–83 pp. 584–585.

THE KUWAIT CRISIS AND SADDAM HUSSEIN'S ATTEMPT TO ATTAIN DOMINATION IN THE AREA

By the end of the Gulf war Iraq was not only the leading power in the Gulf area, but was on the point of catching up with the major military power in the Middle East, Israel. The prerequisite for reaching strategic balance with Israel was the possession of weapons of mass destruction, especially poisonous gas, rather than a huge arsenal of conventional arms. Obviously Saddam Hussein felt strong enough to claim a leading position for his country within the whole area of the Middle East. Such a policy was bound to bring about a confrontation with Israel. Saddam Hussein for the first time clearly expressed his claim to leadership at the meeting of the Arab Cooperation Council in Amman on 23 February 1990. In his address he urged the Arab states to take measures against American influence in the Gulf area. Control of the Gulf and its oil was to be exercised by Arabs, or more precisely, by Iraq.[12] In another speech of 1 April, Saddam Hussein warned Israel not to attack military and armament installations in Iraq, otherwise half of Israel would be destroyed with binary weapons.[13] With this threat against Israel Saddam Hussein acted as an advocate for the Palestinians in the Arab-Israel conflict. The threat to extinguish Israel increased Saddam Hussein's popularity not only with the Palestinians, but with the whole Arab world.

Remembering the bombardment of the Iraqi nuclear reactor by Israel in 1981 and being faced with a growing campaign—particularly in the United States and Great Britain—against the construction of nuclear weapons and super cannons by Iraq, Saddam Hussein feared another Israeli attack on establishments of the Iraqi arms industry, this being the reason for his repeatedly using threats against Israel. However, he was well aware that he was not yet in a position to risk a direct military confrontation with Israel, since he could not yet deploy nuclear weapons. Actually he was pursuing another aim as later developments have shown. On account of a difficult financial position he urgently needed further credits from the Arab oil producing countries in order to carry on his ambitious programme of restoring the Iraqi economy after the Gulf war and of establishing a modern

---

12. BBC, Summary of World Broadcasts, London, 26 February 1990.
13. BBC, Summary of World Broadcasts, London, 4 April 1991.

armament industry capable of producing long-range missiles and weapons of mass destruction (ABC weapons). The mobilization of Arab public opinion which became increasingly alarmed about the possible immigration of more than a million Soviet Jews to Israel and their settlement in the occupied territories was to strengthen the position of the Iraqi administration and of Saddam Hussein within the Arab world and to deter any criticism of their policy. The propaganda against Israel was to predispose the Arab public towards a justification of Iraqi demands on the Arab oil producing states for comprehensive financial aid, an Arab Marshal Plan for Iraq. With the same argument he soon demanded the cancelling of all debts resulting from the war with Iran. The war with Iran had not been waged for the defence of Iraq alone but of all Arabs. As the other Arab countries had withheld from shedding their blood in the defence of arabism against the Persian assault, they should at least show their gratitude in the form of financial aid. Those were his arguments.

In the past he had repeatedly declared that war was to him a legitimate means of attaining political objectives.[14] As a rule he made such remarks in connection with the Arab-Israeli conflict, thus implying that his remarks referred to Israel only. However, the invasion of Kuwait on 2 August 1990 showed that this maxim was of general validity and that it was related to his policy towards the Arab states. Thus the Iraqi ruler had returned to a policy pursued before the outbreak of the war with Iran when he openly worked for the overthrow of the conservative régimes in the Arabian peninsula. While in the 1970s this end was to be achieved by supporting the opposition movements, now several reasons induced Saddam Hussein to take a straight course of action. On the one hand it was caused by financial difficulties, on the other hand his immense army enabled him to carry out his plans. To a certain degree external circumstances for realizing his claim of Iraqi predominance were very favourable now that Iran no longer represented a danger.

But also with the end of the east–west conflict and the weakening of the Soviet Union Saddam Hussein saw a certain peril for the independence of the states within the area. He feared absolute control by the United States which would strengthen the position of Israel and simultaneously weaken that of the Arab world.[15] These apprehen-

14. Saddam Hussein, *op. cit.*, p. 106.
15. See Saddam Hussein's speech in Amman on 24 February 1990 (BBC, Summary of World Broadcasts, 26 February 1990).

sions accelerated his decision to bring forward his own claims. The invasion of Kuwait was the first step on his way to achieve hegemony. The annexation of Kuwait, following the aggression, disclosed that he would not have contented himself with the granting of financial aid and the annulment of debts. With the incorporation of Kuwait he intended to heighten and secure Iraq's predominance in certain respects. First he could markedly improve his country's access to the Gulf by coming into possession of the harbour of Kuwait. Thus he could considerably reduce his dependence on other countries with respect to oil export (via pipelines through Turkey and Saudi Arabia). Furthermore, actions of the Iraqi navy and with them control of the Gulf were now easy. What might have counted most, however, was the financial wealth of Kuwait amounting to more than 100,000 million dollars including investment holdings. Kuwaiti financial means would have been sufficient immediately to pay back Iraq's total debts and to provide additional funds for an ambitious Iraqi industrial development programme. Of similar importance for Saddam Hussein would have been the possession of the immense Kuwaiti oil reserves. Together with the Kuwaiti resources Iraq's oil reserves would amount to about 220,000 million barrels and this would come near to the Saudi reserves. The possession of the Kuwaiti oil deposits would have markedly improved Iraq's position within OPEC and given Iraq the opportunity of having a substantial say in price fixing. Saddam Hussein would have obtained an important means of determining the oil policy altogether. The incorporation of Kuwait would have strengthened Iraq's position within the area to a degree that its dominance could hardly have been disputed. Iraqi requests, for example for higher oil prices, would scarcely have been opposed by the other countries.

The ownership of Kuwait with its funds and oil reserves would have advanced Iraq's power to a new dimension which would have enabled the state, provided that it had attained dominating influence on Arab oil policy and the Arab countries in the area on the whole, to become a serious counterpart of Israel, the United States and Europe. According to Baath ideology this is the very aim of pan-Arab policy. United, the Arab states would achieve a potentiality, especially because of their oil resources, entitling them to an equality of status with the two superpowers, the European Community and Japan. With the annexation of Kuwait Saddam Hussein might have hoped to come substantially closer to this end.

Iraq After the Kuwait Crisis

The crisis over Kuwait and the subsequent war with the allies led by the United States deeply affected the military and economic strength of Iraq as well as its political status in the area. For the time being Iraq lost its military advantage over its neighbours. Through the destruction of its non-conventional weapons and the industrial plants for their production Iraq is farther away from acquiring a strategic balance with Israel than ever before. At the same time Iraq lost its status as a leading political power, even as a political actor in the region. The adventurous policy of Saddam Hussein in Kuwait deprived Iraq of its capacity to act in the international field for the near future.

The economic and military weakness of Iraq, however, will not continue over long periods of time. Its oil wealth will help Iraq to reconstruct the economy and to develop the country into a major economic power in the area. As soon as Iraq reaches this stage, it will automatically be able to bring its political influence to bear on the countries in the area. To what degree Iraq will again arise to major military power status depends on whether the United States will maintain its arms embargo against Iraq. In the long run, however, it will hardly be possible to prevent Iraq from developing its military potential according to its economic and financial resources. The future political development in Iraq and the status of Iraq within the area will to a great extent depend on the question of whether Saddam Hussein remains in power. If he did, economic recovery and the reintegration of Iraq into the Middle East community of states would certainly be retarded. But even if Saddam Hussein remained in power he could not be boycotted in the long term. There is no doubt that in the long run Saddam Hussein will succeed in reestablishing his country as a major economic, military and political power. In the case of his overthrow, however, the danger of an internal destabilization might arise restricting the ability of the Iraqi government to play a leading role in the region. Moreover, another administration is hardly likely to push forward economic and military development as consistently as did Saddam Hussein. Therefore, the opinion held by many politicians that Iraq will remain dangerous as long as Saddam Hussein is in power is certainly right.

On account of the economic potentialities based on its rich oil reserves Iraq will also in future hold a prominent position within the Middle East irrespective of the administration ruling the country. A normalization of Iraq's relations with the Arab states could be speeded up if the area were again to be confronted with a serious political crisis. Such a crisis already exists in the Arab-Israeli conflict. If the expectations of a settlement of the Palestine problem aroused after the recent Gulf crisis are not fulfilled, the political climate could soon deteriorate drastically. Then the Arabs would not be able to get along without Iraq, and Saddam Hussein, if still in power, would have a chance for a comeback.

In addition, the sharpening dispute over water could rapidly expand to a crisis which might offer a chance to Iraq or Saddam Hussein to regain status. The great dam projects of Turkey in southern Anatolia and the resulting reduction in the quantity of water remaining for Syria and Iraq have already provided political explosive. In the long run Iraq cannot be denied a dominant role in the area.

Relations between Iraq and Kuwait

Habib Ishow

Relations between Iraq and Kuwait have known frequent periods of tension resulting from Iraq's territorial and economic claims on the latter. These disputes also have serious and manifold international repercussions. On 2 August 1990 tensions reached a climax when Iraqi troops invaded Kuwait. This invasion was the principal cause of the war which lasted from 17 January to 28 February 1991 and which brought the united forces of the international community into opposition with Iraq, a war commonly referred to as the Gulf War. It has had numerous economic, political and human consequences, critical above all for Iraq and Kuwait, but to some extent, too, for the other countries of the Middle East.

The state of Kuwait is a small desert territory of 17,818 square km. Its importance, its significance in contemporary history, is due to two main factors: namely, the designs of the major powers in the late nineteenth and early twentieth centuries which focussed on its geographical position in that part of the Gulf, and to the discovery of immense oil reserves.[1]

These advantages led Iraq to claim Kuwait as an integral part of its territory in the name of an historical right. Iraq's argument may be summarized as follows: Kuwait used to be part of the Ottoman province of Basra. The present state of Iraq, as the successor to the Ottoman Empire in Mesopotamia, has a claim on Kuwait, which is only a part (a sub-prefecture) of the province of Basra, now in Iraq.[2]

1. For further details on these two points see H. Ishow, *Le Koweit; Evolution politique, économique et sociale*, (Paris, 1989), pp. 17–20 and 81–9.
2. Iraqi Ministry of Foreign Affairs, 'The truth about Kuwait', Baghdad, official report, vol.I, July 1961, pp. 5–7. See also P. Salinger and E. Laurent, *Guerre du Golfe. Le dossier secret*. (Paris. 1991), pp. 195–6.

In order to appreciate the merits of this claim and to understand the nature of the relations between the two countries, it is important to place the problem in its historical context and to examine Kuwait's relations with the Ottoman Empire and Great Britain. For Kuwait, like Iraq, was subject first to Ottoman and then to British influence.

KUWAIT'S RELATIONS WITH THE OTTOMAN EMPIRE

The history of Kuwait begins with the arrival in around 1715 of the Al Sabah family, originally from Najd (central Arabia), fleeing famines and tribal wars.[3] The Al Sabah belonged to the Utub clan of the Arab tribe of Anza.

At that time the city of Kuwait was a small market town, inhabited by Arab nomads and Persian fishermen. After governing the town of Kuwait and its surroundings from 1716 to 1756 with three other tribes, the Al Sabah took power in 1756 and founded their dynasty. It was during this period that the town of Kuwait became the capital and gave its name to the entire emirate. At the time this was limited to the city, its immediate surroundings and a number of islands, including Failaka, which is situated at the entrance to the Bay of Kuwait and which served as a refuge for the inhabitants during periods of unrest and raids on their town. Power has rested almost entirely in the hands of the Al Sabah family since 1756.[4]

Despite its small size the emirate flourished during the second half of the eighteenth century, thanks to its maritime activities of sail boat building and pearl fishing. The importance of these activities was already attested by the German explorer Carsten Niebuhr during his voyage around the Persian Gulf and the Arab peninsula in 1762. Niebuhr described the town of Kuwait as a city of 10,000 inhabitants, with 800 boats, making a living from commerce, fishing and pearl fishing.[5]

The prosperity of the emirate increased again following the arrival of rich merchants, driven from Basra by the plague in 1773–

3. Husain Khazal, *Tarikh al-Kuwait al-siyasi*. [The political history of Kuwait]. (Beirut, 1962), pp. 40, 42.
4. *Ibid.*, p. 43.
5. A.J. Cottrell, ed., *The Persian Gulf states; a general survey*. (John Hopkins University, 1980), p. 112. See also R.M. Burrell, 'Al-Kuwayt', in *Encyclopédie de l'Islam*, (Leiden, 1982), p. 578.

1774 and by the occupation of their town by the Persians from 1776 to 1779.[6] These merchants brought with them money and commercial *savoir-faire*, thus contributing to the development of the country. The port of Kuwait superseded that of Basra and then became the major commercial centre of the region for merchandize which was transported from India by boat and then by caravan to Aleppo in Syria and to the Mediterranean. Finally, following a conflict with the Ottoman authorities in Basra, the English East India Company transferred its agency to Kuwait from 1793 to 1795.[7]

This short stay enabled the Emir of Kuwait to establish good relations with the British. Nevertheless, the British were forced to leave Kuwait for Basra following repeated attacks by the supporters of Wahhabism, a Sunni religious movement founded in Najd in central Arabia by Muhammad Abd al-Wahhab (1703–1792). He preached a puritan and fundamentalist Islam, demanding strict adherence to Koranic law. He met Emir Muhammad Ibn Saud, founder of today's ruling dynasty in Saudi Arabia, and the two men formed an alliance. Religion and politics united in wars waged against all those who refused to accept their doctrines and authority.

Roused to fanaticism, the Wahhabi armies conquered the major part of the Arabian peninsula, relentlessly attacking the principalities of the Gulf and southern Iraq, encouraging acts of piracy and posing a serious threat to the commercial routes between the Gulf and the Mediterranean. Wahhabism remains in force in Saudi Arabia today.

Kuwait was repeatedly attacked from 1793 onwards. It seems that it was thanks to the military protection of the English East India Company that it escaped Wahhabi occupation.[8] Yet later, when the English had left, the Emirs of Kuwait Abd Allah (1762–1812) and his son Jabir (1812–1859) paid tributes to and adopted a benevolent attitude towards the Wahhabis, in order to avoid the annexation of their principality.[9]

Throughout these events the Emirs of Kuwait acted in their own

6. R.M. Burrell, *op. cit.*
7. *Ibid.* See also Hassan A. al-Ebraheem, *Kuwait: a political study*, (Kuwait University, 1975), pp. 28–30.
8. Ahmad Mustafa Abu-Hakima, *Tarikh al-Kuwait* [The history of Kuwait], (Kuwait, 1967), vol. 1, part 1, pp. 213, 253–63. See also Stanford Research Institute, *Area Handbook for the peripheral states of the Arabian Peninsula*, (Washington, D.C., 1971), pp. 18–19.
9. *Ibid.*, pp. 55–7.

self-interest according to individual circumstances. Until 1871 they sometimes behaved like sovereign princes towards the Ottoman Empire and at other times like vassals. In general, they had wide freedom of movement. Even if on certain occasions they recognized an allegiance to the Sublime Porte, in fact, this allegiance had no legal basis. At any rate, throughout this entire period the Ottomans exercised no effective control over Kuwait.[10] The emirate had not yet acquired the strategic importance it would gain for the great powers during the last quarter of the nineteenth century.

Faced with the penetration of the Western and Russian powers into the Gulf, the Ottomans attempted to consolidate their power in the region. In 1871, accompanied by an army, the Ottoman Governor of Baghdad Midhat Pasha embarked on a journey to al-Hasa, another emirate in the Gulf, with a view to subjecting it to Turkish authority. At the time al-Hasa was part of the province of Basra. Today it lies to the south of Kuwait and is part of Saudi Arabia, containing the principal oil fields of the country. In this respect Iraq would be able to make similar claims on al-Hasa to those it has on Kuwait.

On his journey Midhat Pasha stopped at Kuwait, where he was received by the Emir Abd Allah with full honours. Following the success of his military expedition, in 1871 Midhat Pasha made the emirate of Kuwait a district, dependent on the province of Basra. He named Emir Abd Allah an Ottoman head of the district and entrusted the administration of Kuwait to him. The Emir of Kuwait also received the title of Pasha and agreed to pay tribute and to take part in Ottoman military expeditions.[11] The Turkish authorities awarded him vast lands around the town of Fau on the Shatt al-Arab, today part of Iraq. Kuwait flew the Ottoman flag until 1914.

Following these various events, the Emir of Kuwait recognized Ottoman sovereignty over his emirate in 1871. But in reality the relations between Kuwait and the Ottoman Empire were relations of force. A tiny state such as Kuwait would never have been in a position to refuse to recognize Ottoman sovereignty on pain of military occupation. It was far more prudent to recognize this sovereignty, whilst endeavouring to make it as theoretical as possible.

10. R. Mantran, 'Les Ottomans, le Kuwait et l'Iraq', in *Crise du Golfe; La 'logique' des chercheurs, Revue du Monde Musulman et de la Méditerranée*, February 1991, p. 16.
11. Khazal, *op. cit.*, pp. 136–8.

In fact the Ottomans never exercised any real authority over Kuwait and even after 1871 the Emirs of Kuwait acted on their own. For example, in 1896 Emir Mubarak introduced a customs duty of five per cent on the value of all merchandize entering Kuwait, including that which came from Turkish ports. The emirate of Kuwait continued to behave in this way until the end of the Ottoman Empire.

KUWAIT'S RELATIONS WITH GREAT BRITAIN

As we have just seen, Great Britain had an interest in Kuwait from the end of the eighteenth century. Already installed in India, its main concern was to safeguard its imperial commercial routes, one of which passed through the Gulf. Like the other emirates, Kuwait constituted an important link for British politics in the Gulf.

Indeed, during the course of the nineteenth century many British military or commercial missions were dispatched to Kuwait. Its excellent natural position on the Gulf made Kuwait a prized possession for the great powers at the end of the last decade of the nineteenth century.

Following the assassination in 1896 of Emir Muhammad by his half-brother Mubarak, links between Mubarak, who now became Emir, and the British were reinforced. Indeed, in order to escape Ottoman control Mubarak repeatedly attempted to place his state under British protection. He first requested this between 1896 and 1899, but in vain. Britain's interests were not threatened and she could see no good reason for entering into open conflict with the Ottoman Empire. Subsequently, however, the strategic and economic designs of the great powers in the Gulf would completely change British policies towards Kuwait. The Ottomans continued to attempt to consolidate their position in the Gulf region. They even attempted the military occupation of Kuwait in 1898[12] and the emirate was only saved from annexation by British military action and diplomacy. The Germans and Russians also caused the British some concern, with their respective railway line projects, of which the famous German Berlin-Baghdad project was to end in the Gulf region, and therefore in Kuwait.

12. B.C. Busch, *Britain and the Persian Gulf, 1894–1914*, (University of California Press, 1967), p. 103.

In view of these threats of penetration into the Gulf and the repeated requests of Mubarak, Great Britain finally decided to establish its protectorate over Kuwait.

The protectorate treaty was signed on 23 January 1899. By it the Emir of Kuwait committed himself and his successors and heirs not to receive any representative of any other power without the prior permission of Her Majesty's Government. He also committed himself not to cede, sell or grant bases or lease any part of his territory to other states, including the Ottoman Empire, without the British Government's prior consent.[13] This treaty governed relations between Great Britain and Kuwait until the latter's independence in June 1961. Learning of the conclusion of this treaty, the Ottomans, encouraged by the Germans, made repeated attempts to occupy Kuwait between 1899 and 1902. These attempts were thwarted by the diplomatic and military resolve of the British government. In order to show that the Emirate would henceforth form part of the British sphere of influence, Lord Curzon, Viceroy of India, made a visit to Kuwait in 1903. This was followed by the nomination in 1904 of Colonel S.G. Knox as the first British resident political minister in Kuwait.[14]

These privileged relations between Great Britain and Kuwait were further reinforced at the outbreak of the First World War. At the beginning of the war Mubarak sent a letter to Colonel Knox on 18 August 1914 offering military aid to the British. For his part, in a letter dated 13 November 1914, Colonel Knox promised in the name of his government that should the allies be victorious he would recognize the emirate as an independent state under the protection of the British.[15] Kuwait thus entered the war on the side of the allies against the Ottoman Empire and attacked southern Iraq (the region of Umm Qasr, Safwan and the island of Bubiyan).

Constantly consolidating the advantage of its position, Great Britain signed a treaty with Ibn Saud on 26 August 1915, in which the latter committed himself to no acts of aggression against Kuwait. Despite this treaty, however, Ibn Saud's army launched repeated attacks on Kuwait in 1919 and throughout the 1920s. Once again it was British military intervention which saved the emirate from annexation.

13. J.C. Hurewitz, *Diplomacy in the Near and Middle East*, (Princeton University Press), 1956, p. 218.
14. Busch,*op. cit.*, pp. 225, 229–230.
15. Khazal, *op. cit.*, vol II, pp. 153–5.

The peace settlements (1919–1923) broke up the Ottoman Empire. The Asiatic territories removed from the Empire were placed under the rule of Mandates created by the League of Nations. In Mesopotamia, the three provinces (vilayets) of Mosul, Baghdad and Basra were grouped together and placed under British mandate at the conference of San Remo in 1920. It is from the regrouping of these three provinces that the modern-day state of Iraq was born in August 1921.

In order to avoid misunderstandings or statements not based on historical facts, it is important to emphasize that Kuwait was not included in the system of mandates. It did not form part of the territories which constituted Iraq in 1921. Kuwait had its own political identity long before the creation of contemporary Iraq. The peace settlements of 1919–1923 therefore made no change to the status of Kuwait, since the allies recognized the British protectorate over it.

In the Treaty of Lausanne concluded with the Allies on 24 July 1923, Turkey renounced all rights to and claims on territories outside the frontiers defined by the aforesaid treaty. The country no longer had any right, any claim of any nature on Kuwait. The latter's fate was to be settled by the interested parties; and under the circumstances the interested parties were the British, signatories of the Treaty of Lausanne. Thus, Iraq has no claim on territories which Turkey renounced in an international treaty. Iraq itself exists by virtue of this treaty. Certainly, the fate of the two countries depended on Great Britain. If they had so wished they could have joined Kuwait to Iraq without difficulty, although this would not have been in their interest.

Anxious to protect the political identity of his state from the possible acquisitiveness of his neighbours, the Emir of Kuwait, Ahmad Al Sabah (1921–1950), insisted that Britain should define the borders of the emirate with Saudi Arabia and Iraq. To this end a conference was held in Uqayr, with Kuwait and Iraq represented by Sir Percy Cox, a British official, and Najd (Saudi Arabia) by Ibn Saud himself. Negotiations led to a series of accords, referred to as the Uqayr accords of 1922–1923, in which the borders between Kuwait and Saudi Arabia were drawn up, to the clear advantage of the latter. In fact the expansionist kingdom of Ibn Saud was awarded around two thirds of territory belonging to Kuwait.[16] This

16. A.M. Abu-Hakima, *The modern history of Kuwait 1750–1965*, (London, 1983), p. 153.

did not, however, prevent Saudi Arabia from pursuing a hostile policy towards Kuwait during the 1920s, as has been previously pointed out. It was only with the treaty of friendship of 1940, signed by Saudi Arabia and Great Britain, acting in the name of Kuwait, that the border between the two countries was finally guaranteed.[17]

Kuwait's northern borders with Iraq were also drawn up in the Uqayr accords, just as they had been defined by the Anglo-Turkish convention of 1913, a convention which was never ratified, but which was clearly to the advantage of Kuwait, since the two islands of Warba and Bubiyan were included in Kuwaiti territory, which prevented Iraq from gaining important access to the Gulf. This subsequently became one of the causes of tension and conflict between Iraq and Kuwait. The north-western and western borders of the emirate were defined by the Iraqi-Kuwait convention of 1932. It should be noted that this was concluded after Iraq's independence. Despite these accords between 1936 and 1939 Iraq began to make claims on Kuwait following serious political unrest which arose in the emirate in favour of a political union between the two countries.

After the discovery of important oilfields in 1938 and their exploitation on a grand scale from 1946 onwards, Britain decided to set Kuwait's independence in motion. This political development was also motivated by unexpected major events in the Middle East in 1958. On 1 February 1958 the United Arab Republic (UAR) was born from the union of Egypt and Syria under the aegis of President Nasser, leader of Egypt. The aim was eventually to include the other Arab states in this union. President Nasser's pan-Arab nationalist propaganda was of great concern to the countries of the region and threatened their political régimes. To the danger of Nasser was added another far more serious threat to the Gulf countries. On 14 July 1958, under the command of General Qasim, the army overthrew the Hashimite monarchy and proclaimed the Iraqi Republic. King Faisal and the Prime Minister Nuri al-Said, allies of Britain, were assassinated. In 1959 revolutionary Iraq denounced the Baghdad pact and assumed a new hostile political attitude towards Britain.

These new events led Britain to safeguard its interests by establishing friendly relations with Kuwait and the other Gulf emirates,

---

17. *Revue de la Défense Nationale*, Paris, December 1961, p. 2000.

based on the treaties concluded with the sovereign states. To this end, from 1959 onwards, the British government brought about important changes in the status of the emirate by according it sovereign powers.

In terms of foreign policy, in 1959 Kuwait became a member of the following organizations: the International Telecommunications Union, the Universal Postal Union, the International Civil Aviation Organization, UNESCO and the ILO.[18] In terms of domestic politics, from 1 April 1961 onwards Kuwait assumed jurisdiction over foreign residents, who were from now on subject to Kuwaiti tribunals and not to British jurisdiction as had hitherto been the case. On the same day it introduced its own currency, the dinar, valued at the time at one pound sterling, to replace the Persian Gulf rupee, issued by India.

And finally on 19 June 1961 the Emir of Kuwait, Abd Allah al-Salim Al Sabah and the British resident minister in the Persian Gulf, W. H. Luce, exchanged two letters on the status of Kuwait and future relations between Kuwait and Britain. These two letters constituted the new treaty by which the British government recognized the independence and sovereignty of Kuwait, thus rescinding the protectorate treaty of 23 January 1899.[19]

Thus it emerges from this account of Kuwaiti relations with the Ottoman Empire and Great Britain that Kuwait progressively became a state and gained independence, like other contemporary states. From 1961 onwards Kuwait's independence and sovereignty was recognized by these states. For these various reasons on a legal level, therefore, Iraqi claims on Kuwait are indefensible.

RELATIONS BETWEEN IRAQ AND KUWAIT AFTER KUWAIT'S INDEPENDENCE

Following independence relations between Kuwait and Iraq are chiefly characterized by two Iraqi attempts to annex the emirate, one in June 1961 and the other in August 1990. The same reasons can be found for both attempts:

1) To hold sway over the emirate's important oil reserves since Kuwait is in possession of around ten per cent of world oil

18. Ebraheem, *op. cit.*, p. 130.
19. For the complete text of these two letters see Husain M. al-Baharna. *The Arabian Gulf States*, (Beirut, 1978), pp. 374–5.

reserves. In this way Iraq hoped to be able to influence OPEC policy. Such control would have enabled Iraq to rectify to some extent its serious economic, financial and social problems, the result of the disastrous general policies of successive governments.

2) To occupy a geo-political and strategic position of great importance in this part of the Gulf region and at the same time to counterbalance the influence of Iran and Saudi Arabia. The Bay of Kuwait has excellent natural conditions: deep water, protection from the winds and easy year-round access. In contrast Iraq has no site on the Gulf with favourable natural conditions. The port of Basra is situated inside the shallow Shatt al-Arab. Each year it and its mouth are congested with millions of tonnes of alluvium. The Iraqi coastline is also very narrow, extending only to a length of nineteen km obstructed to a large extent by the two Kuwaiti islands of Warba and Bubiyan and their territorial waters.

3) To establish itself as leader of the Arab population of the Middle East and North Africa.

Soon after Kuwait's independence a serious crisis exploded with Iraq. On 25 June 1961 General Qasim, the Iraqi leader, claimed the emirate as an 'integral part of Iraq'. Denouncing the Anglo-Kuwaiti treaty of 19 June 1961 as null and void, he proposed to annex Kuwait without delay.[20]

Frightened by Qasim's claims and faced with the concentration of Iraqi troops on his borders, on 30 June 1961 the Emir of Kuwait lodged a complaint against the Iraqi threat with the Security Council of the United Nations. On the same day he appealed for Great Britain's diplomatic and military aid in accordance with the Anglo-Kuwaiti treaty of 19 June 1961.

To defend their interests and in response to the request of the Emir of Kuwait the British government dispatched to Kuwait part of their armed forces based in the region. On 1 July 1961 British troops arrived in order to dissuade Iraq from invading the emirate.[21]

The threat of the annexation of Kuwait by Iraq engendered lively reaction from international opinion. Most countries, including Iran,

---

20. *Revue Orient*, Paris, no. 19, third quarter, 1961, p. 8.
21. Ebraheem, *op. cit.*, p. 127.

Saudi Arabia, the United Arab Republic, Great Britain, and the United States pledged their support for the emirate against Iraqi claims. It is interesting to note here that Nasser's Egypt found itself in the same camp as Great Britain and the United States, though it wrapped its decision within flowery language.[22] On no account did President Nasser wish to see Iraq annex Kuwait and take control of its important oil resources or to assume an important strategic position in the Gulf, a position which might counterbalance that of Egypt in the Middle East. There was, after all, intense rivalry between Baghdad and Cairo.

This first great crisis between Iraq and Kuwait receded gradually, thanks to military and diplomatic pressure from Western and most of the Middle Eastern countries.

Despite Iraq's strong opposition on 20 July Kuwait was admitted as a member of the Arab League. Following lengthy negotiations between the members of the Arab League and Great Britain, the British forces which had been sent to Kuwait on 1 July 1961 were replaced by those of the Arab League from 14 September of the same year. Most of these forces were formed from UAR contingents and from Saudi Arabia, respectively 1,200 and 1,600 soldiers out of a total of 4,000 men. Under the name of the 'green berets', on 23 September 1961 the forces of the Arab League took up positions along the border between Kuwait and Iraq. On 10 October 1961 the Emir of Kuwait announced the complete evacuation of British troops and the Arab League forces also left the emirate. In fact, following the Syrian coup d'état of 28 September 1961 and its break with the UAR, President Nasser asked the Arab League to withdraw its army from Kuwait because of the dissension between the states concerned and the frictions developing within the Arab league forces: the Jordanian and Syrian troops were in conflict with the Egyptian contingents.[23] The other countries involved also gradually withdrew their troops. On 4 February 1963 the Arab League force sent to Kuwait was totally broken up. Once again Kuwait found itself alone and exposed to potential attack from Iraq.

The crisis between Kuwait and Iraq was temporarily settled by the military coup d'état of 8 February in which General Qasim was

22. *Revue Orient*, no. 19, 1961.
23. M. Khadduri, *Republican Iraq; a study in Iraq politics since the revolution of 1958*, (Oxford University Press, 1969), p. 172.

overthrown. This coup was organized by supporters of Nasser and Baathists and, it would seem, with the aid of the United States. The Emir of Kuwait welcomed the news with relief. In order to attract the sympathy of the new Iraqi government he formally recognized it on 10 February. For its part, the Iraqi government also recognized the independence and sovereignty of Kuwait in a joint communiqué issued in Baghdad on 4 October 1963.[24] On this occasion Kuwait accorded Iraq an interest-free loan of $100 million.[25] Finally, since the USSR was no longer opposed, on 14 May 1963 Kuwait was admitted as a member of the United Nations.[26] It was now recognized by the entire international community.

Despite this recognition, however, Iraq continued to make claims on Kuwait in the form of a demand for the adjustment of the borders between the two countries, laying particular claim to the region of Umm Qasr and the two islands of Warba and Bubiyan.[27] These claims, each of which was rejected by Kuwait, led to serious incidents in 1973 and 1976. In an attempt to settle the crisis in a spirit of good neighbourliness Sheikh Saad Abd Allah Al Sabah, Kuwait's Minister of Interior and Defence at the time and present Prime Minister, made an official visit to Baghdad on 27 June 1977. Following this visit, on 3 July of the same year, the two countries decided to proceed along the lines of a 'partial withdrawal' of their respective troops which were massed along the frontier and to form a committee comprised of their interior ministers, charged with defining common boundaries and settling any disputes which might arise in the region.[28] No settlement was ever achieved.

Despite meetings between the officials of the two states, attempts at mediation by other countries in the region and massive logistical and financial aid accorded by Kuwait to Iraq in its war against Iran from 1980 to 1988, Baghdad continued to demand the modification of its borders with the emirate, which the latter categorically refused. In addition, the Iraqi demand to lease the islands of Warba and Bubiyan for strategic reasons was rejected by Kuwait

24. Baharna, *op. cit.*, pp. 384–5.
25. P. Bonnenfant, 'Utilisation des recettes pétrolières et stratégie des groupes sociaux en péninsule Arabique', *Maghreb-Machrek*, no. 82, October/November 1978, pp. 63–4.
26. *Le Monde*, 6-7 October 1963.
27. *Fiches du Monde arabe*, Beirut, no. 381, 16 September 1975 and no. 1143, 19 December 1978.
28. *Ibid.*, no. 1143, 19 December 1978.

in November 1984. In the context of the time Iran exercised continuous pressure on Kuwait not to respond favourably to the demands of Iraq, with whom it was at war. Thus, it made known to Kuwait in November 1984 that the lease of these two islands to Iraq would be considered as a 'declaration of war'.[29]

Iraq refused to moderate its claims on the emirate. On the eve of the crisis of summer 1990 a high Kuwaiti official said that 'Saddam Hussein not only wants the two islands which it has claimed and which would allow it access to the Gulf; it covets the whole of Kuwait'.[30] Indeed the Iraqi demands to reassert the 'historical claims of Iraq on Kuwait' became particularly insistent and menacing during the course of July 1990 and clearly heralded the crisis. On 2 August 1990 Iraq invaded and on the 8 of the same month officially annexed Kuwait.[31]

Because of the importance of the economic and major political stakes, the conflict assumed an international dimension, placing the community of nations in a critical position, a conflict with very serious and multiple human, economic and political consequences, particularly for Iraq and Kuwait.

One might ask why the Western powers, and the United States in particular, with their allies in the Middle East, did not react in time to dissuade Iraq from invading Kuwait, as they had done in 1961.

The Western countries and those of the Middle East were well aware of Iraq's military preparations. Iraq's vociferous and repeated threats towards the emirate during July 1990 and the concentration of Iraqi troops on the Kuwaiti border were a clear announcement of Bagdad's intentions.

Even if we do not have all relevant information at our disposal, it is nevertheless possible to formulate the following hypothesis: the allies were trying to lure the Baghdad régime into a trap, with a view to destroying its military potential, in particular its non-conventional potential, which would, in time, pose a serious threat to oil reserves in the Gulf and the region's countries.

In any case the Americans' ambiguous and contradictory statements, including those of John Kelly, Under-Secretary of State and those of April Glaspie, United States ambassador to Baghdad

29. *Maghreb-Machrek*, no. 107, January/February/March 1985, pp. 61, 72.
30. Salinger and Laurent, *op. cit.*, pp. 22 and 195–6.
31. *Le Monde*, 3,4 and 10 August 1990.

during the period of tension between Iraq and Kuwait and the months which preceded the crisis in the summer of 1990, would seem to suggest that they were deliberately encouraging Saddam Hussein to realize his project for the annexation of the emirate.[32]

In the same way the reports of Muhammad al-Mashat, Iraq's ambassador to Washington, to the Iraqi government during the months preceding the invasion of Kuwait on 2 August 1990, also encouraged the Iraqi leaders to take decisive action against Kuwait, referring to 'the minor risks of an American reaction in the event of intervention in Kuwait'.[33] Towards the end of January al-Mashat then asked for political asylum in Canada.[34] One might suppose that he acted in collusion with the United States to bring about the downfall of Saddam Hussein in the Kuwaiti snare. The events which followed support this hypothesis.

Despite numerous attempts at mediation on the part of Middle Eastern and North African countries, of the West and the Security Council of the United Nations, Iraq refused to leave Kuwait. And so, on 17 January 1991 the coalition of allied forces, under the aegis of the United States of America delared war on Iraq in order to liberate Kuwait.[35] Kuwait was liberated at the end of February of the same year and Iraq compelled to accept the 12 resolutions of the United Nations Security Council (resolutions 660, 661, 662, 664, 665, 666, 667, 669, 670, 774, 677, and 678). On 28 February 1991 George Bush, President of the United States announced the end of the war.[36]

Before withdrawing from Kuwait, in addition to the pillaging and extortion committed against the inhabitants of the emirate, the Iraqi army set fire to some 700 oil wells causing catastrophic pollution, destroying most of Kuwait's infrastructure, practising a true scorched earth policy.

The cost of the war to Kuwait, in terms of reconstruction and loss of earnings, is valued at around eighty billion dollars.[37]

In accepting the various United Nations Security Council resolutions Iraq is bound to:

32. Salinger and Laurent, *op. cit.*, pp. 11–12 and 68–91.
33. E. Laurent, *Tempête du désert; les secrets de la Maison Blanche*, (Paris, 1991), vol. 2, p. 27.
34. *Le Monde*, 11 May 1991.
35. *Le Monde*, 18 January, 1991. See also *Le Figaro*, Paris, 17 and 18 January 1991.
36. *Le Monde*, 1 March 1991; *Le Figaro* 28 February 1991.
37. *Le Monde*, 31 July 1991.

1) recognize the independence and the sovreignty and territorial integrity of Kuwait.

2) settle its differences with Kuwait through negotiation, good offices or arbitration.

3) recognize its responsibility for the destruction, damage and injustices suffered by Kuwait and the third-party states, their nations and societies following the invasion of Kuwait (resolutions 674 of 29 October 1990 and 686 of 2 March 1991).

In order to effect the reimbursement of war damages the United Nations Security Council created a commission charged with managing the compensation funds on 20 May 1991. These funds will be supplied by a levy of between thirty per cent and fifty per cent on Iraqi oil exports. In principle the importing countries ought to deposit the cost of Iraqi oil in an account blocked by the UN.[38]

Thus, in order to repair the damages of the second Gulf War, and in particular its effects on Kuwait, Iraq will have to pay considerable sums valued at many billions of dollars for several decades. This compensation will have extremely detrimental effects on the Iraqi population, the victim of the folly and tyranny of its leaders.

As regards relations between Kuwait and Iraq, they cannot but remain ambiguous and conflict-laden, even if in the near future the two countries settle their differences on the border by means of the accords duly concluded under the aegis of the United Nations, other nations or regional or international organizations. For the reasons mentioned above Iraq will always be attracted by the riches and the geographical position of Kuwait and will constitute the most serious threat to the very existence of the emirate. In this respect we should also mention Saudi Arabia. For we must not forget the tensions which exist between Saudi Arabia and Kuwait. Beyond its economic interests Saudi Arabia has similar territorial claims on the emirate, in particular on its excellent bay which would serve as an entry to the Najd region.

In this part of the world accords and rights are not always respected. The law of the strongest is imposed whenever local and international conditions are favourable. In the long term only institutions and political régimes founded on democratic principles will permit the rule of justice and peace to be established in these societies. Otherwise social and political structures, characterized by

38. *Le Monde*, 2–3 June and 1 August 1991.

fundamentally anti-democratic tribal mentalities and by religious principles, will not only hinder the evolution of these societies towards democracy, but worse still, will engender optimum conditions for successive autocratic and dictatorial régimes.

Iraq and Saudi Arabia: from Rivalry to Confrontation

Andreas Rieck

The Gulf War of January–February 1991 marked a new nadir in the impotence and conflict the Arab world has suffered since its liberation from direct European colonial rule. Saddam Hussein's 'mother of all defeats' at the hands of the superior combined force of Western military technology not only set back by many years Iraq's candidacy for political and military leadership in the Arab East, but also further intensified the existing divisions between Arab states with differing social systems and regimes. This is particularly true of Iraq and its neighbour Saudi Arabia.

Without the Saudi monarchy's swift decision to make its own country available as a deployment zone to the American-led alliance against Saddam Hussein, Iraqi troops might still be in Kuwait, and an Iraq militarily superior to all its neighbours would still be defying inadequate international economic sanctions. The military expulsion of the Iraqis from Kuwait, let alone the destruction of a major part of Iraq's military forces and of the country's civil infrastructure would never have been possible without Saudi Arabia's assistance.

The existence in the same region of two neighbouring and competing Arab regimes, one of which saw its very survival at risk, created the conditions for the heaviest blow to Arab efforts towards emancipation from Western superiority since Israel's victory in the Six Day War of 1967.

IRAQI-SAUDI RELATIONS BEFORE 1958

When in April 1920 the modern state of Iraq was founded as a British League of Nations mandate in the provinces of Basra, Baghdad and Mosul, all of which had been Ottoman until the First

World War, the third independent state was already in existence at the centre of the Arab peninsula (Najd and al-Hasa), under the leadership of the Al Saud. As had been the case with its predecessors of 1744–1818 and 1824–1891, both of which had been crushed by the Turks, the expansion of the third Saudi kingdom under Abd al-Aziz Ibn Saud (from 1902) rested on the mobilization force of the purist Wahhabi interpretation of the Islamic religion. This was used to direct the warlike energies of the central-Arabian Bedouin tribes against the Al Saud's rivals, who were identified as 'enemies of Islam'. The proclamation of the Kingdom of Saudi Arabia (on 18 September 1932), which followed twelve years of further campaigns of conquest, almost exactly coincided with the formal independence of Iraq (3 October 1932).

From the very beginning the Hashimite dynasty in Iraq, brought in by the British in 1921, found itself in conflict with the Al Saud, who snatched the Hejaz from their control in 1924–25. Great Britain had allowed its first World War ally, the Hashimite Sharif of Mecca, Husain Ibn Ali to be ousted by Ibn Saud, and further allowed the annexation of the Hejaz, which had only become independent in 1916. However, it set limits to the further expansion of the Wahhabi kingdom to the north, east and south of the Arabian peninsula.

Initially, the new state of Iraq was forced to seek British aid in order to defend its territories against attacks by the Wahhabi Bedouin warriors. In the spring of 1922 the Bedouins led major raids against Shi'i settlements in southern Iraq, including the town of Karbala, which had been attacked and looted by the Wahhabis as far back as 1801, at the time of Ottoman rule.[1] In November of the same year the British negotiated with Ibn Saud the border treaty of Uqayr, in which a relatively large part of the desert area of northern Najd was awarded to Iraq. In compensation, Ibn Saud received almost half of the territory of Kuwait as it then was'.[2]

The new border between Iraq and Saudi Arabia divided traditional Bedouin pasturelands in the Najd and remained controversial until the 1970s.[3] Right up until 1929 the Wahhabi *Ikhwan*, Ibn Saud's raiding parties, inspired in particular by the central ideas of

1. P-J. Luizard, *La Formation de l'Irak contemporain*, (Paris, 1991), p. 441.
2. N. Safran, *Saudi Arabia; the ceaseless quest for security*, (Harvard University Press, 1985), p. 45; see also H. Ishow's article in this volume, pp. 303–318.
3. In April 1975 Iraq and Saudi Arabia divided between themselves a 'neutral zone' created in 1922. A treaty which included all border disputes was not signed until December 1981.

the *jihad*, had continued their sporadic attacks on Iraqi territory. In contrast to Saddam Hussein sixty years later, Ibn Saud accurately judged the superior might of Western imperialism—British in his time—in the Near East, and moved against the *Ikhwan* himself when their aggression became burdensome. Following the suppression of the *Ikhwan* rebellion in Najd in 1929, in February 1930 Britain was able to arrange the first meeting between the Iraqi King Faisal and Ibn Saud, at which the two agreed to be 'good neighbours'. And in April 1936 an Iraqi-Saudi treaty of friendship was even agreed.[4]

Nevertheless, relations between Ibn Saud and the Hashimites in Iraq and Jordan remained tense, with the Saudi King in a weaker position and on the defensive. In the early 1930s the lack of state income intensified the problem of retaining the loyalty of the armed Bedouin tribes and other important population groups in the large conquered territory. The threat of insolvency was only averted by the award of oil concessions to the Standard Oil of California Co., and after 1938 to the American consortium ARAMCO. As far as possible, since the late 1920s Ibn Saud had avoided conflicts with Great Britain and its other allies in the peninsula in order to prevent the Hashimites from exploiting Saudi Arabia's internal weaknesses.[5]

In the 1940s plans for a 'Greater Syria', or to unite the entire 'fertile crescent' under the leadership of the Hashimites, revived Ibn Saud's fear of revenge on the part of the Hashimites. And so it was Ibn Saud himself who made intensive efforts during the final years of his life to obtain a defence alliance with the USA and American arms aid, while the USA showed little enthusiasm for the idea.[6] His successor Saud Ibn Abd al-Aziz (1953–1964), however, had more faith in an alliance with Egypt and Syria as a counterbalance to Hashimite ambitions. The fear of a militarily superior Iraq (in alliance with Jordan) even prompted King Saud for some years to imitate Nasser's anti-imperialist and Arab nationalist rhetoric, and to oppose the Baghdad pact concluded in 1955. Only after the Suez crisis of 1956, when Nasser's popularity began to pose a threat to the monarchy in Saudi Arabia, did Saud adopt anti-Nasser policies

4. Safran, *loc. cit.*, p. 54; M. Khadduri, *Independent Iraq 1932–1958; a study in Iraqi politics*, (Oxford Unversty Press, 1960), p. 322f.
5. Safran, *loc. cit.*, p. 57–61.
6. Safran, *loc. cit.*, p. 62–68; B.L. Grayson, *Saudi-American relations*, (Washington, D.C., 1982), pp. 37–63, 77–85.

which led to rapprochement with the Hashimites shortly before their fall in Iraq (July 1958).[7]

TENSE CO-EXISTENCE, 1958-1979

Six months after the great boost to Nasser's power and prestige following the uniting of Egypt with Syria (February 1958) the Iraqi monarchy was overthrown by a 'revolutionary' Arab-nationalist régime. Initially this appeared to place the Saudi monarchy in a precarious position. This danger was soon intensified by the rivalry between Nasser and the new Iraqi ruler Abd al-Karim Qasim (1958-1963). Although, like Nasser, Qasim rejected the Saudi régime on ideological grounds, Iraq's domestic political problems and its political isolation abroad forced him to be restrained, and relations with Saudi Arabia remained cool without major conflicts. In June 1961 Saudi Arabia expressed its solidarity with Kuwait against Iraqi annexation plans, and provided a major part of the troop contingent which the Arab League dispatched between September 1961 and February 1963 to protect Kuwait.[8]

The real challenge for the Saudi régime in the early 1960s came from Nasser, who had won wide support amongst those dissatisfied with the family oligarchy, particularly amongst intellectuals and the officer class. In 1960 a group of 'liberal princes' from the Saudi clan went as far as to plan their own coup with Egyptian assistance.[9] The later King Faisal Ibn Abd al-Aziz (1964-1975) who, as Prime Minister had exercised a decisive influence on Saudi policies since 1958, concentrated on the internal consolidation of the monarchy and its security organs, but initially avoided open conflict with Nasser. In order to appease Nasser, in 1961 Faisal refused an extension to the USA's right to use the air force base at Dhahran.[10] As a counter to Nasser's pan-Arab nationalist propaganda Faisal made use of pan-Islamic fundamentalist slogans. With the foundation of the *World Muslim League* he introduced a policy, which still continues today, aimed at raising the status of Saudi Arabia, with its

7. Safran, *loc. cit.*, p. 77-87.
8. Safran, *loc. cit.*, p. 92; M. Khadduri, *Republican Iraq; a study in Iraqi politics since the Revolution of 1958*, (Oxford University Press, 1969), p. 171f.
9. Safran, *loc. cit.*, p. 90f.
10. Safran, *loc. cit.*, pp. 89, 92; D.E. Long, *The United States and Saudi Arabia; ambivalent allies*, (Boulder, Co., 1985), p. 39f; the last Saudi-American treaty on the use of the base built in 1945, was concluded in 1957 and expired in April 1962.

holy cities of Mecca and Medina, to a kind of Vatican of the Islamic world.[11]

The conflict between Nasser's Egypt and the Saudi monarchy reached its climax with the Egyptian intervention following the coup in Yemen in September 1962 and in the ensuing civil war between Yemeni republicans and the supporters of Imam Muhammad al-Badr, who were backed by Saudi Arabia. The pressure on Saudi Arabia was intensified by guerrilla war in the British colony of Aden, which at the end of 1967 led to the withdrawal of the British and the foundation of the 'People's Democratic Republic of Southern Yemen', and an uprising in the west of the Sultanate of Oman (Dhofar) after 1965.

Iraq did not play an important role in these conflicts in the extreme south of the Arab peninsula. Although Abd as-Salam Arif, who assumed power in 1963, was a pro-Nasser officer, who in 1964 called for 'political unity' with Egypt, this was never achieved, and Iraq's hesitant policies towards Saudi Arabia hardly changed under his rule or that of his successor Abd al-Rahman Arif (1966–1968). Even Iraq's support for the National Liberation Front (from 1967 onwards the National Front) in South Yemen and the Dhofar Liberation Front (which changed its name in 1968 to the Popular Front for the Liberation of the Occupied Arab Gulf, PflOAG),[12] cannot be regarded as serious attempts to destabilize Saudi Arabia, comparable with Nasser's war with Yemen. The influence of the Soviet Union and China on these revolutionary groups was far more important than that of Iraq.

In December 1967 the last Egyptian troops withdrew from Yemen and a year later Saudi Arabia was able to come to an arrangement with the Republican régime. For the next two decades Saudi policies in Southern Arabia were focussed on promoting conflicts between North and South Yemen in order to minimize the influence of Marxist South Yemen.[13]

Following his defeat in the June war of 1967, Nasser no longer

11. J.P. Piscatori, 'Islamic values and national interest; the foreign policy of Saudi-Arabia', in A.I. Dawisha ed., *Islam in foreign policy*, (Cambridge University Press, 1983), pp. 33–53.
12. On the subject of the guerilla war in Dhofar in which Iran also intervened between 1973 and 1977, see F. Halliday, *Arabia without Sultans*, (Harmondsworth, 1974), pp. 304–60; A.H. Cordesman, *The Gulf and the search for strategic stability*, (Boulder, Co., 1984), pp. 428–39.
13. Cf. F. G. Gause III, *Saudi-Yemeni relations; domestic structures and foreign influence*, (Columbia University Press, 1990).

represented a threat, and from 1970 to 1977 under his successor Sadat, Egypt became Saudi Arabia's most important ally. At the same time the rise to the leading Arab power in the Gulf of Iraq, which had been unharmed by the 1967 war, brought with it new dangers.

Even the seizure of power by the Arab Socialist Baath Party in Iraq (July 1968) changed little in the officially normally 'fraternal' relations between Iraqi and Saudi government representatives. The Iraqi Baath régime under Ahmad Hasan al-Bakr and Saddam Hussein rarely aimed direct propaganda attacks against the Saudi royal household, leaving polemics against the 'lackeys of US imperialism' to the various revolutionary groups it supported, such as those referred to above in southern Arabia and to George Habbash's Popular Front for the Liberation of Palestine. From the end of the 1960s onwards, however, it is possible to trace an intensified Iraqi-Saudi power struggle, which was conducted on two main levels: on a regional and political level in the Gulf, and within OPEC on the level of oil prices and export policies.

With the withdrawal of the British from their military bases in the Gulf, announced in 1968 and completed by end of 1971, the three most important Gulf neighbour states (Iran, Iraq and Saudi Arabia) began a race to fill the 'strategic vacuum'. Saudi Arabia, which could not compete on a military level with either Iraq or Iran,[14] approved the USA's increased involvement in the Gulf. For its part the USA put its faith in Saudi Arabia and Iran as the 'twin pillars' of its new Gulf security policy, whereby Iran was naturally the more important Western ally.[15] The Saudis' receptivity to American efforts to strengthen its own position in the Gulf brought it into conflict with the Iraqis, who initially demanded a Gulf free of superpower bases and zones of influence. Following the failure of this demand they signed a treaty of friendship with the Soviet Union in April 1972 which also provided Soviet war ships with a port of call in the Gulf (Umm Qasr).[16]

Saudi Arabia's régime quite openly preferred a 'policing' role for Iran in the Gulf to the spread of Iraqi influence to the Arab Gulf emirates, and shortly before the withdrawal of the British, won the Shah's tacit consent that the Gulf emirates should remain a Saudi

14. See a table comparing the military strength of the three states 1969–1982 in Cordesman, *op. cit.*, p. 156.
15. Cordesman, *op. cit.*, pp. 154–62.
16. Safran, *op, cit.*, p. 138.

sphere of influence. In return Saudi Arabia tolerated Iran's occupation of the islands of Abu Musa and Tumb almost without protest, whilst Iraq posed as 'the defender of Arab rights' in the 'Arab Gulf' with sanctions against Iran and Great Britain.[17] In the 1970s, however, the Saudis also frustrated Iran's plans to unite their Gulf neighbours in a security pact under its own leadership and did not hesitate to exploit Iraqi-Iranian rivalries.[18]

In 1971 Saudi Arabia achieved the division of the British protectorate of 'Trucial Oman' into three sovereign states (Bahrain, Qatar, United Arab Emirates) and later was able to assert territorial claims on the United Arab Emirates.[19] However, Iraq's renewed attempt in 1972/73 to improve its position in the Gulf to the detriment of Kuwait remained unsuccessful. Following Iraqi attacks on Kuwaiti territory and demands for the surrender of the islands of Warba and Bubiyan, Saudi Arabia dispatched 15,000 troops to defend the emirate.[20]

To some extent Saudi Arabia was also able to check Iraq's efforts in the 1970s through its oil policies. Throughout the 1960s Iraq had suffered as the oil concerns introduced measures to combat its revocation of almost all the Iraq Petroleum Company's concessions.[21] Whilst other OPEC members had profited from this pioneering act—including Saudi Arabia, which was able to reduce ARAMCO's concession in 1963 by eighty per cent[22]—it was only in the years 1971 to 1973 that all OPEC countries pulled together to force through oil price rises from US$1.8 to US$9.8 a barrel. Saudi Arabia and Iran played a key role in promoting Iraqi interests, too, in the price hike at the end of 1973 which was connected to the Arab oil boycott during and after the October war. But as early as the beginning of 1974 their ways parted again. Using politico-economic arguments Saudi Arabia resisted the new price increases demanded by Iraq and Iran in particular, and instead increased its production capacity. In reality, Saudi Arabia, with its massive oil reserves and small population, also had other reasons

17. Safran, *op. cit.*, p. 136. Cordesman, *op. cit.*, p. 417f.
18. Safran, *op. cit.*, pp. 268–72.
19. Safran, *op. cit.*, pp. 135–7; Cordesman, *loc. cit.*, p. 416.
20. Safran, *op. cit.*, p. 138; T. Niblock, 'Iraqi policies towards the Arab states of the Gulf, 1958–1981', in T. Niblock, ed., *Iraq; the contemporary state*, (London, 1982), pp. 125–49 (p. 143 f.).
21. P. Stevens, 'Iraqi Oil Policy: 1961–1979', in Niblock *op. cit.*, pp. 168–90; see also M. Chatelus' contribution in this volume.
22. Stevens, *op. cit.*, p. 183.

for preventing the oil price from rising too steeply: Iraq and Iran were in a better position to turn oil export profits into military strength, while Saudi Arabia had additional problems of internal security to overcome, caused by the millions of guest workers which the oil boom had brought into the country. The Saudis therefore preferred to play the role of 'teacher's pet' of its western protectors in OPEC, particularly since as far as possible they and the Gulf Emirates invested surplus capital in the USA and in Europe.

Compared to the lean 1960s, Iraq had made above average profits from the oil price and production increases of the 1970s, and from 1978, as a result of the Egyptian President Sadat's policies towards Israel it gained for the first time the position of a leading political power in the Arab world. Saudi Arabia was able to resist the demands formulated by the 'Steadfast Front' of radical Arab states proclaimed in Baghdad for economic sanctions against Egypt and renewed deployment of 'the oil weapon' against the USA. But it had to distance itself clearly from the Camp David treaty and therefore from the USA. In this situation the victory of the revolution in Iran (February 1979) evoked completely new dangers for all monarchies on the Arab peninsula, which were clearly demonstrated by the occupation for several weeks of the Great Mosque in Mecca (November 1979) by fundamentalist zealots.[23]

THE IRAQI-SAUDI ALLIANCE AGAINST IRAN 1980–1988

From the Saudi point of view, the fundamentalists' takeover in Iran and their aggressive propaganda in favour of the 'export of the Islamic revolution' to Arab neighbour states at least had the advantage of creating a new community of interests with Iraq.[24] Far more than Saudi Arabia, it was the Iraqi régime, with its politically disadvantaged shi'i majority, towards which Iranian subversion and propaganda campaigns were directed from 1979 onwards. As early as the late 1960s members of the Shi'i underground movement *Hizb al-Dawa* had been active against the Baath Regime, which, for its

23. Cordesman, *op. cit.*, pp. 231–8; on the subject of Shi'i unrest in Saudi Arabia 1979/1980 see *ibid.*, pp. 239–42.
24. Thus Iraq and Saudi Arabia signed a treaty of cooperation on questions of 'internal security' as early as February 1979; see *Neue Zürcher Zeitung*, 7 February 1979.

part, was closely allied with the Iranian opposition in exile around Khomeini.[25] After Khomeini's victory in Iran the new Iranian rulers and like-minded Iraqis believed that the time had come for an 'Islamic revolution' in Iraq too.

As early as the spring of 1980 the Baath régime had suppressed the Shi'i fundamentalist opposition to the extent that Saddam Hussein's decision to mount a war of aggression against Iran in September 1980 can hardly be interpreted as a preventive measure to defend itself against an acute threat. At the time he actually regarded Iran as so weakened by internal conflict and by the paralysis of its regular troops that he hoped military action would permanently favour Iraq in the Iranian oil province of Khuzestan—at the very least providing free access to the Gulf, and at best the annexation of large parts of the province with its at one time Arab majority.[26]

There are indications that the Saudi régime should bear some responsibility for the Iraqi attack on Iran which extended to an eight-year war with more than a million dead. US secret service information on Iran's military weakness caused by 'the sanitization' of its troops and lack of replacement parts are said to have been leaked to the Saudis so that they would pass them on to Iraq.[27] At the beginning of August 1980 Saddam Hussein visited Saudi Arabia, the first Iraqi leader to have done so since 1958, and it was during this visit, it is believed, that the planned war against Iran was discussed.

Following the outbreak of war the Saudi media and politicians for the most part adopted the apologist Iraqi version of its causes and aims, particularly regarding Iraq's readiness to find a 'friendly solution' to the conflict. However, Saudi Arabia refused Iraq use of its own territory for military ends, including the transport of arms, so as to give Iran no excuse for major retaliatory measures against its vulnerable oil processing plants and other infrastructure in the eastern part of the country. Even at a level below that of a military alliance Saudi Arabia gave Iraq valuable, if not vital help: with the export of oil paid for by Iraq, the construction of a pipeline for Iraqi oil to the port of Mujizz (near Yanbo) on the Red Sea,[28] and

---

25. H. Batatu, 'Iraq's Underground Shi'a movements; characteristics, causes and prospects', *The Middle East Journal*, 35 (Autumn 1981) 4, p. 578–94.
26. A detailed discussion of the Iraqi strategy (and miscalculations) in the attack on Iran can be found in Cordesman, *op. cit.*, p. 646–65.
27. D. Hiro, *The longest war; the Iran-Iraq military conflict*, (London, 1989), p. 71.
28. Construction work on the US$2.7 billion project began in December 1984. The first phase, with a capacity of 500,000 barrels/day was completed in September

above all with financial support which, according to Saudi figures, amounted to almost US$26 billion (thousand million) by the end of the war.[29]

For the Saudis, who had initially expected Iraq's rapid military victory over Iran, the entanglement of the two states in an ever-increasing war of attrition brought additional risks as well as strategic advantages. When in 1982 and again in 1986 the acute threat of an Iraqi defeat loomed, they vigorously supported Arab solidarity with Iraq, but for most of the war they avoided burning all their bridges with Iran. The losses their more powerful neighbours in the Gulf were inflicting on each other was in the interest of the Saudis, even if they regarded revolutionary Iran as the greater and more direct danger to their régime.

As early as February 1981 Saudi Arabia profited from the Iran– Iraq stalemate by founding the Gulf Cooperation Council under its leadership. The Saudis had been planning this institutionalized alliance of all Gulf monarchies, with the conscious exclusion of Iraq, since 1971. They made efforts to pacify the disgruntled Iraqis with symbolic gestures—such as their promise to finance the re-construction of the 'Osirak' atomic reactor, destroyed by Israel in May 1981—but the impression remained that the Gulf Cooperation Council had been conceived as much to oppose Iraq as Iran.

The Iran–Iraq war also provided Saudi Arabia with an alibi for the renewal and strengthening of its strategic alliance with the USA, which it had been forced to weaken two years beforehand following the Camp David Treaty. Already in the first week of the war (September 1980) four American AWACS planes were deployed from Saudi territory for air surveillance. In the 1980s American arms exports to Saudi Arabia, which spent more money per capita on arms and interior security than any other country in the

1985, the expansion to 1.65 millon barrels/day only in January 1990; see *Arab News* 3 January 1990.

29. In a message to Saddam Hussein on 15 January 1990 on Radio Riyad, King Fahd declared: 'Oh leader of Iraq, Saudi Arabia has given you sums totalling $25,734,469,885, comprised of the following amounts: $5,843,287,671 in aid which does not have to be repaid; $9,246,575,342 in the form of easily re-payable loans; $95,890,410 in developmental loans; $3,739,184,077 in the form of military and transport equipment; $6,751,159,583 in oil aid; industrial products to the value of $16,722,800 for the reconstruction of Basra; $20,266,667 for the legitimate claims of SABIC on Iraq; and $21,333,333.5 for tractors for asphalting'; see *Deutsche Welle Monitor Dienst Nahost*, 17 January 1991, p. 7.

world, reached record heights.[30] The deployment of American warships in the Gulf for the protection of Kuwaiti tankers from March 1987 onwards further strengthened the Saudi-American alliance and represented additional security for the Saudi régime.

NEW TENSIONS: AUGUST 1988–JULY 1990

The end of the Iran–Iraq war in August 1988 was welcomed by Saudi Arabia and the smaller Gulf states, but it also rapidly led to the renewal of old fears of Iraqi expansionism. Saddam Hussein, who regarded himself as the 'victor' over Iran and who had now equipped his country to become the largest military power in the Middle East, was behaving in an increasingly arrogant manner towards Saudi Arabia and the Gulf emirates. He regarded the credit and aid which he had received from these states during the Gulf War (approximately US$45 billion of US$80 billion of Iraq's foreign debt) not as 'normal debts', but as an obligatory contribution to the Iraqi war chest, since the Gulf monarchies 'had been saved from the Persian danger by the blood of the Iraqi people'.

The Saudi rulers did not share this view and made Iraq no public offer of a major remission of debt over the next two years. In contrast to the Kuwaitis, however, they seemed prepared *silently* to write off their aid to Iraq during the war years; at any rate they avoided provoking Iraq with express demands for repayment.[31] The visit of King Fahd to Baghdad in March 1989 was regarded as a sign of weakness in so far as 'the creditor went to the debtor' and not vice versa.[32] On this occasion Fahd and Saddam Hussein surprised their neighbours by signing a treaty of non-aggression and mutual non-intervention in the internal affairs of each other's state, quite unusual for two long-time quasi-allies.[33]

One of the reasons for the treaty was Saudi concern over a new alliance which Iraq had entered into with Egypt, Jordan and (North) Yemen in February 1989. As a counterbalance to this so-called Arab Cooperation Council, Saudi Arabia further extended

30. Safran, *op. cit.*, p. 420–47; A.H. Cordesman, *Western strategic interest in Saudi Arabia*, (London, 1987), pp. 126–233.
31. A. Darwish and G. Alexander, *Unholy Babylon; the secret history of Saddam's war*, (London, 1991), pp. 239, 247.
32. *Frankfurter Allgemeine Zeitung*, 14 April 1989.
33. The treaty of 27 March 1989 contained only four short paragraphs; Verbatim in *Deutsche Welle Monitor-Dienst Nahost* 30 March 1989.

its traditionally good links with Syria. During the campaign against the Syrian occupation in Lebanon, supported by Iraq and led by General Michel Aoun from March 1989, and which met with a good response in the Arab League, it was Saudi mediation in particular which finally intensified the crisis for Syria, and which led to the friendship treaty of Taif in October 1989.[34] In spring 1990 Egypt, too, distanced itself from Saddam Hussein's aggressive claims to the leadership, whereby the Arab Cooperation Council became *de facto* untenable, even before it had been able to develop to form a true 'encirclement' of Saudi Arabia through the uniting of North and South Yemen in May 1990.

Whilst offical Iraqi-Saudi relations remained good and 'fraternal'—demonstrated perhaps by the opening of a new Saudi pipeline for Iraqi oil in January and by Saddam Hussein's state visit to Saudi Arabia in March 1990—behind the facade tensions were increasing. Oil prices, which fell further during 1988–89, made it more and more difficult for Iraq to fulfil its obligations towards its international creditors, especially since it was continuing its programme of re-armament unabated. At the latest from March 1990 onwards an initially secret test of strength began between Iraq and the Gulf monarchies: Saddam Hussein not only demanded full remission of debts, but also additional emergency aid of US$10 billion whilst, for their part, those he was trying to blackmail wanted Iraq to remain under financial pressure so that it would be unable to accelerate its growth in military strength.[35] Since the spring of 1990 Saddam Hussein had also been leading a confrontational propaganda course against the 'imperialistic Western powers', which, it was later established, was apparently the political preparation for his planned attack on Kuwait.[36] This must have further alienated the Gulf monarchs.

As usual the Saudis acted with the utmost caution; they kept to the production quotas allotted them by OPEC and even went some way to meet Iraqi price demands at the OPEC conference of 26–27 July 1990.[37] Ten days previously Saddam Hussein had dramatically

34. T. Koszinowski and H. Mattes, eds., *Nahost Jahrbuch 1989*, (Opladen, 1990), p. 107f, p.137.
35. Darwish and Alexander, *op. cit.*, p. 256; P. Salinger and E. Laurent, *Guerre du Golfe; le dossier secret*, (Paris, 1991), pp. 46–9. In 1989 the Kuwaitis had even hoped through financial pressure to wring from the Iraqis contractual recognition of the existing borders; *ibid.*, p. 292.
36. Darwish and Alexander, *op. cit.*, pp. 228–32, 243–6.
37. *Ibid.*, p. 271.

made the conflict public, and had accused Kuwait and the United Arab Emirates of putting pressure on the oil price by increasing their production quotas without authorization in order to 'strangle Iraq economically'.[38]

Iraq accepted Saudi Arabia as a mediator in the conflict with Kuwait which had intensified overnight, and it appears that the Saudis advised the Kuwaitis to make concessions, while the USA encouraged them to be intransigent, despite the threatened Iraqi troop advances. Whether, amongst other things, Saddam Hussein's personal promise to King Fahd not to apply force against Kuwait led to the neglect of the acute threat of invasion, or whether the USA consciously laid a trap for Iraq, as has been frequently suggested since the end of 1990,[39] is an open question. If the conspiracy theory is correct, the Saudis probably had no part in it, but rather, in the face of the Iraqi threat, they relied to the end on their decades-old practice of appeasement and diplomatic neutralization of Arab opponents.

OPEN CONFLICT: AUGUST 1990–FEBRUARY 1991

One indication of Saudi Arabia's unpreparedness for the Kuwait invasion of 2 August 1990 was the state-controlled Saudi media's complete silence for several days on the subject of this dramatic event. Shocked by the unexpected speed and decisiveness with which Saddam Hussein carried out his aggressive plans, and fearful of becoming his next victim, the members of the Saudi royal household refused for almost a week to make any clear statement on the invasion, except within the framework of a declaration from the Gulf Cooperation Council on 3 August.[40]

The turning point did not come until after the visit of the US Defence Secretary Richard Cheney to Riyadh on 6 August and the landing of the first US troops on Saudi soil on 7 August. At a press conference on 8 August King Fahd condemned the invasion of Kuwait as 'the most vile aggression known to the Arab nation in its

---

38. Speech of 17 July, See *Financial Times*, 18 July 1990; the day before Foreign Minister Tariq Aziz had presented Iraq's accusations against Kuwait in an open letter to the General Secretary of the Arab League; see Salinger and Laurent, *op. cit.*, pp. 279–88.

39. See, for example, K. Pakradouni, *Le piège; de la malédiction libanaise à la guerre du Golfe*, (Paris, 1991), pp. 275–312.

40. *Jordan Times*, 5 August 1990.

modern history' and rejected Saddam Hussein's assurances that he would never attack Saudi Arabia as implausible.[41]

It must be assumed that even this late decision to defy Saddam Hussein and to accept the consequences of adopting such a stance must have required considerable skills of persuasion, if not behind-the-scenes pressure on the part of the USA. The Saudis would probably have preferred to wait for the Arab League summit in Cairo, planned for 10 August, to link their position to a wider Arab agreement, but were pressurized by the USA—with the invocation of American aid—to act before this conference, giving a signal to other Arab states.

Satellite photos of Iraqi troop concentrations on Saudi Arabia's borders are said to have been decisive. It is with these that Cheney was able to convince his Saudi opposite number of the necessity of acting quickly. The Saudi Chief of Staff Khalid Ibn Sultan later asserted that Iraq had moved into Kuwait with seven divisions when two divisions would have been sufficient to conquer the small country.[42] Right until the end of September 1990 the USA is said to have feared a preventive attack by Iraq on the Saudi ports and oil fields in the Gulf, which would have severely impeded the deployment of its own troops.[43]

But it was not only the pro-Iraqi side which doubted that the danger of an Iraqi attack on Saudi Arabia existed in August 1990.[44] Militarily this would have been possible without great risks, but it must have been clear, even to Saddam Hussein, who had fatally underestimated the readiness of the Western world to take countermeasures both before and after the invasion of Kuwait, that Iraq would not be able to withstand the consequences of such an enterprise.

Nevertheless the American decision to mount the 'desert shield' operation was probably vital for the Saudis to secure the medium-term survival of its régime and the inviolability of its territory. A consolidation of the Iraqi attack on Kuwait would sooner or later have encouraged Saddam Hussein, and in all probability any successor from the ranks of the Baath party, to further expansion in

---

41. BBC, *Summary of World Broadcasts, Middle East* (hereafter referred to as SWB ME) 0839, 10 August 1990, i(a).
42. *Arab News*, 28 August 1990.
43. Declaration of US Chief of Staff Colin Powell, *International Herald Tribune*, 18 March 1991.
44. Darwish and Alexander, *op. cit.*, p. 237.

the direction of the Saudi oil sources in the Gulf. This would have been particularly the case if Iraq had had at its disposal a nuclear deterrent, the development of which was not so far off in 1990, as has since been established. In a message to the Iraqi people and the 'glorious Arab nation' on 7 August Saddam Hussein made his ambitions public in a manner whch forced even the Saudis to set aside their remaining doubts:

> The malicious Westerners, when partitioning the Arab homeland, intentionally multiplied the number of countries, with the result that the Arab nation could not achieve the integration needed to realise its full capability . . . they intentionally distanced the majority of the population and areas of cultural depth from riches and their sources . . . The wealth centred in one place, in the hands of a minority lacking in cultural depth—or, more accurately, having no record of cultural depth . . . This malicious act resulted in the minority becoming so corrupt that it was cut off from its nation . . . The wealth in the hands of this minority did not come as a result of legitimate hard work.[45]

In the same speech he described the invasion of Kuwait as '. . . the only way to deal with these despicable Croesuses . . . who were guided by the foreigner instead of being guided by virtuous standards, principles of pan-Arabism and the creed of humanitarianism in relations between the sons of the same people and nation'.[46] Before this Saddam Hussein's polemics had not yet been expressly aimed at the Saudi ruling family. Once they had made their position clear on 8 August he could no longer be restrained, and Iraq began a massive propaganda campaign aimed above all at destroying the long-cherished reputation of the Saudis as 'guardians of Islamic values'. Grotesquely the Iraqi régime took over the arguments and style of its Iranian opponents, whom it had previously mocked as 'madmen' and 'fanatical Mullahs'.

In a lengthy radio message on 10 August Saddam Hussein called upon 'the Arab masses and all Muslims' 'to stand up to defend Mecca, which is captive to the spears of the Americans and Zionists . . . Keep the foreigners clear of our sacred places! . . . revolt against whoever deems it acceptable . . . to allow Arab women to be exposed to harm and driven to obscenity'.[47] On the same day the so-called

---

45. SWB ME 0838, 9 August 1990, A/2.
46. SWB ME 0838, 9 August 1990, A/1.
47. SWB ME 0841, 13 August 1990, A/8-A/10 (here A/9).

'Radio Holy Mecca' began broadcasting from Iraq with the charge that 'The Saudi régime, when it invited the foreigners, committed an unforgivable sin against the sentiments and sanctities, against Arab and Islamic histories . . .'.[48] On 12 August the following statement by the Iraqi Minister for Religion was broadcast:

> God has honoured the Arab peninsula as the land of revelations, messengers and prophets. He made this land sacred by the existence of the holy mosque. But this land is now held hostage by the forces of evil and atheism, and it is now the scene of their armies and their amusement and insolence . . . The rulers of Saudi Arabia have betrayed the trust of safeguarding the Muslim sanctities by bringing in forces of tyranny and atheism, represented by the crusader and Jewish, US and British armies . . .'.[49]

On 15 August Radio Baghdad reviled King Fahd as 'no more than a sinful libertine who filled the earth with sins and debauchery before he came to his throne through plotting and treachery . . .',[50] and from 27 August onwards Iraq's 'Radio Holy Mecca' described the Saudi King only as 'the traitor of both holy mosques' (*khain al-haramain al-sharifain*),[51] a play on the title 'Servant of the Two Holy Mosques' (*khadim al haramain* ..), the title Fahd had adopted in favour of 'majesty' since 1986. Already on the 23 August the same radio had called on 'the Muslims in Najd and Hejaz' to rise up against the 'criminal' King Fahd.[52]

In contrast to the Iraqi propaganda, which became increasingly abusive over the subsequent period, Saudi counter-propaganda remained primarily defensive and refrained from any personal insults to the Iraqi dictator. The arrival of the US troops was declared as 'a purely defensive measure imposed by the current circumstances', with the assurance that they were to be there only temporarily and would leave at any time if the Saudis so wished.[53] The Saudi dynasty made every effort to have their call for aid to non-

---

48. SWB ME 0841, 13 August 1990 i(b).
49. Radio Baghdad (12 August 1990), quoted in SWB ME 0842, 14 August 1990 A/11.
50. SWB ME 0845, 17 August 1990, A/7.
51. SWB ME 0855, 29 August 1990, A/3.
52. SWB ME 0852, 25 August 1990, A/6. Saudi Arabia was consciously only referred to in the form of the geographic name of its provinces. The same call also contained the offer: 'choose another member of the (Saud) family—whom we cannot blame entirely and whom we cannot accuse of ill intent—to replace him and save what we can of Arab sanctities, honour and entity in Najd and Hejaz' (*ibid.*).
53. SWB ME 0839, 10 August 1990, i(a).

Muslim troops sanctioned by the religious authorities. And so, as early as 11 August the General Secretariat of the Muslim World League made it clear from its headquarters in Mecca that '... the two pure noble sanctuaries ... are not under American or any other occupation ... and they are only touched by the foreheads of worshippers when they kneel in prayers'.[54] On 13 August the 'Supreme Council of the Islamic "Ulama" in Saudi Arabia' expressly supported '... the bringing of forces equipped with instruments capable of frightening and terrorizing the one who wanted to commit aggression against this country...'[55] On 12 September 1990 the Saudis brought together 300 Muslim scholars from sixty countries to legitimize their decision. Amongst others, they constructed the analogy of a Muslim who is attacked by robbers, who could allow himself to be defended by a dog (according to Muslim rites, unclean), and thus the use of non-Muslim troops could be allowed to defend an Islamic country (*halal*) according to the Islamic *sharia*.[56]

Certainly most members of the Saudi royal household initially hoped that 'Operation Desert Shield' really could remain defensive, or that the mere threat of military force would be sufficient to move Iraq to withdraw from Kuwait. The defence Minister Sultan Ibn Abd al-Aziz in particular attempted to find a peaceful solution. On 1 September his declaration that 'Saudi Arabia is not a theater for any action that is not purely defensive for itself'[57] challenged the inconsistency of the American Defence Secretary.[58] Despite the malicious Iraqi commentary that 'the US government and not their slave Sultan would make decisions regarding aggression against Iraq',[59] on 22 October Prince Sultan even suggested that Kuwait should make territorial concessions to Iraq, which could be negotiated after the occupying troops had withdrawn. Following American pressure he was forced to correct himself several days later.[60]

It was not so much Saddam Hussein's wild threats—for example that 'in the decisive battle the heads of these traitors to Arabism

---

54. SWB ME 0841, 13 August 1990, A/13.
55. SWB ME 0843, 15 August 1990, A/3.
56. *Frankfurter Allgemeine Zeitung*, 30 November 1990. The construction of an analogy (*qiyas*) is a central legal instrument in Muslim religious law (*fiqh*).
57. *The Jordan Times.*, 2 September 1990.
58. *Financial Times*, 5 September 1990.
59. *Al-Thawra* of 3 September 1990, quoted in *Deutsche Welle Monitor-Dienst Nahost*, 5 September 1990.
60. *Neue Zürcher Zeitung*, 24 October 1990; *DW Monitor-Dienst Nahost*, 24 October 1990

would fall even before the destruction of their thrones'[61]—which caused the Saudis concern, as the prospects for the Middle East region following a total Iraqi defeat. They feared that Israel and Iran would profit the most from the destruction of Iraqi military might, and that more than before Iran would be in a position to destabilize their régime.[62] In view of the growing intransigence of Iraq, however, the Saudis changed their minds, and at the end of 1990 became convinced that war would be unavoidable, even though King Fahd tried until the final day of the ultimatum to move Saddam Hussein to yield peacefully.

In the international alliance's war against Iraq from the 16 January to the 28 February 1991 it soon became clear that the military and political risks for Saudi Arabia were not nearly as serious as many had predicted. It is true that the Iraqis fired a few dozen Scud missiles at Saudi towns—most of which missed their targets—and were even able to occupy the border town of Khafji for two days (30–31 January) and to release a slick of oil on the Saudi coast. But in view of the size of the Iraqi military machine, the damage inflicted on Saudi Arabia was minimal. For their part the Saudis deployed their air force together with the allies against the Iraqis from the first day of the war and later took an active part in the land offensive. It seemed that the Saudi forces had overcome their inferiority complex towards the Iraqis.

The most important thing from the Saudi point of view was, however, that the Arab and Muslim states of the anti-Iraqi alliance should remain loyal until the end of the war. Saddam Hussein's supporters in the Islamic world, even in states such as Morocco and Pakistan, whose governments had dispatched troops in support of Saudi Arabia, may have been more numerous, but they remained condemned to powerlessness. Iraq's deficient military resistance quickly took the wind out of the sails of the initial enthusiasm for Saddam amongst the 'masses' in many Islamic countries, and there was no danger whatsoever of this enthusiasm spilling over into Saudi Arabia.

President Bush's decision to end the war 'prematurely', against the wishes of the military leaders on the spot, and the passivity of the American invading troops at the suppression of the Kurdish and Shi'i uprising against Saddam Hussein in April 1991, were

61. *DW Monitor-Dienst Nahost*, 8 November 1990.
62. C. Murphy, 'Saudis fear chaos in Mideast if Iraq is annihilated', *International Herald Tribune*, 13 November 1990.

surely also influenced by Saudi warnings. On no account did Saudi Arabia want to risk the break-up of Iraq or a pro-Iranian Shi'i seizure of power. Along with the USA, it wanted a 'tamed' Iraq with the old régime more or less intact, though without Saddam Hussein. Like Syria, Saudi Arabia had its own preferred candidate for a seizure of power in Iraq,[63] but had to come to terms with the consolidation of Saddam's régime as a temporary 'minor problem'.

TAKING STOCK AND PROSPECTS FOR THE FUTURE

The 1990–91 climax of the conflict between the anachronistically overly pious oligarchy in Saudi Arabia and the despotic, brutal, but in many respects 'more progressive' régime of the Baath Party in Iraq was no mere side-show to the Kuwait crisis. On the contrary, the Iraqi invasion of Kuwait may be regarded as a chess move, albeit one with very severe consequences, within the wider framework of the generations-old battle between Saudis and Iraqis for supremacy in the Arab Middle East. The emirate of Kuwait, which could not even defend itself against the Iraqi invasion for half a day, really only played the role of a valuable piece of booty. Since the withdrawal of Britain in 1961 it had owed its continued existence mainly to Saudi Arabia, which had been able to give it little protection, but which together with its smaller neighbour has for decades stood under the growing protection of the USA and Western Europe due to its importance as a country with the largest known oil reserves in the world.

Following the landing of US troops in August 1990 Iraqi propaganda condemned Saudi Arabia as 'vassals of US imperialism'. Despite its military weakness and a population only half the size of Iraq's[64] Saudi Arabia has always been a serious rival of Iraq. It has always made clever use of its oil wealth and possession of the holy Islamic sites in order to spread its influence widely across the

63. E. Sciolino, 'Saudis court exiles to replace Hussein', *International Herald Tribune*), 23-24 February 1991. The article named Talib Shabib, formerly a prominent representative of the Baath party and Iraqi Foreign Minister in 1963, and General Hasan Naqib, former commander of the Iraqi troops in Jordan, sacked in 1971.

64. At the end of 1990 a Saudi deputy minister gave the population of Saudi Arabia as 8 million (excluding 4 million foreigners), a figure which was probably exaggerated; see *Arab News*, 18 December 1990. Iraq's population (including Kurds and Turkomans etc.) probably reached 18 million in 1990.

Arabian peninsula and to neutralize opponents. By contrast, through senseless wars of aggression which it could not win, the Iraqi Baath régime has twice gambled away its advantageous position in a bid for supremacy in the Arabian peninsula. Thanks to Western and Saudi aid and Iran's isolation, Iraq was able to emerge from the eight-year war against Iran in a position of improved military strength, but it immediately entered a debt crisis, which finally led Saddam Hussein to invade Kuwait. This, together with the grave error of not using the breathing space of nearly six months to yield to the more powerful international alliance, led to the loss of its military superiority.

The end of the second Gulf War not only saw the military balance shift for many years in Saudi Arabia's favour, but also saw the Saudi régime able to consolidate its political position. The call for help to the 'infidel' protective powers had damaged its reputation as 'guardian of the holy sites of Islam', but not to the extent that its opponents had predicted. During the Mecca pilgrimage season (*hajj*) from June 1991 onwards once again a record number of foreign pilgrims appeared as if nothing had happened, including, for the first time since 1987, more than 100,000 Iranians whose 'Death to America' slogans were even permitted without risk to internal security.[65] During the course of 1991 Saudi Arabia not only resumed diplomatic relations with Iran, but also became reconciled to a great extent with Jordan and the PLO, which had supported Iraq during the Gulf War. Its relations with the important Muslim allies such as Egypt, Syria and Pakistan were better than ever before.

The alliance with the USA, tested for the first time in an emergency, did not develop into an oppressive dependency for the Saudis. Indeed Saudi Arabia was able to escape the American desire for a permanent military presence and the establishment of major material bases and instead win American support for the further expansion of its own army.[66] The Saudis left the potential scapegoat role of a guest country for American military bases to Kuwait and Bahrain, whilst almost all of the more than 500,000 US troops had withdrawn from their country before the end of 1991.[67]

65. *Neue Zürcher Zeitung*, 21 June 1990.
66. K.D. Frankenberger, 'Irritationen zwischen Washington und Saudi-Arabien' *Frankfurter Allgemeine Zeitung*, 19 November 1991; J.M. Goshko, 'U.S. nears approval of jet fighter sale to Saudis', *International Herald Tribune*, 25–26 January 1992.
67. Frankenberger, *op. cit.*

Even if Iraq were to succeed over the next few years—perhaps under new leadership—in shaking off the stranglehold of international economic sanctions and demands for reparations, and renew its struggle for a leading position in the Gulf, it would have to deal with a strengthened Arab rival. Saudi Arabia has had to pay a high financial price for the temporary neutralization of the Iraqi threat, it is true,[68] but it has been able to improve its position economically by filling the gap left by the absence of oil exports from Iraq and Kuwait by increasing its own oil production capacities.[69]

We do not know whether Saddam Hussein's 'mother of all battles' will be regarded in the future by the majority of the now more than 200 million Arabs as 'heroic steadfastness against Western imperialism' and as a milestone in the battle for Arab unity, or whether one day Saddam Hussein will be blamed by his present-day admirers for the real enough set-back in the quest for Arab unity. Iraqi 'revenge'—even if it comes only after decades—and a repetition of the Iraqi–Saudi confrontation under other circumstances is, however, quite conceivable.

---

68. According to Saudi figures, almost US$60 billion; see *Financial Times*, 30 January 1992 (Survey 'Saudi Arabia').
69. M. Nicholson and R. Matthews, 'Saudis strive to retain OPEC dominance', *Financial Times*, 24 January 1992.

Relations between Iraq and its Turkish Neighbour: from Ideological to Geostrategic Constraints

Elizabeth Picard

A comprehensive study of the relations between the Arab countries and Turkey conjures up confused images, in which over the last few years economic projects have shrivelled to nothing, in which banking networks have more political influence than financial power, in which comparisons underline profound differences,[1] and in which discourse on rapprochement hardly masks ignorance, indifference and diverging preoccupations. The image becomes less confused when one examines the relations between Iraq and its large neighbour to the north. Here, geography and history define the contours of the subject. The two states are separated by a mountainous border on the southern side of the Taurus mountains. Important rivers cross the border, the Euphrates (after a detour through Syria) and the Tigris, across which roads, railways and pipelines are superimposed, weaving a network of communications. Moreover, history is close, a shared destiny at the heart of the Ottoman Empire, some of the principal figures of which were still present not long ago: intellectuals such as the Aleppan Sati al-Husri, statesmen such as Nuri al-Said, who were ministers in Baghdad until the 1950s.

The political split and the establishment of international borders between Iraq and Turkey in the early 1920s were all the more

---

1. See in particular the proceedings of the colloquium *Modernisation et nouvelles formes de mobilisation sociale: Turquie-Egypte*, (Cairo 8-10 June 1990), to appear in the *Cahiers du CEDEJ*.

distinct because they corresponded to the firm wish of the occupying European power, Great Britain. The rift between Anatolia and the former Arab provinces of the Empire was further deepened by the difference between the full independence of the Turkish Republic on the one hand, and on the other the colonial situation which shaped the political development of Iraq, at least until the Second World War.[2] After 1945 the distance between Iraq and Turkey widened following the entry of Ankara into the North Atlantic system, while Iraq, together with the others member states of the Arab League, struggled against the new state of Israel. The post-war years are characterized by fixed borders and indifferent relations, so much so that current troubles seem to be the result of sudden changes, of which the causes are largely external, to be found in changes in the international equilibrium. History, however, allows us to take a more subtle view of these present developments.

This history is marked by the territorial controversy surrounding Mosul. But the Mosul crisis was followed by a process of interstate normalization. On both sides of the frontier a 'border' culture began to develop, where familial and community relations were renewed and placed in the service of a 'modern' logic.

Separated, Arabs and Turks maintained their distance, seeing each other through the interpretation of constructed images rather than tangible experience, so much so that Iraq lived for a time under the influence of a Kemalist model, first imitated then challenged.

The strategies of the great powers and the ideology of the Cold War left their mark on bilateral relations without, however, hindering the normalization of Iraqi-Turkish relations and even cooperation in the face of the Kurdish rebellion. The end of the bipolar world marks the return of geostrategic priorities in the region, focussing on the two questions of security and water, both of which are central issues throughout the Middle East, to the point where they helped bring about a reversal in Iraqi-Turkish relations following the Gulf crisis.

THE LEGACY OF MOSUL

It is not surprising that the drawing up of international borders between Iraq and Turkey following the fall of the Ottoman Empire

---

2. Elizabth Picard 'Les nationalistes arabes de Syrie et d'Iraq et le kémalisme: convergences, occultations et influences', *Cahiers du GETC*, no 3, pp. 40–59.

was a painful process, that it gave rise to bitter controversy and even today still fosters irredentist claims. Five centuries of history cannot be erased with the ink of a treaty, more so because the point of contact between the Arab and the Turkish worlds is not a tangible line, but a geographical area with imprecise borders, with diverse and vital identities, both ethnic (Turkish, Arab, Kurdish and others) and religious, since, like Christians, Muslims belong to a variety of confessions. This zone includes Gaziantep (Aintab) in the north, until recently a prosperous and important village in the vilayet (province) of Aleppo. In the south it includes Kirkuk, which still numbers several thousand turcophone Turkomans today.[3] This is an area particularly rich in ancient life and prosperous artisan traditions, close currents of trade, an area in which the division at the beginning of the century brutally disrupted continuity.

In practice the territorial dispute between Iraq and Turkey regarding the vilayet of Mosul lasted from 1920 to 1926. In a study published in *Maghreb-Machrek*,[4] François Georgeon recalls the issues, current at the beginning of the century, as to the Arab character of this Ottoman province and the possibility of defining an equitable solution to the problem of the border between the Turkish and the Arab world, in a region where ethnic and religious communities overlap. The Turkish National Pact of January 1920 refers in this context to the 'Arab majority' of the southern provinces of the Empire, the fate of which should be settled by a plebiscite. Throughout the bilateral negotiations with London, and then under the aegis of the League of Nations, the Kemalists argued that Mosul was not occupied by the British at the time of the Armistice of Mudros (30 October 1918), and therefore rightly belonged to Turkey. Eventually it was neither the respect exhibited for popular self-determination, nor the fear of seeing the Kurdish revolt in eastern Anatolia extend to Arbil and Sulaimaniya which prompted Ankara to capitulate, following a League of Nations arbitration in December 1925 favourable to Iraq.[5] Rather it was the sound assessment of diplomatic, and above all military, relations at the time: the fragility of the young Turkish state at the end of a war which saw its foundation,

---

3. Estimates vary considerably, in general they are around several hundreds of thousands. J. Javernac speaks of 2,500 people in 'Les Kurdes entre la Turquie et l'Irak', *Balkans*, April–May–June 1991, p. 17.
4. F. Georgeon, 'De Mossoul à Kirkouk; la Turquie et le Kurdistan irakien', *Maghreb-Machrek*, 132, April–May–June 1991.
5. F. Husayn, *Mushkilat al-Mawsil*, Baghdad, 1955, pp. 237–243.

faced with a powerful Great Britain determined to retain control of the oil region of Kirkuk. It is true, as François Georgeon once again points out, that Turkish public opinion was rallied in favour of keeping Mosul in 1920–1925, and certain irredentists made loud noises to the effect that the Turks were justified in claiming not only the province of Mosul and that of Aleppo, but also the entire Mediterranean coastal strip—as far as Port Said. But on the whole the keynote policy of 'peace within, peace outside' prevailed and, secure in the knowledge of its oil supplies, Kemalist Turkey accommodated itself to the Treaty of Ankara (June 1926). However, one should not forget that the division was imposed by an external power, and above all that it was foreign to the imperial conception of open spaces, where borders are not of a territorial but community nature, and where trade is the basis of the economic system.

This is why, before considering the development of state relations between Iraq and Turkey, it is interesting to explore the effects of a territorial division, of the inclusion of the province of Mosul in the Iraqi state, on the local communities and cultures, on human and economic exchanges on the Arab-Turkish borders. Whilst the British alternated cooperation with repression with regard to Kurdish movements such as that of Sheikh Mahmud, the rich town of Mosul suffered an appreciable decline, a 'provincialization' in the shadow of Baghdad, during the decades which followed. Would the 'political' logic of the Middle Eastern states allow the ancient societal logic to survive? How far is there a contradiction between them? And is societal logic today capable of taking its 'revenge', that is to say presenting itself as an alternative, when the states in authority are revealing their limitations and experiencing failure? We have asked these questions with regard to Syria; an inquiry in Alexandretta (1982)[6] and another in Aleppo (1988),[7] supply a number of lines of thought. A similar research project in Mosul by the Centre of Turkish Studies in this town has evidently not been brought to a successful conclusion. Is it wrong to suppose that we would have found there a number of tendencies and characteristics also found in Aleppo?

6. E. Picard, 'Retour au Sandjak', *Maghreb-Machrek* 99, January–March 1983, pp. 47–64.
7. E. Picard 'Aux confins turco-arabes; de l'histoire à la géostratégie' in *Le Moyen-Orient dans les années 1990; le nouveau cours des relations turco-arabes*, 1992.

THE IMAGE OF THE OTHER

It must, however, be recognized that on the whole over a number of decades mutual images reflected on both sides of the new Arab-Turkish border are blurred, sometimes tainted with hostility. In particular there is a repertoire of satirical stories alluding to ethnic characteristics attributed to one or the other, which are similar to the settling of scores still encountered today between Germany and France. More seriously, the content of scholarly historical works reveals the permanence of the disputes and the mutual desire to maintain a distance.[8] But at a state level and at that of political élites the vision of the great Turkish neighbour in Iraq and the vision of the new Arab state in Turkey have followed their own courses, which owe much to the dominant ideologies of the era: that of the nation state on the one hand and that of the Cold War on the other.

We have attempted to show the role model which the new Turkish state played for nationalist Arabs in Iraq.[9] After a period of eclipse which persisted beyond the Second World War until 1958, when Iraq lived under the domination—by that we mean ideological too—of a European power, the republicans in Baghdad turned to their Kemalist neighbour, which had a twenty-year head-start on the road to political modernization. Was it possible to say that the nationalist régime of Iraq was still seeking to borrow and reappropriate elements of universal culture—progress, secularization, the construction of a 'nation state' etc—from the Kemalist system? Or, more pragmatically, did it hope to find in Turkey specific answers already tested in the social and political stresses and strains of its Middle Eastern society?

The influence of the model does not imply similarity. Certain irreducible characteristics of Turkish and Iraqi experiences stem from historical differences; during the period in which revolutionary changes were in train in the Arab world, Turkey had already left its second authoritarian phase, that of the İnönü regime (1938–1946) and was attempting a democratization and pluralism. The international context had completely changed from that in which the Kemalist experience had been forged at the time of European fascism. The international system was henceforth dominated by a

8. See in particular E. Copeaux, 'L'image des arabes et de l'islam dans les manuels d'histoire turcs depuis 1931', *CEMOTI* 12 (1991), pp. 163–194.

9. E. Picard, 'La modernisation autoritaire par les nationalistes arabes, écho et test de l'expérience kémaliste', in *Modernisation autoritaire en Turquie et en Iran*, ed. Semih Vaner (to appear).

bipolar division and by an economy far more radically internationalized, so much so that one may say that Iraq, like the other Arab regimes of the Middle East, entered the international scene with a time delay on the 'global clock'.[10] Other characteristics must be considered in the context of the difference in nature between Atatürk's 'anti-clerical secularization' and the 'independent religiousness' of Arab leaders such as Qasim[11] or the Baathists, whose aim was rigidly to control religious instruction and above all to destroy the economic power of the men of Islam, which they achieved through the takeover of clerics and the nationalization of the *waqf*. Despite this, it is still possible to find several similarities with, and indeed explicit references in Iraq to the 'Kemalist model' of modernization: first of all the utilization, or manipulation of history in the construction of a national ideology. Indeed it is interesting to note the renaissance in Iraq of archaeological and historical interest for the pre- Islamic period and even the pre-Christian era, comparable to the exhumation of the Hittite past of Anatolia on the part of the Kemalists,[12] the writing (re-writing) of Turkish history served as an example to the educated élite of the Arab East. Next one can bear in mind the centrality of the one party, the experiences of modernization 'from the top' initiated by this party-state which took society and the economy in hand: nationalization; industrialization; even, in the case of the Baath Party, agrarian reform. The role of the charismatic leader in the revolutionary experience, as well as the negative effects of the personalization of power, should also be noted. Finally, we must not forget the military in these authoritarian structures; it holds a central position, even when the army is subordinated to civilian power, as it is in Baathist Iraq. In Iraq, as in Turkey, emergency powers legislation and the use of coercion are constantly practised by the government. There is another practice which is also inspired by the Kemalist and post-Kemalist experience; that of the participation of the army in the role of institution and the involvement of senior officers in a personal capacity in economic activities. This process was accelerated during the *infitah* phase, in a reorientation in which social

10. On this idea and its application to the new international situation, cf. the works of Zaki Laïdi and the 'Ordre mondial relâché' group at the CERI.
11. M. Rodinson, *Marxisme et monde musulman*, Paris: le Seuil, 1972, p. 185 and 186.
12. Cf. in particular A. Baram, *Culture, history and ideology in the formation of Ba'thist Iraq, 1968-1989*. New York, 1991, 196 p.

priorities were abandoned in favour of collaboration with businessmen and entrepreneurs in the private sector from 1979 onwards. It is no small paradox that, even in their failures or their attempts to escape the model of a nation state, the republican experiences of Iraq still owe a great deal to those of Turkey.

THE COLD WAR AND GOOD NEIGHBOURLINESS

The other ideological reference which helps to shape the mutual images of the Iraqi and Turkish states is that of the bipolar division of the world and the confrontations between the liberal Western world and the socialist Soviet bloc from 1945 onwards. More than in any other region of the world perhaps, the divisions of the Cold War have determined inter-state relations in the Middle East. Thus Iraq, kept under the wing of Great Britain until the revolution of 1958, after the revolution became an ally of the Soviet Union, with which it signed a treaty of friendship and cooperation in 1972, whilst Turkey, advanced post on NATO's eastern front line, became an ally of the United States.

However, during the 1980s when the Iranian revolution and the invasion of Afghanistan highlighted the east-west split even more sharply, Iraq gradually slipped into a position of 'positive' neutrality and then into a *de facto* alliance with the Western powers, who began to consider and treat it as another pillar of Middle Eastern stability. In a number of ways Iraq revived its tradition of alliance with the West (the Pact of Saadabad, Baghdad Pact, CENTO), which dates back to the early years of its independence. With the birth of the 'Second Baathist Republic', dominated by Saddam Hussein from July 1979 onwards, the exclusion of the Communists of the National Progressive Front was radical; the *infitah*, an encouragement to the private sector, and great overtures towards Western enterprises, coincided with the second oil boom, whilst the attack on Iran in September 1980 met with a rebuke from Moscow and provoked a rapid cooling in Iraqi-Soviet relations.

From that time relations between Ankara and Baghdad improved. But it is useful to recall that earlier years, the decisive revolution of 1958 and General Qasim's denunciation of the participation of his country in the Baghdad Pact, did not create fears amongst the Turkish leaders, and that it did not occur to anyone in Ankara to challenge the Mosul accords concluded at the time of the monarchy and the British Mandate.[13] The desire to forget and for appeasement prevailed. Thus, in April 1979 General Evren, who was only Chief of Staff in the Turkish army, turned to Baghdad where he evoked a spirit of co-operation with the Baathist leaders against Kurdish rebels on either side of the border. Even if during the Iran-Iraq conflict Turkey succeeded in maintaining a neutrality with regard to the two adversaries, the sympathy of the secular and pro-West Kemalists visibly leaned towards the Iraqi position, faced with the Islamic Republic.

Despite the prism of the Cold War, the Baathist state of Baghdad with its pan-Arabist ideology, its dictatorial governmental methods, its regional ambitions, its economy dominated by an ossified and unproductive public sector, its intensive efforts to equip and prepare the army, was seen in Ankara as a potential and sufficiently rational ally, as an examination of the economic agenda, territorial disputes and the Kurdish question confirm.

Throughout the Arab east (Egypt, the Fertile Crescent and the Arabian peninsula) economic and financial exchanges with Turkey far from answered the hopes to which the two oil shocks of 1973 and 1979 had given rise. Indeed, no more than 11.25 per cent of foreign investment in Turkey registered on 31 December 1988[14] originated from Arab countries. The participation of a qualified Turkish work force in developmental projects in the Gulf countries was drastically reduced as a result of the oil recession which began in 1984. However, Iraq has a special place in this scene.

Throughout the 1980s the war with Iran provided an incentive for co-operation and civil exchanges between Iraq and Turkey, which has now become the third client of Baghdad, from whom it buys sixty per cent of the oil it consumes. The Kirkuk-Yumurtalik pipeline, inaugurated in 1977 provided a substitute for the former IPC pipeline to Banyas and Tripoli, closed by Syria in April 1982. Its capacity doubled in 1984 and a second parallel pipeline was inaugurated in 1987, carrying the Iraqi export capacity of 1.5 million barrels/day via Turkey, an output which will soon be insufficient, as a result of which the two countries are planning the construction of a refinery as a joint venture, either in Iskanderun or Basra. The two partners are taking on more and more joint-ventures, a railway line to Zakho, the inter-connection of electricity

13. I. Soysal, 'Le Pacte de Bagdad', *Studies on Turkish Arab Relations* 5, 1990.
14. Cf. 'Arap sermayesi atakta', *Ekonomik Panorama*, 1 January 1989, pp. 8–14.

networks etc., so much so that Iraq, which has been sacrificing its civil economy to the war effort, has become Turkey's second client.[15]

The same tendency towards normalization is found in the treatment of the Mosul question, which Baghdad and Ankara refuse to make into a political issue, in contrast to what is happening in Syrian-Turkish relations with regard to Alexandretta. Throughout the 1980s Ankara and Baghdad shared the same conservative analysis concerning the lines of their borders, adopted after a lengthy controversy during the 1920s. This position, reaffirmed by Saddam Hussein in 1984, when the war with Iran gave rise to speculations on the future of his country, was shared by Turgut Özal three years later in 1987, when Iraq was threatened with collapse under the battering of the Iranian advance. Kamran Inan, an ardent nationalist and Minister of State and member of the Motherland party, ventured to recall in public that forty per cent of the oil supplies of his country came from the region of Kirkuk.[16] In order to avert a possible Iranian advance in the region, and to signify his country's pre-emptive right in the event of the break-up of Iraq, he confirmed that no less than one and a half million Turks and Turkomans lived in the province of Mosul. The following year, in April 1988, the Turkish army was placed on a war footing in response to news of the advance of forces of the Islamic Republic towards Sulaimaniya. However, the adoption of these positions remained isolated and was, moreover, strongly contradicted in the sphere of Turkish politics. In President Özal's entourage, as in the opposition, the view prevailed that 'the question of Mosul is an historical one'[17] and should not be reopened. For the Turkish leaders this assertion was in keeping with a broader global logic, not contradicted by military intervention in Cyprus, since this was analysed as a defensive measure, in the face of the danger posed by *Enosis*. Doubtless one should add two factors in order to explain the minimalist position of President Özal's Turkey: the first concerns the relative marginalization of the oil in the north of Iraq, which had been exploited for almost seventy years, in relation to the new producing regions of the Shatt al-Arab. The second is none other than the presence of a strong Kurdish minority in the north of Iraq.

15. Cf. H. Akder, 'Turkey's export expansion in the Middle East, 1980–1985', *Middle East Journal*, vol. 41, no. 1, Autumn 1987, pp. 553–567.
16. Quoted by *FBIS*, 14 January 1987.
17. Turgut Özal in Washington, quoted by *SWB*, 25 September 1990.

Clearly the key to relations between Iraq and Turkey is to be found neither in economic exchanges nor in the choice of whether or not to pursue territorial claims again. During the 1980s it was necessary to regard it rather in the context of the reawakening of the Kurds, who took up arms once more against the central Iraqi power with the support of the Islamic Republic,[18] and of Hafiz al-Asad's Syria. According to some sources,[19] Baghdad had resumed contact with Ankara at the end of the 1970s to prevent any reorganization in Iraq of Kurdish opposition movements, crushed in 1975. In the clashes with the Iranian army on its borders Saddam Hussein's régime welcomed the first large-scale Turkish operation on its territory in May 1983. In any event the bilateral security protocol signed the following year[20] made co-operation against the Kurdish movements official and prepared the way for the two Turkish interventions of August 1986 and March 1987 against the militants of the PKK and the DPK in the mountains of Zakho and al-Amadiya. While it was necessary to place the ground and aerial attacks in a context of extreme emergency, since Iran had succeeded in turning the military situation around by carrying the battle onto Iraqi territory, the signing of the 1984 accord and its implementation testify to a rare convergence of views between the Iraqi and Turkish leaders and to a surprising degree of confidence on the part of Saddam Hussein. What guarantees could he have hoped for at the time from his large Turkish neighbour on the intangible nature of the borders of the region, when he himself was attempting to challenge the accord of Algiers signed with Iran in 1975? In return, the moderation displayed by President Özal stemmed more from a true appreciation of the explosive nature of the situation in Iraqi Kurdistan, than from his desire to test international legalism. Regarding the difficulties with the insurrections in south-east Anatolia, he refused to accord refugee status to some 60,000 Iraqi Kurds in 1988 and unquestionably feared taking control of a region peopled by almost four million Kurds, mobilized for many decades around prestigious leaders such as Barzani or Jalal Talabani.

18. E. Picard, 'L'Irak et l'autonomie kurde' in *La question kurde*, (Brussels), 1991.
19. Kurdish sources quoted by the *Financial Times*. of 28 May 1983.
20. On 15 October, according to the *Iraqi National Agency*, 24 October 1984. Cf. A. Fuat Borovali, 'Kurdish insurgencies, the Gulf War and Turkey's changing role', *Conflict Quarterly*, vol. 7, no. 4, Autumn 1987, pp. 29–45.

Thus, paradoxically, the influence of a bipolar international environment led to an Iraqi–Turkish rapprochement in the last decade of the bipolar era. The pragmatism of the leaders of the two countries counted for much in this unfolding development, as did the relations between the international forces: in this period Saddam Hussein's Iraq, allied with the monarchies of the Gulf and with Egypt was the favoured partner of the Western powers, not only of France, but also of the United States, who thought highly of its attempts to open up and its modernity.

RETURN TO GEOSTRATEGY

Although it is still hazardous to trace the contours of a 'new world order', the current manifestations of which are really those of extreme disorder which will cost the people of the Middle East dear, the 1980s saw the gradual disappearance of the bipolar order founded on ideological certainties and on the balance of power from 1945 onwards between the United States and the Soviet Union. One by one the states of Eastern Europe have broken free from Soviet influence, rendering the Warsaw Pact null and void. At the same time it is the very concept of NATO which has been challenged, and with it the position of Turkey in the Western alliance and the evolution of its European ambitions, damaged by the dilatory response of the Brussels Commission in December 1989. In opposing, but not exactly symmetrical ways, Baghdad and Ankara reconsidered their international environment at the end of the decade. Pragmatically, the two capitals attempted to compensate for the relaxing of their relations with a Super Power, by joining a new and complex Middle Eastern dynamic, marked henceforth by security problems in which the war with Iran will serve as a stumbling-block for many years. Indeed, with the disqualification of the Communist model and the collapse of Soviet power, the Baathist state lost both the guarantees and the justification for its strategic orientations of the preceding decades. Not only Arab socialism, one of the three strong points of its official doctrine (unity, liberty, socialism) became suspect, but Iraq clearly appeared, in the same way as Turkey, as a nationalist state, in competition for the control of material and symbolic resources in the region. In this new context the former influence of Kemalism on the authoritarian regimes of the Arab east takes on a new pertinence: Turkey and Iraq (and Syria) tend to portray themselves as developmentalist states, whose role models American political scientists such as Daniel Lerner have traced to the 1950s. But this orientation implies another definition of their hierarchical relations. The ideological determinants give way to geostrategic imperatives, which give a new dimension to Turkish-Arab relations: the question of development, of the control of natural resources in particular and that of security are from now on the crucial factors.

The appearance of water as a central issue in the relations between Turkey and its two Arab neighbours—Iraq and Syria—is the most obvious sign of the triumph of geostrategic considerations at the turn of the decade. In the past many crises have had many premonitory signs of the seriousness of the problem. Thus, from 1973 onwards, the filling of the first great Syrian dam on the Euphrates, the al-Thawra dam in Tabqa, led to a drop in the level of the water as it flowed through the Iraqi desert. At that time the leadership contest between the two Baathist leaders in Damascus and Baghdad did more to intensify the crisis than the technical questions themselves, and the mediation proposed by Saudi Arabia to settle the problem equitably was unsuccessful.[21] When the Turkish dams in Keban (1974) and Karakaya (1977–1987) were filled the drop in the river flow was limited, because these hydroelectric dams did not have large reservoirs. However, the advance of major work in south-east Anatolia and simultaneous projects in Syria and Iraq led to the three riverain neighbours meeting at the end of 1983 in a technical committee in which Turkey challenged the advice of the World Bank on the necessity of agreeing to an accord with its two partners, playing on Iraqi-Syrian discord to its own advantage.[22]

In addition, the *Guneydoğu Anadolu Projesi* has recently been accelerated now that work has started on thirteen secondary dams intended to irrigate an additional 1.6 million hectares in the regions of Urfa, Mardin and Harran, the construction of seventeen power stations and two pressure pipeline tunnels, each 16 km long,[23] and above all the massive Atatürk dam. The first phase of filling the latter, from 13 January to 13 February 1990, was intentionally preceded by the opening of sluice gates which led to the flow of the Euphrates climbing to 780 m³/s for several weeks. But then the flow

---

21. Cf. E. Kienle, *Baʻth versus Baʻth, Syrian-Iraqi Relations between 1968 and 1989*, (London, 1990).

22. *Middle East Economic Survey*, 1, p. 645.

23. J. Kolars, 'The hydro-imperative of Turkey's search for energy', *Middle East Journal*, vol. 40, no. 1, Winter 1986, pp. 53–67.

fell to 120m³/s and Ankara envisages maintaining it at around 500m³/s. At this level Iraq could lose eighty per cent of its part of the Euphrates[24] in 1994, the year of Turkey's maximum pumpage on the Syrian border.

Without wishing to return to the details of the Iraqi agroalimentary deficit (sixty per cent of its consumption), to its demographic growth, or to its ambitious irrigation projects (one million hectares) from the Euphrates and the Tigris, we should note the incompatibility between the needs of the Baathist states and the hegemonic posturing of Turkey on the question of the sharing of water. Having unilaterally guaranteed a flow of 500m³/s Ankara, defending its use of the 'water weapon', had nevertheless already made it the object of bargaining during President Özal's official visit to Damascus in 1987.[25] He opposed Iraq's objection, arguing that the Tigris and its tributaries, the large and small Zab and the Diyala, had abundant resources.[26] To aggravate matters, Turkey was planning an ambitious project to sell 'by way of compensation' the water from the Seyhan and Ceyhan rivers to all the states of the Middle East, up to Oman and Egypt, and including Israel, by constructing two aqueducts at a total cost of $20 billion, according to the estimates of the American firm Brown and Root, who carried out the feasibility studies for Ankara.

The muffled character, the technical formulations, and the 'civil' nature of the conflict surrounding the question of water should not give a false impression. The depletion of the water levels, at any rate its relative depletion with regard to demographic growth, will represent a crucial problem in the next century, in particular in the Middle East where it is a question which not only surrounds the Euphrates and the Tigris, but equally the Litani and Jordan basins, and that of the Nile too.[27] The analyses of the Center for Strategic and International Studies in Washington (1988) as well as those of Amon Sofer, researcher at the University of Haifa (1989) highlight the explosive nature of the problem in the medium term, and the direct relation between the aspirations of the states in the region

24. Syria could lose forty per cent.
25. *Al-Alam* (Cairo) 31, 20 January 1990.
26. We should note that this river's source is in Iran and could become the subject of new tensions.
27. *Middle East Economic Digest.*, 26 March 1988 and 13 October 1989, *Al-Hayat*, 9–15 November 1989 ('Mushkilat al-mawarid al-maiya fi al-sharq al-awsat'), *Financial Times*, 3 January 1990, *Jerusalem Post*, 9 June 1990.

regarding development on the one hand, and on the other the political regimes' control of national security; in other words, on the close relationship between the economy and the military.[28]

The appearance of this new key issue provoked a radical change in Iraqi-Turkish relations from 1990 onwards, even before the outbreak of the Gulf crisis. After the first few months of 1990 Iraq signalled its move or that which it announced as its move towards a strategic parity with Israel: the launch of a missile in three stages in December 1989, the extension of the range of Scud missiles to more than 800 km and the official announcement that it had developped missiles with chemical warheads.[29] After the long war with Iran, which left the country drained, Baghdad declared itself ready to take on the regional leadership of the Gulf as far as the Lebanon, where it was arming the opponents of Damascus.[30] At the same time, since its role of extreme Eastern pillar of NATO had just been brutally discredited and it had suffered an official rejection from the EC, Turkey found itself having to find a new role, if not in a position of weakness.

On an official visit to Baghdad on 5 May the Iraqi President firmly asked the new Turkish Prime Minister Yildirim Akbulut for a negotiation on the waters of the Euphrates, and also the Tigris. In addition, his request for authorization for renewed Turkish armed intervention within the borders of the two countries, motivated by the increase in PKK terrorist operations in the neighbouring Turkish provinces met with refusal: since the end of its war with Iran, Saddam Hussein's regime, playing on the terror inspired by the Halabja massacre, had gradually regained control of its Kurdish regions of Dohok, Arbil and Sulaimaniya, under the command of the President's cousin Ali Hasan al-Majid, Minister of Local Administration. With the powerful aid of the Kurdish troops of the *jahsh*, its intention was to exercise full sovereignty. It demanded from Ankara, which officially undertook talks with the Iraq Kurdish chiefs on the occasion of the massive exodus of Autumn 1988, the extradition of DPK militants who formed part of the many millions of refugees waiting in temporary camps north of the border. But at

28. Cf. The introduction to *Dilemmas of security and development in the Arab World*, ed. R. Brynen, B. Korany and P. Noble (London, 1991).

29. In a speech by Saddam Hussein threatening to destroy half of Israel in the event of an attack by the latter, 2 April 1990.

30. E. Picard, 'Le régime irakien et la crise; les ressorts d'une politique', *Maghreb-Machrek* 130, Oct–Nov–Dec 1990, pp. 25–35.

the same time, to some extent it took over from Syria—which closed the area it had opened to the Kurdish guerrillas, on its territory and in the Beka, with the intention of regaining international legitimacy—by encouraging PKK commandos based in Syria and operating in Turkey to cross its own territory. Denouncing the Ankara accord of 1984, Saddam Hussein clearly showed that, following Syria's example, he is ready to use the blackmail of security concerns to reinforce its position in negotiations surrounding the question of water.

AFTER THE GULF WAR

Under these conditions the Gulf crisis provoked a veritable reversal of relations between Iraq and Turkey, who became adversaries on the verge of confrontation and unequal partners on the Middle East stage.

Turkey maintained an extreme position in the international coalition. From early August onwards it decided to close the Iraqi oil pipelines to the Mediterranean, which Saddam Hussein had however already stopped using. Throughout the offensive Turgut Özal hoped to involve his country in the war in order to engage the solidarity of his NATO partners, who were using the Incirlik and Batman bases to bombard Iraq, and to provoke the re-evaluation of the Turkish presence at the eastern and southern borders of the Alliance. The response to this ambition was German military aid, international financial aid, principally Japanese, in order to compensate the losses Turkey had suffered under the blockade. But he obtained no more, and in any case there was not a single Scud attack which would have given him the ideal pretext to order the advance of the 300,000 men on alert in the south-east into Iraqi territory.

The second phase of the Gulf war, as it unfolded between the Iraqi regime and its population, gave him the opportunity to set out his projects to the detriment of its Prime Minister and the commanders of the army. At the beginning of March 1991 Özal proposed nothing less than to transform Iraq into a tripartite 'Arab-Turco-Kurdish' federation, with Turkey ready to accord its protection to the two latter parts of the trio! Next came the official welcome of the leaders of the Iraqi Kurdistan Front in Ankara and the suggestion of establishing an 'international protection zone' for the Kurds, which would later be taken up again by the allies under the guise of 'safe havens'. Then Özal obtained the participation of the

Turkish army in the rapid intervention force which the US was putting into place provisionally in south east Anatolia. But it was on its own initiative, and despite the signals of discontent reiterated in Washington and Bonn, that the Turkish army invaded Iraq for more than a week in August, deploying vast combing operations against the PKK militants.

If we are witnessing the end of the regional status quo in the Middle East, established after the first World War and maintained afterwards by the colonial powers, and then by the two superpowers, Özal's Turkey is preparing to 'sit down at the negotiating table', by initiating on the domestic plane overtures at once timid and audacious towards the Kurds. Certainly it cannot hope to reestablish the Empire, all the less so because it has lost its rich cosmopolitan culture. But its territorial size, its demographic and military strength, its abundant waters, its economic growth, single the country out for a hegemonic role in the Middle East, especially now that the Iraqi ambitions have evaporated for a long time and that the Kurds have not taken advantage of the situation to mobilize in a united fashion, and that neither Syria nor Saudi Arabia holds enough trump cards to take over from them.

Paradoxically, it is the United States, supporters of the status quo in the Middle East and the non-Arab regional powers such as Israel and Iran who are checking the Turkish appetites, whilst the international community is not as radical in its position on the inalienable nature of the borders. Iraq itself has few resources with which to resist—the sound security machine of its President and above all its oil, which Tariq Aziz once again offered to Ankara in June 1991. But its ethnic communities are so divided that they have the greatest difficulty in resisting the pull of the centre and reveal themselves to be incapable of building a common charter of government. Since, after the fashion of other 'progressive' ideologies, the Baathist discourse has been considerably devalued, seventy years on history and geopolitics are at the meeting point of the Iraqi–Turkish border and of the fulcrum of the nation states in the Middle East.

The Limits of Fertile Crescent Unity: Iraqi Policies towards Syria since 1945

Eberhard Kienle

More than thirty years after the death of Nuri al-Said in the 'revolution' of 1958 Iraqi policies towards Syria are still largely seen in the light of the 'Fertile Crescent' scheme elaborated and propagated by this politician who incarnated the *ancien régime* as much as its Hashemite sovereigns. The aim to bring about a union of sorts between the two countries which was one of the main tenets of this scheme continues to haunt politicians as well as analysts and observers gravitating around them. And indeed, their suspicions seemed to be vindicated by the abortive unity scheme of 1978–79 which repeated some of the features known from the old days. At any time a union or even merger of Syria and Iraq, most likely under the latter's domination, would certainly have had far-reaching practical consequences for the politics of the Middle East. From another point of view such an event could also reveal a fundamental rejection by political actors in Iraq of the state borders imposed on them by the European powers after World War One. Hence the demand for uniting the two countries could indicate that Iraqis, at least those in power, do not accept the territorial shape of their state and seek to redraw the borders in the region. In this sense, Iraqi policies could be seen as attempts to overcome the 'artificial' divisions of the Arab nation and to unite it or part of it in one nation-state. By implication, this would be yet another proof that at present Iraq does not qualify as a nation-state.

On the following pages an attempt will be made to sketch Iraqi government policies towards Syria since the Second World War and to identify the factors and aims that determined them. It will thus be seen that unity schemes, though recurrent, neither always dominated the Iraqi agenda, nor ultimately reflected a desire to replace 'artificial' with more 'natural' borders. Unlike similar schemes formulated in Syria, those devised in Iraq did not primarily aim at dissolving this particular state in some wider Arab entity.[1] This should not be taken as an indication of Iraq being a nation-state in the proper sense of the term;[2] rather, it illustrates that the foreign policies of merely territorial states[3] need not be obsessed with the creation of nation states, even if surface phenomena seem to confirm this. In the Iraqi case, simpler considerations of geo-political power politics account for much of the unity discourse, even though a sense of belonging together can be detected here and in other policies.

THE LAST YEARS OF THE MONARCHY, 1945-1958

In the days of the monarchy the most noteworthy features of Iraqi policies towards Syria (and to some extent vice-versa) certainly were the recurrent proposals to establish some sort of union between the two countries. These were often subsumed to the famous Fertile Crescent scheme proposed by Nuri al-Said, ex-Sharifian officer, many times Prime Minister, and pillar of the *ancien régime*.[4] The last in a line of proposals that initially focused on 'unity' with Transjordan and Palestine, this scheme was elaborated in late 1942 and then distributed to a selected circle of supposedly influential people in early 1943[5].

    1. For Syria cf. M. Seurat, 'Les populations, l'Etat et la société', in A. Raymond, ed., *La Syrie d'aujourd'hui* (Paris, 1980).
    2. This means a state co-extensive with a population perceiving itself as a nation, i.e. as an imagined community in the sense of Anderson: B. Anderson, *Imagined communities: reflections on the origin and spread of nationalism*, (London, 1983). It implies not only differentiation of some sort from people living outside the state's borders, but also a similar degree of internal homogeneity. Basic loyalties must be focused on a group co-extensive with the population of the state, not to any other larger or smaller one. In the Iraqi case this would entail people considering themselves as Iraqis first and only then as Kurds, Sunnis, Banu Tamim, etc.
    3. Distinction in the sense of Korany: B. Korany, 'Alien and besieged, yet here to stay: the contradictions of the Arab territorial state', in G. Salamé, ed., *The foundations of the Arab State*, (London, 1987).
    4. For a historical narrative of Syro-Iraqi relations in this period cf. P. Seale, *The struggle for Syria; a study in post-war Arab politics*, (London, 1965); and G. Torrey, *Syrian politics and the military* (Ohio State University, 1964).
    5. For its history see H.G. Balfour-Paul, 'Iraq; the Fertile Crescent dimension',

Al-Said's scheme essentially called for the merger of Syria, Lebanon, Palestine, and Transjordan into one state which together with the Iraqi state should form the nucleus of an Arab League then open to other Arab states as well. This Arab League—distinct from the one that was formed on Egyptian initiative in 1945— would be headed by a joint council responsible for defence, foreign affairs, communication, currency and customs as well as the protection of minority rights. The Jews in Palestine, and to a lesser degree the Maronites in Lebanon, were to be given some degree of autonomy.

Though aiming at a union of sorts between Syria and Iraq, the scheme clearly distinguished between the merger of Syria with its western and southern neighbours and the more loosely conceived league this new state would enter with Iraq. Both states would continue to have their own governments, however reduced their prerogatives would be; and Syria would even be able to retain its republican régime.[6] A somewhat different scheme was proposed in January 1954 by the then Iraqi Prime Minister Fadil al-Jamali who sought a federation comprising Iraq, Syria and Jordan.[7] Like al-Said, al-Jamali implicitly accepted the existence of the Sykes-Picot line. Abd al-Ilah, Regent until 1953 and then Crown Prince, largely preferred to wait in the wings, but clearly supported the schemes publicized by others; the young king in turn supported the Crown Prince.[8]

Sometimes in the late 1940s and early 1950s Iraqo-Syrian union seemed not too remote from realization. However, its fortunes were changing continuously and at times rapidly, depending on the strength of its advocates in Syria. Although at times these prevailed upon the opponents of any such idea, their advantage was never

in T. Niblock, ed., *Iraq; the contemporary state*, (London, 1982); Y. Porath, 'Nuri al-Said's Arab unity programme', *Middle Eastern Studies*, XX, 172–89; Y. Porath, *In search of Arab unity 1930–1945*, (London, 1986).
    6. For the complete text see N. al-Said, *Istiqlal al-arab wa-wahdatuhum*, (Baghdad, 1943); J.C. Hurewitz, *Diplomacy in the Near and Middle East*, 2 vols., (Princeton, NJ, 1956); details are also given in Balfour-Paul, *loc. cit.*; E. Dawn, *The project of Greater Syria* (unpublished Ph.D. thesis, Princeton University, 1948); Porath (1984), *op. cit.*, pp. 89 ff.; Porath (1986), *op. cit.* and Seale, *op. cit.*, pp. 11 f.
    7. For details see Seale, *op. cit.*, pp. 139 f.
    8. More modest border revisions were never an issue in these days, and the question debated after World War One whether Dair al-Zur should be part of Syria or Iraq was not reopened; for this episode cf. E. Tauber, 'The struggle for Dayr al-Zur; the determination of boundaries between Syria and Iraq', in *IJMES*, Vol. 23, No. 3, pp. 361–85, 1991.

clear-cut nor lasting, not least because they failed to seize opportunities and at crucial moments remained undecided. The question of unity with Iraq was a central issue in Syrian politics that divided the country and repeatedly led or contributed to changes of government and military coups. Iraqi actors often attempted to influence such events and so did Egypt and Saudi Arabia who sought to offset Iraqi influence. They all benefited from strong tendencies among Syrians to consider their state as entirely artificial and their ensuing lack of loyalty to it. The old ruling classes were divided among themselves between friends and foes of the Iraqi régime, partly for economic reasons, partly because of the special treaty and then the Baghdad Pact that linked it to Britain. But the growing numbers of Syrians who challenged these classes from below had an obvious penchant for anti-imperialism and social reform as advocated by Nasser. As the 'struggle for Syria' went on, prospects for Fertile Crescent unity receded. However, while Iraqi leaders did not cease to plan for it behind the scenes,[9] Syria continued to strengthen its ties with Egypt, culminating in the United Arab Republic (UAR) of 1958–61.[10]

During this period large amounts of money poured into the pockets of Syrian politicians whom the one or the other side thought to be ready to further its case.[11] Iraqi investment in the portfolios of Syrian politicians was significantly helped by the 1950 agreement on profit-sharing with the still foreign-owned Iraq Petroleum Company (IPC). After 1958 when the new Qasim régime tried representatives of the monarchy many such instances came into the open. Though certainly not impartial, several of the allegations made at these trials could be substantiated. At one point for instance the Syrian veteran politician Sabri al-Asali had received 15,000 ID (Iraqi Dinars) while his colleague Maruf al-Dawalibi claimed to have refused similar offers from Nuri al-Said and the Regent.[12]

9. Cf. W. Gallman, *Iraq under General Nuri; my recollections of Nuri al-Said 1954–1958*, (Baltimore, 1964); and Seale, *op. cit.*, pp. 166 ff.

10. For a detailed account of the 'Struggle for Syria', cf. Seale, *op. cit.*; Shikara adds hitherto unknown information. A.R. Shikara, 'Iraqi foreign policy in the 1950s; an analysis of trends and policies in Public Record Office documents', Paper submitted to the Quinquennial Conference of the International Association of Middle Eastern Studies, Tunis, September 1991.

11. For details see Seale, *op. cit.*, pp. 24–148, 266; also E. Penrose and E.F. Penrose, *Iraq; international relations and national development* (London, 1978), p. 129; R. El-Sayed, *The Baghdad Pact in world politics*, (Geneva, 1971), pp. 33–42.

12. Seale, *op. cit.*, pp. 168 ff.

When financial and moral support for plots, be they parliamentary or military, seemed to be inadequate, Iraqi leaders also countenanced overt military intervention, particularly from 1953 onwards. This was the year when the Jamali government asked its military attaché in Damascus to devise the detailed 'Plan X' for armed intervention. Temporarily shelved, it reappeared in June 1954 when Jamali and some of his allies in Damascus, including Prime Minister Sabri al-Asali, thought of uniting the two countries through an Iraqi attack on Syria. In March 1955, after the signature of the Baghdad Pact, Iraq—and Turkey—actually concentrated troops on their borders with Syria. Back in power, Nuri al-Said played his part in a major plot involving Great Britain, the USA and Syrian exiles in 1956 and in 1957 instructed the Iraqi Chief of Staff to support a planned coup in Syria with a three-pronged attack on Aleppo, Homs, and Damascus; however, as previously the army hierarchy was less than keen to cooperate.[13]

These plans of bringing about some sort of political union with Syria or of otherwise controlling and influencing decisions made in Damascus were concocted and pursued at different levels in the Iraqi state apparatus. Far from implementing each others' orders, their authors were guided by their own, partly diverging interests; these, however, they sought to realize through policies whose common denominator seemed to reflect the consistent policy of a single state actor. Indeed, the Iraqi state apparatus in these days was highly fragmented not only on the inferior levels of its bureaucracy but even at its top where decisions were made.

Abd al-Ilah and Faisal II, who always remained under his uncle's influence, neither with regard to Syria nor in general always shared the concerns of the prominent politicians in Parliament. In their overwhelming majority the latter represented the propertied classes including a number of ex-Sharifian officers whose upward mobility, however, often resulted from royal favours. These new and 'old landed and commercial classes'[14] were certainly divided among themselves, but increasingly united during the 1950s to contain the rise of the middle and working classes[15]. Their ambiguous

13. These plots and plans are described in great detail in Seale, *op. cit.*, pp. 122 ff., 137 f., 166 ff., 266–82, 297 ff.; cf. also Gallman, *op. cit.*, pp. 161 f.
14. Cf. the title of H. Batatu, *The old social classes and the revolutionary movements of Iraq; a study of Iraq's old landed and commercial classes and of its communists, Ba'thists and Free Officers*, (Princeton, 1978).
15. As to the social structure of Iraq under the monarchy and the relations

relationship with the Palace is illustrated by Nuri al-Said himself, the 'chief arbiter and executive of these [propertied] classes'[16] who continuously vied with the Regent for the control of Parliament. Each of them attempted to pack it with his own cronies, a process in which al-Said increasingly distanced himself from the Hashemites, particularly the Regent.[17]

Concerning Syria, the Hashemites and their internal competitor- allies nonetheless agreed as to the necessity to entertain some sort of unilaterally privileged relations with the government of that country. This attitude in part derived from the perceived zero-sum logic of the 'struggle for Syria', in which the antagonists, Egypt, Saudi Arabia and Iraq, were convinced that control over that country was the key to regional hegemony and influence.[18]

In addition to that Iraqi oil exports, the largest part of which throughout the 1950s came from the Kirkuk area in the north,[19] depended on the cooperation of Damascus. The only outlet for these exports were the pipelines from Kirkuk through Syria to Banyas and Tripoli on the Mediterranean.[20] The amount of royalties had been a subject of debate between the IPC and the Syrian government ever since the pipelines were built[21]. Syria certainly had an interest in maintaining the flow of oil as it received substantial amounts of transit dues, but after all was less dependent on these than Baghdad was on its export earnings.[22]

Beyond this common denominator, however, different priorities

between class and state, cf. Batutu, *op. cit.*, p. 11 f., Part II, and p. 113 ff.; Hopwood in this volume; M. Farouk-Sluglett and P. Sluglett, *Iraq since 1958; from revolution to dictatorship* (London, 1987), p. 35 ff.; R. Fernea and W.R. Louis, eds., *The Iraqi revolution of 1958; the old social classes revisited*, (London, 1991); and R. Owen, 'Class and class politics in Iraq before 1958; the "colonial and post-colonial" state' in Fernea and Louis, eds., *op. cit.*, pp. 154–71.

16. Batatu, *op. cit.*, p. 352.
17. *Ibid.*, p. 349 ff.
18. For details see Seale, *op. cit.*
19. Penrose, *op. cit.*, p. 148.
20. As to Iraqi anxieties, cf. Gallman, *op. cit*, p. 41; earlier such designs on the part of Nuri are mentioned by J. Kimche, *The second Arab awakening*, (London, 1970), p. 147.
21. Penrose, *op. cit.*, p. 390 ff.
22. Syria in 1955 received £414,000 in royalties while Iraqi oil revenue amounted to some £73 million; in 1956 after a new agreement with the IPC Syria received royalties worth £4.9 million while Iraq's oil revenue reached about £69 million; figures from Penrose, *op. cit.*, p. 390 ff; B. Shawdran, *The Middle East, oil and the Great Powers*, (London, 1973), p. 270. In the 1950s oil revenue amounted to about sixty per cent of the annual state budget in Iraq while in Syria royalties paid by oil companies

dominated. For al-Said the 'struggle for Syria' in the 1950s became increasingly interwoven with his policy of containing communism as an ideology and the country that served as its major base, the Soviet Union, as a geopolitical power. Syria, from this perspective, had to adhere to the Baghdad Pact but instead the country drifted ever more to the 'left'. On the other hand, Abd al-Ilah and Faisal, though not less anti-communist, were particularly interested in Syria in order to enhance their position in the intra-dynastic rivalry with Abdallah in Jordan and their inter-dynastic rivalries with the Saudis who in the 1920s had expelled them from the Hejaz.[23] Finally, there was also some concern in the Iraqi military and elsewhere that Israel might attack Syria if it became too close an ally of Egypt. Hence, not only Arab powers had to be kept out of Syria.

The most elegant way of achieving these objectives would have been some sort of Syro-Iraqi union derived from Nuri al-Said's Fertile Cresent scheme. Yet its full implementation in the originally proposed form that encompassed also Lebanon, Jordan and Palestine was no longer either practical or necessary for the intended purpose. Stopping short of a complete merger, the scheme would have had the double advantage of keeping Iraq out of the complexities and intricacies of Syrian politics while at the same time tying the country closer to Iraq.[24]

However, that the proposals more or less explicitly left it to the Syrians to decide on their form of government not only shows an intention to make them more acceptable to people whose political leaders in their majority were republicans, but in Nuri al-Said's case also betrays that his concern was not identical with Abd al-Ilah's who desperately sought to climb on a yet to be created throne in Syria. Towards 1953 as Faisal's majority approached Abd al-Ilah, faced with the threat of redundancy, became ever more jittery[25] and, though for other reasons as well, projects of military intervention were more seriously envisaged (cf supra). However, al-Said's scheme did not prevent Syria from becoming a monarchy

certainly increased gradually, but as late as 1960 only amounted to about twenty-five per cent of budget revenue; cf. C. Issawi and M. Yeganeh, *The economics of the Middle East*, (London, 1962), p. 147.

23. Balfour-Paul, *op. cit.*, p. 10.

24. Al-Said apparently considered the Austro-Hungarian empire as a model for the future Iraqo-Syrian entity; cf. minutes of a meeting with al-Said by the then British Ambassador Sir Henry Mack, as quoted by W.R. Louis, *The British Empire in the Middle East 1945–1951* (Oxford, 1984), p. 306, note 1.

25. For Abd al-Ilah's plans cf. Balfour-Paul, *op. cit.*; Seale, *op. cit.*, p. 47.

and thus the Regent from becoming King. Thanks to its non-committal nature it could be presented to the latter as an astute and cunning device to further his interest without antagonizing public opinion in Syria.

From the point of view of the Regent an Iraqo-Syrian union would have been the perfect arrangement. It would have allowed for sufficiently strong ties with Iraq to allow his new country—hopefully—to benefit from Iraq's oil wealth, yet not entailed a complete merger under which quite obviously no second monarchy would have been possible or needed.[26] From the point of view of al-Said union projects moreover served the more cynical purpose of keeping the Regent busy and out of Iraqi politics proper.[27] Yet other Iraqi politicians indulged in these projects merely to ingratiate themselves with either the Regent or Nuri. In any case, for many in Iraq, talking about another Hashemite throne in Syria on top of some sort of union between the two countries remained a tactical ploy at best. However, even the more genuine advocates of the various Iraqi designs repeatedly failed to seize opportunities when they arose. Sometimes their Syrian allies seemed cumbersome, sometimes Syria altogether too complicated, and some other time Saudi Arabia, Egypt and others too hostile to bring about unity or instal a client régime in Damascus. When, a few months before the Iraqi 'revolution' in 1958 Syria and Egypt formed the United Arab Republic (UAR), power shifted to Cairo and into the hands of Egyptians. The 'struggle for Syria' was temporarily decided and policies towards Syria became part and parcel of those vis-a-vis Egypt.

The Qasim Regime

As the 'revolution' of 14 July did not split the UAR, the republican régime too had to accommodate its policy towards Syria with effective Egyptian rule there. From the point of view of Abd al-Salam Arif, who led the coup together with Abd al-Karim Qasim, such an accommodation did not pose major difficulties. Already four days

---

26. According to Seale (*op. cit.*, p. 80 f.), Saddiq Shanshal, an Iraqi politician involved in secret unity talks with Syria in 1949 claimed that following instructions from the Regent the Iraqi envoys insisted on uniting the two countries under one throne. Nothing of course would have prevented the Hashemites to split up the new country again in 1953 upon the majority of Faisal II.

27. Their diverging policies and alliances with Syrian actors are well illustrated in Seale, *op. cit.*, p. 267.

after the coup in Iraq he met Nasser in Damascus to discuss closer ties with the UAR.[28] Also, when he became President some five years later, relations with Nasser were generally good, but then of course the UAR had already ceased to exist (except for the name which continued to designate Egypt alone). However, Qasim, who later in 1958 discarded Arif, decided to follow his own course and to maintain Iraq entirely independent. Consequently, his relations with Egypt were tense at least, if not frankly hostile.[29]

Under Qasim the Iraqi position vis-a-vis the UAR continued to be marked by the same relative weakness as under the monarchy. As well as trying to set the agenda in Syria as before, Iraqi leaders now had to defend themselves against hostile forces operating from the northern province of the UAR. Syria's transformation from a bilateral battleground into an Egyptian outpost profoundly changed the Iraqi situation. This became particularly evident in March 1959 when the leaders of the Mosul uprising received weapons and other support from across the border. Similarly, after the attempt on Qasim's life in autumn 1959, its Baathi authors escaped into Syria and were granted asylum in the UAR.[30]

In September 1961 Qasim cautiously welcomed Syria's secession (*infisal*) from the UAR and later met its new president; however, he was careful not to overplay his hand and prevented the normalization of relations with Damascus from turning into a serious challenge for Nasser and his régime.[31] That such a policy excluded any unity scheme was of no concern to Qasim whose interest focused entirely on Iraq[32]. In its modest form, the rapprochement served him to defend his position against Nasserist encroachments and attacks. Hence, Iraqi policy was again determined by the constraints inherent in the regional balance of power.

28. Batatu, *op. cit.*, p. 817, referring to the Memoirs of Abd al- Salam Arif, *Ruz-al-Yusuf*, 30/5/1966.
29. For details, see M.H. Kerr, *The Arab cold war; Gamal Abd al-Nasir and his rivals 1958–1970*, (London, 1971); also U. Dann, *Iraq under Qassem* (London, 1969), p. 348 ff.
30. For details, cf. Batatu, *op. cit.*, pp. 866–89, 1084 ff.; Dann, *op. cit.*, p. 156 f.; Kerr, *op. cit.*, p. 16, ff.; M. Khadduri, *Republican Iraq; a study in Iraqi politics since the revolution of 1958*, (London, 1969), p. 128 ff.. Conversely, there is little evidence confirming Iraqi support for Syrian communists as denounced by the UAR, cf. e.g. Haykal in *Al-Ahram*, 20/1/1959.
31. For details, cf. *Middle East Record*, Vol. II (1961); Dann, *op. cit.*, p. 330.
32. Earlier references to the old Fertile Crescent scheme such as in November 1959 solely served to spice the propaganda war with Nasser; they were not resuscitated after the break-up of the UAR.

The *mashriq* had indeed reverted to a lesser version of the situation prevailing prior to the creation of the UAR. An injured Egypt and a prudent and self-centred Iraq were again the major antagonists; Syria as always found itself in between them, but thanks to their and its own experience slowly emerged, though with hitches, towards greater independence.

THE FIRST BAATH REGIME IN IRAQ, 1963

Policy again changed—and more substantially than ever before—when on 8 February 1963 a group of officers overthrew Qasim, resulting in the first Baath régime of Iraq. Entirely new considerations now entered the formulation of Iraqi policies towards Syria. No longer the balance of power between the masters in Baghdad and those ruling over Syria, be they Syrian or Egyptian, dominated the approach. Although the issue was never entirely absent from the actors' minds, other concerns now became paramount.

Until 8 March 1963 when another coup in Damascus brought the Syrian Baath party to power as well, the new Iraqi leaders by various means attempted to further the chances of their party colleagues on the other side of the border.[33] There was certainly some genuine party solidarity, but a Baath régime in Damascus could also be seen as an additional support for that in Baghdad which was far from being uncontested in the country or the armed forces; in due course this fact then indeed led to its demise.[34]

After 8 March the Baathis in power in Baghdad were guided by yet different concerns in their dealings with their Syrian counterparts. First, tripartite unity negotiations were embarked on with Syria and Egypt.[35] Apart from spontaneous enthusiasm, the Iraqi Baathis, though to a lesser extent than some of their Syrian colleagues, thought of unity as a means to enhance their own Arab national credentials, especially as Nasser still represented Arab legitimacy incarnate. If negotiated with the necessary—more or less confederal—safeguards, this would consolidate their own position

---

33. For details and the reasons of the Syrian government's acquiescence, cf. Kerr, *op. cit.*, p. 42.

34. Cf. Batatu, *op. cit.*, pp. 1003–1026; Devlin, *op. cit.*, pp. 255–79; Farouk-Sluglett/Sluglett, *op. cit.*, p. 85 ff.; Kerr, *op. cit.*, pp. 41–96; I. Rabinovich, *Syria under the Ba'th 1963–1966: the army-party symbiosis*, (New York, 1972), pp. 75–108.

35. For the course these negotiations took and their chronology, cf. Kerr, *op. cit.*, pp. 44–93; also Devlin, *op. cit.*; Rabinovich, *op. cit.*

at home and then perhaps enable them to get rid of their internal competitors, including the local Nasserists. Under favourable circumstances, of course, unity would also produce some of the effects ascribed to it by Baathi ideology and strengthen the three countries regionally and vis-a-vis the forces of imperialism.

When the tripartite unity scheme collapsed in July, only three months after it had been agreed on, Syrian and Iraqi Baathis decided to negotiate a bipartite arrangement excluding Egypt. Fragile as they were, this would still strengthen them both internally, and also vis-à-vis Nasser whose goodwill under the new circumstances could no longer be counted on. At the same time, however, the Iraqi as well as the Syrian Baath were deeply divided among themselves and each of the main Iraqi factions was closer to certain Syrian groupings than to its inner-party opponents in Iraq. The Iraqi 'left' around Ali Salih Sadi was closer to the Syrian 'left' around Hamud al-Shufi than to fellow Iraqis of the conservative 'right' such as Talib Shabib and Hazim Jawad who sought to ally themselves with Michel Aflaq, the party leader, and his supporters.[36] Hence, often close links across the border were considered as a means to strengthen the position of a faction rather than that of the party as a whole. Within these alliances support by Baathis from the one country mainly served a purely instrumental purpose, but generally fell short of their authoritative participation in the affairs of the other country.

The cooperation between Sadi and Shufi, for instance, focused on defeating their conservative opponents at the Baath's Sixth National Congress in October 1963 where a new National Command was to be elected[37] and a new programme to be adopted. However, the aim was not only as it appeared on the surface to put greater emphasis on socialism, but at the same time to give greater independence to the party leadership of each individual country. The *theoretical points of departure (Ba'd al-muntalaqat al-nazariya)* which the congress passed as the party's new programme explicitly acknowledged the differences between Arab countries or

36. For details, cf. Batatu, *op. cit.*, p. 1020 ff.; Devlin, *op. cit.*, pp. 260–77; Rabinovich, *op. cit.*, pp. 75–108.

37. Consistent with its claim to be an Arab nationalist movement the Baath party's highest authority was the so-called National Command (*Qiyada qawmiya*) which comprised members from all the different Arab countries, in Baathi parlance *regions* in which the party had branches. The National Command retained a number of reserve powers vis-à-vis each Regional Command (*Qiyada qutriya*) which presided over the Syrian, Iraqi etc. branches.

'regions' and that they could only be overcome gradually.[38] Such independence was particularly dear to the Iraqi party who did not fancy sharing Iraqi oil wealth—an issue that seems to have been the subject of some debate at the Sixth National Congress.[39]

Consequently, the bilateral union which the congress called for was to be a federal one and therefore just the minumum one should expect from an Arab nationalist party.[40] Earlier decisions, taken in September, could, but need not, have indicated a desire to go further along the road to union. The rather vague agreement on economic union was perfectly compatible with a looser form of co-operation and so was the military charter establishing joint armed forces headquarters in Damascus. To its signatories the latter probably meant no more than a rhetorically enhanced alliance of sorts which then allowed a Syrian brigade to fight against Kurdish troops in Iraq. The limits of the union were strictly defined by the necessities of survival.

When at the Iraqi Regional Congress immediately after the National Congress the conservatives attempted a coup and bundled off to Spain a number of leftist members, among them Sadi himself, two Iraqi members of the National Command, Ahmad Hasan al-Bakr and Salih Mahdi Ammash, called on this highest party body to take over direct control of affairs in Iraq. Though ideologically closer to the conservatives, Bakr and Ammash probably thus sought to prevent the party from self-destruction. This time non-Iraqi Baathis, mostly Syrians like Aflaq, Jadid and Hafiz, were supposed to save the Iraqi party as a whole, not one particular faction; yet, the guiding thought was once more to consolidate the position of a (however divided) group or movement in Iraq. Again, this did not necessarily involve any role for the non-Iraqis beyond such transitory crisis management.[41]

At its crisis meeting in Baghdad the National Command exiled to Beirut a number of Iraqi Baathis responsible for the previous

38. The 'Theoretical Points of Departure', whose complete title is *Ba'd al-muntalaqat al-nazariya alati aqraha al-mutamar al-qawmi al-sadis fi tishrin al-awwal 1963* are available in numerous Iraqi and Syrian party publications or brochures; they are reprinted in *Nidal al-Baath*, IV, 169 ff; for extracts in English and a discussion see Rabinovich, *op. cit.*, p. 81 ff.
39. Cf. also Rabinovich, *op. cit.*, p. 82, note 16.
40. Cf. Resolutions of the Sixth National Congress, in: *al-Baath*, Damascus, 28/10/1963; translated in *Arab Political Documents 1963*, pp. 438–44.
41. For a chronology and details see Rabinovich, *op. cit.*, and J.F. Devlin, *The Ba'th Party: a history from its origins to 1966*, (Stanford, CA, 1976).

expulsion of the leftists and filled the five cabinet posts now vacant. Only a day later, on 18 November, a military coup led by Abd al-Salam Arif put an end to the Baathi turmoil. The authors of the coup certainly disapproved of the National Command's decision to maintain the National Guard, the party militia, which was still controlled by the Sadi faction. At the same time, however, the chaos spread by a party not limiting itself to Iraq had negatively affected key institutions of the Iraqi state such as the Cabinet; on top of that, non-Iraqis, among them Hafiz who was president of Syria, had interfered in the appointment of major representatives of this state. Such an interference in one's own 'internal affairs' could not be tolerated[42], not least of course as under the circumstances it tipped the balance of power against one's own factional interests.

THE ARIF REGIMES, 1963-1968

With the advent of Abd al-Salam Arif's régime, followed by that of his brother Abd al-Rahman, Syria no longer served as the recruiting ground for auxiliary troops that it had been during the nine months of Baathi rule. Instead it was again regarded entirely as another country ruled by another régime, completely independent of that in Baghdad, and with its own interests. In this respect the situation resembled that of the 1940s and 1950s when rulers in Baghdad had to co-exist with independent-minded régimes in Damascus, but it differed inasmuch as pro-Iraqi forces in Syria now hardly existed. Yet more importantly, unlike then the régime in Damascus now—despite all internal turmoil—sufficiently consolidated itself to equal that in Baghdad in terms of strength and resources. Combined with the demise of Nasserist forces in Syria this entailed the end, at least for the time being, of the 'struggle for Syria'. A certain however limited sense of cooperation between Syria and Egypt no longer posed a threat to the latter's generally good relations with Iraq.

However, if the Baath's successor régime in Iraq no longer regarded Baathi Syria as an area from which support could be mobilized, there was some concern that Baathis in Iraq might be able to enlist Syrian support to return to power. Such support could not be ruled out, especially as long as Aflaq and the conservative nationalists retained some influence in Damascus. They seemed close

42. For details see Devlin, *op. cit.*, and Rabinovich, *op. cit.*

to the leaders of the new clandestine Iraqi Baath Regional Command appointed by Aflaq some time after Arif's coup. Following an abortive coup in 1964 some of them were arrested,[43] but it is not known whether this attempt involved any Syrian Baathis. At any rate, their successful coup in 1968 underscored their independence from Syrian support. The 1968 coup was staged two years after the 'Movement of 23 February' had ousted all members of the Aflaq wing from power and office in Damascus and installed a régime there that would not even recognize its Iraqi counterparts as genuine Baathis.[44]

Throughout the Arif period Iraqi relations with Syria remained difficult. In summer 1966 Damascus sought to obtain higher transit dues for Iraqi oil exported via the trans-Syrian pipeline to the Mediterranean. Although the dispute involved the still foreign-owned Iraq Petroleum Company (IPC), the three months of pipeline closure imposed by Damascus and the subsequent increase in royalties negatively affected Iraqi government revenue. Since 1952 the Iraqi government received a share of roughly fifty per cent of IPC profits by which token any loss for the company implied a loss for the government.[45] As Syria challenged an imperialist oil company Iraq had verbally to support it, but in reality was just as much dismayed. As in the 1940s and 1950s the issue was again one of incompatible régime interests, but now expressed in terms of benefit and not in terms of power (which of course is convertible into benefit).

In comparison this was, nonetheless, a calm period. Tensions with Syria never led to more than verbal exchanges, even though they sometimes were acrimonious. Unlike previous and later periods mutual subversion remained minimal and no troops were concentrated on the common border.

THE SECOND IRAQI BAATH REGIME

Since July 1968 when Iraqi Baathis and officers took power in

43. Devlin, *op. cit.*, p. 275.
44. As to events in Syria, cf. Devlin, *op. cit.*, Rabinovich, *op. cit.*, and N. Van Dam, *The struggle for power in Syria; sectarianism, regionalism and tribalism in politics 1961–1978*, (London, 1979).
45. The pipeline episode is best described in Penrose and Penrose, *op. cit.*, pp. 390–4; cf. also E. Kienle, *Ba'th v. Ba'th; the conflict between Syria and Iraq 1968–1989*, (London, 1990).

Baghdad the country has been ruled by régimes claiming to represent Baathi values and to pursue Baathi policies[46]. For some three or four years this claim to Baathi authenticity heavily burdened relations with Baathi Syria. Even later it never completely disappeared from the Iraqo-Syrian agenda, although by then it had become a secondary matter superseded by other issues. In the first years after the 1968 coup Iraqi policy towards Syria was again heavily influenced by the potential efficacy of cross-border ties and loyalties between Baathis in the two countries. However, it was so in a different way from before. In 1963 different Iraqi Baathi factions had actively developed and used these ties in order to enhance their own position back home in Baghdad through support from Syria. Now, in and after 1968, they were reserved at best vis-a-vis those in power in Syria who in February 1966 had ousted the 'historical leadership' around Aflaq. They certainly remained close to the remaining supporters of their former sponsor in the Syrian party, but these had to operate in clandestinity and were of little help to prop up the régime in Baghdad. Who were useful, however, were those former Baathi leaders like Aflaq himself, who in 1966 had escaped from Syria and now lived in exile, either in Lebanon or further away. Many among these supported the new Baath régime in Iraq, visited Baghdad and even settled there permanently. While they thus strengthened the Baathi and more widely the Arab nationalist credentials of the Iraqi régime, their presence there reinforced fears of subversion in Damascus. Whether the Iraqi régime right from the outset sought to help the Aflaq wing back to power in Syria cannot be ascertained. It could be concluded from past patterns dating back to the 'struggle for Syria', but on the other hand there is sufficient evidence (not least from 1963) that the Iraqi Baath—be it only to ensure its immediate survival in power—had become largely Iraq-centred.

Be this as it may, visibly the Iraqi attitude towards Syria only changed late in 1968 after the régime in Damascus had launched a violent propaganda campaign in which it denied any Baathi legitimacy to its Baghdad counterpart. By doing so the régime in Damascus sought to defend its own Baathi legitimacy and indeed survival which it saw threatened by disappointed Syrian party

46. For a detailed account and analysis of Syro-Iraqi relations in this period cf. Kienle, *op. cit.*; Baram is more concise but the present author disagrees with a number of his views. A. Baram, 'Ideology and power politics in Syrian-Iraqi Relations 1968–1984', in M. Ma'oz and A. Yaniv, eds., *Syria under Assad*, (London, 1986).

members. These, it feared, might consider the new régime in Baghdad more attractive and thus erode its own position from inside. Apart from supporters of the 'historical leadership' also two other—partly overlapping—categories of party members were considered as potential deserters. The one was formed by all those angered by the conduct of the 1967 war against Israel and the heavy defeat of the Arab side in which the Syrian régime bore a heavy responsibility while the Iraqi Baath had precisely replaced a régime associated with this defeat; the other comprised those members of the Syrian party who grew increasingly resentful over the appropriation and monopolization of political power by Alawite officers.[47]

The Iraqi régime finally responded in kind, probably to prevent the erosion of its own Baathi legitimacy under the attacks from Syria. Even though there was not much pro-Syrian sympathy in the Iraqi Baath, constant Syrian attacks might in the end have prompted the communicating channels between the two parties to reverse the flows of legitimacy. From now on Baathi ties across the border had to be managed in two different ways: they had to be severed inasmuch as they produced dissaffection in Iraq and they had to be stimulated inasmuch as they helped to replace the cumbersome and dangerous régime in Damascus with a more friendly one. Hence, Baathi legitimacy was denied to the régime in Damascus and generally the propaganda war was stepped up. The same applies to subversion in Syria, but compared to previous and later periods hostile acts remained limited. Again, however, the aim was different from 1963 as influencing cross-border ties between Baathis only indirectly served to stabilize the rulers in Baghdad. At the same time, it now increasingly involved controlling Syria and thus partly resembled the 'struggle for Syria', with the difference that it was waged against Damascus itself, no longer against Cairo.

The communicating vessels of Baathi legitimacy became largely clogged by the early 1970s, and the perils as well as opportunities linked to the existence of another Baath régime in Damascus ceased to have a large-scale influence on Iraqi policies towards Syria. Largely this was the result of new policies pursued in Damascus where in another intra-Baathi coup in November 1970 Hafiz al-Asad had taken over. Asad's policy of economic

47. It is important to omit the definite article before Alawite(s); cf. Kienle, *op. cit.*, pp. 31–60.

liberalization (*infitah*) not only served the Syrian business community, but also those on whose direct support the survival of the régime rested: party officials as well as army and 'security' officers. These *apparatchiks* now benefited from the commissions and bribes they could charge to business people for the many licences and authorizations that were necessary to take advantage of the new economic openings. Material benefit thus replaced legitimacy as the major source of régime stability; consequently, the régime felt less compelled to insist on its Baathi credentials and to denigrate its potential competitor in Baghdad. The latter in turn no longer had to defend its own Baathi legitimacy, nor would such insistence have enabled it now to gain support among Baathis in Syria.

Although the existence of an ideological competitor time and again affected bilateral relations throughout the 1970s and 1980s it ceased to be a major issue. With the growing consolidation of the Iraqi régime and the tightening of its grip over the country, paralleled by similar developments in Syria, two disputes over clearly defined material issues became more prominent, but were rapidly eclipsed by an ever more violent competition for regional influence. First, in 1972–73 Iraq, after nationalizing the IPC, was faced with a Syrian demand to double the royalties for oil exports through the trans-Syrian pipeline. More vulnerable than the IPC in 1966, Baghdad had to give in but, much embittered, began to build alternative pipelines from its northern oilfields to the Gulf and through Turkey.[48] The second dispute erupted in the spring of 1975 when Syria filled lake Tabqa, thus greatly reducing the flow of the Euphrates into Iraq and causing considerable harm to the country's agriculture.[49]

Corresponding to their new stability, the two régimes were able to mobilize greater resources and to resort to harsher means in their conflict. Propaganda warfare was increasingly accompanied

48. For an extensive discussion of this matter cf. M.E. Brown 'The nationalization of the Iraqi Petroleum Company' in *International Journal of Middle East Studies*, X, 1979, pp. 107–24; Farouk-Sluglett. *op. cit.*, p. 145 ff.; Kienle, *op. cit.*, p. 66 ff.; Penrose and Penrose, *op. cit.*, pp. 405–20; C. Whittleton, 'Oil and the Iraqi economy', in CARDRI, eds., *Saddam's Iraq; revolution of reaction?*, (London, 1986).
49. For details see Z. Bari, 'The Syrian-Iraqi dispute over the Euphrates waters' in *International Studies*, (New Delhi), XVI, 2, 227–44, 1977; P. Beaumont, 'The Euphrates River; an international problem of water resources', in *Environmental Conservation*, V, 1, 35–43, 1978; Kienle, *op. cit,*, p. 97 ff.; and T. Naff and R.C. Matson, *Water in the Middle East; conflict or cooperation?*, (London, 1984).

by support for oppositional movements in the neighbouring country and at times by terrorist acts there. Repeatedly also troops were dispatched to the common border but without engaging in combat. The escalation in terms of conflict behaviour largely reflected the exacerbation of the competition for regional incluence. Particularly in the late 1970s and early 1980s Iraq granted significant support to the Islamic opposition in Syria in its armed struggle against the régime. Also, plots to overthrow the neighbouring régime became more elaborate. Finally, communications between the two countries were interrupted, and economic relations almost entirely severed.

The first indication of the regional competition between the two régimes is provided by the October War of 1973. Prepared by Egypt and Syria who preferred not to associate Iraq, the latter's troops, called in when the situation became extremely critical, nonetheless arrived quickly and played a major role in arresting the Israeli advance into Syria.[50] As successes were hushed up and Baghdad not consulted for the cease-fire, it repatriated its forces immediately and without much ado. But it knew how to turn events to its advantage and emphasizing its readiness to fight when others 'capitulated' helped to illistrate its devotion to the Arab and Palestinian cause.

Iraq's main criticism was not directed against Egypt, but against Syria. Egypt, so Iraqi declarations, at least admitted its limited war aims and its search for a peaceful solution to the Arab-Israeli conflict; Syria on the contrary was hiding in Egypt's shadow, waiting for it to blaze the trail[51]. Accusations against Damascus intensified not only with every one of its own steps away from military confrontation such as the Golan disengagement agreement; they also intensified with Egypt's growing and more far-reaching rapprochement with Israel[52] which then Syria was blamed for. Partly, it seems, attacking Egypt was still too dangerous; partly also growing reservations in Damascus about the speed and scope of Cairo's rapprochement with Israel afforded Iraq the opportunity to settle accounts with Syria first and perhaps successfully reopen the 'struggle for Syria'.

50. A detailed account is given in E. O'Ballance, *No victor, no vanquished; the Yom Kippur war*, (San Rafael, CA, 1978).
51. E.g. *al-Thawra*, Baghdad 31 December 1973, 14 January 1974.
52. For instance when Egypt signed the second Sinai disengagement agreement in 1975, cf. e.g. *al-Thawra*, Baghdad 5 September 1975.

Central to Iraq's renewed regional ambitions was its growing oil wealth after the price increases in 1973/4 and again in 1979/80. These resources enabled the country's leaders to try and realize the Napoleonic designs that are reflected in Saddam Hussein's speeches in the late 1970s when he did not hesitate to compare the strength of Iraq to that of the USSR and the USA.[53] With the Algiers agreement between Iraq and Iran in 1975 Baghdad rid itself of the last shackle that still prevented it from its bid for regional hegemony. Relations with Tehran improved and deprived of Iranian support the Kurdish resistance in Iraq collapsed. Ironically, it was this agreement that let Iraq gather the strength which in 1980 enabled it to attack Iran. The war against Iran like the later one against Kuwait illustrates a shift of Iraqi interest, perceptible from the late 1970s, from Palestine and Israel to the Gulf. Certainly, the Iranian revolution contributed to this shift, but it also closely followed the failure of the Iraqo-Syrian unity scheme of 1978–79 (cf. infra).

Such reorientation notwithstanding, Iraqi policy towards Syria was characterized by the same search for regional influence. This was not only visible in the preferential treatment given to Cairo in matters pertaining to Arab-Israeli affairs. In Lebanon, especially in the so-called civil war after 1975, Iraq persistently supported forces opposed to Syria. The most conspicuous instance was Iraq's military and financial support for General Aoun whose troops in 1989–90 opposed the imposition of the *pax siriana*.[54] Similarly, Iraqi attempts to influence the PLO and support for it often served to weaken Damascus, especially after 1983 when the rift deepened between Asad and the PLO majority.[55]

Once, in October 1978, Iraq seemed closer than ever to its aim of prevailing upon Syria. Almost overnight the violent propaganda war was stopped on both sides and negotiations announced that were to lead to a yet ill-defined union of the two countries. Trying to exploit Syria's weakness after the Camp David agreement between Egypt and Israel, Iraq sought to achieve by peaceful means

---

53. A.Y. Ahmad, 'The dialectics of domestic environment and role performance; the foreign policy of Iraq', in A.E.H. Dessouki and B. Korany, eds., *The foreign policy of Arab states*, (Boulder, CO, 1984), p. 159; Kienle, *op. cit.*, p. 94 f.
54. For detailed and extensive coverage cf. e.g. *Middle East International*, September 1988 onwards and particularly from August 1989.
55. Cf. e.g. coverage in *Middle East International* and in *Middle East Contemporary Survey*, Vols. VII (1982–3) onwards.

what it had failed to achieve through hostility. If accepted by Damascus as a means to balance the 'defection' of Egypt, a unity scheme at that particular moment would have inevitably led to Iraqi domination over Syria and ultimately thus over the entire Arab East. This design was clearly expressed in the Iraqi position which went far beyond the old Fertile Crescent scheme and even further beyond anything proposed under the second Baathi reign. While there had been no talk of union with Syria since 1968,[56] the aim now all of a sudden was the complete merger of the two countries. Oil revenue which in 1963 was eagerly protected by 1978 had grown to an extent that the absorption of Syria seemed easily digestible. The rulers there, however, sought to temporize, to sort out technical problems first, and to limit the scheme to a confederation of still largely autonomous constituents. As in the days of the monarchy, union with Syria was supposed to extend the influence of the régime in Baghdad and to enhance its regional position. However, the aim was no longer to contain Egypt which by now had isolated itself thanks to the Camp David accords, but to decide the struggle for its succession before Syria might regain some of its strength. Moribund since spring 1979, the scheme fell apart in early summer when Iraq tired of Syrian procrastination and events in Iran gave rise to new apprehensions and designs.[57]

When in 1980 Iraq-Iran relations degenerated into a fierce war, it was only logical for Damascus to support Tehran. As shipping in the Gulf became increasingly dangerous, Baghdad sought to reopen the trans-Syrian pipeline which, however, it obtained for a brief period only. In April 1987 King Hussein with Soviet support finally succeeded in arranging 'secret' talks between Hafiz al-Asad and Saddam Hussein. These again failed to produce lasting results, even though Iraq showed signs of exhaustion in its war against Iran. Its former position of strength vis-à-vis Syria turned into one of inferiority, and Iraqi policy now merely aimed at arresting this decline. As the attempt to regain the initiative by occupying Kuwait lamentably failed, Iraqi foreign policy became a sheer search for survival. In the first serious military encounter ever between the

56. Not counting Iraq's propagandistic and still-born attempt in 1972 to redefine and join the Federation of Arab Republics comprising Egypt, Syria and Libya, cf. Kienle, *op. cit.*
57. For details cf. Kienle, *op. cit.*, pp. 135–51; *Middle East Contemporary Survey*, Vol. VIII; L. Rokach, 'I passi verso l'unificazione fra Iraq e Siria; un disegno politico che tende alla "restaurazione"', in *Politica Internazionale*, luglio/July 1979

two countries Syrian troops during the *reconquista* of Kuwait at one stage even repelled an Iraqi incursion into Saudi Arabia. Lastly, the Damascus Declaration signed between Syria, Egypt, and the countries of the Gulf Cooperation Council after the end of the Kuwait war is a further sign of the demise of Baghdad and the rise of Damascus.

CONCLUSION

This outline shows that Iraqi rulers basically pursued two sorts of aims in their policies towards Syria. Although over certain periods of time these aims were pursued simultaneously, most periods—and these only to a limited extent coincide with the rule of this or that régime—were dominated either by the one or by the other.

Maintaining or tipping the bilateral balance of power in the interest of Baghdad was the chief aim until the advent of the first Baath régime in Baghdad in February 1963; this included attempts at generally indirect territorial control. More diluted, this aim returned to the top of the Iraqi agenda nine months later, after the overthrow of the Baath in Baghdad. Relegated to background during the period immediately following the second Baathi takeover in Iraq, it has, however, dominated bilateral relations since the early mid-1970s. The major difference between these three periods lies in the growing resourcefulness of régimes in Damascus which increasingly enabled them to challenge Iraqi designs.

In the remaining periods from February to November 1963 and from July 1968 to the early 1970s (corresponding to periods in which both countries were ruled by Baathi régimes, except for the month between 8 February and 8 March 1963) when Iraqi policy towards Syria (and vice versa) was predominantly marked by attempts to manage, control and exploit cross-border loyalties existing between the Baathi constituencies of the two countries the objective was a more modest one. Whilst earlier appeals from Iraq to pro-Hashemite or wider Arab sentiments in Syria had aimed at bringing the one country under the influence of the other, appeals to Baathi loyalties in ther 1960s and early 1970s largely served to protect and consolidate the internal position of the rulers in Baghdad. From March to November 1963 the chief purpose was to strengthen one Iraqi faction against another, while after 1968 it was to secure the survival of the Iraqi régime as a whole. In February 1963 the idea was certainly to help the Syrian Baath to power, but mainly in order to consolidate Baathi rule in Iraq. The same motif guided Iraqi Baathis when at times in the late 1960s they sought to help to power in Damascus Baathis other than those who had taken over in 1966.

The need to manage cross-border loyalties indicates that some Iraqi actors did not consider the border with Syria as a boundary between them and others consistent with the 'us-vs.-them' logic that nationals of nation-states are supposed to display. They were ready to shift their allegiance to Syrians instead of granting it to Iraqis, thus denying the relevance of this border for limiting political participation and for distinguishing between insiders and outsiders, or internal and external affairs. However, as we have seen, the number of 'defectors', real or potential, was rather small in Iraq, especially if compared to Syria. In fact, when activating cross-border loyalties Iraqis mainly sought to mobilize additional support for their own interests or, what comes down to the same, to impair their adversaries. They were rather reluctant in associating non-Iraqis to actual decision-making and when some of them did so in autumn 1963 others quickly and decisively moved to stop it. There was a domain in politics that remained largely reserved for Iraqis.

To this unity schemes with Syria were no exception. First of all, they were, in spite of their recurrent nature, less of a distinguishing feature of bilateral relations than commonly assumed. After all, there were lengthy periods of time when no union was sought by the rulers in Baghdad. More importantly, however, though perhaps less obviously, the unity schemes that were put forth either in the 1940s and 1950s or in 1963 or again in 1978 were never premised on the authoritative participation in politics of actors so far excluded. Under the monarchy and in 1963 the idea was not a unitary but a sort of federal state. Prior to 1963 this included an element of domination and participation in other people's affairs, but certainly not by Syrians in Iraqi affairs. The Iraqi state in these years largely remained the 'political field'[58] within which competing interests jockeyed for influence and power. Only in 1978, as oil had doped the leading minds in Baghdad, the idea was that of a unitary state, but clearly under the domination of those already dominating Iraq. The border posts between the two countries would—possibly—

---

58. S. Zubaida, *Islam, the people and the state; essays on political ideas* (London, 1989), p. 145 ff. For Syria cf. M. Seurat, 'Les populations, l'Etat et la société', in A. Raymond, ed., *La Syrie d'aujourd'hui* (Paris, 1980).

have disappeared, but not the boundary separating the ruling clientele in Baghdad from the rest of Iraqis now including the Syrians as well. The rulers' chief aim was not to break down unnatural borders, unite an artificially divided people, and come closer to an Arab nation state; in the logic of petro-despotism it was to increase their say in regional and world affairs by adding strategically important square miles and a few millions of disenfranchized subjects.

Relations between Iraq and Iran

Paul Balta

'Geography dictates the politics of a country', asserted Napoleon. 'Geography is the eye of history', as Pierre Dabezies was fond of saying.[1] Both statements are particularly relevant to Iraq and Iran. Since the dim and distant past the Indo-European peoples of the high plateaux of Iran have fought with the Semitic populations of Mesopotamia, the country 'between two rivers'. In Genesis (II, 8–15) the Garden of Eden or Paradise on earth is situated here, between four rivers, including the Tigris and the Euphrates.

In this geographically, ethnically and culturally 'fractured zone', where it is easy to go down to the plain from the Zagros mountains, which form Iran's western border, the past continues to weigh heavily on relations between the two countries. Each country seeks historical and religious references and symbols to justify its actions and territorial claims. It is for this reason that we have devoted the first part of this chapter to the principal events and historical milestones which help to explain relations between Baghdad and Tehran in modern times, and in particular at the time of the first Gulf War (1980–1988) and Iraq's invasion of Kuwait in August 1990, which subsequently led to the Second Gulf War (1991).

It is in Elam, in the south-west of the Iranian plateaux that the Susa civilization was born at the beginning of the third millennium BC; immediately it clashed with that of Sumer and the Sumerian founders of Ur in Mesopotamia. Sumer invented the first alphabet and cuneiform writing, and bequeathed us the Gilgamesh epic. In 2350 BC the Akkadians founded Babylon (Bab-yl), the Port of

---

1. See *Approches polémologiques, conflits et violence politique dans le monde au tournant des années quatre-vingt-dix*, Fondation pour les études de défense nationale, Paris, 1991.

God, but also the Port of Science. We owe them the calculus, cosmogony and the Code of Hammurabi, the first judicial principles characterized by a concern for equality. After his death, King Hammurabi's kingdom fell under the attacks of the Assyrians, founders of Nineveh (close to present-day Mosul), capital of the Empire of Assurbanipal (669–627 BC).

In turn, the Kassite mountain dwellers of Zagros advanced on and captured Babylon. Nebuchadnezzar the Great (604–562 BC) liberated his kingdom, returned it to its former glory and took back from the Kassites the statue of the God Marduk. This pendulum movement continued with Cyrus II the Great (558–528 BC). He began by attacking the Medes, another Indo-European people, inhabiting the north of the Iranian plateaux, a people whom the Kurds regard as their ancestors. (In modern times the Iranian Shahs have frequently invoked this ethnic relationship to justify their claims on Kurdish territories against the claims of the Arabs and the Turks.) Cyrus reunited the two kingdoms under his own crown and formed the first world empire when he annexed the Kingdom of Babylon and the whole of Asia Minor.[2]

On a spiritual level, Zoroastrianism, preached by Zarathustra or Zoroaster (660–583 BC), dominated the life of the Persian Empire in various different forms and organizations of the Magi for thirteen centuries until the fall of the Sassanids.[3] It therefore influenced the soul and society of Iran for the same amount of time as Islam has from its beginnings in the seventh century to the present day. (It is for this reason that throughout the Iran-Iraq conflict, the Baghdad leaders and press always referred to Ayatollah Khomeini and the Iranians as 'Zoroastrians', using the term to mean 'non-believers' and 'barbarians'.)

After the defeat of Darius III Codomannus, Alexander the Great hoped to rebuild the illustrious city which Xerxes had destroyed. But death surprised him in 323 at the age of thirty-three. The Macedonian's name was nevertheless involved during the 1950s in the controversy which brought first Cairo and then Baghdad into opposition with Tehran, and which concerned the naming of the Persian Gulf. The Arabs pointed out that the Greeks—and in particular the geographer Strabo—and then the Romans—especially the historian Pliny the Elder—used the

---

2. D. Wilber, *Iran: past and present*, 8th ed. (Princeton University Press), 1978.
3. J. Duchesne-Guillemin, *La religion de l'Iran ancien*, (Paris, 1962).

expression 'Arab Gulf'.[4] The term 'Persian' had previously been used, principally by Niarkos, one of Alexander's generals who had explored the eastern (Persian) coast, judged more favourable than the western (Arab) coast. Other names were subsequently used; the term *sinus arabicus* reappears in a Mercator map of 1595. It seems that the term 'Persian Gulf' became established with the rise to power of the Safavid dynasty at the beginning of the sixteenth century and the decline of the Arabs. We have dealt with this subject elsewhere.[5]

The Battle of Qadisiya is another important milestone. After the death of the prophet Muhammad in 632 the Muslims fought two decisive battles, that of Yarmuk (636) in Syria, which opened the route for them to Egypt and the Maghreb; and the battle of Qadisiya (636), which brought the Persians over to Islam, and which later allowed Allah's troops to reach the banks of the Indus.[6] (Baghdad referred to the first Gulf War as the 'Second Qadisiya' and the 'Qadisiya of Saddam'; it was presented as the present-day battle of the Arabs against the Persians. For Tehran on the other hand, the battle of 636 represented a victory of Muslims over infidels and that of 1980 was, in the same vein, a battle of Good against Evil, of believers against the atheist Baathists.)

Another symbolic event which has served as a point of reference for both imperial Iran and the Islamic Republic proclaimed in 1979 is the martyrdom of Ali and his son Hussein. As is well-known, the fourth caliph Ali, nephew and son-in-law of the prophet was captured in 657 at Siffin by Muawiya, Governor of Damascus, which led to the Shi'i schism. In 680 his son Hussein and his companions were massacred by Caliph Yazid, son of Muawiya, and interred in Karbala. Since then Ali and Hussein have become tragic symbols of right persecuted by tyranny, of the weak conquered by the strong. (In the twentieth century the Shahs of Iran laid claim to the sites of the Shi'i saints; Najaf, where Ali is interred, and Karbala in the south of Iraq. The Pahlavis claimed at the very least oversight of their administration. Ayatollah Khomeini summarized his own position with the slogan 'the route to (or, according to other versions, 'the liberation of') Jerusalem passes through Najaf and

---

4. In *L'Enquête d'Hérodote*, (Paris, 1964), the Arab Gulf corresponds to the Red Sea; on maps the Tigris and the Euphrates flow into what he calls the Erythrean Sea.

5. P. Balta, *Iran-Irak, une guerre de 5000 ans*, 2nd ed. (Paris, 1988).

6. In reality the battle of Qadisiya is the last of seven conflicts beginning in 633.

Karbala'. It is also interesting to note that the Iranian press has consistently referred to Saddam Hussein by the name Saddam Yazid.

New issues arose at the beginning of the sixteenth century, with the foundation of the Safavid dynasty, which restored Persia to its former glory, and the consolidation of the Ottoman Empire, which extended its authority to the majority of the Arab peoples of the Middle East. These issues concerned not only religious beliefs and the power of the caliphs, but also became strategic, taking place on both a territorial and an ethnic level.

The most important of these concerns Mesopotamia, which was coveted by Persia and consequently the 204 km long Shatt al-Arab (The Arab shore), formed by the confluence of the Tigris and the Euphrates, between Kurna in the north and the port of Fau on the Arabo-Persian Gulf. Unable to win back Mesopotamia, it laid claim to this waterway, with the intention of ensuring at the very least that the *talweg* (the median line of the river) should mark the border between the two empires, and in the twentieth century between Iraq and Iran.

Linked to this issue was the problem of Arabistan or the Arab countries, which the Sublime Porte regarded as a continuation of Mesopotamia, referred to as Lower Mesopotamia,[7] which as such should be under its sovereignty. Conversely, the peacock throne wanted it in its own territory.

Another issue was gradually established; that of the territories populated by the Kurds, also disputed by the two empires. This became a serious cause of tension during the nineteenth and twentieth centuries. (Formed by the British in 1920, modern Iraq regards itself as the heir to the Ottoman Empire in its disputes with Iran. For its part, every time it has wanted to obtain an advantage, or has believed Arabistan to be threatened, Iran has encouraged rebellions in Iraqi Kurdistan; its support has always been substantial enough to embarrass the Baghdad government, but at the same time sufficiently limited to avoid any confirmation of autonomy, or indeed the proclamation of independence, which might spread to Iranian Kurdistan.)

These issues gave way to a series of conflicts punctuated by Peace Treaties, which we will outline briefly, since they show how

---

7. L. Massignon, 'Mohammera', in *Revue du monde musulman*, no 11, November 1908; A. Wilson, *South-West Persia; a political officer's diary 1907–1914* (Oxford, 1941).

Persian diplomacy has achieved its aims through persistence and obstinacy:

The Treaty of Amasia (1555) forced the Shah of Persia to renounce Mesopotamia (Iraq) and the Shatt al-Arab to the Sublime Porte;[8]

The Treaty of Qasr-i-Shirin (1639), or the Treaty of Zuhab, confirmed the terms of the latter, after which the Persians occupied the Shatt al Arab region for fifteen years.

Article 7 of the Treaty of Amir Ashraf (1727) states: 'The Persian Empire undertakes not to interfere in the affairs of Arabistan';

The Treaty of Nadir Shah (1747) repeated this clause and put an end to the cause of the new confrontation. Peace was established until Persia launched hostilities in 1818;

The Treaty of Erzurum I (1823) confirmed that the Shatt al-Arab belonged to the Ottoman Empire and confirmed the power of Hajj Yusuf Bin Mirdao over the Emirate of Muhammara (Arabistan) from the name of the port which he created;[9]

The Treaty of Erzurum II (1847) marks a turning point. The English and the Russians, who had gained a foothold in Iran, demanded a permanent and stable frontier in order to safeguard their own interests and imposed their own border plans on the two declining empires. For the first time the Sublime Porte 'positively undertakes that the town and surroundings of Muhammara, the island of Khizr (later Abadan), the moorings and lands on the left bank of the Shatt al-Arab (. . .) are in the possession of the Persian government, who has full sovereignty'. In return the latter 'will desist from any kind of claim concerning the province of Sulaimaniya (Kurdistan)';

The Protocol of Tehran (1911) clarified the details but did not settle the fundamental problems associated with the borders which had been left in abeyance;

The Protocol of Constantinople (1913) defined with extreme precision, in texts and on maps, the line of the border. It sanctioned the sovereignty of the Sublime Porte over the Shatt al-Arab, with the exception of some ten islands, including that of Abadan, situated between Muhammara and the sea;

8. Abdelkader Benabdallah, *La question du Chatt el Arab* (Montreal, 1981).
9. Louis Massignon, *op. cit.*

The Minutes of the Commission for the Demarcation of the Turko-Persian borders (1914). England and Russia had put into effect on land their plan of the border running from the Shatt al-Arab in the south to Ararat in the north; they specified that these frontiers were 'definitive and recognised' by the two parties;

The Treaty of Tehran (1937) re-established the power struggle. Indeed, Reza Shah denounced the protocol of 1913 as an 'imposed treaty' and launched an appeal to the League of Nations. Concluded under the aegis of the League of Nations, the accord of Tehran is entitled *The Treaty of the Borders between Iraq and Iran with appended protocol.* Tehran succeeded in extending its sovereignty to that part of the Shatt al-Arab opposite the oil city of Abadan for seven kilometers, as far as the *talweg*. However, the text confirms that the kingdom of Iraq controls navigation on the river, the frontier being fixed on the eastern (Iranian) shore.

Meanwhile, Reza Shah proceeded with the intensive Persianization of Arabistan: the area was renamed Khuzestan ('Land of Towers'), Muhammara became Khorramshahr and the Arabic names of towns, rivers and mountains were replaced with Persian names. The Arabic language was prohibited in local courts and Iraq accused the Tehran government of displacing Arabs and encouraging the settlement of non-Arabs in the province. For their part the Iranians accused Baghdad of encouraging and fomenting rebellion. These polemics did not prevent the status quo from being established on a long-term basis, to the extent that after World War II London and Washington succeeded in bringing the two monarchies together in the Baghdad Pact (which also included Great Britain, Pakistan and Turkey), formed to join forces against the Communist threat and the wave of various different forms of nationalism, in particular Arab nationalism and its Nasserist version.

The overthrow of the Iraqi monarchy on 14 July 1958 by General Qasim, the proclamation of the Republic and Iraq's withdrawal from the Pact worried Tehran, London and Washington. Moreover the new regime decided by decree to 'restore' to the Persian Gulf its 'true name of the Arab Gulf' which it had already been given by the 'Voice of the Arabs', a radio station broadcasting from Nasserist Egypt.[10] Muhammad Reza Shah immediately reopened the issue of

10. P. Balta, *op. cit.*

the Shatt al-Arab, defining Iran's position as follows: 'The accord of 1937 is unacceptable and without precedent (. . .) It is evident that a river which flows at the border of two countries cannot in the twentieth century be the object of use and of sovereignty of a sole party'. And in order to reinforce his claims the Shah encouraged a rebellion in Iraqi Kurdistan.

Faced with increasing difficulties General Qasim chose relentlessly to pursue the gratification of Iraqi nationalism, asserting Iraq's rights over the emirate of Kuwait, which was a sub-governornate of Basra under the Ottoman Empire. On 19 June 1961, to avert danger, the British Resident and Emir Abd Allah Al Sabah exchanged a number of letters in which Great Britain recognized Kuwait's independence. On 25 June Qasim denounced this treaty and claimed the emirate as 'an integral part of Iraq'. In the most perceptive work dedicated to this country Pierre Rossi has defined the issues at stake: 'The affair (of Kuwait) is so complex that it actually embraces the future destiny of Iraq; on its result depends whether Baghdad will be the capital of a major power or merely the first city of Mesopotamia'.[11]

The overthrow of General Qasim on 8 February 1963 brought about a respite in relations with Tehran as well as Kuwait. The new Baathist government, whose very foundation was fragile (it would be overthrown in November by the nationalist Abd al-Salam Arif) recognized the independence and sovereignty of the emirate in a communiqué published on 5 October 1963. A document to the same effect was also signed by Hasan al-Bakr, leader of the government, and Emir Abd Allah, but was never ratified.

On 18 July 1968 the Baath party returned to power in Baghdad, renewing fears in Tehran. On 19 April 1969 Muhammad Reza Shah unilaterally denounced the 1937 treaty and declared that it was the *talweg* which defined the border. Iraq turned to the United Nations Security Council, proposing that the dispute be submitted to the International Court of Justice at The Hague. Tehran refused, calling for a new treaty, under the terms of which the Shatt al-Arab 'is a non-Iraqi border river'.[12]

In order to put an end to the latent unrest in Iraqi Kurdistan, the

11 P. Rossi, *L'Irak des révoltes*, (Paris, 1962).
12. *Some facts concerning the dispute between Iran and Irak over Shatt-el-Arab*, Ministry of Foreign Affairs, Tehran, May 1969. Iraq replied in July with a commentary on Iranian claims and allegations in Khalid al-Izzi, *The Shatt el Arab river dispute in terms of law*, (Baghdad, 1972).

Baathist government signed an accord recognizing the autonomy of the region on 11 March 1970. The accord was to become definitive in 1974 after a trial period. Taking advantage of this respite, Baghdad was able to resist pressure from Tehran. At the end of 1971 the régime, which saw itself at the forefront of Arab nationalism, denounced Iran's occupation of the three strategic islets controlling the straits of Hormuz: Abu Musa and the Tumbs. The affair was cleverly buried by the Security Council, but Iraq continued to uphold the view that these islets should return to Arab sovereignty.

Openly supported by Iran and secretly by Israel and the United States, Iraq's Kurds, led by Mustafa Barzani, resumed hostilities at the expiry of the accord of 11 March, which they refused to ratify in 1974. Saddam Hussein, then Vice President, cherished great ambitions for his country on the level of both internal development and links with the outside and dreaded being caught in the trap of Kurdistan.[13] At the end of January 1975, therefore, he agreed to pursue negotiations with Tehran initiated by Egyptian diplomacy in the greatest secrecy. These led, at the end of the first OPEC summit on 6 March 1975, to the Algiers Accord, signed by the Shah of Iran and Saddam Hussein. Reasons of state had prevailed in both men.

Noting that the pursuit of the war was beginning to have repercussions in Iranian Kurdistan, Muhammad Reza agreed to halt his aid to Barzani, who ceased combat within a fortnight. In return he realized an old imperial dream: that is that the border should correspond to the *talweg* of the Shatt al-Arab. The Algiers Accord was reduced to a Joint Iraqi-Iranian Declaration, but it was completed by a series of treaties and protocols fixing the land and river borders.[14] Whatever might subsequently be declared by the leaders of the two countries, these texts were progressively applied. And if they were not applied in their entirety it was because from 1978 onwards Iran embarked upon a revolutionary process which turned the country upside down and transformed the regional equilibrium with the overthrow of the monarchy and the proclamation of the Islamic republic on 31 March 1979.

No serious or irremediable incident occured between the two countries until the end of 1979. Nevertheless, the occupation of the United States embassy in Tehran on 4 November by supporters of

13. P. Balta, 'L'Irak à la recherche de nouvelles alliances', *Le Monde*, 7,8,9 April 1972.
14. The complete text can be found in *Le conflit Irak-Iran 1979– 1989*, ed. P. Balta, *La Documentation française* (Paris, 1989).

the 'line of the Imam' (Khomeini) and the hostage-taking of the diplomats marked a turning point in the régime's policies; the régime was becoming increasingly radical and could not hide its desire to export its revolution. It was now the turn of Iraq (and the oil-monarchies of the Gulf) to be concerned. From the beginning of 1980 onwards tension continued to mount between the two capitals. It began with the war of the waterways and continued with subversion,[15] which gave way to armed incidents. It is in this context that on 17 September 1980, Saddam Hussein, who had become President one year before, announced the unilateral abrogation of the Algiers Accord, described as an unfair treaty 'dictated by circumstances' and imposed on Iraq at a time of weakness.

On 22 September the Iraqi Revolutionary Command Council ordered its armed forces to attack Iranian military targets. They entered Khuzestan. War broke out. Strictly speaking Iraq was the aggressor. But in order to avoid this accusation the Iraqi government complained—after the event—of Iranian provocation, maintaining that Tehran had started the hostilities on 4 September and that on the 22 its own troops had done nothing more than counter-attack. At this time Saddam Hussein and his team seemed convinced that they were mounting a 'ten-day war' which would bring about the fall of the Imam Khomeini and his régime. This rather dangerous gamble was thwarted by Iranian resistance.

The war took place on three levels: national, religious and ideological. It set two men against one other who were opposites in every respect: in their view of the world, their philosophy of history, their vision of man, their ideologies. Saddam Hussein, an Arab nationalist, secularizer and socialist, saw himself as the heir of Sumer and the Abbasids. At the beginning of the conflict *al-Thawra*, the organ of the Iraqi Baath Party, had depicted him in parachutist's uniform with Nebuchadnezzar, who had conquered Cyrus, and Saladin in the background, the latter was a symbolic figure, since he was a Kurd and he re-established Sunni orthodoxy against schismatic Shi'ism. Khomeini on the other hand had given new life to radical Islam; in his eyes Arabism and modernism were nothing but reprehensible deviations inspired by the west, a west

---

15. Let us give a few examples. On 1 April 1980 an assassination attempt was organized against Tariq Aziz, Christian by religion, at the time Vice Prime Minister; *al Dawa*, supported by Iran, was implicated. Conversely, the former Prime Minister Shapur Bakhtiar and General Oveissi fomented plots at the heart of the Iranian army. Baghdad encourgaed unrest in Khuzestan and Teheran, also in Iraqi Kurdistan.

dominated by the United States, described as 'Great Satan' and supporting 'Little Satan' Saddam Hussein.

The course of the conflict may be divided into three major phases, each of which also includes several shorter ones. The first phase (1980–1982) is characterized by the Iraqi offensive which took the 'enlightened war' into the 'war of attrition'; from September 1981 the Iranians recaptured Khuzestan and put the Iraqi army on the defensive. In this weak position Saddam Hussein was ready 'to accept the borders as defined by the Algiers Accord', on condition that Iran unite its forces with those of Iraq to oppose the Israeli troops which had invaded the Lebanon on 6 June 1982. Threatened with a coup d'état, the Iraqi president would be saved by the intransigence of Khomeini, who launched the slogan 'From Basra onwards to Baghdad!' This in turn led the Iraqis to unite around Saddam Hussein.

During the second phase, which lasted from summer 1982 to summer 1987, Iran applied constant pressure on its enemy. However, the victory periodically promised by Khomeini remained out of reach, despite the fact that Iran was three times larger in size and population than Iraq, and that Baghdad was only around a hundred kilometers from the border, on flat land. Refusing to allow an Islamic regime to be imposed on them, the Iraqis resisted every inch of the way. In actual fact, this prolonged conflict represented a strategic respite for Israel, and the regional powers and most of the great powers were not exactly unhappy to see the two enemies' mutual weakening of one another. The Karbala offensives (end 1986–beginning 1987), launched by Iran with arms provided by the United States and Israel (as the Irangate scandal later revealed) had three objectives: to capture Basra in order to bring about the fall of the Baghdad regime; to cut off the route to Kuwait and to win over two or three of the Gulf emirates to weaken and isolate Saudi Arabia; to prevent the summit of the Organization of the Islamic Conference from being held (at the end of January 1987 in Kuwait), which was proposing to tighten the ranks of the Arab states and to condemn Tehran.

This failure marked a decisive turning-point and intiated the final phase of the conflict (March 1987–August 1988). Through the systematic use of SCUD missiles and, on occasion, chemical weapons, Iraq demoralized the Iranian population before engaging its troops in the battle to win back the peninsula of Fau and to penetrate Iranian territory. Parallel to this, various factors contributed to the internationalization of the conflict, which until now had been limited to regional dimensions: the obstinacy of Iran in wanting to win a total victory in order to install an Islamic republic in Baghdad; the threat that such a dominantly Shi'i republic would represent to Saudi Arabia and the Sunni emirates—the vulnerable states of the region—allies of the United States, and also the Soviet Muslim republics; the intensification of hostilities in the Gulf, which threatened navigation and therefore Western oil supplies; the fear of seeing chemical arms spread throughout the Third World, becoming the 'atomic bomb' of the poor.[16]

The UN, whose various resolutions had gone unheeded in many respects, intensified its pressure; on 20 July 1987 the Security Council unanimously adopted the 'obligatory' text of resolution 598, which called for an immediate cease-fire, the halting of military activity and the retreat of all forces to internationally-recognized borders.[17] This was favourably received by Baghdad, but Tehran took a year to comply. Following pressure from the President of the Parliament, Ali Akbar Rafsanjani, and those pragmatists who feared a crushing defeat, on 20 July 1988 Ayatollah Khomeini declared that he would accept resolution 598 'as one takes poison'. The cease-fire came into effect on 20 August. An initial phase of negotiations opened in Geneva under the supervision of Perez de Cuellar, Secretary General of the UN.

All observers believed that the negotiations would be long and arduous. But they stalled immediately on the first point of resolution 598 and the reference to international borders. Iran saw these as those defined by the Algiers Accord; but Iraq, which had denounced the accord, claimed sovereignty over the Shatt al-Arab and demanded that it be cleared, since it represented the country's main access to the Gulf. Iran refused. Thus the seeds of a new conflict were present in these negotiations, which did not progress even though the two belligerents had been bled dry by the eight-year confrontation, which had seen around a million deaths, a quarter of whom were Iraqis.

In summer 1989 I wrote:

> The Baghdad government wishes to have at its disposal a less limited maritime space, where it can deploy its fleet; it has therefore proposed to Kuwait an exchange of the island of Bubiyan for a plot of territory

---

16. For a detailed description of the battles and a thorough chronology of events see *Iran-Irak; une guerre de 5000 ans*, and *Le conflit Irak-Iran 1979–1989*.
17. The complete text can be found in *Le conflit Irak-Iran*.

in southern Iraq which is rich in oil. The emirate has refused, but will it be able to resist its neighbour's pressure in the long-term? Instead of exchanging territories, will it agree to lease the island or to authorize the installation of a naval and military base there? Parallel to this Iraq has pointed out to its creditors in the Gulf that it has helped them to avoid falling into the Iranian orbit by paying 'the price of blood', and has said this in such a way that it would be unseemly for them to demand repayment of the debts incurred during the war; in the name of fraternity, solidarity and gratitude, it has also asked them to grant the country new loans to ensure the reconstruction of the areas affected by the war (Basra and Fau in particular), a reconstruction which has been accelerated since the end of the conflict.[18]

We should not forget that the cost of reconstruction was estimated at $60 billion and that Iraq's debt was estimated to be between $60 and $70 billion, of which around half had been lent by the Gulf states. In addition, Saddam Hussein demanded of the Emir of Kuwait a donation of $10 billion, but the Emir let him know that he could not go beyond nine!

Another consequence of the Iran-Iraq war was that the arms technology increasingly mastered by the Iraqis had got the better of the 'miracles of faith', the basis of Khomeini's hopes and sense of certainty.

From then onwards it was possible to observe, even before the death of the Imam on 3 June 1989, that reason of state led the country progressively towards revolutionary logic. The election of Rafsanjani to the Presidency of the Republic on 28 July only confirmed this course, and was subsequently illustrated by the victory of the 'pragmatists' over the 'radicals' in the legislative elections in spring 1992. On the other hand Saddam Hussein tended to over-estimate his victory, his military potential and the abilities of his army. To this misjudgement was added another, concerning the consequences of the end of the Cold War and the weakening of the USSR's power, which changed the international balance of power to the advantage of the United States. This twofold error led him to invade Kuwait on 2 August 1990, provoking the Second Gulf War[19].

The deterioration in relations between Iraq and its Arab

18. See *Le conflit Irak-Iran*.
19. P. Balta, 'La nouvelle crise du Golfe et ses antécédents', *Hérodote*, No. 58–59, 1990; Chapour Haghighat, *Histoire de la crise du Golfe*, (Brussels, 1992). This work contains an appendix of the chronology of events and the essential extracts of resolutions adopted by the UN Security Council from 2 August 1990 to 11 October 1991.

neighbours, in particular Saudi Arabia, on the one hand and the lack of progress in negotiations with Iran on the other, led Saddam Hussein to establish a strategic connection between the problem of the islands of Bubiyan and Warba, under Kuwaiti sovereignty, and that of the Shatt al-Arab. In this context a brief summary of the origin of the dispute with Kuwait is appropriate, in order to clarify events.

The name Kuwait, the diminutive of *kut* (fort) did not appear on maps until the beginning of the 19th century. The Al Sabah tribe, the current ruling family had arrived there in around 1715 and had imposed its authority over other tribes in 1750–1752.[20] Since the emirate's independence in 1961 it has emphasized the continuity of the dynasty to justify its legitimacy. But Iraq read history in a different way, emphasizing that the principality was part of the Ottoman province of Basra, as had been confirmed by Midhat Pasha, Governor of Baghdad, in the name of the Sublime Porte in 1871. He had also named Emir Abd Allah Al Sabah *qaim maqam* (sub-prefect) and granted him the title of Pasha. In return the Emir had agreed to pay tribute.[21]

Following the fall of the Ottoman Empire in 1918, the British had attempted to consolidate their position in the region. Sir Percy Cox, the British High Commissioner, representing both Kuwait and Iraq, negotiated a series of accords which led to the Treaty of Uqair on 2 December 1922. He had already accorded King Abd al-Aziz Ibn Saud two thirds of Kuwaiti territory, compensating this loss by re-drawing the northern border of the emirate to the detriment of Iraq, which now saw itself deprived of a large opening into the Gulf. In 1926 the oil-rich vilayet of Mosul had been joined to the Kingdom on Iraq, and now became Iraqi Kurdistan.[22]

Neither the monarchy installed by the British in 1920, nor the Republic proclaimed in 1958 accepted the terms of the treaty. As for the Baath Party, which returned to power in 1968, it continued to demand the rectification of the borders and the restitution of the islands of Warba and Bubiyan in accordance with the document signed in 1963 by Colonel Abd al-Salam Arif, who had become President, and Emir Abd Allah, but which had never been ratified. In 1975, after the signing of the Algiers Accord, on a visit

20. Ahmad Mustafa Abu-Hakima, *The modern history of Kuwait, 1750–1965*, (Montreal, 1982).
21. See the chapter by H. Ishow in this volume, pp. 303–318.
22. S. Yerasimos, 'Frontières d'Arabie', *Hérodote*, no,. 58–59, *op. cit.*

to Tehran Saddam Hussein had declared during the course of a press conference: 'We do not wish to extend the Iraqi domain, we want to extend the Gulf nature of Iraq in such a way that our country may defend itself and the other countries of the Gulf against all foreign aggression. If one day Iraq and Kuwait form but one part of the Arab region, this would certainly be in the interest of Iraq, but also of Kuwait and all other parties in the large Arab nation'.[23] Then, in November 1984, fully at war with Iran, he had (already) requested permission to lease the two islands. But in vain.

He returned to the attack in 1989. As we have seen, at the time Tehran was opposed to the clearing of the Shatt al-Arab, which made difficult the use of the river port of Basra, the main window of the country onto the Gulf. Baghdad then envisaged diverting part of the waterway on its territory, so that it would end more to the west, near the small port of Umm Qasr, where its war fleet was anchored. However, this solution, intended to put pressure on Tehran, had one serious disadvantage: Umm Qasr is only accessible through the narrow straights of Khor Abd Allah, wedged between the south of Iraqi territory and the Island of Bubiyan, uninhabited, uncultivated, but a highly strategic position dependent on Kuwait. The government of the Islamic Republic of Iran had been vigilant and had already warned Emir Jabir Al Sabah against any transfer of the islands in any form whatsoever.

In order to help his neighbour and ally out of the impasse, King Hussein of Jordan had tried mediating between Baghdad and Kuwait between January and March 1990. Jabir would have agreed to lease Warba and Bubiyan to Iraq, to renounce its debts and to award it $9 billion of the $10 billion demanded. He would also have agreed to begin discussions on the demarcation of the borders, but imposed the condition that the 1963 document recognizing the sovereignty of the emirate should first be ratified. Saddam Hussein, however, demanded satisfaction before ratification. The mediation failed and Iraq reiterated its financial demands at the Arab summit in Baghdad at the end of May 1990, accusing its neighbours, Saudi Arabia and Kuwait in particular, of mounting an economic war against Iraq by reducing the price of a barrel of oil.[24]

In the weeks preceding the invasion of Kuwait on 2 August, Iraq

23. According to agency dispatches, cited in *Hérodote*, no. 58–59, *loc. cit.*
24. P. Balta, 'La nouvelle crise du Golfe . . .'.

endeavoured to improve its relations with Iran. A rapprochement of some kind could be detected at the beginning of July in Geneva, on the subject of the exchange of prisoners of war. On the 20 of the same month, Saddam Hussein asked President Rafsanjani to receive Tariq Aziz, his Minister of Foreign Affairs. Tehran agreed, on condition that Baghdad should recognize the Algiers Accord. Events started to move quickly.

The Iraqi President, who manifestly had not foreseen the strength of international reaction, and who had underestimated the solidity of the American-Soviet rapprochement as well as the new world order, found himself in a serious position. On the morning of 15 August he offered Iran unconditional peace. He accepted the 1975 Accord dividing the Shatt al-Arab and the evacuation of Iraqi troops who still occupied 1500 km^2 of Iranian territory, despite the cease-fire of 1988. In order to prove 'his good intentions', he announced that Iraq was withdrawing 'all its forces facing Iran all along the border'. He also agreed to the exchange of all prisoners of war: 70,000 Iraqis for 30,000 Iranians. In return he asked Iran to 'cooperate in the face of the manoeuvres of the forces of evil'.

Iran accepted the advantages it had been granted, but condemned the invasion of Kuwait. During a visit to Tehran on 9 and 10 September, Tariq Aziz achieved the normalization of relations between the two countries, but his interlocutors refused to help Iran break the embargo ordered by the UN. Indeed, the Iran of Rafsanjani, which, without actually admitting it was for the first time attempting to make overtures to the West to safeguard its own development, adopted a stance of strict neutrality, and was taking full advantage of it. It maintained this line, despite the attempts of the 'radicals' to relaunch the 'anti-imperialist' dynamic of Khomeini, abandoned in order to form an alliance with Saddam Hussein, or at least to support him. In any case the wounds of the first Gulf War were far from being sufficiently healed for the people to allow such a volte-face. In addition, just like Ankara, Tehran was already looking to the Muslim republics of central Asia, which were in the process of proclaiming their independence as the USSR began to disintegrate.[25]

Rafsanjani thus gambled on the weakening of Iraq and the safeguarding of its territorial integrity, for fear that any dismemberment

25. P. Balta, 'Nouveaux enjeux en Asie musulmane', *Géopolitique*, no. 29, Spring 1990.

would spread to his own country, which was threatened, amongst other things by a possible secession of Kurds (Sunnis) and Azeris, who were Shi'i, but turcophone, and who looked to ex-Soviet Azerbaijan, with Baku as its capital.[26] The Iraqi planes which had taken refuge in Iran on the eve of the anti-Iraq coalition's offensive on 17 January 1991 were immediately confiscated. On the other hand Tehran showed great prudence when, following an appeal launched by President George Bush, the Iraqi Kurds rose up, as did the Shi'i of the south.

Of course, the Iranian régime could not ignore Mahdi al-Hakim, one of the leaders of the Iraqi Shi'i opposition, installed in Tehran, but the support which it had agreed to was actually only verbal. President Rafsanjani and his Minister for Foreign Affairs, Ali Velayati, were well aware that, one way and another, and spurred on by Riyad, the United States were opposed to al-Hakim or his like seizing power in Baghdad: the *de facto* if not *de jure* constitution of a unit which included the Shi'i of Iraq (fifty-five per cent of the eighteen million forming the population) and of Iran (eighty-five per cent of the fifty-five million Iranians) would simply have been unacceptable to Saudi Arabia. Tehran had preferred to revive relations with the conservative Arab countries and in March 1991 to reestablish diplomatic relations with Riyad, having obtained an increase in the quota of Iranians permitted to visit Mecca on pilgrimage. In practice many decisions were made which buried the ideas of the 1979 Islamic revolution, dear to Khomeini, even if, to allay suspicion, to ensure a certain continuity and to take account of subtle internal games, the services answerable to the regime abroad eliminated various famous opponents, such as Shapur Bakhtiar, condemned to death in an expeditious fashion several years later (August 1991) by 'revolutionary courts' or by one of Khomeini's *fatwas* (religious judicial proclamation).

Faced with Iran which was putting in place a new regional and international strategy, Iraq, which in Spring 1992 was still subject to UN sanctions, found itself particularly isolated. Worse still: the representatives of the UN Security Council decided to rectify the border in Kuwait's favour; they allocated to the emirate part of the oil-field of north Rumeila, cut in two the port of Umm Qasr and further reduced the opening from Iraq to the sea, when, even in

---

26. O. Roy, 'Asie centrale: une zone géostratégique en formation', in *Approches polémologiques*.

normal times, the river port of Basra was no longer able to meet the needs of a country whose population and economic development had increased markedly during the course of a single generation. The reaction of Iran was circumspect; Saudi Arabia, which knew perfectly well how the frontiers were drawn up in 1922[27] questioned the justification for this decision. Most observers saw in this a form of provocation or 'punishment', containing the seeds and in time the danger of a new conflict. The lessons of the Treaty of Versailles, whose draconian conditions imposed on Germany prepared the ground for Nazism, seem to have been forgotten or ignored by the international powers, though not by Iraq's neighbours, other than Kuwait, who remember what happened after the Treaty of Sèvres (1920), concluded with the representatives of the dismembered Ottoman Empire and the Treaty of Lausanne (1923), signed with Atatürk.[28]

27. S. Yerasimos, 'Frontière d'Arabie', *Hérodote, loc. cit.*
28. *Les nouvelles questions d'Orient*, (Les Cahiers de l'Orient, Paris, 1991).

Index

Abd al-Rashid, Mahir 106
Aflaq, Michel 61, 63, 106, 367–71
agrarian reform 171–91
Agrawi, Aziz 43
agriculture 125–7, 171–91, 198, 213, 227–9
Al Bu Nasir 96
Algiers treaty 101, 183, 291, 393
Ammash, Salih Mahdi 368
Arab Cooperation Council 295, 296, 329
Arif, Abd al-Rahman 28, 369, 370
Arif, Abd al-Salam 23, 27, 28, 364, 365, 369
army 20–3, 26, 29, 104–8, 292, 293
Asad, Hafiz 372, 373
Askari, Jafar 79
atabat 82, 83

Baath Party 22, 24–6, 28, 30–4, 337–43, 44, 47, 49, 51, 53, 59–63, 65, 67, 68, 70, 72, 87, 90, 97, 100, 104, 107, 206–10, 287, 366–73
Baghdad Boycott Conference 288, 289
Bahri, Muna Yunis 72
Bakr, Ahmad Hasan 31, 368
banking 216
Barzani, Masud 43
Barzani, Mustafa 77
Barzani, Ubaid 209
Barzinji, Mahmud 77, 344
Basra Petroleum Co. 124, 145, 149, 150
Bazzaz, Abd al-Rahman 27
Bint Huda 88

Britain 6–12, 52, 84, 305, 307–13, 320

Christians 4, 7, 15, 16, 185
Code of Personal Status 69
Communists 22, 24, 25, 29, 37, 44, 52–6, 64, 67, 85, 86, 173, 174, 210

Dawa al-Islamiya 85
Dortyol 124, 212

education 219, 220, 231, 232
Egypt 257–82, 288
employment 199, 200
Euphrates 120, 127–9, 130–2, 352, 353, 373

Fahd, King 329, 331, 334
Faisal ibn Husain 9, 10, 21
foreign trade 200
France 148, 149, 158, 211
Free officers 22–4, 31
Futuwa 44

General Federation of Iraqi Women 45, 46, 65–7, 71–3
Gulf Cooperation Council 328, 331

Hakim, Muhammad 85
Hakim, Mahdi 396
Hammadi, Saadun 41
Hashimi, Yasin 79
Husri, Sati 79, 87
Hussein, Saddam 31–5, 39–42, 44, 45, 48, 49, 57, 58, 60, 68, 89, 91–115, 148, 286–301, 327, 330, 332, 333, 335, 336, 349,

375, 376, 384, 390, 392, 394, 395

Ibn Saud 320, 321
industry 119, 198, 199, 203, 211, 214, 226, 229, 230, 231, 233
intisab 93–5
Iran 91, 97, 99–104, 107, 109, 114, 290–2, 326–9, 381–97
Iraq Petroleum Company 124, 142–52, 360, 362, 370, 373
Iraqi National Oil Company 148, 151, 157
Istiqlal 22

Jamali, Fadil 359, 361
Jawad, Hazim 367
Jews 3, 7, 15, 16
Jordan 295

Karbala 80, 83, 88, 89
Kashif al-Ghita, Muhammad 85
Kashshaf 45
Khabur, river 128, 130
Khalid ibn Sultan 332
Khalisah 264, 271–4
Khalisi, Muhammad Mahdi 84
Khomeini 103, 109, 383, 389, 390
Khuzestan 100
Kirkuk 124, 145, 152, 199, 214, 228, 362
Kubba, Ibrahim 173
Kurdish Democratic Party 43, 350, 354
Kurdish Revolutionary Party 43
Kurds 3, 14, 15, 27, 35, 43, 44, 76–8, 86, 87, 99, 101, 205, 206, 343, 348, 350, 355, 368, 384, 388
Kuwait 236–42, 297–300, 303–18, 330–3, 335, 337, 387, 393, 394

landowning 172–91, 228
League for Defence of Womens' Rights 64

Lebanon 294

Mahabad 77
Majid, Ali 106
Maktab Khalid group 190
Mesopotamia 34, 100, 111, 287, 381, 382
migrant labour 257–82
Mina al-Bakr 212
Mosul 199, 214, 229, 342–4, 347, 349, 365
Muhammad Reza Shah 386–8

NATO 347, 351, 354, 355
Najaf 80, 83, 85, 88, 89
Nasser, Jamal Abd al- 26
National Assembly 32, 47, 209
National Democratic Party 22
national income 196, 201–4, 216–9, 223, 225, 226, 232–6
National Patriotic Front 86
National Progressive Front 44, 210
nationalization 55

OAPEC 154
OECD 158
OPEC 141, 149–51, 153–7, 160, 325, 326, 330
oil 123–5, 134, 141–68, 211, 212, 224, 225, 238, 348
Ottoman Empire 304–9

Patriotic Union of Kurdistan 43
Popular Army 46
population 122, 123

Qadisiya 108, 383
Qasim, Abd al-Karim 23–7, 29, 53, 146, 312, 347, 364, 365, 387

Rabita 64, 67
Rajsanjani 395, 396
Ramadan, Taha Yasin 41
Reza Shah 386

Revolutionary Command Council
31, 32, 35, 46–9, 58, 87, 98,
112, 209
Rikabi, Fuad 87
Rumeila 157, 396

Sadi, Ali Salih 367
Sadr, Baqr 85, 86, 88
Said, Nuri 79, 357–64
Saudi Arabia 305, 308–10, 313,
319–39
Shabib, Talib 367
Sharif, Abd al-Sattar Tahir 43
Shatt al-Arab 101–3
Shawi, Hamid 37
Shi'a 12, 13, 35, 43, 80–90,
99–101, 109
Shufi, Hamud 367
Shu'ubiya 109, 110
Sudan 296
Sunnis 78–80, 96, 108, 109
Suwaidi, Naji 79
Syria 128–31, 286–9, 294, 295,
330, 352, 357–79

Takrit 31, 55
Takriti, Hamid Shaban 106
Takriti, Hussein Kamil 106
Tigris 120, 127–32, 137, 352,
353
tribes 13, 14
Tulfah, Adnan 106, 190
Turkey 127–32, 341–56

USSR 173, 186, 211, 347
Umar, Faruq 110
United States 149, 158, 205, 237,
238, 313, 315, 328, 335–8

Womens' League against Fascism
64, 67

Yasin, Murtada 85
Yemen 294, 295

Zahawi, Asma 64